Jews
and Australian Politics

Contents

Part III   Issues and Controversies

ACKNOWLEDGEMENTS

In producing this book we have benefited from the assistance of many people and institutions, which it is now our pleasure to record. Our first debt is to our contributors, who needed no persuading as to the importance of the project, and who executed their commissions in a timely fashion and accepted the editorial process with good cheer. This is a peer-reviewed book of new essays, and we would like to thank both our anonymous readers and the other individuals who kindly read drafts of particular chapters or sections (indicated at the conclusion of the chapters concerned). Clive Kessler and Konrad Kwiet offered suggestions at critical junctures that lent shape to the project. Rodney Smith generously shared his expertise on a number of points. Staff at various institutions diligently responded to our inquiries, including the Office of Prime Minister of Australia, Parliamentary Library of the Parliament of Australia, Library of the Parliament of New South Wales, Council for Multicultural Australia, Jewish Care Victoria, and Community Relations Commission for a Multicultural New South Wales. We are grateful to the *Australian Jewish News*, its Sydney editor, Vic Alhadeff, and photographer Ingrid Shakenovsky for allowing us to reproduce the jacket photographs, and to Professor Stephen Whitfield of Brandeis University for his early endorsement of the project. Dr Bernard Freeman, editor of the *Australian Jewish Historical Society Journal*, kindly granted us permission to include a revised excerpt from a *Journal* article that forms our Appendix.

We extend special thanks to our publisher Tony Grahame of Sussex Academic Press for his unstinting support for the project, to editorial consultant Tim Andrews for his diligent oversight, and to the Press's Australian agent, Eleanor Brasch, for her efforts in promoting the product locally.

In addition, PM would like to thank his colleagues in the Social Work Department at Monash University for understanding the obvious connection between social policy and the Jewish question; the people in his various policy, campaign and friendship networks who have encouraged him to continue blending scholarship with activism, particularly Itiel Bereson, Dawn Cohen, Viviana Cohn, Ian Katz, Doug Kirsner, David Mendes, Bernard Rechter, Bill Rubinstein, Shimon and Jenny Senator, Danny

Shavitsky, Michael Stevenson and Harold Zwier; and most importantly, his cherished wife Tamar and precious children Lucas and Miranda for their constant support, and spirited if at times bemused enthusiasm.

GBL confines himself here to acknowledging two life-long supporters, Phyllis and Victor Levey. Vic would have been, were it possible, this book's first and most studious reader.

Jews
and Australian Politics

INTRODUCTION

Jews and Australian Politics

GEOFFREY BRAHM LEVEY AND PHILIP MENDES

Jews have been political actors in Australia ever since a handful arrived as convicts on the "First Fleet" of British settlement in 1788.[1] While at this time an impassioned public debate was under way in Western Europe over whether Jews should be admitted as citizens in the new liberalizing states, Jewish free settlers and emancipated convicts in the Australian colonies enjoyed full civil and political rights as a matter of course. With few exceptions, this easy and untroubled acceptance has been the overwhelming pattern of the Australian Jewish experience to this day.

Judged by numbers alone, the Jewish presence in Australia has always been miniscule, consistently hovering under one percent of the total population. By 1841, there numbered an estimated 1,183 Jews – convicts and free settlers – on the continent, mainly from England. Today, after additional waves of Jewish immigrants from Europe pre- and post-World War II and more recently from South Africa and the former Soviet Union, there is an estimated 100,000 or so Jews in a total Australian population of 20 million.[2] Numbers alone, however, belie the Jewish impact on Australian life. In its cover story of 15 October 1996, *The Bulletin* magazine surveyed what it called "the extraordinary contribution of Australia's Jews" to business, the arts, the professions, and public service.[3] As a quick indication of Jewish acceptance and achievement Down Under, few discussions of Australian Jewry fail to note that Sir John Monash was commander of the Australian Corps during World War I, and that Australia has had two Jewish Governors-General or quasi-Heads of State, including the first Australian-born Governor-General, Sir Isaac Isaacs (1931–6).

One aspect of the Jewish presence in Australia that has not received the scholarly attention it deserves is Jews' involvement in Australian politics. This, ironically, is perhaps even more true of the past few decades, when Australian Jews arguably have been at their most politically engaged, than of earlier periods. In recent years, Jews have been at the centre of some significant Australian political and ideological debates, including those over War Crimes legislation and the associated Helen Demidenko controversy; anti-vilification legislation and broader concerns over multiculturalism and racial tolerance; and the on-going Israeli–Arab conflict, and its local manifestations such as the recent Hanan Ashrawi and Sydney Peace Prize affair. There is a strong public perception that Jews are an influential group in terms of their social and economic resources, and access to key political groups and players. The perception is not without foundation, as is suggested by the bipartisan motions in 2004 condemning anti-Semitism in Australia and abroad moved by the House of Representatives and the Senate of the Australian Parliament and by the Parliaments of New South Wales and Victoria.[4] More problematic is how popular literature portrays Australian Jews monolithically, as speaking with a single voice rather than as a diverse community with many different factions and perspectives.

This book aims to contextualize, illuminate and explain the contemporary politics of Australian Jewry. It draws attention to the various and often conflicting positions held within the Jewish community. And it situates the politics of Australian Jews through comparisons with general patterns in Australian politics, the politics of other minorities in Australia, and the politics of other Western Jewish communities.

Hampering any inquiry into contemporary Australian Jewish politics is the absence of up-to-date survey data on Jewish political attitudes and behaviour. Being such a small minority, general social and political surveys of Australians typically fail to identify Jewish respondents and, in the few cases that do, the numbers constitute too small a sample on which to base reliable generalizations. At the same time, the Australian Jewish community has not invested the same resources in studying itself as have, for example, American and British Jewries, where national surveys of Jewish opinion and trends are conducted regularly. As far as political research goes, we have modest surveys of political allegiance among Melbourne Jews in 1947, 1958, 1961, 1967, and 1991, of Sydney Jews in 1969–70, a national survey of 231 Australian Jewish students' vote choice in the 1990 federal election, and a 1995 national survey of 706 Jewish leaders' voting intentions – and not much else.[5] Our answer to this limitation has been to rely, in addition to this survey evidence, on case studies, interviews, and a wide variety of source material.

Our hope is that the following chapters will contribute to a better understanding of Jewish political activities and agendas, and of the factors and forces that shape them in the Australian context. As will be evident, the authors themselves represent a diverse range of perspectives – a fact that further underscores our point about the political heterogeneity of the Jewish community. Several issues not treated or canvassed only in passing in this book might also have been explored in their own right. Chapters on War Crimes legislation, Jews and the media, marginalized Jewish groups, and the academic boycott of Israel were, for example, planned or considered, but, for one reason or another, did not eventuate.

The book is organized around three principal themes: identifying the demographic features of the Australian Jewish community and which bodies are and are not authorized to speak in its name; the impact of ideologies such as liberalism, socialism, conservatism, Zionism, and anti-Semitism on Jewish politics and Jewish political allegiances; and the involvement of Australian Jews in specific political issues and controversies.

Identifying the Jewish Community

Public discourse often presents Jews as uniformly affluent and influential, and as speaking with a single voice on issues. The reality is rather more complex.

As noted by John Goldlust in **chapter 1**, Australian Jewry is a socio-economically diverse community. To be sure, Australian Jews generally have higher educational levels and higher incomes than the Australian median. Some Jews are significant donors to political parties,[6] and there remains a significant (albeit declining) number of Jews on the *Business Review Weekly's* "Rich 200" list.[7] However, Goldlust also confirms that a significant minority of Jews have incomes well below the Australian median. Jewish immigrants from the former Soviet Union appear to be particularly disadvantaged. Many Jews find themselves socially marginalized from and unable to participate in the organized activities and institutions of the Jewish community. Goldlust also points out that while most Jews in Australia have acculturated to the Australian way of life and "feel accepted and at ease" in mainstream urban Australia, most also strongly identify as Jews.

Of considerable political significance is Australian Jewry's relatively small size, estimated by Goldlust to be between 105,000 and 112,000 persons. This figure clearly has implications for the political influence of Australian Jewry, particularly when compared to the much larger Australian-Arab and Australian Muslim communities.[8]

The question of Jewish political representation is equally complicated. Suzanne Rutland in **chapter 2** traces the historical emergence of the Executive Council of Australian Jewry (ECAJ) and the associated state roof bodies as the official representatives of Australian Jews. However, she also notes the important roles played by the Zionist Federation of Australia and the independent think tank, the Australia/Israel & Jewish Affairs Council (AIJAC), and other bodies. Rutland identifies a number of problems with this representative structure, including the tendency to exclude minority or dissenting groups from representation, and the absence of professional funding for the ECAJ. In practice, the Jewish leadership appears to operate as a rather ineffective plutocracy, with AIJAC contentiously playing a leading role due to its professional structure and funding.

Partisanship and Ideologies

Modern Jewish history has had three epochal events, two of them within the space of a single generation: the admission of Jews as citizens in Western societies from the late eighteenth century, the Holocaust, and the establishment of the State of Israel in 1948. Each of these events has profoundly shaped Jewish political commitments and behaviour. The ideological orientations and political choices of Australian Jews repeat patterns found among other modern Jewish communities, albeit with some local variations.

The **chapters** by Sol Encel (**3**) and Philip Mendes (**4**) focus on Jewish involvement in the political left. Encel examines the record of Jewish involvement in the Australian Labor Party (ALP), and the complexities and tensions in the relationship between Jews and the ALP. He notes that since World War II, Jewish participation in the ALP has far exceeded Jewish contributions to the conservative parties, yet ironically Jewish electoral support for the ALP has progressively declined.

Mendes explores the history of Jewish involvement in the international left, and also draws attention to Jewish involvement in the broader Australian left, and to Australian Jewish left groups. He argues that most left-wing Jews experience an ongoing tension between their specific Jewish loyalties and their commitment to broader universalistic causes. This tension reflects the impact of left-wing anti-Zionism which sometimes deteriorates into outright anti-Semitism. Nevertheless, he agrees with Encel that Jewish involvement in the Australian left has far exceeded the Jewish contribution to conservative causes.

Peter Baume and William Rubinstein explore the relationship between Jews and the mainstream political right in Australia. In **chapter 5**, Baume documents the participation of Jews in the Liberal Party since its inception in the 1940s, and concludes that such involvement has been minimal, at least at the parliamentary level. His examination of the record suggests that the increased conservatism of Australian Jews identified by Rubinstein will have to overcome something of an "historical absence" if it is to be politically institutionalized.

In **chapter 6**, Rubinstein argues that Australian Jewry has become increasingly conservative in its voting preferences. He attributes this right-wing drift to a number of factors, including the growth in Jewish religious Orthodoxy, the high Jewish day school attendance, the centrality of Israel to Australian Jewish identity, and the generally affluent socio-economic status of Australian Jewry. Nevertheless, Rubinstein acknowledges the paradox that most prominent Jewish political activists are still associated with the left rather than the right, and equally that most Jewish leadership bodies adopt left-liberal positions on symbolic issues such as gender equality, Aboriginal rights, and support for immigrants and refugees.

Chapters 7 and **8** examine how specific Jewish concerns around anti-Semitism and Zionism or "pro-Israelism" influence Jewish politics more generally. Andrew Markus provides an historical overview of Australian Jewish responses to anti-Semitism and the impact of anti-Semitism on Australian Jewry. He discusses the traumatic legacy of the Holocaust for Australian Jews, and their heightened sense of vulnerability and sensitivity to the dangers of anti-Semitism. Whilst this post-war trauma may have subsided for subsequent Jewish generations, he argues that such concerns have been revived by the current perceived threat of terrorist attacks on Jewish schools and organizations. Markus also notes the persistence of internal Jewish divisions based on ideology, region, and personality regarding responses to anti-Semitism.

Danny Ben-Moshe considers the impact of identification with the State of Israel on Australian Jewish politics. He argues that Israel dominates the Jewish political agenda, but that other concerns such as Jewish education, communal security, Nazi war crimes, and broader human rights are also significant. Ben-Moshe suggests that support for Israel significantly influences voting outcomes in the heavily Jewish-populated federal seats of Melbourne Ports and Wentworth, but that support for Israel alone is no guarantee of Jewish support at the voting box.[9]

Issues and Controversies

In addition to their voting patterns and broad ideological orientations, the politics of Australian Jews are revealed in their engagement – or lack of engagement – with specific political movements and issues.

Barbara Bloch and Eva Cox in **chapter 9** dissect the relationship between Australian Jews and feminist politics. Drawing on a survey of Jewish women actively involved in "second wave feminism", they argue that many Jewish activists have a sense of being outsiders both within feminism and the Jewish community. Bloch and Cox identify a number of common factors behind this Jewish political activism, including Jewish social justice traditions, experiences of strong Jewish women, growing up in a minority group, anti-Semitism, and Jewish sexism.

Colin Tatz (**chapter 10**) critically examines the supposed "tradition" of Jewish concern for Aboriginal Australians. He argues provocatively that compared to the prominence of Jews in the American civil rights and South African anti-apartheid movements, Australian Jewish support for Aboriginal rights has been minimal. Tatz attributes this relative disinterest to the lack of physical interaction between the mainly urbanized Jewish community and Aborigines.

In **chapter 11**, Geoffrey Brahm Levey considers Jews' relation to multi-culturalism. He argues that the arrival of multicultural policies in Australia in the 1970s forced Jews to rethink their longstanding *modus operandi* as a religious minority and private association in Australian society, a challenge that helps explain why Jews were generally followers rather than leaders in the movement toward a multicultural regime in this country. Levey notes the shifting dualism in Australian Jewish identity, reflected in how Jews choose to call themselves: "Australian Jews", used within the Jewish community to emphasize the primacy of Jewish identity; and "Jewish Australian", typically used in public discourse to emphasize a common identity with other Australians. Levey explores this dualism through a number of case studies, including church–state separation, racial vilification and anti-discrimination legislation, ritual slaughter, and symbolic recognition. He concludes that despite their initial ambivalence, Australian Jews are now strong supporters of multiculturalism.

The discussion of Jews and multiculturalism returns us to the subject of democratic and pluralist politics, and of how Jews mobilize in support of their perceived interests.

Chanan Reich in **chapter 12** explores the political outlook and activities of the Australian Jewish lobby group, AIJAC. After sifting AIJAC publications and interviewing its Director, Colin Rubenstein, Reich describes AIJAC as an effective lobby group both on the Middle East and on domestic issues such as Nazi war criminals, anti-Semitism and racism, multiculturalism, terrorism, and Jewish security, although he concludes that measuring the overall success of such lobbying activities is elusive. Reich argues that AIJAC works cooperatively with the peak Jewish bodies at national and state level, and represents the views of mainstream Jewry. He notes that some left-wing Jews resent what they consider to be the "biased and overzealous" activities of AIJAC, and particularly its unflinching defense of Israeli government policies. AIJAC's activities also seem to provoke a backlash from those who fear the power of the so-called "Jewish lobby." However, Reich accepts the AIJAC perspective that successful lobbying for Israel and other Jewish concerns depends on a public presentation and perception of communal unity. This emphasis on public unity is also not uncommon in other Australian ethnic communities.

A more critical view of AIJAC is presented by Geoffrey Brahm Levey and Philip Mendes in their discussion of the Hanan Ashrawi affair in **chapter 13**. They accept the view that the unduly aggressive and ideological lobbying activities of AIJAC played into the hands of those who wish to paint the Jewish community as a disproportionately powerful lobby group. However, they argue that the Ashrawi affair reflected features endemic to Australian Jewish politics more generally, and some attitudes in the broader Australian community. In this sense, Hanan Ashrawi and her award of the Sydney Peace Prize were incidental to the controversy. Levey and Mendes point to the disjuncture between Jews' own sense of insecurity and vulnerability and general perceptions of them as affluent, privileged, and influential. They also question the unqualified public defence of Israeli policies by local Jewish bodies, and highlight the diversity of Jewish opinion on how these concerns should be operationalized in the Australian political context. Levey and Mendes conclude by asking whether the conventional assumptions and modes of Australian Jewish politics best serve the interests of Australian Jews today.

Peter Medding concludes the discussion by considering the politics of Australian Jews in comparative perspective. He identifies four primary Jewish group needs – identity, autonomy, security and survival – and traces the impact on these of four major post-World War II developments, including the establishment of the State of Israel, memory of the Holocaust, the collapse of communism and the rise of globalization, and the advent of multiculturalism. Picking up on themes addressed throughout the book, Medding identifies what is both common and distinctive about Jewish politics in Australia. He also offers an explanation for the shift towards conservatism in the party allegiances of Australian and British Jews from the late 1960s, in contrast to the continued support of American Jews for the Democratic Party.

Finally, in the Appendix, Hilary Rubinstein has compiled a useful roster of Jewish parliamentarians in Australia from 1849 to the present day. Two impressions quickly emerge from this list: First, the significant number of Jews who have held parliamentary seats in this country; even though, as Medding notes, Jewish representation in Australian legislatures and cabinets may not have reached the disproportionate involvement witnessed in the United States and Britain; and Second, the decline in this involvement in recent decades compared to previous periods. This latter trend may reflect a preference among contemporary Jews for professional and organizational roles in the political process and, perhaps, for local rather than state and national political offices,[10] although a few prominent community figures have, in recent years, sought preselection for federal seats. The coming years will tell whether the relative paucity today of Jewish parliamentarians is a passing or confirmed trend in Australian Jewish life.

Notes

1   John S. Levi and G. F. J. Bergman, *Australian Genesis: Jewish Convicts and Settlers, 1788–1860*, new edn (Carlton South, Vic.: Melbourne University Press, 2002).

2   See Hilary L. Rubinstein et al., *The Jews in the Modern World: A History Since 1750* (London: Arnold; New York: Oxford University Press, 2002), pp. 273–4, and chapter 1 this volume.

3   Damien Murphy, "Star Quality: The Extraordinary Contribution of Australia's Jews", *The Bulletin* 15 October (1996): 18–21.

4   For the House (16 February 2004), see: http://parlinfoweb.aph. gov.au/piweb/view_document.aspx?id=856541&table=HANSARDR. For the Senate (22 March 2004), see: http://parlinfoweb.aph.gov. au/piweb/view_document.aspx?ID=953833&TABLE=HANSARDS. For the NSW Parliament, see: www.parliament.nsw.gov.au/prod/parlment/

hansart.nsf/all/0FEF09A7A5B1F653CA256E50002727AD?openDocument &Highlight=2,la,anti-semitism. The Victorian Parliament passed its resolution against racial and religious vilification – a government initiative openly assisted by B'nai B'rith's Anti-defamation Commission – on 2 June 2004.

5 For citations and discussion of these surveys, see chapters 3, 6, and 8, this volume.

6 Michael Cavanagh, "Most funds went Liberals' way", *Australian Jewish News* 13 February 2004.

7 Simon Segal, "Jews on Rich 200 list declining", *Australian Jewish News* 30 May 2003.

8 Cameron Stewart, "Falling out with friends", *The Australian* 5 September 2003.

9 See also Philip Mendes and Geoffrey Brahm Levey, "Jewish vote is not so easily categorised", *Sydney Morning Herald*, 1 October 2003.

10 See Aviva Bard, "Jewish candidates out in force", *Australian Jewish News* 19 March 2004, which reports that at least 30 Jewish candidates – "an unprecedented number" – were standing in the New South Wales local council elections in March 2004.

PART

I

Identifying the Jewish Community

1 | Jews in Australia: A Demographic Profile

JOHN GOLDLUST

A Question of Numbers

A great deal of the sociological discussion surrounding Jewish life in the modern Diaspora has focussed on the decidedly murky numerical and definitional problems that immediately confront any observer seeking to describe and analyze local and/or national Jewish "communities."[1] Do Jews constitute a "religious", "national", "ethnic" or "cultural group", or some unique combination of all of these? In modern, secular nation-states does "being Jewish" indicate an "ascribed characteristic" or is it a "voluntary" component of personal identity? Can a person "born Jewish" cease to "be Jewish" during their lifetime? By what recognized authority or principle might an "objective" observer determine if a person is clearly "Jewish" or "not-Jewish"? It would be fair to conclude that despite the mountain of research, debate and verbiage expended on these issues, all continue to remain open questions.

In Australia, Jewish demography has been heavily reliant upon the Australian population census and, in particular, on the regular census question included that asks respondents to nominate their "religion." In this context, being counted as "Jewish" in the census has therefore relied firstly on honest self-disclosure and, secondly, on the preparedness of individuals to formally acknowledge a religious identification with "Judaism" or the "Jewish religion." This is further complicated by a number of other factors. Most generally, while the level of reliability of the data collected in the national census is undoubtedly reinforced by the weight of bureaucratic and governmental authority, the veracity of individual information provided in response to any of the questions is never checked or challenged. More importantly, since 1933 the question that asks for the respondent's religion has been clearly designated as "optional" – the only question in the Australian census for which the right to voluntary disclosure is formally granted.

As a result there is considerable dispute amongst demographers, sociologists and community leaders as to the "actual" size of the Australian Jewish community. Since 1933 the proportion of the Australian population who reply either "no religion" or choose not to answer the religion question has steadily increased, reaching 25.3 percent in 2001. Over this period there has undoubtedly been a corresponding increase in persons who were "born Jewish" but who, given the choice, prefer not to designate themselves as "Jewish by religion" in reply to the census question. Some do not adhere to religious beliefs or practices and therefore consider themselves "secular" Jews.[2] Some have immigrated to Australia from countries, and in circumstances, where government knowledge about the identity of Jewish residents led in the past to tragic personal outcomes, and therefore have remained understandably cautious about divulging this sort of information to the "authorities" in Australia. Some, like a considerable number of other Australians, may perceive the Australian census as another example of governmental and bureaucratic "invasion of privacy" and therefore will opt not to answer any question they are not required to answer.

On the other hand, for political and strategic reasons, before each national census Jewish organizations, media and community leaders strongly encourage all "communally oriented" Jews to identify themselves through the census religion question in order to provide accurate and reliable data on the size and demographic characteristics of the community. Particularly, in the context of Australia's multiculturalist policies and programs, the question of numbers is of critical importance to ethnic or minority group organizations preparing submissions for support and funding for communally organized welfare, education and social services from local, state and federal agencies.

Taking into consideration the implications of the above qualifications, the following points may be made:

- The data on "Jews by religion" drawn from the Australian Census (and in particular from each national census since 1933) probably understates the total Jewish population.
- Demographers and sociologists who have considered the issue carefully have concluded that, at least since 1991, the "real" number of Jews is probably between 20–25 percent higher than the figure suggested by the Australian census religion question.[3]
- So, at the 2001 Census, the "core" of 84,000 self-identified "Jews by religion" residing in Australia more than likely reflects a certain level of under-enumeration. My cautious, but still speculative, "adjusted" estimate of the "real" number of Jews in Australia, would be a figure somewhere between 105,000 and 112,000.[4]
- However, for the more detailed discussion of the demographic charac-

teristics of Jews in Australia set out below, I consider the validity of undertaking this sort of "data adjustment" exercise (particularly at the level of individual cells within a cross-tabulation) to be highly questionable. So, all subsequent figures, percentages and cross tabulations cited in this chapter are based on Australian census data that includes only persons who chose to identify themselves as "Jewish by religion" in the census.

Residential Distribution

Since the beginning of the twentieth century, at least 80 percent of Australia's Jewish population have continuously resided in the two largest cities of Sydney and Melbourne. Furthermore, most of the pre- and post-World War II Jewish immigrants also chose to settle in or near the already existing Jewish neighbourhoods in the larger state capital cities. Consequently, by 1961 the proportion of Australia's Jewish population concentrated in these two cities had increased to almost 90 percent. Since then, this figure has remained fairly constant, and at the time of the 2001 census had declined only very slightly to 88 percent.

Table 1.1 Jews by State and Territory, selected census data, 1841–2001

Persons who identified as "Jewish by religion" by State/Territory of residence

Year of census	NSW	Vic	WA	Qld	SA	Tas	NT	ACT	Australia
1841	856	57	1	—	10	259	—	—	1,183
1901	6,447	5,907	1,259	733	786	107	—	—	15,239
1933	10,305	9,500	2,105	1,041	528	70	—	—	23,553
1961	24,026	29,932	2,782	1,334	985	136	23	111	59,329
2001	34,608	39,185	5,068	3,298	1,069	170	120	485	84,003

Persons who identified as "Jewish by religion" by State/Territory of residence (percent)

Year of census	NSW	Vic	WA	Qld	SA	Tas	NT	ACT	Australia
1841	72.4	4.8	0.1	—	0.8	21.9	—	—	100.0
1901	42.3	38.8	8.3	4.8	5.2	0.7	—	—	100.0
1933	43.8	40.3	8.9	4.4	2.2	0.3	—	—	100.0
1961	40.5	50.5	4.7	2.2	1.7	0.2	0.0	0.2	100.0
2001	41.2	46.7	6.0	3.9	1.3	0.2	0.1	0.6	100.0

Sources: W. D. Rubinstein, *Judaism in Australia* (Canberra: AGPS, 1995), p. 23; W. Lippmann, "The Demography of Australian Jewry", *Jewish Journal of Sociology* 8, 2 (1966): 213–39; 2001 Census Classification Counts – First Release Data, *Australian Bureau of Statistics* website (www.abs.gov.au).

By the later half of the nineteenth century, there were a number of smaller towns and regional centres in each Australian state with small Jewish populations, some large enough to sustain rudimentary religious and community organizations. However, throughout the twentieth century the trend in most of these regional centres has been one of declining Jewish numbers, often accompanied by the neglect and closure of synagogues and the virtual disappearance of public signs of Jewish communal life. So, in 2001, the Jews of Melbourne, Sydney, Perth and Adelaide represented more than 90 percent (and in the case of Melbourne as high as 96 percent) of the total number of Jews residing in each respective Australian state.

Overall, there are the two large Jewish communities of Melbourne and Sydney (40,000–50,000 each), and then two "medium sized" communities in Western Australia and Queensland (with more than 3,000 persons in each). The number of Jews in Perth has been boosted by immigration from South Africa over the past two decades; also, since the 1960s, there has been considerable in-migration to Queensland of Jews from other states, with the Gold Coast area in particular becoming a popular Jewish retirement destination.

As indicated in table 1.1, there are only very small numbers of Jews in each of the other Australian states and territories (mostly concentrated in Adelaide, Hobart, Canberra and Darwin). In 2001 the number of Jews in South Australia was just over 1,000, most living in Adelaide. In marked contrast with the other mainland states, in numerical terms this community has shown almost no growth since the 1960s. The Jewish population of Tasmania has always been tiny and, indeed, it peaked numerically in the nineteenth century. The total number of persons in Tasmania who identified as Jewish in the 2001 census was 170, and while this represents a considerable increase from the 70 Jews living there in 1933, it is still well below the figure recorded in 1841.

Within each of the major cities Jewish residential patterns are concentrated even further. Since the 1960s Jews continue to remain residentially most heavily concentrated in a handful of southeastern suburbs of Melbourne, the harbour side eastern suburbs of Sydney and selected sections of Sydney's North Shore. Well over half of all the Jews in Perth reside in the Local Government Area of Stirling. Similarly, more than half of Melbourne's Jews live within the municipality of Glen Eira. Located in the southeastern region of Melbourne, the City of Glen Eira is home to by far the largest number, as well as the densest residential concentration, of Jews anywhere in Australia. The more than 20,000 Jews living there represent a little over 17 percent of all residents of this municipality. Similarly, the 10,000 Jews who reside in Sydney's eastern suburbs municipality of Waverley represent more than 16 percent of the total population of this Local Government Area.

Indeed the extent of Jewish suburban residential concentration is perhaps best illustrated in the data presented in table 1.2 below. From the

2001 census information, if we add together the number of Jews residing in the 10 local municipalities with the largest Jewish populations in Australia (five in Melbourne, four in Sydney and one in Perth), the combined total represents more than 71 percent of all Jews in Australia.

Table 1.2 Local Government Areas in Australia with highest numbers of "Jews by religion": 2001 Census

Local Government Area of usual residence	Number of Jews	% of Jews in State	% of Jews in Australia
New South Wales			
Waverley	9,660	28.0	11.5
Woollahra	6,779	19.6	8.1
Ku-ring-gai	3,975	11.5	4.7
Randwick	3,645	10.5	4.3
Victoria			
Glen Eira	20,137	51.4	24.0
Stonnington	4,697	12.0	5.6
Port Phillip	4,002	10.2	4.8
Bayside	2,377	6.1	2.8
Boroondara	2,217	5.7	2.6
Western Australia			
Stirling	2,722	53.8	3.2
All Local Government Areas	60,211	—	71.6

Source: Analysis of data set from the Australian Bureau of Statistics prepared at the request of the Jewish Community Council of Victoria Demography Committee.

Birthplace

A little over half of Australia's current Jewish population was born overseas. Australia's large-scale immigration program of the past six decades notwithstanding, the proportion of overseas-born Jews (53 percent) is still significantly higher than the overseas-born component in the Australian population (22 percent).

The proportion of Jews born in Australia was quite high prior to World War I. However, from a low-point of 39 percent in 1961 (reflecting the volume of post-World War II Jewish immigrants), the component of the Jewish population born in Australia has steadily increased to reach 47 percent in 2001. The 2001 figures also highlight more recent Jewish immigration patterns. With the inevitable decline in the number of surviving Jews from the pre- and post-World War II immigrant generation, there has been a corresponding decrease in the overall proportion of European-born Jews since 1961, and a concomitant increase in the number who were born in South Africa and the former USSR. Indeed, the significance of South African Jewish immigration has been such that this group now represents almost 13 percent of the Australia's Jewish population and has clearly replaced the post-World War II Polish-born as the largest overseas-born cohort within the active Jewish community.

Age and Sex Distribution

The continuing demographic impact of the large group of Jewish immigrants who arrived in Australia between the 1940s and 1960s (and their children) is again clearly illustrated in the age distribution of Jews at the time of the 2001 census (see figure 1.1). In comparison to the general Australian population the Jews are an especially aging community (the median age for Jews in 2001 was 42 years compared to 35 years for all Australians). This is further emphasized by the group 65 years or older who now represent more than 19 percent of all Jewish persons, compared to 12.5 percent of the general Australian population. The numerically largest Jewish age cohort is made up of persons between 40 and 55 years, who make up almost a quarter of Australia's total Jewish population.

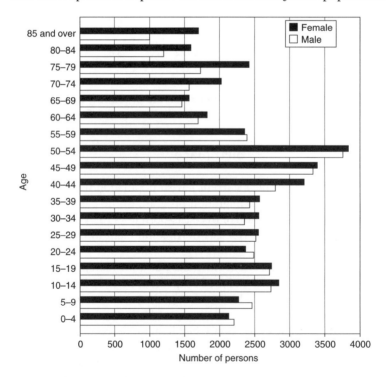

Figure 1.1 Jews by religion: 2001 census age by sex
Source: Analysis of data set from the Australian Bureau of Statistics prepared at the request of the Jewish Community Council of Victoria Demography Committee.

In Australia Jewish females (51.9 percent) significantly outnumber Jewish males (48.1 percent), and this is true across virtually all age group-ings, except for the very youngest. The gender imbalance is more pronounced for the Jewish population aged 60 years and older, amongst whom 56 percent are females. Within the smaller Jewish cohort aged 75 years or older the proportion of females is even higher (59 percent).

Education, Occupational Status and Socio-economic Position

During the latter half of the twentieth century, as Robert Wistrich has observed:

> [Jews] have largely become a middle class people, inhabiting the core areas of the world's economic and political systems. To a much greater degree than in 1939, they are generally to be found in advanced industrial countries that have high per capita incomes, health standards, literacy rates, and cultural achieve-ments.[5]

This is certainly an accurate description of the Australian situation. Firstly, since the 1920s, there has been a consistently high rate of upward socio-economic mobility between each immigrant Jewish cohort and succeeding generations. As a consequence, as one overview recently suggested, Australian Jewry is "by and large, an upper-middle-class group", with higher than average family incomes. This has occurred as a result of "Jews' occupational concentration in the higher managerial and professional cate-gories", with the pathway to achieving this status the considerable number and increasing proportion of young Jews who have completed post-secondary educational and professional qualifications.[6] Certainly the analysis of data from the most recent Australian census strongly reinforces this general picture.

According to the 2001 census the proportion of Australian Jews (both male and female) who have completed a tertiary or post-graduate degree (34 percent) is almost three times higher than for the general Australian population (13 percent). The proportion with an undergraduate or post-graduate degree is even higher for the "younger" Jewish age groups – more than half aged 25–44 years, and 42 percent of the 45–64 year-old age group. Among Jews aged 25 years or older, a slightly higher proportion of those born in Australia reported having completed a university or post-graduate degree (46 percent) than Jews who were born overseas (35 percent). What is more significant is that in both of these sub-groups the proportion with such qualifications is considerably higher than in the general Australian population. In this respect, it would seem that the post-World War II Jewish immigrants to Australia were similar to the early twentieth century Jewish immigrants to the USA. Both groups "took advantage of free public education for their children as a tool of acculturation and as a stepping stone to upward mobility." Consequently, in both countries Jewish children stayed in school longer than did children of other immigrant groups.[7]

This high level of educational qualifications among the Australian Jewish population is clearly reflected in the data on distribution of occupations and median levels of household income. According to the 2001 census information, around two-thirds of the 40,000 Jews employed in Australia's workforce are concentrated in more highly remunerated occupations, either as managers or administrators (15 percent), professionals (38 percent) or associate professionals (14 percent). The extent to which the Jewish occupational distribution is heavily skewed towards higher status and better paid jobs is further reinforced by noting that, according to the 2001 census, fewer than 40 percent of all employed Australians are in these occupational categories.

Not surprisingly, analyses of income data in Australia over recent decades consistently confirm that, as a group, Jews have incomes well above the national average. This is given considerable anecdotal support with the publication of the annual *Business Review Weekly* "rich lists." In these, the proportion of Jewish individuals and families among the nation's highest income earners (recent estimates are around 20 percent) far exceeds what one might expect, given the extremely modest numerical representation of Jews in the Australian population as a whole (one person in every 200 Australians is Jewish). It must be noted that income data from social surveys – and this includes the census – are based on self-reporting and are therefore considered notoriously unreliable. Still, a good index of the *relative* socio-economic position of Jews as a group may be derived from a comparative analysis of the household income data reported in the 2001 census. So, for example, whereas at that time the median household income for all Australian households was calculated at around $39,000 per annum, the median for the more than 34,000 Jewish households identified in the 2001 census was $61,400 per annum. Couple families (with and without dependents) make up over 62 percent of all Jewish households, and it is in these categories that we find particularly high median household incomes (see table 1.3 below).

However it would of course be misleading to suggest that high incomes are universal for Jews living in Australia. More than 27 percent of Jewish households reported incomes below $32,000 per annum. Table 1.3 shows relatively much lower median household incomes for a number of subgroups within the Jewish community, in particular for lone-person households. These tend to include a high proportion of both the young and the elderly. Similarly, household incomes are lower among one-parent families with dependent children. The census data also indicate generally higher incomes for households in which there are Jews who were born in Australia and among households with Jewish immigrants from English-speaking countries (particularly from South Africa, Zimbabwe and North

America). As a group, the generally less affluent socio-economic situation of the cohort of Jews from the former Soviet Union who have settled in Australia in recent decades is also very apparent. Their median household income is conspicuously well below that of most other sub-groups in the community, and their level of socio-economic success quite a contrast with the experience of the Jews from Southern Africa – the other Jewish immigrant group to enter Australia in significant numbers during the same period.

Table 1.3 Median annual household income reported for Jewish households[1] by family/household type – Australian Census 2001

Family/household type	Median annual household income ($)	Total households
Couple family with dependents	$92,800	9,757
Couple family without dependents	$71,100	11,570
one-parent family with dependents	$35,400	1,558
one-parent family without dependents	$49,200	744
One Family Household: Other family	$42,600	342
Multiple Family Household	$104,000+	193
Lone person household	$27,600	8,599
Group Household	$66,500	1,552
All 'Jewish' Households	$61,400	34,315

[1] Jewish household is defined here as any household that includes at least one Jewish person.
Source: Analysis of data set from the Australian Bureau of Statistics prepared at the request of the Jewish Community Council of Victoria Demography Committee.

It is also of interest that while the majority of Jewish immigrants from South Africa have embraced existing Jewish institutions and community norms and appear to have become extremely well integrated into Jewish community life in Australia, the same is not generally true of immigrants from the former Soviet Union.[8]

It has been suggested that one less frequently acknowledged aspect associated with the widespread upward socio-economic mobility among Jews in Australia is the concomitant tendency towards the social marginalization of less affluent Jews. A Sydney report commissioned to examine the "threat" to future Jewish continuity noted that, in a community where being upper-middle class is the norm there is also an expectation that those who wish to purchase kosher food, participate in organized community life, contribute to Jewish charities and send their children to fee-paying Jewish Day schools and on extended school or group visits to Israel, are financially able to so. Furthermore financial constraints inevitably influence area of residence and therefore many of the less affluent Jews tend to live a considerable distance from the more expensive suburbs in which many of the community resources are located.[9]

Jewish Education and the Jewish Day School Phenomenon

The Jewish Day school movement was itself a leading initiative of, and strongly supported by, many among the post-World War II immigrant cohort. One of its primary goals was an inter-generational strengthening of Jewish identity and thereby, it was assumed, an increased likelihood of future Jewish continuity.

In Australia where, since the late nineteenth century, state education systems had been providing universal access to secular, free, primary and secondary education, a new generation of Jewish community leaders and educators was determined to establish a "Jewish alternative." They drew their model both from their own experiences of separate Jewish school systems in Europe, and from the alternatives to state education previously established in Australia – the various Protestant denominational private fee-paying schools and Church-supported Catholic school system. The first Jewish Day School, Mount Scopus College, opened in Melbourne in 1949. The concept continued to expand its base of support among Jewish parents so that by the 1990s there were a total of 18 Jewish Day schools (nine in Melbourne and six in Sydney) with at least one primary-level Jewish school in every major Australian city, except Canberra. At this time, almost three-quarters of all Jewish children in Melbourne and half of those in Sydney were spending at least some of their primary or secondary school years as students of one or more of these private, fee-paying Jewish day schools. The success in attracting such a high proportion of the target group is widely perceived as "the community's most significant effort towards ethnic continuity."[10]

Also, since the 1960s, a rise of the Jewish Day schools in Australia has coincided with a decline in levels of support and resources provided by state governments for the centrally funded universal education systems, and a more general movement by middle-class parents towards securing a private school education for their children, particularly at secondary level. Indeed, census figures confirm that in 2001, of the more than 10,000 Jewish children attending school, around 70 percent of Jewish children (across infant, primary and secondary levels) were in non-Government fee-paying schools (of course not all of these were students at Jewish Day Schools). This is the inverse of the situation within the general Australian population among whom more than two-thirds of school-age children attend Government or "state" schools.

Marital Status, Family Relationships and Household Types

A little over three quarters of all Jewish persons enumerated in the 2001 Australian census were living in couple family households. More than half (54 percent) live in families that include one or more children with a further 23 percent in couple families without children. The next largest category is "lone-person" households, accounting for a further 12 percent. This figure is slightly higher than in the general Australian population, and this is partly due to the peculiarities of the Jewish age distribution that includes a higher proportion of elderly within the Jewish community. It is also consistent with the relatively high proportion of widowed persons in the Australian Jewish population (see table 1.4 below).

Table 1.4   Marital Status by Sex in percentage: Census 2001

Persons aged 15 years or older	Married	Separated	Divorced	Widowed	Never married	Total (millions)
Male						
All Australia	52.4	3.2	6.6	2.5	35.3	7,347,379
Jewish persons	60.0	2.5	5.9	3.3	28.3	33,045
Female						
All Australia	50.1	3.6	8.1	9.7	28.5	7,690,960
Jewish persons	52.9	2.3	7.8	14.4	22.6	36,436
All						
All Australia	51.2	3.4	7.4	6.2	31.8	15,038,339
Jewish persons	56.3	2.4	6.9	9.1	25.3	69,481

Sources: Basic Community Profile Australia 2001 Census, *Australian Bureau of Statistics*, Catalogue No. 2001.0; Analysis of data set from the Australian Bureau of Statistics prepared at the request of the Jewish Community Council of Victoria Demography Committee.

Table 1.4 compares the marital status for Jewish persons with the Australian population as a whole at the time of the 2001 census and, on the whole finds the two groups to be quite similar. Overall, a slightly higher proportion of Jews are married and a slightly lower proportion have never been married, but again both these findings may be attributed to the significantly higher median age of the Jewish population compared to the Australian population as a whole. The proportion of Jews separated or divorced is very close to the national norm and also follows the widespread recent trend in western societies of a higher rate of divorce among females than males. This is in contrast with the findings of demographic studies of Australian Jews prior to the 1990s that consistently reported a lower rate of divorce among Jewish couples than in the general population. Currently, the Jewish divorce rates are noticeably highest among the 45–64 year old age cohort with 15 percent of females and 13 percent of males in this age group divorced (and a further 4 percent of both males and females separated).

Overall, 92 percent of Jewish couples are in registered marriages with 8 percent in de facto marriage relationships, with these proportions identical for both males and females. The proportion of de facto marriage relationships among couple families in the Australian population as a whole is slightly higher at 12 percent. However, consistent with general societal trends, de facto relationships are noticeably more prevalent among the younger age groups. These were reported by 12 percent of Jewish respondents between 25 and 44 years of age (and also by half of the small number of Jews aged between 15 and 24 years in couple relationships).

Of all family households in Australia that include at least one Jewish adult, around 16,000 also include children. There are a total of 29,000 children living in these households. Of these, 61 percent are aged 14 years or less, 32 percent are aged between 15 and 24 years and 7 percent are 25 years or older. There is one child in 38 percent of family households, in 40 percent there are two children, 15 percent of families have three children and 7 percent have four or more children. The evidence suggests that again following general "first world" norms, Jewish families are, on average, having fewer children and that the "fertility rate" among Jewish women in Australia remains below the "replacement" figure of 2.1 children per adult female.[11]

Intermarriage Patterns

There is no topic that arouses greater concern among Jewish religious leaders, educators and community leaders than the rising rate of intermarriage between Jews and non-Jews. Most tend to support the views articulated by one of the pioneers of the demographic and sociological study of modern Jewry, Arthur Ruppin, who, as early as 1940, had undertaken a careful and extensive examination of the "post emancipation" trends in Jewish/non-Jewish marriage rates. After considering the large body of longitudinal data available since the mid-nineteenth century in a number of European countries and, in particular, the available evidence on the likelihood that children of such unions will "remain Jews", Ruppin's forceful conclusion was that:

> Mixed marriages constitute the final and decisive step in the process of assimilation of Jews to their non-Jewish environment . . . As soon as inter-marriage on a large scale becomes customary, the last barrier that divides the Jews from their neighbours has fallen, and therewith their fate as a community is ultimately sealed. Probably the disappearance of the Jews in many countries, in which they existed in ancient times and in the Middle Ages, is accounted for by the fall of this last barrier.[12]

Ruppin's interpretation and prognosis still represent the essence of the widely shared "common-sense" understanding of the implications of rising intermarriage rates on the "continuity prospects" for Jewish life, both at the levels of the survival of particular local communities and for the Jewish Diaspora in general. Indeed, the most recent expressions of serious concern for future Jewish survival were triggered by the findings of the 1990 National Jewish Population Survey in the United States which reported that the intermarriage rate of Jews there had risen steeply in the previous two decades and was rapidly approaching 60 percent.[13]

An increasing proportion of Jews choosing to marry non-Jews was already evident in Australia by the early decades of the twentieth century. Drawing on the available census data it is possible to tabulate the number of partner relationships in which both males and female partners identify as "Jewish" in response to the census religion question. A longitudinal overview of these results for selected Australian censuses between 1911 and 2001 is reproduced in table 1.5 below.

Table 1.5   Jewish In-Marriage rate in Australia, in percentage: 1911–2001

Census year	Married Jewish males with Jewish partners	Married Jewish females with Jewish partners
1911	73.0	87.0
1921	71.0	84.0
1933	80.0	89.0
1961	88.0	94.0
1981	86.0	89.8
1991	85.5	88.8
1996	84.4	87.7
2001	78.6	80.1

Sources: W. Lippmann, "The Demography of Australian Jewry", pp. 213–39; W. D. Rubinstein, *The Jews in Australia*, Vol 2, (Port Melbourne: William Heinemann, 1991), p. 94; A. C. Gariano, "Religious Identification and Marriage", *People and Place* 2, 1 (1994): 41–47; A. C. Gariano and S. D. Rutland, "Religious Intermix: 1996 Census Update", *People and Place*, 5, 4 (1997): 10–19; Analysis of data set from the Australian Bureau of Statistics prepared at the request of the Jewish Community Council of Victoria Demography Committee.

The table shows a higher rate of Jewish in-marriage for females than males, a pattern that remains consistent over time. The data also document the earlier trend in Australia towards an increasing number of Jews marrying non-Jews, with the out-marriage rate reaching a "high-point" in 1921, when more than a quarter of all Jewish males had non-Jewish spouses. However, following the influx of European Jews before and after the World War II, this trend had sharply reversed by the 1950s. The "low-point" for Jewish out-marriage in Australia was recorded at the time of the 1961 census when 88 percent of Jewish males and 94 percent of Jewish females in

Australia were married to Jewish spouses. This relatively low rate of Jewish out-marriage continued until the 1970s, and then began to climb again, although, at least up to the late 1990s, increasing at a fairly slow rate.

While the data in table 1.5 illustrate long-term trends, establishing a precise "rate" of intermarriage has always been an extremely problematic exercise. The major difficulty in assessing Australian data is once again an artefact of the presence in the census of the "non-compulsory" religion question. It seems reasonable to assume that if, in the 2001 census, up to a quarter of all Jews in Australia either indicated they had "no religion" or chose not to reply to this question, then the same logic would suggest that in some couple relationships one partner replied "Jewish" to the religion question while the other, perhaps from a very similar background, chose not to do so. The "religiously non-identifying" partner, might therefore appear in the "no religion/not stated" category. In 2001 this category accounts for around 6 percent of the spouses of Jewish partners and may suggest that the "real" intermarriage rate remains somewhat below the 20 percent otherwise indicated.[14]

However, an analysis of the census data by age group does suggest an intergenerational shift in the likelihood of Jews in Australia "marrying out." In 2001, for the 65 years and over cohort, 86 percent of Jewish males and 91 percent of Jewish females had Jewish partners; the equivalent figures for the 25–34 year old group were 70 percent and 72 percent respectively.

Another continuing trend is the much higher out-marriage rates for Jews living outside of the major urban centres of Jewish population. In 2001 the proportion of Jewish in-marriages in Victoria and New South Wales, was reported at 85 percent and 78 percent respectively. It was lower in Western Australia (74 percent), South Australia and Queensland (around 50 percent); and much lower still among the smallest Jewish communities in the ACT (40 percent), the Northern territory (30 percent) and Tasmania (15 percent).

However, certainly in the larger Australian cities, where the overwhelming majority of Australian Jews reside, the current rate of intermarriage remains below that recorded for Jews in Australia in the 1920s. It is also still nowhere near the Jewish intermarriage rates of 50 percent and higher reported for the US and most countries in Europe in the 1990s.[15]

The Future: Jewish Growth, Stagnation or Decline?

What can this brief demographic snapshot tell us about the current state of the Australian Jewish community, and is it possible to make any projections about its future? Much of the evidence presented above runs counter to any suggestion of imminent community stagnation or decline. Certainly, in the first decade of the twenty-first century the Australian Jewish community would appear to be in a very "healthy" state, particularly when compared with the picture currently being painted of much larger national Jewish communities in the United States, Britain and Argentina.[16] At the most basic level of numbers, since the initial European settlement more than 200 years ago, the Australian Jewish community has been continually growing and, with a Jewish population of well over 100,000, it is currently the tenth largest national Jewish community in the world. More significantly, Australia stands out as one of very few countries in the Jewish Diaspora in which the Jewish population continues to increase.

However, as the current Jewish birth-rate in Australia indicates that the Jewish population is not replacing itself, a number of demographic questions follow. Will there continue to be enough future Jewish immigration to Australia to sustain the current rate of growth, or at least maintain the current size of the community? From where might such immigration come? Will the rate of intermarriage between Jews and non-Jews in Australia stabilize, or continue to increase? And if it does increase significantly will this inevitably lead to a net Jewish "loss" in future generations?

A very small percentage of Jews worldwide would currently exhibit the stringent level of religious observance traditionally associated with the term "strict Orthodoxy." In Australia, the proportion is around 5 percent. Even if the notion of "religiosity" were expanded to include all whose principal "mode" of Jewish identification is religious (rather than ethnic/communal or cultural) the proportion of Australian Jews in this category would probably not rise above 15 percent.[17] Among the remainder, a further 40 percent maintain some on-going connection with Jewish religious traditions, adhering to at least some of the religious observances associated with the most important festivals and holy days, and also in relation to the rituals associated with significant life-cycle events (birth, circumcision, *Bar-* and *Bat-Mitzvah* ceremonies, marriage and death). Nor should it be assumed that all of the 45 percent of Jews who prefer to consider themselves "Jewish but not religious" are necessarily aggressively "secularist" in their orientation. It is therefore important to distinguish the majority within this "secular" group who might also occasionally participate in some Jewish religious rituals and customs and who continue to identify themselves ethnically or culturally as Jews, from a minority for whom "being secular" implies both a weakened Jewish identity and little interest or concern with Jewish continuity.

Apart from experiencing little anti-Semitism and few if any barriers to economic mobility, by the 1980s and 1990s, most Jews in Australia exhibited a high level of general acculturation. Almost all, apart from small groups located within the "strictly Orthodox" section of the religious spectrum, are well integrated into the broader Australian community. Almost all now use English as their primary language of communication. (Yiddish is still in evidence, but it remains the *lingua franca* only amongst the now elderly post-World War II generation, while Russian is widely spoken by recent immigrants from the former Soviet Union.)

More importantly, most Australian Jews participate, both actively and as audiences/consumers, across the full range of available sporting, artistic, musical and cultural activities. It is perhaps not surprising, then, that most Jews, particularly those born in Australia or who arrived as young children, generally feel accepted and at ease in "mainstream", middle-class, urban, Australian society. Yet, in terms of patterns of social relations and attitudes to group identity, a 1991 research study in Melbourne found that most still mixed extensively (although not exclusively) with other Jews, and expressed a firm commitment to their identity as Jews, and to Jewish continuity into the future (with little variation between Australian-born Jews and those who came to Australia as immigrants, as well as across all adult age groups).[18]

Notes

This chapter includes analyses of demographic data on the Australian Jewish community drawn from the most recent Australian Census of 2001. The author wishes to express his gratitude to Mr Grahame Leonard who, in his role as Chairman of the Jewish Community Council of Victoria's Demography Committee, arranged for the purchase of a specially commissioned data set to which he kindly granted me complete access. This was of enormous assistance in the preparation of this chapter.

1 See for example the discussion by the leading Israeli demographer, Sergio Della Pergola in the section "Main Problems in Jewish Population Research" of his article "World Jewish Population, 2001", *American Jewish Year Book* 101 (New York: American Jewish Committee, 2001).

2 In a comprehensive Jewish community survey of 640 adults undertaken in Melbourne in 1991, 45 percent of those interviewed instead chose to describe themselves as "Jewish but not religious". This would suggest that a considerable proportion of Jews in Australia do not consider affiliation with any contemporary version of religious Judaism as a necessary component of their identification as Jews. More significantly, the percentage that gave this response in 1991 was more than double the 22 percent who had replied this way in a similar 1967 survey. See John Goldlust, *The Jews of Melbourne: A Community Profile* (Melbourne: Jewish Welfare Society Inc, 1993), p. 212.

3 My preference is for the relatively simple technique of adjusting the "Jews by religion" figures in each census by a factor reflecting the overall percentage of the total Australian population who either replied "no religion" or gave no answer to this question. This proportion has increased in each Australian census from around 11 percent in 1933 to 25.3 percent in 2001. That this approach provides reasonable and defensible estimates of the level of "under-enumeration" of Jews living in the larger communities is supported by reference to other communal sources; for example, the detailed "community registers" kept over the years by Jewish welfare organizations in Melbourne and Sydney, community organization membership files, information available

from Jewish Day schools and community fund-raising lists. See the discussions of "under-enumeration" by Sol Encel, "The Changing Face of Australian Jewry", *Australian Jewish News*, Special Report, Melbourne edn, 24 January 1992; W. D. Rubinstein, "Jews in the 1996 Australian Census", *Australian Jewish Historical Society Journal* 14, 3 (1998): 497–8; and Gary Eckstein in his report, *Sydney Jewish Community: Demographic Profile*, prepared for the New South Wales Jewish Communal Appeal (February 2003).

4 The 2001 Australian Census included the question: "What is the person's Ancestry?" Analysis of responses indicates that "Jewish" was written in as the first choice "ancestry" by only 15,664 persons and as second choice by 6,889, for a total of 22,553 persons (and that this included only 18 percent of all persons who identified themselves as "Jews by religion"). However the question did reveal that there were 6,819 persons in Australia who claim a Jewish "ancestry" but who did not reply "Jewish" to the religion question. What we do not know is how many in this group falls into the category of "secular Jews", and how many may be merely acknowledging a Jewish grandparent or other Jewish ancestor, but have little or no current sense of a personal identity with "Judaism" or "Jewishness".

5 See Robert S. Wistrich, "Do the Jews have a future?", *Commentary* 98, 1 (1994): 23.

6 See Rubinstein, *Judaism in Australia*, pp. 37–42.

7 See Paula E. Hyman, "National Contexts, Eastern European Immigrants and Jewish Identity: A Comparative Analysis", in Steven M. Cohen and Gabriel Horencyk, eds, *National Variations in Jewish Identity: Implications for Jewish Education* (Albany, NY: State University of New York Press, 1999), pp. 111–12.

8 For an extended discussion of Jewish immigrants from the former Soviet Union, see my article "Soviet Jews in Australia", in James Jupp, ed., *The Australian People: An Encyclopedia of the Nation, Its Peoples and Their Origins* (Cambridge: Cambridge University Press, 2001), pp. 543–7.

9 See Helen Pitt, "Being Jewish is so costly", *Sydney Morning Herald*, 16 April 1997.

10 Leon Glezer, "Jews in Australia in the Twentieth Century", in Jupp, ed., *The Australian People*, p. 541.

11 Although this varies from state to state, with the fertility rate among Jewish women in Victoria, at least in the early 1990s, almost at "replacement level". See Rubinstein, *Judaism in Australia*, p. 29.

12 Arthur Ruppin, *The Jewish Fate and Future* (London: Macmillan, 1940), p. 114.

13 In the 1990 National Jewish Population Survey in the United States, of the 5.5 million "core" Jews (defined as those who were "born Jewish"), 31 percent had married a non-Jewish person. For marriages between 1985 and 1990, however the rate was 57 percent. See Stephen Sharot, "Judaism and Jewish Ethnicity: Changing Interrelationships and Differentiations in the Diaspora and Israel", in Ernest Krausz and Gitta Tulea, eds, *Jewish Survival: The Identity Problem at the Close of the Twentieth Century* (New Brunswick, NJ and London, UK: Transaction, 1998), p. 85.

14 An interpretation consistently argued by W. D. Rubinstein. See, for example,

his discussion, "Jews in the 1996 Australian Census", *Australian Jewish Historical Society Journal* 14, 3 (1998): 595–6.

15 Paralleling the already cited intermarriage trends from the United States, Bernard Wasserstein reports: "In most of Europe a third to a half of Jews who marry have non-Jewish spouses. Most of the children of such marriages cannot be expected to identify themselves as Jews". See his *The Vanishing Diaspora: The Jews in Europe since 1945* (London: Hamish Hamilton, 1996), p. 282.

16 See, for example, the overviews of these, as well as of a number of other, national Jewish communities in a recent cross-national comparative volume: Sol Encel and Leslie Stein, eds, *Continuity, Commitment, and Survival: Jewish Communities in the Diaspora* (Westport, Connecticut: Praeger, 2003).

17 The proportion of "highly observant" Jews within the Australian community is indicated by the following data reported in the 1991 Jewish Community survey in Melbourne: 14 percent of respondents attended synagogue several times a month or more; 11 percent attended synagogue at one of the "strictly orthodox" congregations; 9 percent strictly observed Sabbath; and 17 percent "try to keep all the dietary laws" (See Goldlust, *The Jews of Melbourne*, pp. 126–30).

18 See *ibid.*; and John Goldlust and Jewish Welfare Society Inc., Melbourne, *The Melbourne Jewish Community: A Needs Assessment Study* (Canberra: Australian Government Publishing Service, 1993).

2 | Who Speaks for Australian Jewry?

SUZANNE D. RUTLAND

In recent years, Australian Jewry has emerged as one of the most vibrant of Jewish communities in the world, with most Jews having a strong sense of Jewish identity. The community has developed a rich network of Jewish communal organizations. Its major features include its flourishing Jewish day school movement which attracts a very high percentage of school age children and the strength of its Zionist movement which manifests itself in a high level of fund raising, active youth movements and *aliyah* (emigration to Israel) rates. Constituting around 0.5 percent of the overall Australian population, Jews have experienced a high level of acceptance by the general community and have made outstanding contributions to many aspects of Australian life. While situated on the edge of the Diaspora, the community has come to play an increasingly important role on the world Jewish stage. The plethora of organizations which have emerged in post-war Australian Jewry means that there is a great deal of choice, but creating effective roof bodies to fully represent the community has presented challenges.

Principal Governing Bodies

Until World War II there was no federal body representing Australian Jewry. When the Australian colonies federated in 1901 an attempt was made to create a federal structure for Australian Jewry, but this failed.[1] The community was dominated by an Anglo-Jewish oligarchy, which controlled the communities from the synagogues, as Peter Medding has shown in his seminal study *From Assimilation to Group Survival*.[2] He argued that "the struggle to organize a communal roof body . . . was basically a fight for supremacy within the community, in which control by the

specifically religious institutions and their leaders was challenged and overcome by institutions and leaders committed to other aspects of Jewish
identification".[3]

The Zionists, then a peripheral group within the community, were the
first to federate in 1927.[4] Two years later under the leadership of Dr Fanny
Reading, the National Council of Jewish Women (NCJW) was founded.[5]
Dr Reading was one of the interwar Australian feminists who fought for
full equality for women on the basis of traditional attitudes of justice and
concern for others in what she described as "The Law of Loving
Kindness".[6]

Australian Jewry's organizational structure changed radically following
Hitler's rise to power and the enormous refugee crisis, which emerged
after 1933, challenging the comfort and complacency of the established
Australian Jewish leadership. It was during the war years, as the enormity
of the disaster of the Holocaust and the devastation of European Jewry
became known, that a fully representative federal body for lay leadership
was created in August 1944.[7] Named the Executive Council of Australian
Jewry, its formation marked a watershed in Australian Jewish history.

Thus, the two main federal governing bodies for Australian Jewry are
the Executive Council for Australian Jewry (ECAJ) and the Zionist
Federation of Australia (ZFA). Other federal bodies include the NCJW,
the federal body of WIZO (Women's International Zionist Organization),
the Federation of Australian Jewish Welfare Societies, federal B'nai B'rith,
the federal United Israel Appeal (UIA) and the federal Jewish National
Fund (JNF). This multiplicity and complexity of organizations is a feature
of Australian Jewry and is both a strength, being part of the rich fabric of
the community, and a weakness, as there have been over time internal
conflicts that have mitigated against effective leadership.

The Executive Council of Australian Jewry

The formation of the Australian Council of UNRRA (United Nations
Relief and Rehabilitation Association) to assist in the restoration of liber-
ated Europe proved to be the catalyst for the formation of the ECAJ. The
Department of External Affairs convened a meeting of this new organiza-
tion in February 1944. Representatives of three Jewish organizations, the
Australian Jewish Welfare Society, the Jewish Advisory Boards and the
United Emergency Committee for European Jewry, attended this meeting.
Subsequently two further organizations sought to affiliate: the World
Jewish Congress (Australian Section) and United Jewish Overseas Relief
Fund in Victoria; but the Department was reluctant to have too many
Jewish organizations. The departmental secretary stressed that "You will
appreciate that it is necessary to restrict membership to the most repre-
sentative organizations, otherwise the membership of the Council would

increase to a number which would make its effective working most diffi-cult".[8] Two Jewish representatives were finally chosen, Dr Leon Jona of Melbourne and Gerald de Vahl Davis of Sydney. The Jewish community's experiences with the Australian Council of UNRRA, combined with its concern for the tragedy of European Jewry, led to the decision to hold an interstate meeting to form an all-Australian Jewish Council.[9]

The first ever official meeting with either direct representation or support from all the Jewish communities scattered across Australia took place in Melbourne on the weekend of 5–6 August 1944, hosted by Alec Masel, as president of the Victorian Jewish Advisory Board. The main aims of the meeting were to affirm the creation of an Australian roof body, finalize the constitution, and discuss the major issues facing the commu-nity at the time. These were relief and rescue of the surviving remnant of European Jewry, the creation of a Jewish Commonwealth in Palestine, anti-defamation and the status of the ex-internees in Australia.[10]

As the *Sydney Jewish News* later commented, the delegates were "seized by a realization of their heavy responsibilities" and "quickly set-tled to their business".[11] The meeting unanimously approved the formation of a body representing Australian Jewry that would be called the Executive Council of Australian Jewry (ECAJ). The aims of the ECAJ were set out as follows:

- To represent and speak officially on behalf of Australian Jewry;
- To take such action as it considers necessary on behalf of Australian Jewry in matters that concern Australian Jewry or Jewry in other parts of the world.

At the second conference of the ECAJ in Melbourne in January 1945 the constitution was formally ratified and the first committee of management based in Melbourne was elected with Alec Masel as president.

The formation of the ECAJ was a vital development for Australian Jewry. The editor of the *Jewish Herald* wrote that a united national body was needed to deal with key issues such as anti-Semitism, immigration and relief and the absence of such a body "has entailed a very severe hand-icap". He stressed:

> Such consultation as did exist between the states was at best a vague and shadowy thing. There was not only the absence of common counsel with all that meant in the way of hesitancy and confusion, but there was also the disservice rendered at Canberra and in other official quarters, by the spectacle of the Jews speaking with a dozen voices. By consultation and discussion there can be no doubt that we shall all of us gain in thought and action, and it is gratifying to see the imminent fulfillment of a step long demanded by common sense and self-interest alike.[12]

During the early post-war period, the immigration of Jewish Holocaust survivors to Australia was a major concern for the Executive Council, as was the creation of the State of Israel.

Over time, the ECAJ has become involved with a variety of issues relating to Australian and world Jewry. On the local scene these have included refugee immigration, the issue of Nazi war criminals in Australia, combating religious and racial bigotry and creating interfaith dialogue. On the international scene, the ECAJ has assisted communities in the Asia-Pacific region, played a key role in the campaign for Soviet Jewry, assisted oppressed Jewish communities in other countries and represented Israel's case in relation to the Arab–Israeli conflict. More recently the issues of terrorism and communal security have come to the fore.

The constitution established the structure for the Executive Council of Australian Jewry. It has remained basically the same since that time. The work of the ECAJ has been based on the principle of rotation between the two major Jewish centres of Melbourne and Sydney. There are significant problems associated with this structure, but every attempt to change the constitution in any radical way has failed. As a result, the ECAJ has faced constant problems throughout its history. As Robert Goot, president of the New South Wales Jewish Board of Deputies, summed up in March 1982:

> The ECAJ has never been, in my view, an ideal organ for the representation of Australian Jewry. It is very much a compromise body – compromising its head-quarters between Sydney and Melbourne; compromising its programs by abysmal funding; compromising its national representation by distance, cost of travel and inadequately funded administration and communal facilities but ultimately relying on compromise to ensure a consensus on political attitudes.[13]

These may sound like harsh criticisms of the ECAJ's structure, but the various crises in its history illustrate their validity.[14] Yet, as Robert Goot also pointed out, the structure of the ECAJ "may be imperfect, but it is still the most representative organ of Australian Jewry".[15] In all key issues, the ECAJ has been recognized as the official representative body of Australian Jewry, its leaders have been outstanding personalities and it has been able to present in an effective manner the major concerns of the community throughout its history.

How are ECAJ Leaders Elected?   The constituents of the ECAJ are the various roof bodies of the states of Victoria, New South Wales, Western Australia, Queensland and South Australia, together with the Hobart Hebrew Congregation, and later the Australian Capital Territory. Initially Victoria and New South Wales elected five councilors each. This was increased to eight in the 1950s and finally to ten in the early 1960s. Western Australia had two councilors, Queensland and South Australia two, and Tasmania and the ACT one each; these numbers have remained unchanged, apart from Queensland, which now has three. The ECAJ also has a small number of honorary life members with voting rights.

The structure of the ECAJ is built on the state representative councils. The formation of Boards of Deputies in New South Wales, Victoria, South Australia, Queensland and Western Australia, changed the organizational structure of Australian Jewry. This process mainly took place after the formation of the ECAJ in 1944 and, in the case of the smaller Jewish communities, was a consequence of the need for equivalent structures across the different states. These roof bodies are the central lay authority and official mouthpieces of the respective Jewish communities and their aims include the promotion of unity and co-operation within the community. Among their many activities they deal with policy matters relating to Jewish immigration, support of Israel, co-ordination of appeals in the community, ex-servicemen, public relations – involving defence work against the growth of anti-Semitism, and the promotion of goodwill between Jews and non-Jews. In recent years, community security has become a major concern. In addition, they are concerned with developments in overseas Jewry. In this way, they covered a wide variety of communal activities representing a broad spectrum of Jewish activities in Australia.

In 1945 the New South Wales Jewish Advisory Board was reconstituted on a broader basis as the New South Wales Jewish Board of Deputies (NSWJBD). In the first elections held in 1945, 25 Jewish organizations were represented and the contest was portrayed as the synagogues opposing the Zionists.[16] By 2003, the Board had 62 constituent organizations representing almost every aspect of organized Jewish communal life in New South Wales.

Initially the NSWJBD only represented Sydney Jewry's organizational structure and there was no direct franchise for Board deputies. As a result of the constant demands for further democratization of the Board, spearheaded by the controversial Viennese lawyer, Dr Hans Kimmel, a constitutional committee was established in 1948 to review the situation. It was decided that one quarter of the Board's deputies would be elected by direct, general franchise. In 1954 this was extended to fifty percent of the deputies. New South Wales is the only state to have direct general franchise, the other Boards continuing to be based on an indirect system of deputies being chosen through the affiliated organizations. In 1967, Sydney Jewry created a local community appeal structure, known as the Jewish Communal Appeal (JCA). Over the years, the fundraising capacity of the JCA has expanded, and it provides significant financial support for the Board enabling it to function effectively.

The struggle for constitutional change of the Victorian Jewish Advisory Board had occurred earlier than in the NSW equivalent, with major reforms being introduced in 1938 and again in 1942. At this time, the base of the VJAB was widened to include all representative Jewish organizations in Victoria. In 1947, following the New South Wales example, the VJAB changed its name to the Victorian Jewish Board of Deputies (VJBD) and in 1988 it became the Jewish Community Council of Victoria (JCCV). Standing committees were created for finance, public relations, organization, education, immigration and other such matters as were established by a two-thirds majority of the Board.[17] From 1947 the Board met on a monthly rather than a quarterly basis.

Demands for further democratization were also made in Melbourne. These demands were met in 1955 when a number of changes were proposed, including direct representation for each 150 voters.[18] These proposals were later slightly altered so that the registration fee was increased to £1 and there would be one representative for each 250 members rather than 150.[19] The first ballot under this new system was held in October 1955[20] but direct general franchise was not maintained in Melbourne. Also, unlike New South Wales, there is no central fundraising structure and the JCCV has faced ongoing funding problems in recent years.

The ECAJ also established closer links with overseas world Jewish organizations such as the World Jewish Congress (WJC), founded in 1936 in Geneva to represent Diaspora Jewry. In 1941 an Australian section was established but at its annual conference of April 1947, the ECAJ leadership decided to affiliate directly with the WJC and the WJC section was closed.

Despite all the flaws of the ECAJ's structure and the failure to rectify these over the years, the ECAJ has still managed to represent the Australian Jewish community effectively. The major factor in the success of the ECAJ has been in the calibre of its presidents. Since 1945 there have been 15 presidents, of whom three[21] served only a one-year term during the early years of the ECAJ, and a further two served only a two-year term.[22] Three presidents, Maurice Ashkanasy and Isi Leibler, both of Melbourne, and Sydney Einfeld of Sydney, served a total of four terms each. Indeed, Ashkanasy and Einfeld alternated for almost a twenty-year period, from 1948 to 1968. Their outstanding personalities in many ways set the mould for Australian Jewry's key leadership position. In December 2001, Jeremy Jones was elected to the ECAJ presidency. This election meant that, for the first time, Australian Jewry has followed the American pattern of moving from "wealthy men who validated their title to authority in the ethnic community by philanthropic generosity"[23] to leadership from a community professional.

The structure of the ECAJ is very different from roof bodies in other parts of the English-speaking world. Australian Jewry drew many of its origins from the model of Anglo-Jewry, but because of the small size of the community in the nineteenth century and the traditional Melbourne/Sydney rivalry, it did not imitate the structure of the British Board of Deputies, which is located in London with a permanent secretariat. It is also different from the United States model, where there are a plethora of organizations that operate on a federal level.

The two most pertinent comparisons for Australia are the Canadian Jewish Congress and the South African Jewish Board of Deputies. Both communities have provincial divisions similar to the Australian states, and both have two main communities – in Canada, Montreal and Toronto and, in South Africa, Johannesburg and Cape Town. However, in both Canada and South Africa the provincial boards function as committees of the central organization, and this allows for policies to be established on a central basis. They also both have their headquarters located permanently in one place, Toronto for Canada and Johannesburg for South Africa, and both have a permanent, centralized secretariat. However, the honorary officers do not have to reside in the headquarter city. There are significant advantages from every point of view for having the headquarters of a national organization located in one center. In the 1970s, ECAJ councilor, Ted Whitgob, pointed out:

> One other problem that this [biennial migration] has caused is that the ECAJ has not been able to develop a "personality" of its own – and has been dependent on the host State for its secretariat and almost non-existent research facilities. If the ECAJ is to develop then it may well be essential to consider the establishment of an independent permanent secretariat.[24]

The roof bodies of Canada, South Africa and the United Kingdom are not faced with these problems.

The roof bodies in both Canada and South Africa also have a much better fundraising structure. In South Africa, the Board raises funds for both local and Israeli causes, and is responsible for the allocation of funds for all local needs, and the Canadian Jewish Congress operates on a similar basis. This system of centralized fundraising provides for a professional structure and avoids duplication and additional administrative costs. While the basis for such a structure exists in New South Wales with the effective functioning of the Jewish Communal Appeal (JCA), and more recently (2003) in Perth, no parallel structure exists in Victoria.

The Zionist Federation of Australia

By 1945 Australian Jewry had developed a framework for the administration of Zionist activities and this structure has remained largely unaltered. In 1927 the Australian Zionist Federation (later renamed the Zionist Federation of Australia and New Zealand, and then Zionist Federation of Australia [ZFA]) was formed at a combined Zionist meeting held in Melbourne during the visit of Dr Alexander Goldstein, an executive member of the World Zionist Organization. The Federation acted as an umbrella organization for the different branches of the Zionist movement and helped to co-ordinate Zionist activities, improve Zionist publicity within the Jewish and non-Jewish communities, and facilitate the exchange of ideas.[25] In the post-war years, the Federation has worked to assist in the growth of the Zionist youth movements and encourage immigration to Israel (*aliyah*). The ZFA is affiliated with the World Zionist Organization and sent representatives to the Zionist Congresses, held in Palestine/Israel every four years. In November 1952 Max Freilich was appointed a member of the Actions Committee of the World Zionist Organization in recognition of the growing status of the Australian Zionist movement.[26] Since then a number of Australian Zionist leaders have held such positions, with immediate past president Mark Leibler and present president, Dr Ron Weiser, being examples.

The major Zionist organizations are associated with fund-raising. They include the United Israel Appeal (UIA), which holds an annual appeal to raise money to assist in the integration of immigrants into Israel. Australian UIA has a federal structure with a president elected from the state bodies. The Jewish National Fund (JNF: *Keren Kayemet*) raises money throughout the year through blue boxes, tree planting for *simchot* (festive occasions such as weddings and *barmitzvahs*), as well as holding larger functions. With the large number of blue boxes placed in Jewish homes throughout Australia, the JNF was described in 1946 as "the most comprehensive Jewish organization in the Southern Hemisphere".[27] Throughout the post-war years it continued to expand its activities and is still one of the most broadly based Jewish organizations in Australia, which also has a federal structure. WIZO, which carries out fund-raising activities, is also at the forefront of cultural and educational endeavors with its federal structure created in 1938.

How are ZFA Leaders Elected?   A two-tiered system of elected representation and administration is in place for the Zionist movement, following a similar pattern to that which evolved for the ECAJ and the Boards of Deputies.[28] For most of its history, the headquarters of the Zionist Federation alternated every four years between Sydney and Melbourne, while regular biennial conferences were held to discuss matters of policy. The new ZFA executive is elected at the biennial conferences, by set numbers of representatives from each state. This system of rotation meant that the Zionist Federation had neither a permanent general secretary nor administration and this, combined with the large distances in Australia, made its administration more complicated.[29] Despite these difficulties, the Zionist Federation did manage to carry out its various responsibilities because of the dedication of both its voluntary workers and its employees, but the flaws in the system were recognized.

In the 1980s, Mark Leibler established an office in Melbourne under the leadership of executive director, Haya Mond, who retired after a period of 15 years in 2002. Leibler himself served as president for a record 12 years from 1982 to 1994 and the first female president, another Melbournian, Anne Zablud, succeeded him. In 1996, Sydney-based Dr Ron Weiser was elected as president, a position he fills in 2004. When the ZFA moved to Sydney in 1996, Dr Weiser decided it was time to create a permanent secretariat and the ZFA office remained located in Melbourne with Haya Mond continuing as executive director.[30] In this way, the ZFA has introduced the constitutional changes proposed by the Goot/Gersh paper for the ECAJ but which, to date, have not been implemented.

At the state level, the various Zionist organizations are co-coordinated by the State Zionist Councils (SZCs) which function in Victoria, New South Wales, Queensland, South Australia and Western Australia. The SZCs have affiliated membership of the state branches of the United Israel Appeal, the Jewish National Fund, WIZO, Youth *Aliyah* and other Zionist organizations such as the Friends of the Hebrew University, *Magen David Adom* (Israeli Red Cross), Aid for Israel, Ezra and NCJW. The pre-war Jewish refugees established most of these organizations during the 1930s. The SZCs have developed a very broad base of representation, with its affiliate membership being very similar to the ECAJ, including the schools, synagogues and main social and cultural organizations.

Division of Responsibility between ECAJ and ZFA

The division of responsibility between the ECAJ and the Australian Zionist Federation, including the State Zionist Councils, has created problems. This problem has operated at the state and federal levels. For example, in 1949, the Queensland Jewish Board of Deputies wrote to the ECAJ asking who should be responsible for organizing a reception for the Israeli Consul General, Y. H. Levin. The advice was that the function should be organized jointly between the Board and the State Zionist Council.[31] This system has been in operation since, with major functions relating to Israel, such as the annual Israeli Independence Day Cocktail parties held in the major centers, being organized jointly by the lay roof bodies and the SZCs.

In 1953, problems emerged when the Zionist Federation changed its constitution to permit any Jewish individual or group to become a member, whether they were Zionist or not. At a meeting, ECAJ leader, Ashkanasy, and Federation president, Wynn proposed a motion declaring that there was no conflict between the two bodies. During the debate, it was made clear that communications between Australian Jewry and the government in matters relating to the State of Israel should continue to be made through the ECAJ and that Israel's representative, at the time Max Nurock, should communicate with the ECAJ when he felt an approach to the government was required, while the Federation would continue in its important role of consolidating the Jewish state.[32] For many years, this system worked well, with Nurock and his successors being in constant communication with the ECAJ over matters of importance for Israel.[33] However, in the 1980s, the failure to include the ZFA in delegations to the federal government on matters relating to Israel created tensions. A system has developed whereby the ECAJ and the ZFA have jointly met with government officials on all key matters relating to Israel. Under Weiser's presidency, there has been no friction over representation to the federal government as a result of an understanding that there should be joint representation between the ECAJ and the ZFA to the federal government on all matters concerning the Jewish community.[34]

How Representative is the Australian Jewish Leadership?

In theory, the two-tiered system of leadership of both the ECAJ and the ZFA is very representative. At the state level, the Boards/Community Councils and the SZCs represent almost the entire spectrum of Jewish community organizations and religious and political positions. The ECAJ has had active executive members from both the orthodox and reform rabbinate and lay leadership and almost the entire spectrum of the Jewish day school movement. In the ZFA, almost the full range of political opinions are represented, from the left-wing Hashomer Hazair, which still has a youth movement in Melbourne, to the right-wing Friends of Likud and its youth movement, Betar. However, there are groups that have excluded themselves by not applying for affiliation. The ultra-orthodox groups, such as Adath Yisroel (Sydney)/Adass Israel (Melbourne) and the multi-faceted Habad institutions, have not applied for affiliation. This also applies to the secular social Hakoah Club, which has the largest membership of any Jewish organization in Sydney [11,000, of whom 95% are Jewish according to the Hakoah management].

On the other hand, there are groups that have been expelled, such as the left-leaning Melbourne Council to Combat Fascism and Anti-Semitism in June 1952, a complex story which has been analyzed by a number of scholars and which had McCarthyite features.[35] More recently, the Melbourne Community Council has rejected applications for membership. The left-leaning Australian Jewish Democratic Society initially experienced problems when it tried to affiliate in 1987 because of its criticisms of the Likud government in Israel. The Society opposed the prevalent belief among Diaspora leaders that they should support the Israeli government of the day regardless of their own personal beliefs on the basis that they were not living in Israel and facing the difficulties there. With the election of the Rabin government and the Oslo Accords the situation changed and the Society affiliated with the Board in September 1993.[36] As Philip Mendes has written, this whole issue was a debate over "censorship and pluralism".[37] The Gay & Lesbian Society, known as Alef Melbourne, tried to affiliate but was rejected by the plenum in March 1999. In this way, both the ECAJ and the ZFA only represent groups they judge to be within the mainstream viewpoints of the community.

Another problem is the two-tiered system of leadership and the indirect nature of elections for the federal leadership of both organizations. The pyramid structure means that the grass root organizations elect their delegates for the state bodies and the state bodies elect the delegates for the federal bodies, so that there is almost no direct contact between the federal leadership and the broadly based organizations. The New South Wales election structure, with half the deputies being elected by direct franchise, sought to create a more democratic and representative structure. However, the small number of people who vote for the direct franchise has meant that this system has failed to operate according to the aspirations of its initiators.

The divisions between the two major centers – Melbourne and Sydney – also create problems. In 1978 John Higham edited a study of leadership of the main ethnic groups in America. Higham noted the neglect of the study of ethnic leadership and delineated four major areas of basic concern for such leaders. The first related to the relationship between the United States and their homeland; the second to their status in American society; the third to their internal cohesion and integrity of the group; and finally "the elemental issue of survival".[38] In dealing with these major areas of concern, he argued that there were two main responses: leadership of accommodation, and leadership of protest. Historically since the formation of the ECAJ, Sydney Jewry has taken the approach of accommodation, while Melbourne has followed a policy of leadership of protest. Veteran Jewish journalist Sam Lipski described the two approaches in Yiddish as "*Sha Shtill*" ("Softly, softly"), the Sydney way, and "*Shrei Gevalt*" ("Mount the Barricades"),[39] the approach of the Melbourne Jewish leadership. Ensuring effective representation of these two different communities – seen in their ethnic composition, state representative structures and funding, spectrum of Jewish identification and demographic patterns – has been another ongoing challenge for the Jewish community.

Is There a Political Bias in the Representative Bodies?

Both the ECAJ and the ZFA claim to have no political bias with respect to Australian political parties. However, over the years the leadership has manifested definite trends and biases. In the period until 1967 the two main leaders, Maurice Ashkanasy and Sydney Einfeld were both active members of the Australian Labor Party (ALP). Australian Jewry's connection with the ALP will be discussed in depth in the next chapter. In the late 1970s, the Liberal Prime Minister, Malcolm Fraser, became a strong advocate of multiculturalism and assisted the ECAJ leadership in Sydney, under

Dr Joachim Schneeweiss, and Melbourne, under Isi Leibler, a local businessman. For example, during Leibler's visits to Moscow on behalf of "refuseniks" during the late 1970s, Fraser extended the facilities of the Australian embassy there.[40]

Jewish politicians from both sides of the political spectrum have worked closely with the ECAJ as consultants. These have included Sir Asher Joel and Dr Peter Baume from the Liberal Party and Barry Cohen and Joe Berinson from the ALP. Today political affiliation plays a less important role than before, but the community is seen as enjoying a close relationship with the conservative Liberal Prime Minister, John Howard.

Australian Jewish political alliances have been closely linked with the attitudes of political parties to Israel. When Labor leader Gough Whitlam was elected in December 1972, the three years of Labor government caused consternation for the community leadership because of his "even-handed policy" on the Middle East conflict, which the community considered to be pro-Arab. Even prime ministers considered friendly to Israel were criticized if they did not support the position of the Israeli government. For example, Bob Hawke was renowned for his close friendship with the community and Israel, starting with his first visit to Israel in 1971, but from 1987 the Hawke government was perceived as beginning to be "more even-handed" in terms of urging Israel to negotiate with the PLO and support an international conference to resolve the dispute.[41] The tension arose during 1988 when Isi Leibler brought out 15 Jewish "refuseniks" who had battled for the right to emigrate to Israel. At a celebration held in Melbourne, Hawke linked the aspirations of Soviet Jews with those of the Palestinians. He described Israel as "a giant eyeless in Gaza" and repeated his thesis that, if Israel retained the occupied territories, the demographic realities would eventually force Israel to choose between being a democratic state and a Jewish state.[42] This speech was strongly criticized by Leibler and other Jewish leaders.

Relation to Other Jewish Advocacy Groups

Since the mid-1970s specific Jewish advocacy groups have emerged. In 1975, the Zionist Federation, initially in partnership with the ECAJ, established Australia Israel Publications (AIP) with the aim of better informing members of the broader Australian community about the Middle East. In 1984 Leibler and Richard Pratt (another Melbourne businessman), formed the Australian Institute of Jewish Affairs. Its aim was to sponsor intellectual developments and research into issues of the Jewish community. Over the years, the AIJA organized a number of key conferences relating to anti-Semitism, Jewish education and the National Outlook Conferences, as well as producing research studies on a variety of topics. Isi Leibler believed that the AIJA was able to attract a higher level of funding from major businessmen and key philanthropists than the more broadly based ECAJ.

After settling in Israel in 1995, Isi Leibler came to the realization that he needed to ensure that the community had an effective advocacy group. As a result of negotiations, in 1997 AIP and AIJA amalgamated to form the Australia/Israel & Jewish Affairs Council (AIJAC), which has developed as the main Jewish public advocacy body in Australia (see chapter 12 of this volume).

B'nai B'rith in both Melbourne and Sydney have also established Anti-Defamation Units (ADUs), which have also sought to play a research and advocacy role. They publish a monthly bulletin that deals with a specific issue each month relating to key aspects facing the community. B'nai B'rith ADUs have also played an active role in promoting better understanding of racism and the Holocaust, in recent years through its Courage to Care project. The latter aims to highlight the dangers of racism and the important contribution of the Righteous Amongst the Nations, that is, non-Jews who helped save Jews during the Holocaust.

Conclusion

Australian Jewry has developed a complex representative structure that operates on three levels – local, state and federal – following the pattern of general Australian representation. At the federal level, the two peak bodies have cooperated effectively in their representation to the outside community. However, the present system has a fatal flaw due to the lack of funding of the ECAJ that means that it does not have a professional structure. As a result, the Jewish advocacy groups, particularly AIJAC, which is well funded, play a more active role, which can lead to conflict within the community. These are major issues, and need to be addressed by Australian Jewry if it is to ensure that it has an effective representative roof body. The community also needs to become more open to minority positions. This would reinforce its pluralistic and democratic structure and ensure that it functions as a democracy and not a plutocracy.

Notes

1   Suzanne D. Rutland, *Edge of the Diaspora: Two Centuries of Jewish Settlement in Australia*, 2nd edn (New York: Holmes & Meier, 2001), pp. 101–3.

2   Peter Medding, *From Assimilation to Group Survival: A Political and Sociological Study of an Australian Jewish Community* (Melbourne: Cheshire, 1968).

3   *Ibid.*, p. 30.

4   See Bernard Hyams, *History of the Australian Zionist Movement* (Melbourne: Zionist Federation of Australia, 1998), and Eliyahu Honig, *Zionism in Australia 1920–1940: The Formative Years* (Sydney: Mandelbaum Trust

Studies in *Judaica*, No. 7, 1997). Hyams has concentrated on the Zionist Federation's structure, education programs, youth movements and fundraising. The first area of federal activity was sport with the introduction of interstate carnivals in 1923. Brian Kino, *The Carnivals: A History of Amateur Jewish Sporting Competitions, 1924–1974* (Melbourne: York Press, 1974).

5　Marlo Newton, *Making a Difference* (Melbourne: Hybrid Press, 2000).

6　Anne Andgel, "The Law of Loving Kindness: A Tribute to Dr Fanny Reading, Founder of the National Council of Jewish Women of Australian in 1923", *AJHSJ* 14 (1998): 199–257. Marlo Newton's study of the NCJW has shown that while it supported the struggle for full equality for women, it has not supported more radical feminism because of the traditional Jewish stress on home and family.

7　*Sydney Jewish News* (henceforth *SJN*), 11 August 1944.

8　Secretary, Department of External Affairs to Jewish Advisory Board, 5 July 1944, AJHSA, Box 17, 167C.

9　See, for example, letter from Sam Karpin representing the Bureau of Jewish Affairs to Herbert I. Wolff, for the Advisory Board requesting that such a meeting to be held, 22 June 1944, AJHSA Box 17, File 176C.

10　During World War II, the Allied governments defined all immigrants of German and Austrian nationality as "enemy aliens" and placed them in internment camps, without considering the fact that Jewish Germans and Austrians were refugees from Nazism. Jews were later reclassified as "friendly aliens" and permitted to leave the internment camps, but there was still concern about their status after the war.

11　*SJN*, 11 August 1944.

12　*AJH*, 28 July 1944, p. 5.

13　Robert Goot, Presidential Report, Annual Report, NSW Jewish Board of Deputies, 16 March 1982.

14　The controversy over Professor Hanan Ashrawi, discussed in chapter 13, is the most recent example.

15　Robert Goot, Presidential Report, Annual Report, NSW Jewish Board of Deputies, 16 March 1982.

16　*SJN*, 20 April and 15 June 1945.

17　VJBD, Notice of motion for alteration of the constitution, 1947, VJBD Corres. Files, Box 6, La Trobe Library.

18　VJBD Minutes, 4 April 1955.

19　*Ibid.*, 6 June 1955.

20　*Ibid.*, 11 December 1955.

21　Founding president Alec Masel, 1945, Horace B. Newman in 1950 and Ben Green who replaced Ashkanasy for a short period in 1951.

22　Gerald Falk of New South Wales, 1968–70 and Louis Klein, 1972–4. Klein died suddenly in 1975.

23　John Higham, ed., *Ethnic Leadership in America* (Baltimore and London: Johns Hopkins University Press, 1978), p. 12.

24　ECAJ Proposed Constitutional review, E. Whitgob, no date.

25　Suzanne D. Rutland, "The Jewish Community in New South Wales 1914–1939", MA (Hons) thesis, University of Sydney, 1978, p. 93.

26　*SJN*, 21 November 1952.

27　*SJN*, 22 February 1946.

28 In 2003, the ZFA affiliate organizations are: each of the State Zionist Councils, the Australian Reform Zionist Association (ARZI), the Union of Progressive Judaism of Australia, the Australasian Union of Jewish Students (AUJS), the Australian Zionist Youth Council (AZYC), the Jewish National Fund (JNF), the Labor Zionist Movement, Maccabi, Mizrachi, National Council of Jewish Women (NCJW), the Sephardi Association, the United Israel Appeal (UIA), the Women's International Zionist Organization (WIZO), the United Zionist Revisionist Organization (UZRO) and Youth Aliyah. Each of these organizations has one representative on the Executive.

29 Duffield, "Administrative Report", cit. sup.

30 Information supplied by Dr Ron Weiser, e-mail 16 November 2003.

31 M. Ochert to H. B. Newman, 2 December 1949 and Newman to Ochert, 5 December 1949, "Constituent Bodies and Vice-Pres., June 1949–June 1950", Box E25, Archive of Australian Judaica.

32 *SJN*, 21 August 1953.

33 See Nurock to Fink, Senior Vice-President, 24 January 1955, requesting that an approach be made to the Australian government in relation to the arming of the Arab States, "Loose Papers", Box E15, ECAJ Corres. Files, Archive of Australian Judaica.

34 Dr Ron Weiser, e-mail, 16 November 2003.

35 See Philip Mendes's chapter in this volume.

36 Philip Mendes, "Australian Jewish Dissent on Israel: A History of the Australian Jewish Democratic Society", *Australian Jewish Historical Society* Part 1, 15 (1999): 117–38, and Part 2, 15 (2000): 459–74.

37 Mendes, "Australian Jewish Dissent on Israel", Part 2, p. 459.

38 Higham, ed., *Ethnic Leadership in America*, p. 4.

39 *Australian Jewish News*, Sydney edn, 5 December 2003.

30 *Ibid.*

40 Interviews with Isi Leibler, Jerusalem, November 2000.

41 See the communist paper, *Tribune*, 4 February 1987.

42 As reported in the *Australian Jewish Times*, 27 May 1988.

II

Partisanship and Ideologies

3 | Jews and the Australian Labor Party

SOL ENCEL

This chapter canvasses the multiple connections, both positive and negative, between the ALP and the Jewish community. There is an important historical dimension. Until World War II, Jewish participation in politics was mainly on the non-Labor side. Since the early 1940s, this balance has been reversed, and Jewish political activism has been strongly oriented to the left, not only in the ALP but in various other sections of the left-wing spectrum. From 1940 onwards, the participation of Jews in the ALP as parliamentary candidates, MPs, and ministers has far exceeded the small number of counterparts on the non-Labor side. Paradoxically, political activism has coincided with a steady decline, since the 1950s, in Jewish electoral support for the ALP.

Relations between the Jewish community and the ALP are subject to fluctuating pressures and tensions. Although Jewish activists have, on the whole, been welcomed in the ALP, the welcome has not been unqualified. The traditional left-wing identification of Jews with capitalism, deriving originally from Karl Marx, has left its mark in the ALP and in the wider labour movement from which the party draws its strength. This has been reactivated since the 1970s because of left-wing hostility to Israel, which is constantly liable to degenerate into old-fashioned anti-Semitism.

Another source of tension, much less overt and rarely acknowledged, is Christian anti-Semitism. An annual survey of anti-Semitic incidents and references reports that "debate still rages in a number of mainstream churches as to the legitimacy of Judaism in the Christian era".[1] This applies, in the case of the ALP, mainly to Catholics, who have been a major presence in the ALP since it was formed. On the whole, Catholics and Jews have coexisted amicably in the ALP, despite the occasional hiccup, as when Catholic members of the dominant right-wing faction of the NSW party were rumoured to be opposed to the appointment of a Jewish party official, Eric Roozendaal, to the position of state secretary of the party in 1999. Whatever the truth of the matter, Roozendaal was appointed.

Apart from examining both the positive and negative aspects of the relationship between the Jewish community and the ALP, I have highlighted the significant contributions to public policy made by those Jews who have attained ministerial office in both state and federal governments. Accordingly, the chapter is divided into the following topics: The Ministers, the MPs, and the Aspirants; Voting Behaviour; Anti-Jewish Prejudice; The ALP and Israel; and Party and Community Involvement.

The Ministers, the MPs, and the Aspirants

Altogether, fourteen Jews have been members of the Australian Parliament since Federation.[2] Nine of them were Labor members. At the state level, there have been five Labor members in three states – NSW, Victoria, and Western Australia – during the same period. Six of these Labor parliamentarians held ministerial office, including three in Canberra. One of the three also became a state government minister. Four Jews were elected to the Australian Parliament in 1969 alone, all on the ALP ticket – Joe Berinson (Western Australia), Moss Cass (Victoria), Barry Cohen (NSW), and Richard Klugman (NSW). Berinson, Cass, and Cohen each held ministerial office.

Berinson is an observant Jew, whose family has been prominent in the WA Jewish community. He joined the ALP in 1955. Originally a pharmacist by profession, he qualified as a lawyer in 1970. He became a member of the state executive of the party, attaining the position of senior vice-president. Berinson collided with the Labor Prime Minister, Gough Whitlam, during the Middle East crisis of 1973 (described below), which is widely believed to have delayed his promotion to a ministerial post. He was, however, highly regarded within the parliamentary party, and became chairman of committees in 1975. Subsequently, he was elected to the Ministry in July 1975, replacing Moss Cass in the Environment portfolio. He had little time to make a mark, as the Whitlam government was dismissed in November 1975. Berinson lost his seat in the subsequent election. He had a much more significant career in state politics, following his election to the WA Legislative Council in 1980. Between 1983 and 1993, he held a number of ministerial posts. He retired from parliament in 1993.

Dr Moss Cass, a medical practitioner by profession, became involved in politics as an undergraduate at the University of Sydney, where he was a member of the Labour Club.[3] From 1964 to 1969, he was a member of the Central Executive of the Victorian branch of the ALP, and moved on from there to become MP for the federal seat of Maribyrnong, which he retained until 1980. When Labor returned to office in Canberra in 1972, Cass was elected to the ministry, although he was at odds with his party leader, Gough Whitlam. He was given the new portfolio of Environment. As Minister, he was responsible for the first Australian legislation requiring environmental impact statements, and for the creation of important national parks, including Kakadu and the Great Barrier Reef. In July 1975, Cass moved to the portfolio of Minister for the Media, and was responsible for the introduction of public broadcasting. He had links with the Jewish community in Melbourne and was the founding president of the left-wing Australian Jewish Democratic Society in the 1980s, but is not religiously observant.

Barry Cohen was one of the four Jewish MPs elected to the federal Parliament in 1969, and remained in parliament until 1990. He followed in Cass's footsteps and became Minister for the Environment (and later also Minister for the Arts) from 1983 to 1987.

Sydney Einfeld (1909–95) was, arguably, the most successful of Jewish Labor politicians, who managed to combine a leading role in the Jewish community with a career in New South Wales state politics. He was president of the Executive Council of Australian Jewry on four occasions between 1952 and 1966, and president of the Australian Jewish Welfare Society (now Jewish Care) in NSW from 1952 until 1979. He also played a central role in the establishment of the NSW Jewish Board of Deputies in 1945. One of his most important achievements was in facilitating the entry of European Jewish refugees after 1945 and assisting them to settle in Australia.[4]

Einfeld was born in 1909, three weeks after his parents arrived in Australia. He joined the ALP in 1938, and was an active party member from the outset. Between 1944 and 1955, he was president of the Bondi Branch; for nine years, he was also president of the Wentworth Federal Electorate Council (FEC), and subsequently president of the Phillip FEC for fourteen years. He acted as campaign manager for Abram Landa in 1941, when Landa won back the state seat of Bondi which he had lost in 1932. Einfeld was successful in winning the federal seat of Phillip at the 1961 general election. In 1963, the pendulum swung back and Einfeld lost the seat. His next opportunity occurred in 1965, when Abram Landa vacated his seat to become NSW Agent-General in London. Einfeld won, despite the fact that the Labor government lost the general election and was in opposition for the next eleven years.

In 1968 the state parliamentary leader, J. B. Renshaw, resigned and his deputy, P. D. Hills, was elected in his place. At the time, Einfeld was lobbied by some of his colleagues to contest the leadership, but contented himself with the role of deputy leader. (One of the reasons for this decision was his concern that the choice of a Jew as leader would have a negative impact within the party.) When the ALP regained power in 1976, he became the first incumbent of the portfolio of Consumer Affairs, to which was added Housing in 1978. He retired from politics in 1981.[5]

Abram Landa (1902–89) emigrated with his family from Belfast before

World War I. He was admitted as a solicitor in 1927, and was elected to
the New South Wales Legislative Assembly in 1930 at the early age of 28,
winning the seat of Bondi in a Labor landslide. He did not hold the seat
for long, losing it in 1932 when the Lang government was swept away in
the Labor debacle of that year. He regained the seat in 1941, when a further
swing to the left returned Labor to power. In 1952, following the advent
of J. J. Cahill as Premier, he was appointed Minister for Labor and
Industry, to which he added the portfolios of Housing in 1956 and Co-
operative Societies in 1959. In 1965, he resigned from parliament to take
up the post of Agent-General for NSW in London, which he held until
1970.

Landa's ministerial career was unspectacular, unlike that of his nephew
Paul (1941–84). Paul Landa, like his uncle, became a solicitor, and was
admitted to the Bar in 1975. In 1973, he was elected to the NSW
Legislative Council and became government leader in the upper house
when the ALP won the 1976 election. His first portfolio was that of
Industrial Relations. He soon moved to the new post of Minister for
Planning and Environment, which he held until 1980. Among his achieve-
ments in this portfolio, were the prohibition of logging in south-eastern
NSW, the establishment of the Land and Environment Court, the creation
of a number of national parks, and controls on motor vehicle emissions.
Landa's parents were non-observant Jews and he grew up without any
Jewish education. However, he remained conscious of his Jewishness, and
he was sworn in as a minister wearing a yarmulke and using the Hebrew
Bible. In an interview with the *Australian Jewish Times*, he stressed his
commitment to Israel, and declared that he was not prepared to become a
"token Jew". Landa moved to the portfolio of Education in 1980, and
became Attorney-General in 1981. He died prematurely of a heart attack
while playing tennis.

Among Jewish Labor members of the Australian Parliament who did not
hold ministerial office, there was, first, S. M. Falstein (1914–67). Falstein
was of the type referred to in the news media as a "colourful" character.
After graduating from the University of Sydney with a law degree, he went
to New Zealand, where he became an organizer for the Labor Party. He
returned to Sydney in 1940 and was admitted to the Bar. Shortly afterwards, he was elected to Parliament. After the war, Falstein went into
business and travelled to China to develop trade links. In 1948, he was
fined for falsifying documents to understate the value of imported wrist-
watches, and lost his appeal. As a result, he also lost his Labor
endorsement, and ran unsuccessfully as an "independent Labor" candidate in 1949. He died in 1967.[6]

Sam Cohen, Q.C., was elected to the Senate in 1961, and became
deputy leader of the Opposition in the upper house in 1967. He died
prematurely in 1969 (see below).

Richard Klugman made a point of distancing himself from the Jewish community. Born in Vienna in 1924, he trained as a doctor, and was active in student politics at the University of Sydney. Klugman was in parliament from 1969 to 1990, and moved from left to right during that period. He became chairman of the parliamentary party's committee on social security and health, and was also shadow minister for health for several years. In his public utterances, he took pains to oppose the views of the organized Jewish community on a number of issues, including its support for Israel, its endorsement of multiculturalism, and its support for the trials of Nazi war criminals.[7]

Even more detached from the Jewish community was Lewis Kent, *né* Kapolnai. Kent was born in the former Yugoslavia, and lived in Israel for several years before migrating to Australia in 1954. He joined the Socialist Left faction of the ALP in Victoria, and was elected to parliament in 1980, losing his seat in 1990. He became well known for his support for war crimes trials, especially of alleged Yugoslav war criminals.[8] A not dissimilar case is that of David Bornstein, a journalist by profession, and also a member of the Socialist Left, who was a member of the Victorian state parliament from 1970 to 1975. Bornstein worked briefly for the *Australian Jewish News*, and did not evince the same kind of hostility towards Israel, but overall he took little interest in Jewish affairs.[9]

The most recently elected Labor MP is Michael Danby, member for the federal electorate of Melbourne Ports since 1998. Danby was a prominent figure in the Australian Union of Jewish Students (AUJS) in the 1970s. In 1977, he was physically attacked by a group of "Maoist" students after he had criticized the leadership of the Australian Union of Students (AUS). Later, he became an industrial officer with the shop assistants' union, and worked as an assistant to two federal Labor MPs. He also served as editor of the monthly *Australia-Israel Review*. Danby's pre-selection as ALP candidate in 1997 was hotly contested, and a further pre-selection battle took place in 2000, when there were accusations of ethnic branch stacking.[10]

Although many Jews have been active in the ALP, not many have stood for parliament. Maurice Isaacs (d. 1984) was a Sydney solicitor, actively involved in Jewish affairs. He was a leading figure in the Young Men's Hebrew Association (YMHA), which was a significant force in the Sydney community in the 1930s and 1940s, especially in relation to assisting refugees and combating anti-Semitism.[11] He was also a leading supporter of the scheme to settle Jews in the Kimberley region of northwest Australia.[12] In 1961, Isaacs was the ALP candidate for the federal seat of North Sydney, but failed to win election despite an impressive campaign. His namesake, Maurice Allen, also a solicitor, was a leading figure in the NSW Jewish Board of Deputies, of which he was president from 1973 to 1975. (He resigned because of ill health and died shortly afterwards.) Allen stood as a Labor candidate for the NSW parliament on two occasions, but was unsuccessful.

In Victoria, prominent Jewish Council activists Norman Rothfield and Sam Goldbloom unsuccessfully contested House of Representative seats in the 1958 federal election. Rothfield was also an unsuccessful ALP candidate for the state seat of Ivanhoe in 1961. Another Jewish Council activist, Ernest Platz, was the preselected candidate for the federal seat of Balaclava in the same year. In addition, Michael Pakula ran for the federal seat of Goldstein in 1993, also without success.

Undoubtedly the most prominent of unsuccessful parliamentary aspirants was Maurice Ashkanasy, Q.C. (1902–71). Like Syd Einfeld, he was a leading figure in the Jewish community. Between 1948 and 1966, he alternated with Einfeld as president of the Executive Council of Australian Jewry, and was also chairman of the Victorian Jewish Board of Deputies on three occasions between 1947 and 1962. Ashkanasy joined the Labor Party and stood, unsuccessfully, for the safe Liberal seat of Balaclava in 1946. In 1954 and 1958, he was selected as a member of the Labor Senate team, but was again unsuccessful. It was widely believed that he would be given a safe place on the 1961 Senate ticket, but the Victorian state executive of the ALP chose another prominent Jewish barrister, S. H. Cohen, Q.C., instead. The ensuing "Sam Cohen affair" spelt the end of Ashkanasy's active involvement with the Labor Party.

The "affair" has been described by several writers.[13] It demonstrated the complexity of relations which can arise between internal community politics and the affairs of a political party. It was, among other things, an after-effect of the split in the ALP in 1955, which led to the exodus of a large number of conservative Catholic party members, many of whom joined the newly formed Democratic Labor Party (DLP). As a result, the party in Victoria turned decisively to the left. Sam Cohen was on the left of the party and a member of the state executive. Ashkanasy, on the other hand, had become well known for his attacks on Communist influence in the ALP.

After Cohen was selected for the Senate ticket, a campaign was mounted against him involving Ashkanasy, who was president of the Victorian Jewish Board of Deputies at the time, and Isi Leibler, chairman of the public relations committee of the Board. The DLP also became involved through its main organ, *News-Weekly*, which attacked Cohen as a Communist sympathizer. The "affair" came to a head following Cohen's official entry into the Senate in July 1962, when he was embroiled in a debate about the persecution of Jews in the Soviet Union. The tensions within the Jewish community were exploited by the Liberal Party, which attempted to drive a wedge between Cohen and Syd Einfeld, who was at that time a member of the House of Representatives. Einfeld was able to deflect the attack and avoid any appearance of conflict with Cohen. The latter, for his part, made a strong speech attacking the motives of Liberal senators for raising the issue, and he was supported by a number of Labor senators.

Cohen's political career was cut short by his sudden death in 1969 at the age of fifty-one. He became involved in politics as an undergraduate at the University of Melbourne, where he was president of the Students' Representative Council and a founding member of the National Union of Australian University Students. He joined the ALP in 1946. In 1948, he was secretary of the first United Israel Appeal in Victoria, but his main involvement in Jewish affairs was as chairman of the Jewish Council to Combat Fascism and Anti-Semitism.[14]

Cohen was a prominent figure among Labor senators, and was deputy leader of the party in the Senate in 1967–9. He became Labor spokesman on education, science, and communications, and is credited with being the architect of the Whitlam government's education policy. He collapsed and died after an election meeting in Adelaide in October 1969. By a remarkable irony, he was posthumously given the Maurice Ashkanasy Award for Australian Jew of the Year in 1970.

Voting Behaviour

Generally speaking, the voting pattern of the Jewish community has moved from a high degree of support for the ALP to a situation where Jewish voting behaviour does not differ significantly from that of the population as a whole. In 1947, Ronald Taft found that 75 percent of his sample of Jews in Melbourne voted Labor.[15] Fifteen years later, a survey by Peter Medding again showed a clear preference for the ALP. Using a sample of 124, Medding asked his respondents to indicate how they had voted at the 1958 and 1961 Federal elections. For 1958, the figure was 56.5 percent in favour of the ALP, and in 1961, 61.6 percent. The swing to the ALP was consistent with the general movement of voters against the conservative government headed by Sir Robert Menzies, which barely scraped home at the 1961 election. An interesting feature was the sharp movement in the women's vote. In 1958, women voters were equally divided between the two major parties (43.5 percent each), but in 1961 they moved sharply to the left, giving the ALP 56.5 percent of their votes. By 1966, this preference for the ALP had been somewhat eroded, but it still received more than 50 percent.[16]

A detailed study of Jewish voting behaviour was included in a survey of the NSW Jewish community in 1969–70, in which 1020 households provided responses.[17] The question on voting behaviour was treated as optional, and received a total of 1,330 individual responses, divided almost equally between men and women. Respondents were asked how they had voted at the last federal election (1969) and the last state election (1968). The voting pattern was almost identical for the two elections: 40 percent of men, and 37 percent of women, voted for the ALP. The Liberal Party was supported by 53 percent of male voters, and 57 percent of females.

In a more recent commentary, Bill Rubinstein has argued that the "swing to the right" has continued, and cites "informed observers" who maintain that the Fraser government was supported by a 2:1 majority of Jewish voters between 1975 and 1980.[18]

A subsequent study by John Goldlust, based on a sample of 640 persons in Melbourne in 1991, confirmed the relative popularity of the Liberal-National coalition among Jewish voters.[19] In Goldlust's survey, 59.3 percent favoured the coalition parties, as against 22.2 percent for the ALP. The earlier pattern of preference for the ALP is reflected in the fact that persons aged 60 and over were more likely to vote Labor than the average of all Melbourne Jewish voters, whereas those aged under 40 were less likely to do so.

Since Goldlust's survey, there has been no systematic study of Jewish voting behaviour in Australia,[20] but it has undoubtedly been influenced by party attitudes to Israel (discussed below and in chapter 8). It remains clear that the majority preference among Jewish voters is for the Liberal Party. This is not surprising, since Australian Jews are largely middle class or upper middle class in their social position. The Jewish preference for the Liberal Party appears to be rather less marked than among the more affluent sections of the population as a whole. It also represents a trend away from an earlier situation where the proportion of Liberal and Labor voters was almost equal.

Anti-Jewish Prejudice

The ALP has been relatively free of anti-Jewish prejudice. The manifestations which have occurred derive from a variety of sources, reflecting different strands within the party itself. One important source has been a long tradition of linking Jews with capitalism, which goes back to Karl Marx himself and his essays on the "Jewish Question" in 1844. Such ideas were derided by prominent figures in the socialist movement. Friedrich Engels remonstrated with the German Social Democrats for their approval of anti-Semitism, and persuaded the party leader, August Bebel, to publish an official condemnation.[21] Nevertheless, the influence of the idea has been considerable, and it attained a degree of popularity in Australia.

It is important to distinguish between anti-Semitic utterances appearing in the Labour press and other left-wing publications on the one hand, and the situation within the Labor Party. A number of writers have identified examples of anti-Semitic outbursts within sections of the Labour movement, starting from the 1890s. Reviewing this literature, Philip Mendes points out that on balance, philo-Semitism has exceeded anti-Semitism, although the situation has changed somewhat since the 1970s.[22]

Within the ALP itself, there have been a few instances of prominent figures expressing anti-Jewish prejudices. At the time of the South African

War (1899–1903), German-Jewish financiers with mining interests in South Africa were accused of instigating the conflict to protect their profits.[23] The *Bulletin* newspaper invented a character named John Bull-Cohen who was the mastermind of British imperial policy. A similar cry was taken up in the Labor press, and endorsed by W. A. Holman, one of the leaders of the ALP in NSW and subsequently Premier between 1913 and 1920.[24]

The role of Jewish warmongers was taken up again during the 1914–18 war by Frank Anstey, a federal Labor MP from 1910 to 1934. He was deputy leader of the Opposition from 1921 to 1927 and a minister in the Scullin government from 1929 to 1932. As the war progressed, Anstey wrote a series of articles attacking the "money power", which were issued as a pamphlet in 1917 entitled *The Kingdom of Shylock*, complete with a frontispiece cartoon of a hooknosed Jewish moneylender.

Anstey received a string of complaints from his left-wing friends, both Jewish and non-Jewish, and in 1921 he published a revised version entitled *Money Power*, in which most of the anti-Jewish references had been removed and replaced by a "black Masonic plutocracy". However, as Anstey's biographer observes, the anti-Semitic references did not disappear entirely (especially a reference to the Rothschilds). The stereotype of the Jewish moneylender was so deeply embedded in the imagination of Anstey and his readers that it could not be displaced.[25]

The stereotype emerged again during the monetary crisis of 1929–31. The Labor Premier of NSW, J. T. Lang, appropriated Anstey's arguments and claimed that Australia's economic problems were caused by British capital. In particular, he denounced the role of Sir Otto Niemeyer, a director of the Bank of England, who visited Australia as part of a delegation to discuss Australia's foreign debt with the Scullin government. Niemeyer was a member of an Anglo-German Protestant banking family, but his surname lent plausibility to the assertion that he was a Jew acting on behalf of London Jewish speculators. Lang's daily newspaper, the *Labor Daily*, referred to the "London Jews with their fat rake-offs". Lang was dismissed as Premier by the state Governor, Sir Philip Game, in 1932, after refusing to pay interest to foreign bondholders. The *Labor Daily* and its weekly successor, *Century*, continued to fulminate against finance capital, and also opposed Jewish immigration in the 1930s and 1940s.[26]

On the other hand, Jewish MPs have been relatively unaffected by active anti-Semitism. Paul Landa, a minister in the NSW state Labor government from 1976 to 1984, observed in an interview that anti-Semitism existed in political life, and that he had been called a "Jewish bastard" several times. He believed that being a Jew in politics was neither an advantage nor a disadvantage, and it should not be treated as an obstacle – "that's a concession to anti-Semitism".[27] Barry Cohen, a minister in the Hawke government from 1983 to 1987, experienced considerable anti-Semitism in his youth. However, his experiences as a minister were much more positive. On retiring from parliament in 1990, he observed that he had received 100,000 letters during his parliamentary career, but only five contained anti-Semitic remarks.[28]

Moss Cass, a minister in the Whitlam government (1972–5), recalls some anti-Semitic incidents at the time he was selected as candidate for the Victorian seat of Maribyrnong. At the time, this electorate was regarded as a stronghold of the Democratic Labor Party, the predominantly Catholic right-wing organization which had split from the ALP in 1955. After his selection for the seat, a letter was circulated among branch members which attacked Cass on several grounds, including the fact that he was a Jew. Cass also recalled that he had been accosted by a prominent party member at a Christmas party, who asserted that he could not support a Jew in such a Christian electorate.[29]

Ironically again, the Catholic stereotype of the Jew as capitalist is matched by the identification of Jews with the Russian Revolution and international Communism (satirically depicted as the "international Jewish capitalist Bolshevik conspiracy"). The former leader of the ALP, Arthur Calwell, was one who accepted this view and described the Russian Revolution as a Jewish affair.[30] Although there is evidence of Catholic antipathy towards Jews and Judaism, which has its effects as an undercurrent in the Labour movement, it has clearly not damaged the careers of Jewish activists within the ALP.

Nevertheless, there was some Labor opposition to the admission of Jewish refugees into Australia. In November 1938, following Kristallnacht, the ALP federal member for Kalgoorlie, A. E. ("Texas") Green, alleged that the Jews would "grab your farm". He returned to the topic in June 1939, claiming that Hitler was right to rid Germany of the Jewish domination of German culture, commerce, and the professions.[31] Although Green's sentiments were extreme, opposition to the admission of refugees after the war continued, and although it came mainly from right-wing sources, there was also unease in the trade union movement over competition for jobs. Arthur Calwell, Minister for Immigration from 1945 to 1949, endeavoured to maintain a humanitarian policy, but found himself constrained to cut back the refugee intake in the face of such pressures.[32]

The ALP and Israel

Australia has multiple connections with the Middle East. The Gallipoli campaign of 1915 remains a pivotal event in Australian history, commemorated annually by the most distinctive of national holidays, Anzac Day. During the 1939–45 war, Australian troops again took part in the Syrian campaign of 1941, where a joint force of British, Australian and Free French units overthrew the French colonial regime, which had sided with the Vichy French government after France had surrendered to Nazi Germany in 1940.[33]

The crucial link between Australia and Israel was established through the role of the Australian Minister for External Affairs, Dr H. V. Evatt, in the processes leading up to the partition of Palestine on the basis of a United Nations resolution in November 1947. The story of Evatt's involvement in these events has now been told a number of times.[34] A few salient points will be noted here.

Evatt was friendly with Max Freilich, one of the leaders of the Zionist movement in Sydney, and was a frequent visitor to the Freilich household. Freilich, together with other Zionist colleagues, was an active fundraiser for the ALP. A more direct influence was that of Abram Landa, who had been an active member of the ALP since 1925 and became a state Labor MP in 1941. Landa regularly accompanied Freilich and his colleagues on visits to Canberra. Landa visited the United States during the period when the Palestine issue was before the UN. He was also a member of the Australian delegation to the UN General Assembly in 1949 (when Evatt was president of the Assembly). The Assembly admitted Israel as a member of the UN.

Evatt was not, however, influenced only by his Jewish friends. In 1949, when the Labor government was facing an election, Evatt took pains not to alienate the Catholic Church. The Vatican was hostile to the idea of a Jewish state, and was particularly opposed to Jewish control of the Christian holy places. The Vatican line was faithfully followed by the Catholic press in Australia.[35] As a recent biography of Evatt suggests, Cardinal Gilroy, Catholic archbishop of Sydney, may have had more influence than Evatt's Jewish acquaintances.[36]

Recent studies of Evatt's tactics at the UN argue that he exploited the UN committee procedure in order to bring about the partition resolution.[37] However, his biographers stress that the irreconcilable positions of the Arab and Jewish delegations made it clear to him that partition was the only way out.

ALP support for Israel remained solid until 1973, when the Arab oil producing countries imposed an embargo following the Yom Kippur war in October of that year. However, attitudes on the left of the party had already changed following the Six-Day War of 1967, in line with a general shift in left-wing sentiment around the world. The growth of anti-Zionist and anti-Israel sentiment in Australia has been particularly marked among Marxist-oriented groups and their supporters and sympathizers in the union movement and the left factions of the ALP, especially the Socialist Left in Victoria.

Left-wing hostility towards Israel and Zionism has been examined by several writers.[38] Mendes also takes up the controversial relationship between anti-Zionism and anti-Semitism, which has been the subject of much debate by a wide range of commentators from all points of the political spectrum. As Mendes observes, the link between anti-Zionism and anti-Semitism is manifested by the disproportionate hostility of much of the left, not only to Israel but to broader Jewish aspirations, the use of anti-Semitic rhetoric, the stereotyping of all Jews as supporters of Israel's oppression of the Palestinians, and the tendency to minimize or trivialize the reality of the Holocaust.[39] Much of this left-wing hostility emanates from groups outside the ALP. It has, however, surfaced within the ALP itself, most notably among members of the Socialist Left faction within the party in Victoria. Bill Hartley, who was secretary of the Victorian branch of the ALP in the 1960s and 1970s, became well known for anti-Semitic rhetoric as part of his criticism of Israel (although it should be noted that this occurred after he had been ousted from his party secretaryship). Hartley was, for a time, associated with a left-wing union periodical, *Scope*. In 1975, he wrote in *Scope* that supporters of Israel were manipulating the ALP and the Labour movement. Subsequently, Hartley became a regular broadcaster on the community radio station, 3CR, whose anti-Israel and anti-Jewish bias has been the subject of repeated complaints from the Jewish community. In 1982, following the Israeli invasion of Lebanon, Hartley compared the Israeli leaders with Adolf Hitler, adding, "if anything, the situation is worse".[40]

Similar views were expressed by the NSW Labor MP, George Peterson. His wife, Mairi Peterson, well known for her support of the Palestinians, stood as an ALP candidate in the federal election of 1980, but made the strategic error of running in the seat of Wentworth, which has a large Jewish population.

Undoubtedly, however, the most significant involvement of the ALP with Israel and the Middle East has come about through the personal actions of two successive Prime Ministers, Gough Whitlam and Bob Hawke. Whitlam's actions have been the subject of much scrutiny.[41] When the Egyptian army crossed the Suez Canal in October 1973 and launched the Yom Kippur war, Whitlam was approached by his Cabinet colleague, Moss Cass, who tried to persuade him to call for a cease-fire. Whitlam refused, and Cass did not take the matter further. However, the matter was raised in parliament by Joe Berinson, MP for Perth, who incurred Whitlam's wrath as a result.[42] Ironically, Whitlam did call for a cease-fire when the tide of war had turned and the Egyptian army had been pushed back across the Canal.[43] Whitlam's position in public was that his government would be "even-handed", which the Jewish community interpreted as a direct reversal of Labor policy.

Whitlam's motives are not the major concern of this chapter, where we are mainly interested in the effects of his actions on the relationship between the ALP and the Jewish community. They were, clearly, extremely negative. At a meeting with Jewish community leaders in Melbourne in 1974, he addressed them as "you people" and described the recent Israeli reprisal raid into southern Lebanon as a "crime".[44] In his autobiography, Whitlam claimed that he had been subject to "crude blackmail" by spokesmen from the Jewish community, and defended this allegation in a subsequent address to the National Press Club.[45]

In the circumstances, it is not altogether surprising that a number of leading figures in the Jewish community recommended in 1975 that Jewish voters should not support the ALP at the election in December of that year – the only occasion when such action has been taken.[46] These events represent the nadir of relationships between the Jewish community and the Labor Party.

The contrast between Whitlam and his prime ministerial successor, Bob Hawke, could hardly be stronger. As Rubinstein observes, "Bob Hawke's support for Israel and Jewish causes is so well known that it is regularly discussed at length in virtually all accounts of his career and is one of the facets of Hawke's outlook best known to the public".[47] Rubinstein recalls that Hawke, then president of the Australian Council of Trade Unions (ACTU) and also national president of the ALP, publicly attacked Whitlam's "even-handed" policy in November 1973.

Hawke's passionate defence of Israel brought him into direct confrontation with Whitlam and also with some of his colleagues on the federal Executive of the ALP, where an attempt was made to force his resignation. In January 1974, addressing the conference of the Zionist Federation, he again attacked the policy of even-handedness. Paraphrasing John Donne, he concluded: "I know that I am not an island and I know that if we allow the bell to be tolled for Israel it will have tolled for me, for us all".[48] Rubinstein also notes that, despite Hawke's personal commitment to Israel, the Hawke government did not diverge significantly in its Middle East policies from those of the preceding Liberal-National coalition government, and he argues that it was marginally friendlier towards Arab interests. On occasion, however, Hawke made a point of stressing his support for Israel to the extent of disagreeing publicly with his own Foreign Minister, Senator Gareth Evans, who took a much more pro-Arab line. This was particularly the case after a speech at the UN by the Australian ambassador, Dr Peter Wilenski, in April 1989, in which he expressed Australia's regret for the actions of the Israeli government in restricting Muslim religious rights on the Temple Mount in Jerusalem.

It is of particular interest to contrast the behaviour of Senator Evans with that of his predecessor, Bill Hayden, Foreign Minister from 1983 to 1988. While Hayden was leader of the Opposition from 1977 to 1983, he was regarded with some suspicion by Jewish community leaders, especially after a meeting with Yasser Arafat in Beirut in 1980. As Minister for Foreign Affairs, however, he pursued a largely pro-Israel policy in line with that of Bob Hawke. In 1986, he delivered a memorable speech to the biennial congress of the Zionist Federation of Australia in which he dwelt on the links between socialism and Zionism, quoting the works of eminent socialist-Zionist writers such as Moses Hess, Ber Borochov, and Nachman Syrkin.[49]

Under Hawke's successor, Paul Keating, Labor policy continued to be broadly supportive of Israel, but maintaining diplomatic and commercial links with the Arab world. Thus, in 1993, following the Oslo peace accords, the Keating government recognized the PLO as "the representative of the Palestinian people". In an address to the annual conference of the Australian Union of Jewish Students in 1990, Barry Cohen, a former minister in the Hawke government, described the balance of forces within the federal Parliamentary Labor Party as tripartite – one-third friendly to Israel, one-third hostile, and one-third neutral or uninterested. (Other estimates by Jewish Labor activists suggest that the "uninterested" category is considerably larger.) Keating himself displayed little interest in the Middle East, being mainly focused on Southeast Asia.

The temperature rose considerably after the accession of Ariel Sharon to the prime ministership of Israel in 2001, when Israel's policy towards the Palestinians became much tougher. Criticism of Israel from the left of the parliamentary party became increasingly strident. For example, Tanya Plibersek made several speeches attacking Israel as a "rogue state". Criticism also came from right-wing ALP MPs, including Julia Irwin and Leo McLeay.

Simon Crean, leader of the Opposition from 2001 to 2003, hesitated for some time before stating his position on the Arab–Israeli conflict. In September 2003, following a particularly violent suicide bombing in Jerusalem, he spoke to a Jewish audience and assured them of continued ALP support for Israel. Labor, he emphasized, was a "strong and forceful advocate" for a two-state solution based on the principle of land for peace. Labor's support for the right of Israel to exist behind secure borders in a peaceful Middle East remained "unequivocal and unshakeable". He also foreshadowed that a future Labor administration would do more to advance the peace process, which was in Australia's national interest.

Not long after Simon Crean's statement, he was replaced as Labor leader by Mark Latham, who acted quickly to improve Labor's relations with the Jewish community. Latham, who made a private visit to Israel in 2001, is a member of the Australia-Israel parliamentary friendship group, and made a favourable impression on Jewish community leaders during the ALP national conference in January 2004.[50]

The conference resolution on the Middle East was the result of factional negotiations which enabled the resolution to be moved by a leading member of the Left faction in the federal parliamentary party, Anthony Albanese, and seconded by the only Jewish MP, Michael Danby.

The resolution declares, "Labor continues to support the right of Israel to exist in peace and security within secure and recognized borders". It also condemns all acts of terrorism, including Palestinian suicide bombing. At the same time, the resolution criticizes the building of a security barrier by the Israeli government, and supports the right of self-determination for the Palestinian people. In other words, the resolution maintains an "even-handed" approach to the Arab–Israeli conflict, but its emphasis on the legitimacy of the Israeli state has clearly improved the atmosphere between the ALP and the Jewish community.

Party and Community Involvement

Jews have made significant contributions to local government, although most Jewish municipal councillors have not come from the ALP. The most notable Labor councillor was undoubtedly Norman Lee (d. 2000), who was a member of the Waverley municipal council in Sydney from 1983 to 1999, and deputy mayor in 1988. During his term as a councillor, he was instrumental in improving building access for disabled persons. He was also active in promoting the interests of ethnic minorities, and in persuading the council to grant leave to employees for religious obser-vances.[51]

Two other Labor men were elected to the Waverley Council in the 1990s – George Newhouse in 1995 and Sam Einfeld in 1999. (Sam Einfeld is the great-nephew of Syd Einfeld, whose ministerial career is described elsewhere in this chapter.) In the neighbouring municipality of Woollahra, David Bitel was a councillor in the 1970s. Bitel was also president of several ALP branches in the Sydney area in the 1980s and 1990s, and is the current chairman of the NSW Jewish Board of Deputies Social Justice Committee. A solicitor by profession, he has devoted much of his time to issues related to immigration, including the presidency of the Refugee Council of Australia.

Jews have played a variety of parts in the Labor movement for many years. One important and continuing contribution has been as fund-raisers. Arthur Calwell, who was a minister in the Curtin and Chifley governments and subsequently leader of the Opposition (1960–6), had close ties with the Jewish community in Melbourne. Jack Skolnik, a former trade union official who ran a wineshop in the central business district, introduced Calwell to other Jewish businessmen. They raised funds to support Labor's electoral campaigns in 1943 and 1946.[52]

Bob Hawke's well-known commitment to Israel and Jewish cases derives partly from his association with prominent figures in the Jewish commu-nity in Melbourne, including the lawyer and retailer, Lionel Revelman, and Saul Same, head of a large firm of clothing manufacturers and a leading figure in the Zionist movement. During the 1974 election campaign, Same organized some highly successful fund-raising functions where Hawke was the guest speaker.[53]

In NSW, an important fund-raiser for the ALP was Sam Fiszman (d. 2003), who arrived in Australia as a refugee after World War II and built up a highly successful carpet retailing business. Although never a member of the party, he was close to some of its influential figures, in particular Graham Richardson, secretary of the NSW party from 1976 to 1983 and subsequently a minister in the Hawke and Keating governments. One of Fiszman's regular services to the ALP was to fund the opinion polls conducted by the party to test electoral support.

A number of Jews have been active in the party organization and as assistants to Labor ministers. The most notable recent case is that of Eric Roozendaal, secretary of the ALP in NSW from 1999 until mid-2004. Reports suggest he will be the NSW campaign director for the federal election expected in 2004. On 28 June, he took up an Upper House seat in the NSW Parliament vacated by the previous sitting member.[54] Matthew Strassberg, another young activist, was appointed as chief of staff to John della Bosca, a senior member of the Carr government in NSW. An unusual example is that of Walt Secord, director of communications in the Premier's office in NSW, who is a Canadian Indian by birth, but worked for some years as a journalist on the *Australian Jewish News* in Sydney and has close links with the Jewish community. Other examples of Jewish involvement in party affairs are given by Mendes.[55]

Relations between the ALP and the Jewish community in NSW have been cemented by the prominence of Labor lawyers in Jewish communal affairs. Since 1973, six of the eleven presidents of the NSW Jewish Board of Deputies have been lawyers formally involved in, or well disposed toward, the ALP and labor politics.

In 2003 a group of young NSW activists, perturbed by the rift between the Jewish community and the ALP resulting from the anti-Israel stance of some sections of the party and the union movement, organized the Jewish Labor Forum, with the aim of encouraging closer links between the ALP and the Jewish community. The group was formed with the encouragement of Premier Bob Carr, who has been consistently active in encouraging Jews to participate in the ALP. One result of the Forum's activities was a significant increase in the number of Jewish Labor candidates at the local government elections in NSW in 2004.

An earlier project to encourage such participation was mounted in the 1980s through the "McKell schools", named after a former Premier of NSW. The schools, organized by J. R. ("Johno") Johnson, president of the NSW upper house of parliament from 1978 to 1991, were set up to train young Labor activists. Johnson made a point of encouraging young Jews to join, to the extent of ensuring that non-kosher food was not served at social gatherings.[56] In the light of the observations made at the beginning of this chapter, it is relevant to note that Johnson was a loyal Catholic and a member of the dominant right-wing faction in the NSW party. The relationship between Jews and the ALP continues to display multiple facets and interesting contradictions.

Notes

1 Jeremy Jones, *Report on Anti-Semitism in Australia* (Sydney: Executive Council of Australian Jewry, 2001), p. 9.

2 On the historical figures, see Hilary Rubinstein, "Jewish Parliamentarians in Australia, 1849 to the Present", *Australian Jewish Historical Society Journal* [henceforth *AJHSJ*] 10, 4 (1988): 298–316, and the appendix in this volume.

3 Alan Barcan, *Radical Students: The Old Left at Sydney University* (Melbourne: Melbourne University Press, 2002), p. 343.

4 Suzanne D. Rutland, *Edge of the Diaspora*, rev. edn (Sydney: Brandl and Schlesinger, 1997), p. 254; and Anne Andgel, *Fifty Years of Caring: The History of the Australian Jewish Welfare Society, 1936–1986* (Sydney: Australian Jewish Welfare Society, 1988), pp. 89–95.

5 Suzanne D. Rutland, "The Honourable Sydney Einfeld, AO: Builder of Australian Jewry", *AJHSJ* 11, 2 (1991): 312–30.

6 "S. M. Falstein", *Australian Dictionary of Biography*, vol. 14 (Melbourne: Melbourne University Press, 1996), p. 136.

7 *Age*, 31 August 1988.

8 W. D. Rubinstein, *The Jews in Australia: A Thematic History – Volume Two, 1945 to the Present* (Melbourne: Heinemann, 1991), p. 301.

9 Walter Jona, "Jews in Victorian Politics, 1835–1985", *AJHSJ* 10, 1 (1986): 2–14 at p. 12.

10 L. Allan, "Ethnic Recruitment or Ethnic Branch Stacking?", *People and Place* 8, 1 (2000): 54–77.

11 Rutland, *Edge of the Diaspora*, p. 213.

12 Michael Blakeney, *Australia and the Jewish Refugees 1933–194* (Sydney: Croom Helm Australia, 1985), pp. 265–75.

13 See Peter Y. Medding, *From Assimilation to Group Survival: A Political and Sociological Study of an Australian Jewish Community* (Melbourne: Cheshire, 1968); Rubinstein, *The Jews in Australia*; Rutland, *Edge of the Diaspora*; Rodney Gouttman, "The Sam Cohen Affair: A Conspiracy?", *AJHSJ* 15, 1 (1999): 69–79; Philip Mendes, "The Senator Sam Cohen Affair: Soviet Anti-Semitism, the ALP and the 1961 federal Election", *Labour History* 78 (2000): 506–24.

14 Rubinstein, *The Jews in Australia*, pp. 402–10; Rutland, *Edge of the Diaspora*, pp. 327–8. On the Council, see also chapter 4 this volume.

15 Peter Y. Medding, "Factors Influencing the Voting Behaviour of Melbourne Jews", in P. Y. Medding, ed., *Jews in Australian Society* (Melbourne: Macmillan, 1973), p. 143.

16 *Ibid.*, p. 144.

17 S. Encel and B. S. Buckley, *The NSW Jewish Community: A Survey* (Sydney: NSW University Press, 1978), pp. 68–9.

18 Rubinstein, *The Jews in Australia*, p. 135.

19 John Goldlust, *The Jews of Melbourne: A Community Profile* (Melbourne: Jewish Welfare Society, 1993).

20 There have been a couple of small, targeted surveys of Jewish political dispositions. In a 1991 national study of Australian Jewish students, 56 percent reported voting for the Coalition in the 1990 federal election, 28 percent for the ALP, and 9 percent for the Australian Democrats. See W. D. Rubinstein, *Attitudes of Australian Jewish Tertiary Students to Their Jewish Identity* (Melbourne: Australian Institute of Jewish Affairs, 1991). The other such survey was a study of Jewish leaders Australia-wide, and is discussed in chapter 6.

21 Andrew Gladding Whiteside, *The Socialism of Fools* (Berkeley: California

University Press, 1975); Michael Lerner, *The Socialism of Fools* (Oakland: Tikkun Books, 1992).

22 Philip Mendes, "Left Attitudes Towards Jews", *AJHSJ* 13, 1 (1995): 97–127.
23 Peter Love, *Labour and the Money Power: Australian Labour Populism 1890–1950* (Melbourne: Melbourne University Press, 1984), p. 38.
24 Blakeney, *Australia and the Jewish Refugees*, p. 19.
25 Peter Love, "The Kingdom of Shylock: A Case Study of Australian Labour Anti-Semitism", *AJHSJ* 11, 1 (1993): 54–62 at p. 61.
26 Mendes, "Left Attitudes Towards Jews", p. 100.
27 *Australian Jewish Times*, 29 November 1984.
28 Rubinstein, *The Jews in Australia*, pp. 301–4 and 366 n.
29 Dr M. H. Cass, personal communication, 2003.
30 Arthur Calwell, *Be Just and Fear Not* (Melbourne: Rigby, 1978), p. 116.
31 Blakeney, *Australia and the Jewish Refugees*, pp. 77–8.
32 Rutland, *Edge of the Diaspora*, pp. 225–43.
33 G. Long, "Greece, Crete and Syria" in *Australia in the War of 1939–45*, Series 1 (Army), vol. 2 (Canberra: Australian War Memorial, 1950).
34 See H. V. Evatt, "Australia's Part in the Creation of Israel", *AJHSJ* 5, 4 (1961): 157–68; Max Freilich, *Zion in Our Time* (Sydney: Morgan Publications, 1967); Rodney Gouttman, "First Principles: H. V. Evatt and the Jewish Homeland", in W. D. Rubinstein, ed., *Jews in the Sixth Continent* (Sydney: Allen and Unwin, 1987), pp. 262–302; Rubinstein, *The Jews in Australia*; Ken Buckley et al., *Doc Evatt: Patriot, Internationalist, Fighter and Scholar* (Melbourne: Longman Cheshire, 1994); Rutland, *Edge of the Diaspora*; and Chanan Reich, *Australia and Israel: An Ambiguous Relationship* (Melbourne: Melbourne University Press, 2002).
35 Gouttman, "First Principles".
36 Buckley et al., *Doc Evatt*, p. 312.
37 Coral Bell, *Dependent Ally* (Melbourne: Oxford University Press, 1988); and H. Adelman, "Australia and the Birth of Israel: Midwife or Abortionist", *Australian Journal of Politics and History* 38, 3 (1992): 354–74.
38 Rubinstein, *The Jews in Australia*, pp. 441–51; Mendes, "Left Attitudes Towards Jews" pp. 97–127.
39 Mendes, "Left Attitudes Towards Jews", p. 109.
40 *Ibid.*, p. 113.
41 See Alan Reid, *The Whitlam Venture* (Melbourne: Hill of Content, 1976); and Gough Whitlam, *The Whitlam Government* (Ringwood; Viking Penguin, 1985); and Rubinstein, *The Jews in Australia*.
42 Commonwealth Parliamentary Debates, 16 October, 1973: 2224–46.
43 Dr M. H. Cass, personal communication, 2003.
44 Rubinstein, *The Jews in Australia*, pp. 541–3.
45 Whitlam, *The Whitlam Government*, p. 126; Rubinstein, *The Jews in Australia*, p. 542.
46 Rubinstein, *The Jews in Australia*, pp. 541, 545; and Dr Suzanne Rutland, personal communication.
47 Rubinstein, *The Jews in Australia*, p. 547.
48 Blanche d'Alpuget, *Robert J. Hawke* (Melbourne: Schwartz Publishing Group, 1982), p. 267.

49 William Hayden, "Israel: A Contemporary Democratic Socialist Perspective" (Melbourne: Zionist Federation of Australia, 1986).
50 "Latham Impresses Community", *Australian Jewish News*, Sydney edn, 13 February 2004.
51 Mrs Ilona Lee, personal communication, 2004.
52 Rutland, *Edge of the Diaspora*, pp. 212–13.
53 d'Alpuget, *Robert J. Hawke*, pp. 271–2.
54 Aviva Bard, "Roozendaal bound for Parliament", *Australian Jewish News*, Sydney edn, 2 April 2004; and Oryana Kaufman, "Roozendaal becomes the State's newest MP", *Australian Jewish News*, 2 July 2004.
55 Philip Mendes, "From the Shtetl to the Monash Soviet", *Australian Journal of Jewish Studies* 14 (2000): 54–77.
56 Michael Marx, private communication, 2003.

4 | Jews and the Left

PHILIP MENDES

Historically, Jews have been described as a "people of the left". From the early nineteenth century onwards, Jews were prominent in movements for liberal change and reform. For example, Jews played an active role in the 1830 French Revolution, in the Saint-Simonist movement, and in the abortive uprisings of Giuseppe Mazzini's Young Italy movement.[1] Jews were also particularly active in the 1848 revolutionary upheavals, contributing prominently to liberal campaigns for freedom and reform in Germany, Austria, France, Italy, Rumania and Hungary.[2] German Jewish intellectuals such as Moses Hess, Karl Marx and Ferdinand Lassalle were influential in the promotion of early radical and socialist ideas.[3]

Jewish involvement in liberalist movements reflected the support of these movements for Jewish legal and political equality. However, the granting of Jewish rights in much of Western and Central Europe was frequently accompanied by a severe anti-Semitic backlash. In addition, the large Jewish masses in the Russian Empire continued to be subject to severe official disabilities and persecution.[4]

Faced with considerable prejudice and social discrimination in Western and Central Europe and no rights or prospects of emancipation whatsoever in Eastern Europe, many Jews turned to the growing socialist movement. This conspicuous Jewish involvement in socialist and communist parties and movements would last from about 1870 to 1970, and incorporate not only the Russian Pale of Settlement, but also much of Europe, the English-speaking world, parts of Latin America, and even sections of North Africa and the Middle East.

The Jewish alliance with the left reflected a number of complex historical and political factors. One was the class oppression and poverty of many Jews: at the turn of the twentieth century, most European Jews were poor and working class, and struggling to survive. For example, it has been estimated that as many as 20 percent of Russian Jews in the late 1890s were paupers relying on charity.[5] Many saw immigration to the English-speaking world as the solution to their problems, whilst others agitated for radical social and political change.

Another factor was the ethnic/national oppression of Jews by various European right-wing governments and movements. This anti-Semitic persecution of Jews included government-organized pogroms in late nineteenth and early twentieth century Tsarist Russia, the 1894 Dreyfus Affair in "democratic" France, the slaughter of 60,000 Jews by anti-communist Ukrainians during 1918–20, and finally the horrendous murder of six million Jews by Nazi Germany.[6]

An additional influence was the defence of Jewish claims to equality by most left-wing European parties and movements. The early socialist movement – influenced by the popular prejudices of nineteenth-century Europe – had tended to identify Jews with capitalist exploitation. And whilst not all nineteenth-century socialists were hostile to Jews, most regarded anti-Semitism with critical benevolence as a deluded anti-capitalist movement of the declining social classes that would eventually bring them into the fold of socialism, rather than as an inherently hostile ideology.

During the late nineteenth and early twentieth centuries, however, the socialist movement gradually switched to an unequivocal denunciation of anti-Semitism. This adoption of a basically philo-Semitic approach was particularly influenced by the increasing influence of Marxist ideology which precluded any form of national or religious discrimination. An equally important factor was the self-interest of the left in combating anti-Semitic movements as it became clearer that these were actually serving conservative political interests. This basic left-wing sympathy for Jews would later be strengthened further by the rise of Nazism, which pitted Jews and the left against a common enemy.[7]

Jewish support for the left has taken five principal forms. Initially, Jews were active in early to mid-nineteenth century liberal movements for social and political change. Somewhat later there was the prominence of a small number of Jews in early to mid-twentieth century European revolutionary movements. Some of the best-known figures included the Russian Bolsheviks Trotsky, Kamenev, and Zinoviev, the Mensheviks Martov and Dan, Bela Kun in Hungary, Ana Pauker in Roumania,[8] Rudolf Slansky in Czechoslovakia, and Rosa Luxemburg in Germany. In addition, there was the emergence of mass Jewish labor movements in a number of mainly European cities in the late nineteenth and early twentieth century. The best known such movement was the Jewish Labor Bund which was formed in Poland in 1897, and played a key part in the founding of the Russian Social Democratic Labor Party.[9] Similar movements – also influenced by socialist beliefs and often inspired by the Bund – existed in Berlin, Paris, London, New York, Amsterdam, and even Buenos Aires.[10]

A further manifestation was the emergence of specific Jewish left groups often (but not always) affiliated with broader left political parties and movements. For example, the Jewish Labor Bund worked closely, but was not formally affiliated with the Polish Socialist Party during the inter-war period.[11] Similarly, many national communist parties formed specifically Jewish networks or factions as in the Soviet Evsektsiya. There were also numerous left Zionist groups involved in broader left campaigns and activities. In addition, there was significant Jewish electoral support in democratic countries for either social democratic parties, or liberal parties as in the USA. For example, it has been estimated that 90 percent of American Jews supported President Roosevelt's New Deal in 1944, and that Jews have continued to vote for Democratic presidential candidates in numbers greater than any other white ethnic group.[12] Australian Jews also offered considerable support to the Australian Labor Party for a number of years, as reviewed in the previous chapter.[13]

The documented existence of a Jewish-left alliance does not, however, substantiate far-right conspiracy theories that Jews invented or controlled international communism. The concepts of socialism and social revolution were not introduced by Jews. Many of the most important socialist leaders such as Friedrich Engels, Mikhail Bakunin, Jean Jaures and Lenin were not of Jewish origin. Equally, the majority of Jews were never political radicals. Many of the Eastern European communist movements to which Jews belonged in disproportionate numbers were very small movements. Only a small minority of Jews were involved. In fact at the time of the Bolshevik Revolution, an overwhelming majority of Russian Jews expressed a preference for Zionist or conservative religious allegiances.[14]

Nevertheless, a disproportionate number of Jews were involved in politics, and the overwhelming majority of these activists participated in the left. Except in countries such as Great Britain and the USA where conservative groups and parties were not overtly anti-Semitic, Jews had little choice. In this context, the allegations of Judeo-Communism made by European right-wing extremists and often mainstream conservatives became a self-fulfilling prophecy.

For example, Australian novelist Helen Darville/Demidenko gained enormous publicity for her claims that Ukrainian collaboration with the Nazi Holocaust involved a reasonable payback for the alleged prominence of Jews in the Soviet security apparatus responsible for the 1930s famine.[15] Yet this allegation is arguably ahistorical in that it ignores the long history of Ukrainian anti-Semitism that existed well before the 1930s famine, including the infamous Chmielnicki massacres of the 1640s. This history of discrimination culminated in the 1918–20 pogroms under the rule of Ukrainian nationalist leader Simon Petlyura. Some Ukrainian Jews – particularly the Russian-speaking, educated, middle-class intelligentsia as opposed to the mainly Yiddish-speaking working-class mass – responded to this brutal oppression by joining the Bolsheviks, and actively suppressing anti-communist and nationalist views. Yet there is little evidence that Jews as an ethnic group or even Jews as individual Bolsheviks played a significant role in the Ukrainian famine.[16] Rather, this episode demonstrates that the more Jews were persecuted by right-wing parties and governments, the more likely were politically active Jews to turn to the left for defence and support.

The Post-World War II Decline of the Jewish/Left Alliance

In the decade from 1939–48, two profoundly important events took place which progressively eroded Jewish faith in universalistic solutions. The first was the Holocaust, the murder of six million Jews by Nazi Germany. The lesson that many Jews (even radical Jews) drew from the Holocaust was that the great working-class movements of Europe had failed to defend the Jews from genocide, and that any future defence strategy would have to be based primarily on the Jews' own resources. No less importantly, the Holocaust had directly liquidated the Jewish Labor Bund in Poland, the breeding ground of Jewish socialism. The mass Jewish labour movement which promoted a class and ethnic loyalty to socialism was no more.[17]

The second event was the creation of the Jewish State of Israel in 1948. The emergence of a national Jewish entity with a strong and powerful army meant that Jews all over the world could look to their own State for protection, rather than depending on international movements and ideologies. The establishment of Israel tended to unite rather than divide Jews, and so diminished the importance of internal class distinctions that might still have attracted Jews to the left.[18]

The revelations of Soviet anti-Semitism in the early to mid-1950s also undermined Jewish support for universalistic socialism. In the pre-war period, many Jewish intellectuals (not exclusively Marxist) had been impressed by the Soviet Union's apparent outlawing of anti-Semitism, and by its creation of a Jewish national homeland in Biro-Bidzhan. For many, Biro-Bidzhan seemed to present a practical and potentially more viable alternative to Zionism and Palestine. However, Stalin's appalling anti-Jewish campaign of 1948–53 ended any residual interest in Biro-Bidzhan, and permanently disillusioned most Jewish-conscious Marxists.[19]

A further significant influence was the 1967 Six-Day War in the Middle East which galvanized even non-Zionist Jews in support of Israel.[20] Following the war, Jews in many parts of the Diaspora began to act more and more like other national émigré groups. In particular, their political choices and alliances began to reflect the needs and interests of the Israeli State as much as any local issues or concerns.[21]

A number of other circumstances and events have arguably influenced the decline in Jewish identification with left movements and causes. The first is the overwhelmingly middle classing of Jews (at least in the West) since World War II. Today, there are fewer and fewer working-class Jews who have a class basis for supporting socialist ideologies.[22] A second factor is the sharp decline in traditional right-wing anti-Semitism (at least in Western countries) which has provided politically active Jews with new political choices.

A third factor is the rise of left-wing anti-Zionism (and in some cases outright anti-Semitism) which has served to alienate much of Western Jewry from even the mainstream social democratic left.[23] And finally there is the influence of Jewish neo-conservatives (particularly in the USA through *Commentary* and related magazines) who have actively campaigned for greater Jewish support for conservative political parties and agendas.[24] However, none of these factors significantly influenced the initial Jewish move from internationalist to nationalist solutions. What they did do was erode the class and ethnic basis of any remaining Jewish attraction to the left, and provide a rationalisation for some Jews to actively favour right-wing political agendas.[25]

Continuing Prominence: The Vietnam War and Beyond

Jewish involvement in the left remains significant. In many Western countries, Jews continue to figure prominently in various left-wing and radical movements. What has changed, however, is that there is arguably no longer any intrinsically objective underpinning for Jewish commitment to the left. Jewish class and ethnic interests today are arguably not represented by universalistic agendas.[26] Nevertheless, a disproportionate number of Jews continue to be socialized by family and community cultural traditions into involvement with the left.

For example, Jewish involvement in the New Left of the 1960s was particularly significant. In the USA, it has been estimated that roughly one third to one half of New Leftists were Jewish. Jews were prominent in the struggle for black civil rights, in the Free Speech Movement, and in the anti-Vietnam War campaigns. A number of the leading New Left activists and theorists were of Jewish origin. Jews were also prominent in the New Left in a number of other countries including France, Britain, Italy, and Argentina. However, such activists always constituted only a small minority of the larger Jewish student community.[27]

The prominence of Jews in the New Left subsequently spawned a significant and ongoing Jewish contribution to emerging social movements such as feminism and gay rights. Many of the most prominent leaders of these movements were Jewish.[28] Even today a disproportionate number of Jews appears to be involved in movements against war such as the recent American intervention in Iraq.[29]

The post-World War II Jewish left contribution is arguably based on totally different motivations and agendas to the earlier pre-war Jewish left. First, most post-war Jewish leftists have not been influenced by specifically Jewish concerns or interests such as anti-Semitism into seeking involvement with the left. On the contrary, Jewish involvement in the New Left, for example, reflected solely universalistic concerns related to black equality or peace in Vietnam. Secondly, and as a result, the Jewish prominence in the New Left exerted little or no long-term influence on mainstream Jewish political culture. This outcome is distinct from the pre-World War II period when the disproportionate involvement of Jews in left-wing movements directly impacted on Jewish political interests and choices due to the prominence of the "Jewish question" in European political life.

To be sure, the last fifteen years has seen a revival of specifically Jewish/left groups advocating a renewal of the older Jewish/left alliance. The best-known groups include the Tikkun Magazine/community in the US, and the Jewish Socialist Group in the UK. Some groups have been influenced by Socialist/Zionist ideology, and others by Bundist ideas and tradition. Their establishment almost certainly reflects the growing importance of multicultural and identity politics within what was previously a narrowly class-based and monocultural Western left. Whilst such groups have enjoyed some success (particularly in relation to formulating a more Diaspora-linked Jewish identity independent of Zionist or Israeli centrality), they are unlikely to prosper in the long term. The principal reason for this likely failure is that the left today no longer supports objective Jewish interests. In fact on many issues, particularly Zionism and the State of Israel, much of the left is openly unsympathetic to Jewish concerns.[30]

The Australian Jewish Left

The early Australian Jewish left was primarily an immigrant phenomenon associated with the post-World War I arrival of European Jews. It existed principally in Melbourne and Sydney (the two largest population centres of Australian Jewry), had no significant trade union base, and was largely directed by middle-class males, although some activists had a background of European working-class affiliation. The first recorded Jewish left presence is that of the Jewish Workers Association, formed in 1914 by Russian Jewish exiles in Brisbane.[31] However, a serious organized Jewish left did not emerge until the late 1920s in Melbourne.

The first major Jewish left group – the Gezerd – was formed by Polish Jewish immigrants in 1930. The aim of the Gezerd (meaning "back to earth") was to support the settlement of Jews in the Soviet Biro-Bidzhan, a far away Asiatic province of the USSR where the Bolsheviks hoped to establish a Jewish homeland. Similar Biro-Bidzhan support groups were set up by pro-Soviet Jews all around the world. The Gezerd attained considerable support during the 1930s for its anti-Nazi propaganda campaigns, including a call for a boycott of German goods. However, the Gezerd declined during the war due to its blind support of the Soviet Union, particularly at the time of the unpopular Nazi/Soviet pact. It was dissolved in 1944.[32]

The Gezerd was succeeded by the Jewish Progressive Centre, a small pro-Soviet, Yiddish-speaking organization established principally by post-war Polish Jewish refugees in 1946. The JPC members maintained a Jewish communist sub-culture, but few actually joined the Communist Party due to concerns about their alien status, and the threat of potential persecution or deportation. The JPC split over the 1967 Six-Day War, and dissolved soon after.[33]

The most significant Australian Jewish left group was the Melbourne Jewish Council to Combat Fascism and Anti-Semitism, a broad-based organization established in 1942 by a coalition of social democrats, communists and liberals (both immigrant and Anglo-Australian Jews) determined to take a public stand against anti-Semitism. In spite of its overt left-wing sympathies, the Council was a highly influential, if not dominant organization in the Melbourne Jewish community of the immediate post-war years, acting as the official public relations representative of the Victorian Jewish Board of Deputies (VJBD). This meant that the Council took control of all action pertaining to anti-Semitism, communal relations, and political activity undertaken by the Board. The Council was also responsible for the public relations activities of the Executive Council of Australian Jewry whenever that body was based in Victoria.[34]

The Council's emphasis on the joint struggle against the evils of fascism and anti-Semitism reflected the experiences of many Jewish refugees who had experienced persecution under anti-communist regimes. This emphasis suggested that potential dangers to Jews came principally from conservatives and the political Right. Conversely, the Council believed that left-wing groups and organizations were particularly sympathetic to Jews. This position quickly came under attack with the beginnings of the Cold War in 1948. The Jewish political unity of the wartime period began to erode. Jewish support for the Soviet Union collapsed as increasing evidence of Stalinist anti-Semitism began to emerge. In addition, Jews locally and internationally were influenced by the growth of anti-communism, and the pressure to endorse new political alignments against the USSR.

In contrast, the Council rejected the Cold War consensus, and attempted to maintain its existing political links and strategies. As a result, the Council became involved in a series of public disputes and controversies which progressively weakened its previously strong support within the Jewish community. Common to all these controversies was the allegation that the Council was associating the Jewish community per se with communist activities, and therefore creating, rather than combating anti-Semitism.[35]

The allegation that the Council was controlled by Communist or pro-Soviet factions has some merit, but is also strongly linked to the Cold War politics of the period. On the one hand, there is little evidence of direct Communist Party control of the Council. On the other hand, there is little doubt that the Council was significantly influenced by a number of prominent Communist Party members and active sympathizers. The McCarthyism of the period tended to accentuate the significance of these associations, both in terms of exaggerating the extent of Communist involvement, and equally in reinforcing the reluctance of leftist non-Communists to openly join anti-Communists in voicing criticisms of the Soviet Union. These complex internal manoeuvrings within the Council led to repeated conjecture as to whether the Council was sincerely leading campaigns against anti-Semitism, or alternatively and insidiously pursuing veiled political agendas.[36]

For example, particular conflict occurred around the controversial Jewish campaign against German/Nazi immigration to Australia. The campaign, which had been directed by the Jewish Council, was suspended by the Executive Council of Australian Jewry in April 1951. However, the Council resolved not only to continue the campaign against German immigrants, but also a broader campaign against West German rearmament. In contrast, the Jewish roof bodies were increasingly influenced by the State of Israel's reconciliation with West Germany, and the general Cold War concern to include the Germans in the Western alliance. The Council was eventually expelled from the Victorian Jewish Board of Deputies in July 1952 for refusing to cancel a protest demonstration against the new West German Ambassador.[37]

The Council remained an influential body. It had a numerically significant membership including a number of active sub-committees, a vocal Youth Section, and interstate affiliates in New South Wales and Western Australia. In addition, key Council personalities such as Norman Rothfield, Sam Goldbloom, Sam Cohen (later an Australian Labor Party Senator), and Walter Lippmann remained prominent in both the Jewish and broader Australian communities. The Council's robust approach to fighting anti-Semitism from traditional conservative sources continued to attract support from a cross-section of the Jewish community.

However, the Council's inadequate response to Stalinist anti-Semitism destroyed its political credibility. In particular, the Council responded to the anti-Semitic Czech Slansky show trial of November 1952 and the associated USSR Doctors Plot of January 1953 by claiming that anti-Semitism and Communism were a contradiction in terms. According to the Council, any suggestions to the contrary reflected either temporary aberrations arising from the continued existence in Eastern Europe of popular pre-communist prejudices, or alternatively, manifestations of Cold War propaganda. Whilst the Council did not join the Communist Party of Australia in formally endorsing the show trials, it consistently denied that any anti-Jewish manifestations per se were involved. This position, which appeared to prioritize the Council's left loyalties over its Jewish loyalties, eroded the Council's remaining support in the mainstream Jewish community.[38]

The Council remained an active organization until its eventual demise in 1970. It regained some prominence in the late 1950s due to the association of some of its key members with the dominant left faction of the Victorian ALP. However, the unfortunate Senator Sam Cohen Affair in 1962 left the Council once again stereotyped as "soft" on Soviet anti-Semitism. Cohen opposed a parliamentary motion condemning Soviet anti-Semitism, and appeared to defend the Soviet Union's record on this issue.[39] In its later years, the Council continued to be plagued by divisions over the Soviet Union, an ageing leadership, and a failure to attract new supporters despite the emergence of significant Jewish participation in the new radical student and anti-war movements.

The older Jewish left was succeeded by three newer Melbourne Jewish left groups: the Jewish Radical Association (which existed from 1971–3), Paths to Peace (1974–86), and the still extant Australian Jewish Democratic Society established in 1984. All three organizations were convened by former Council leader Norman Rothfield, but were able to address a wider range of issues than the Jewish Council, and establish a more diverse support base including many younger and female activists.[40] However, the Jewish left continued to play a relatively marginal role in the Melbourne Jewish community. In addition, a Sydney Jewish Left group was active from 1987 till 1994. And a small group of Jewish Marxists participated in the Jews Against Zionism and Anti-Semitism group which existed in Melbourne and Sydney from 1979 till about 1985.[41]

The major left opposition to the Jewish Council during the Cold War period came from the social democratic and anti-communist Jewish Labor Bund. The Bund was originally formed in Melbourne in 1928 as a small outpost of the international Bund, sharing its unique commitment to secular Yiddish culture and education, socialism, and anti-Zionism. The Melbourne branch grew significantly after World War II with the arrival of many Yiddish-speaking Polish Jewish refugees. Bundists soon became involved in broader politics, joining the Labor Party and the affiliated New Australia Council (NAC) in significant numbers. Prominent Bundist Bono Wiener became Secretary of the NAC, and his friend Joseph Winkler the Treasurer.

Many of the Polish Bundists had been strongly influenced by the intense hatred which existed between the Communists and the Bund in Poland between the wars. Consequently, they colluded with the Zionist movement to destroy the Jewish Council's influence in the Jewish Board of Deputies and the Kadimah Cultural Centre. They also campaigned against the Council and other alleged apologists for Communism within the Victorian ALP, but with less success. Eventually, the Victorian ALP dissolved the New Australia Council, and established a new committee headed by Jewish Council Secretary, Ernest Platz. Wiener was then expelled from the Victorian ALP following his unsuccessful attempt to discredit Council activist Sam Goldbloom as an alleged secret member of the Communist Party.[42] In later years, many younger Bundists became prominent in the anti-Vietnam War movement despite opposition from the older generation.[43] The Bund continues to exist today as an educational and cultural movement, but with only minimal involvement in political activities.

Jewish Involvement in the Broader Australian Left

Jews have also been active in broader Australian left parties and movements. For example, Jewish support for the now defunct Communist Party of Australia (CPA) appears to have been significant during World War II and the immediate post-war years. This support reflected the Soviet Union's wartime alliance with the Western powers, its rescue of many Polish Jews from the Nazi Holocaust, its strong support for the creation of the State of Israel in 1948, and the Party's strong stand against anti-Semitism in Australia.[44] Conversely, the revelations of Stalinist anti-Semitism in the early 1950s, and the CPA's defence of the Soviet Union's policies quickly eroded much of this support.

Jewish support for the CPA took three principal forms. First, there were two identifiable organized Jewish blocs within the CPA. The earliest Victorian Jewish CPA faction existed in the 1930s, and consisted of approximately a dozen persons. This faction was led by prominent anti-war activist Nat Seeligson, and included both Jews actively involved in the Gezerd, and those whose links with the Jewish community were more tenuous. A similar Jewish faction was formed in Sydney. However, both factions were dissolved by the Party in 1943.[45] Later, a revitalized Jewish faction in the late 1940s and early 1950s included some forty to forty-five mainly youthful and mostly immigrant activists from the Melbourne suburb of Carlton. This faction played a dominant role in the Jewish Council Youth Section, and in the associated Kadimah Youth Organization.[46]

In addition, a number of Jews played prominent roles in the CPA leadership. They included leading figures such as the Aarons family, Bernie Taft, Harry Stein, Judah Waten, and Teachers Federation leader Sam Lewis. Many other Jews were active in Party life, but retained (with some notable exceptions) only minimal links with organised Jewish activities. There is also some evidence of significant Jewish financial support for the CPA during the immediate post-war years.[47] However, once it became clear that the Soviet Union was actually persecuting rather than defending Jews, these donations quickly declined.[48]

Although Jewish support for the CPA declined during the Cold War, Jews continued to be involved in the CPA, and to contribute (at times significantly) to its political and intellectual leadership. During the Vietnam era, there was also a minor revival of Jewish support for the CPA as a number of younger Jews, mostly the children of older leftists, joined the Party. However, in contrast to the older generation, their association with the CPA principally reflected broader universalistic, rather than specifically Jewish concerns.[49]

There is also some evidence of significant Jewish electoral, political, and financial support for the Australian Labor Party particularly in the 1950s and '60s. For example, it has been estimated that two-thirds of Melbourne Jews supported the ALP in the 1961 federal election[50] (although, as Sol Encel discusses in the previous chapter, in more recent years this support seems to have been reversed).[51] Jewish involvement in the Victorian ALP also seems to have been disproportionately high during this period. Many members of the Jewish Labor Bund were active in the ALP, and strongly opposed alleged Communist influences.[52] Conversely, a number of Jewish Council activists were prominent in the dominant left faction.

In addition, a number of Jews have represented the ALP in state and federal Parliament, including most notably Sam Cohen, Barry Cohen, Sid Einfeld, Paul Landa, Whitlam Government Ministers Moss Cass and Joe Berinson, and currently Michael Danby in Canberra, and Marsha Thomson in the Victorian Lower House.

It has also been argued by various media and some academic commentators that Jewish financial support for Labor electoral funds has been influential. This support appears to have been consolidated during and immediately after World War II when the ALP government was active both in granting entry to Jewish refugees from the Holocaust, and in supporting the creation of Israel.[53] Speculation continues that contributions by Jewish businessmen remain significant today.[54] However, no serious research has been conducted to specify either the level of Jewish financial contributions to the ALP, or alternatively how they compare to Jewish donations to the Liberal/National Party coalition.

At present, Jewish support for and attitudes to the ALP appear closely to correlate with ALP policies towards Israel. Although the ALP leadership remains sympathetic to Jewish concerns and is fundamentally pro-Israel, recent high profile attacks by Labor backbenchers Julia Irwin and Tanya Plibersek on Israel may erode Jewish political and financial support for the ALP.[55] It is also apparent that organized Jewish involvement within the ALP is now almost exclusively within the Labor Unity or right-wing faction. This reflects the belief that the ALP left (irrespective of the wide diversity of views within) is hostile to Israel. And it would also appear that most current Jewish activity in the Victorian ALP is based around shoring up branch and political support for Michael Danby, the federal MP who represents the heavily Jewish electorate of Melbourne Ports.[56]

Jews have also been prominent in broader Australian social movements. For example, Jews were involved in significant numbers, both as leaders and as activists within the New Left and anti-Vietnam War student movements at Monash and Melbourne Universities. In addition, Jewish individuals and organizations were prominent within the broader Moratorium movement. Preliminary investigations also suggest a substantial Jewish contribution to the anti-Vietnam movement in Sydney.[57] And NSW Jewish students were prominent in the 1965 Freedom Ride for Aboriginal rights.[58]

Similarly, a considerable number of Jewish individuals – many the children of older CPA and ALP activists and still holding to the beliefs of a leftist Jewish sub-culture – remain prominent in newer movements pertaining to women, gay rights, the environment, animal liberation, multiculturalism, civil liberties, Aboriginal rights, and the peace movement.[59] For example, they include most notably the President of the Refugee Council of Australia, David Bitel, feminist Eva Cox, gay rights activist Denis Altman, International Socialist Organization convenor David Glanz, and animal liberation and Greens activist Peter Singer. It has also been estimated that at least eight of the forty committee members of the Victorian Peace Network formed to oppose the recent American intervention in Iraq were Jewish.[60] And specifically Jewish gay and lesbian groups have been established in both the Melbourne and Sydney Jewish communities.[61]

The Contemporary Australian Jewish Left

Today at least seven Australian Jewish left groups are active. They include the Australian Jewish Democratic Society (AJDS), Jews for a Just Peace, Jews for Refugees, and the Jewish Labor Bund in Melbourne, Ethical Left Action in Byron Bay, and Jewish Voices for Peace and Justice, and Jews Against the Occupation in Sydney. Compared to the older Jewish left, most of these groups are far more diverse in terms of gender, age, and political affiliations. For example, many of the leading figures come from social movements rather than traditional left party backgrounds.

These groups vary significantly both in terms of their views and priorities. Some are concerned only with the issue of Israel and the Palestinians. Some prioritize engaging with the broad Australian left, others more so with the Jewish community. Some are doctrinaire, whilst others prefer inclusion and a plurality of views. Some are overtly critical of the anti-Zionist left, whilst others are less so. Some were formed recently, whilst others such as AJDS and the Bund have existed for many years. However, there still appears to be significant common ground around issues such as support for refugees, endorsement of Aboriginal rights, opposition to the American intervention in Iraq, concern about anti-Semitism, and criticism of Israeli policies towards the Palestinians.

The contemporary Jewish left is almost completely secular, and it is rare to hear of any reference being made to Jewish religious tradition or values. There also appears to be little intervention around socio-economic divisions or inequities within the Jewish community. For example, none of the groups appear to be involved with internal Jewish debates around poverty, unemployment, domestic violence, substance abuse, discrimination against Russian Jews, and inequitable access to Jewish education.

All of the Jewish left groups experience an ongoing tension or conflict between their specific Jewish loyalties, and their commitment to broader universalistic causes. This conflict mirrors earlier Jewish left tensions around Soviet anti-Semitism, but today concentrates around the Arab-Israeli conflict. On the one hand, tribal solidarity with Israel remains the core defining aspect of contemporary Australian Jewish identity. On the other hand, much of the contemporary Australian left is critical of Israel to varying degrees, explicitly rejects Zionist or pro-Israel agendas, and expects left-wing Jews to actively dissociate themselves from Israeli policies. This increasing polarization between Jewish and left perspectives tends to leave those who are both Jewish and leftist on the outer in both communities. For example, many Jewish leftists advocating compromise between Israeli security requirements and Palestinian national aspirations find themselves labelled "traitors" or "self-hating Jews" in the Jewish community, and alternatively dismissed as apologists for the Israeli Government by left groups.[62]

The most significant local Jewish left group is arguably the Australian Jewish Democratic Society.[63] Formed in 1984 by Norman Rothfield and former Labor Party Minister Dr Moss Cass, AJDS has traditionally pursued four distinct objectives: support for peace and nuclear disarmament, opposition to racism and anti-Semitism, support for Aboriginal rights, and a peaceful two-state solution to the Israeli-Palestinian conflict. To progress these objectives, AJDS has engaged with both the Jewish community and the broader left, describing itself as "A progressive voice among Jews" and "A Jewish voice among progressives". It has also maintained an informal alliance with sections of the Israeli peace movement. Most of AJDS' objectives sit relatively comfortably with the mainstream Jewish community. At least in recent years, community leaders have expressed what might be called liberal/left views on social issues such as support for Aboriginal rights, multiculturalism, racial tolerance, refugees, and opposition to the racist One Nation Party. The question of Israel, however, remains a source of regular conflict. AJDS' criticism of Israeli policies towards the Palestinians and its support for Palestinian national rights has been constantly attacked by organizations such as the Jewish

Community Council of Victoria (JCCV), and the Zionist Federation of Australia.

In 1987, for example, an AJDS application to join the JCCV was knocked back due to allegations that the organization was "anti–Zionist". Two years later an AJDS statement calling for "a peace of mutual recognition, based on territorial compromise and self-determination" was signed by over 550 Australian Jews. The statement provoked considerable controversy and discussion in the Melbourne Jewish community, and further attacks from conservatives who questioned AJDS' "Jewish" credentials.[64]

However, the passage of the Oslo Peace Accords in 1993 provoked changes in the politics of Australian Jewry, including a much greater willingness to accommodate diverse opinions. Consequently, AJDS was admitted to the JCCV in September 1993, and became far more involved in mainstream Jewish communal activities. But the outbreak of the second Palestinian Intifada in September 2000 has once again led to a polarization between Jewish roof bodies committed to supporting the Israeli Government perspective, and dissenting groups such as AJDS which argue for a less partisan approach. Equally, AJDS appears to have come under pressure from broader left groups to engage in much stronger criticism of Israel.

In May 2001, for example, AJDS expressed "in principle support for the right of Palestinian refugees to return to their original homes". This statement appeared to place AJDS totally outside the mainstream Jewish and Israeli left. Most Israeli peace activists oppose any Palestinian Right of Return on the grounds that it is seen as representing a denial of the legitimacy of Israel, and hence is incompatible with any two-state solution. Not surprisingly the statement led to conflict with and condemnation from the JCCV and the Zionist movement. The subsequent participation of some leading AJDS activists in a highly publicized demonstration against visiting Israeli right-wing politician Bibi Netanyahu led to further controversy.[65] The relationship between AJDS and the mainstream Jewish community seems sadly to have regressed back to the war of attrition of a decade ago with acrimonious mutual condemnation replacing the potential for constructive dialogue and engagement.[66]

Another vocal group is the Melbourne-based Jews for a Just Peace. Formed in early 2002, J4JP has some members in common with AJDS, but is a single-issue group concerned solely with the Middle East conflict. In contrast to other Jewish left groups, many of its leaders seem to be long-time left activists (including many intellectuals and academics) with at best tenuous links with the Jewish community. For at least some of its members, their Jewish identity seems to be expressed solely through political criticism of Israel. Certainly, the group seems unwilling to tackle the "blaming the victim" arguments of some on the left that the policies of the Israeli

Government are directly responsible for increased anti-Semitism in Australia.

In May 2002, J4JP published a declaration of principles calling for a two-state solution based on an Israeli withdrawal to the pre-1967 borders. The petition, which was signed by almost 250 Australian Jews, provoked considerable publicity and criticism within the Jewish community.[67]

Subsequently, the organization lobbied on behalf of a parliamentary motion submitted by Labor Party MP Julia Irwin calling for an unconditional withdrawal of Israel to the pre-1967 borders. This motion and subsequent statements by Ms. Irwin were regarded by most Australian Jews as unbalanced and anti-Israel, and reflecting views overwhelmingly hostile to the Jewish community.[68] In supporting such sentiments, J4JP seemed to be stating that they had little interest in engaging with Jews who do not share their views.

The NSW Jewish Voices for Peace and Justice formed in 2001 shares most of the ideological assumptions of Jews for a Just Peace, but appears to take a less confrontational approach to other Jewish groups and views. For example, JVPJ aims to "support diverse voices within the Jewish community", and to "create a safe and inclusive" space for Jews who want to be involved in both Jewish and peace movement activities. In addition to campaigns for Israeli–Palestinian peace and reconciliation, JVPJ also advocates for the rights of asylum seekers and indigenous Australians.[69]

A smaller Sydney-based group formed in October 2003 is Jews Against the Occupation (JOP). JOP calls for an Israeli withdrawal from all territories occupied in the 1967 Six-Day War, the dismantling of all Jewish settlements in the territories, the immediate establishment of an international peacekeeping force to end the cycle of violence, and the establishment of a Palestinian state alongside Israel based on the pre-1967 borders, with Jerusalem as the capital of both states.[70] JOP seems to be more concerned with influencing the broader left than the Jewish community, as reflected in its support for the awarding of the Sydney Peace Prize to Palestinian academic Hanan Ashrawi.

A very different left group is the organization Ethical Left Action formed recently by Dawn Cohen and Julie Nathan in Byron Bay to confront new manifestations of anti-Semitism. Whilst Ethical Left shares much of the traditional Jewish left agenda, including support for the creation of a Palestinian state alongside Israel and opposition to the demonization of Palestinians or Arabs, their principal concern is with the increasing tolerance of and acceptance of anti-Semitism on the political left. In particular, they oppose the left's partisan support for Palestinians/Arabs at the expense of Israelis/Jews, and the unethical manner in which subtle anti-Semitism is utilized to enhance Palestinian claims and perspectives.[71]

The inclusive approach taken by Ethical Left Action suggests the potential for a new and potentially more effective Jewish left agenda which incorporates a range of Jewish and left concerns, without giving priority or a higher ranking to one particular concern or one particular issue (e.g. views on Israel and Zionism versus anti-Semitism) over the other. It also suggests that for Jewish left groups to be viable they need to genuinely emerge from and be embedded in the concerns of their own ethnic community, rather than attempting to impose universalistic ideological agendas from outside.

Continued Jewish Support for the Left?

Jews have played a significant role at different times in Australian left political parties and social movements. To be sure, Jewish involvement in the left here may not have been as numerically disproportionate or as ethnically structured as in some other countries. Nevertheless, a large number of individual Jews have been prominent as activists, intellectuals, and donors, reflecting the continuation of a Jewish leftist sub-culture. There has certainly been a far greater Jewish contribution to Australian left causes than to conservative causes.

The future for the Australian Jewish left arguably depends on its ability to confront and resolve numerous challenges and contradictions. On the one hand, cultural factors continue to predispose many Jews towards identification with radical and humanitarian causes. There is some evidence that an increasing number of younger Jews are participating in broader universalistic causes around issues such as racial tolerance, the rights of refugees and asylum-seekers, and support for victims of persecution whether in Bosnia or East Timor.[72] It has been argued, although not yet conclusively demonstrated, that many of these younger people are influenced by family experiences of the Holocaust, and are applying the meanings of the Holocaust to broader political concerns.[73]

Equally, an increasing number of Jews – many from the Vietnam era or even younger – are willing to openly criticize Israeli government policies, and to identify unequivocally with a two-state solution. This process has produced at least a partial revitalization of the Jewish left, which until five or so years ago was still largely dominated by veterans of the Cold War period. Nevertheless, it remains debatable as to whether those younger activists who are Jewish and left-wing will remain involved in specifically Jewish rather than broader left groups.

Two other factors may limit the extent of Jewish identification with the left. First, most Australian Jews are middle class, and generally not sympathetic to left arguments for income redistribution. This tension is likely to restrict Jewish participation in explicitly socialist or Marxist groups.

Perhaps more significantly, much of the Australian left is highly critical of Israel to a greater or lesser degree. Some groups blame Israel solely for the current Palestinian Intifada and associated violence and terror but at least acknowledge the need for a two-state solution, whilst others – mainly, but no longer exclusively, on the Marxist left – go even further and argue that Israel is a racist and colonialist state which has no right to exist. Much of the literature from these latter groups extends the denunciation of all Israelis to include all Jews – Zionist or otherwise – who are supportive of Israel's existence, whatever their actual ideological and political position on solutions to the conflict.[74] This ethnic stereotyping of all Israelis or all Jews as "oppressors" is highly intimidating and offensive to most Jews, and is hardly likely to attract younger Jews to the organized left. For those Jews who wish to support social justice and humanitarian causes, but not at the expense of trashing their own ethnic and national concerns, continued engagement with at least the ideological left is likely to prove a rocky enterprise.

Notes

I am grateful to Bernard Rechter, Geoffrey Levey, Doug Kirsner, Dawn Cohen, David Bitel and Julie Nathan for their helpful comments on an earlier draft.

1 Zosa Szajkowski, *Jews and the French Revolutions of 1789, 1830 and 1848* (New York: KTAV Publishing House, 1970).

2 *Ibid.*, pp. 1058–61; Howard Morley Sachar, *The Course of Modern Jewish History* (New York: Dell Publishing, 1977), pp. 103–12.

3 Robert Wolfe, *Remember to Dream: A History of Jewish Radicalism* (New York: Jewish Radical Education Project, 1994), pp. 89–96.

4 Sachar, *Course of Modern Jewish History*, pp. 221–55.

5 Hadassa Kosak, *Cultures of Opposition: Jewish Immigrant Workers, New York City, 1881–1905* (Albany: State University of New York Press, 2000), p. 18.

6 Sachar, *Course of Modern Jewish History*, pp. 221–60, 302–3, 439–59.

7 Philip Mendes, "Left Attitudes Towards Jews: Anti-Semitism and Philo-Semitism", *Australian Journal of Jewish Studies* 9, 1 and 2 (1995): 7–44.

8 Robert Levy, *Ana Pauker: The Rise and Fall of a Jewish Communist* (Berkeley: University of California Press, 2001).

9 Jack Jacobs, ed., *Jewish Politics in Eastern Europe: The Bund at 100* (Houndmills: Palgrave, 2001).

10 Nancy Green, ed., *Jewish Workers in the Modern Diaspora* (Berkeley: University of California Press, 1998).

11 Piotr Wrobel, "From Conflict to Cooperation: the Bund and the Polish Socialist Party, 1897–1939", in Jacobs, ed., *Jewish Politics in Eastern Europe*, pp. 155–71.

12 Marc Dollinger, *Quest for Inclusion: Jews and Liberalism in Modern America* (Princeton: Princeton University Press, 2000), pp. 3, 229.

13 Peter Medding, *From Assimilation to Group Survival: A Political and Sociological Study of an Australian Jewish Community* (Melbourne: Cheshire, 1968), p. 238.

14 Joseph Nedava, *Trotsky and the Jews* (Philadelphia: Jewish Publication Society of America, 1971), pp. 154–5.

15 Helen Darville, *The Hand That Signed The Paper* (St Leonards: Allen & Unwin, 1994).

16 Philip Mendes, "Jews, Ukrainians, Nazi War Crimes and Literary Hoaxes Down Under", *Patterns of Prejudice* 30, 2 (1996): 55–71.

17 Enzo Traverson, *The Marxists and the Jewish Question* (New Jersey: Humanities Press, 1994), p. 2.

18 Arthur Liebman, *Jews and the Left* (New York: John Wiley & Sons, 1979), pp. 417–18.

19 Arkady Vaksberg, *Stalin Against the Jews* (New York: Alfred A. Knopf, 1994).

20 Ron Taft, *The Impact of the Middle East Crisis of June 1967 on Jews in Melbourne: An Empirical Study* (Melbourne: Jewish Social Service Council of Victoria, 1967).

21 Philip Mendes, "The Rise and Fall of the Jewish/Left Alliance: An Historical and Political Analysis", *Australian Journal of Politics and History* 45, 4 (1999): 483–505.

22 Percy Cohen, *Jewish Radicals and Radical Jews* (London: Academic Press, 1980), pp. 198–9.

23 Philip Mendes, "The Left and Anti-Semitism Part 11", *Australian Journal of Jewish Studies* 19 (1996): 94–130; Philip Mendes, "Left Attitudes to Zionism and Israel", *Australian Journal of Jewish Studies* 11, (1997): 114–25.

24 Bill Rubinstein, *The Left, the Right and the Jews* (London: Croom Helm, 1982), pp. 123–5.

25 Philip Mendes, "The Rise and Fall", pp. 500–1.

26 Stephen J. Whitfield, "Famished for Justice: The Jew as Radical", in L. Sandy Maisel and Ira N. Forman, eds, *Jews in American Politics* (New York: Rowman & Littlefield, 2001), pp. 221–2.

27 Liebman, *Jews and the Left*, pp. 67–9, 540–1; Cohen, *Jewish Radicals*, pp. 35–77; Norman Finkelstein, *Heeding The Call: Jewish Voices in America's Civil Rights* Struggle (Philadelphia: Jewish Publication Society, 1997); Debra Schultz, *Going South: Jewish Women in the Civil Rights Movement* (New York: New York University Press, 2001).

28 Whitfield, "Famished for Justice", p. 222.

29 Mike Marqusee, "No compromise with anti-Semitism", *The Guardian*, 5 May 2003.

30 Philip Mendes, "The Rise and Fall", pp. 504–5.

31 Solomon Stedman, "The Jewish Workers' Association in Brisbane", *The Bridge* January (1973): 26–30.

32 Philip Mendes, "From the Shtetl to the Monash Soviet: An Overview of the Historiography of Jewish Radicalism in Australia", *Australian Journal of Jewish Studies* 14 (2000): 55–6; David Rechter, "Beyond the Pale: Jewish Communism in Melbourne", *Master of Arts Thesis* (Melbourne: University of Melbourne, 1986), pp. 32–72.

33 Mendes, "From the Shtetl", pp. 56–7.

34 On the ECAJ, see chapter 2 in this volume.

35 Philip Mendes, "Jews, Nazis and Communists Down Under: The Jewish Council's Controversial Campaign Against German Immigration", *Australian Historical Studies* 33, 119 (2002): 76–7.

36 Philip Mendes, "The Cold War, McCarthyism, the Melbourne Jewish Council to Combat Fascism and Anti-Semitism, and Australian Jewry, 1948–1953", *Journal of Australian Studies* 64 (2000): 196–206.

37 Mendes, "Jews, Nazis and Communists", pp. 88–91.

38 Philip Mendes, "The Melbourne Jewish Left, Communism and the Cold War: a Comparison of Responses to Stalinist Anti-Semitism and the Rosenberg Spy Trial", *Australian Journal of Politics and History* 49, 4 (2003): 501–16.

39 Philip Mendes, "The Senator Sam Cohen Affair: Soviet Anti-Semitism, the ALP and the 1961 Federal Election", *Labour History* 78 (May 2000): 179–97.

40 Philip Mendes, "The Melbourne Jewish Left 1967–1986", *Journal of the Australian Jewish Historical Society* 11, 3 (1991): 506–24.

41 Philip Mendes, "Denying the Jewish Experience of Oppression: Jews Against Zionism and Anti-Semitism and the 3CR Controversy", *Australian Jewish Historical Society Journal* 16, 3 (2002): 368–82.

42 Rachel Hand, "The General Jewish Labour Bund in the Melbourne Jewish Community, 1920–1961", *Arts Honours Thesis* (Melbourne: La Trobe University, 1995), pp. 31–66; Philip Mendes, "Review Essay", *Australian Jewish Historical Society Journal* 14, 3 (1998), pp. 533–7; Rechter, "Beyond the Pale", pp. 117–19, 130–5, 148–9; Chava Rosenfarb, ed., *Bono Wiener Remembered* (Montreal: privately published, 1997).

43 Philip Mendes, *The New Left, the Jews and the Vietnam War 1965–1972* (Melbourne: Lazare Press, 1993), pp. 136–7.

44 Alan Barcan, *Radical Students: The Old Left at Sydney University* (Melbourne: Melbourne University Press, 2002), pp.182, 233; Philip Mendes, "Left Attitudes Towards Jews", pp. 102–3.

45 Rechter, "Beyond the Pale", pp. 59–60; Stuart Macintyre, *The Reds: The Communist Party of Australia from Origins to Illegality* (St Leonards: Allen & Unwin, 1998), pp. 310–11.

46 Rechter, "Beyond the Pale", pp. 88–99; Barrie Blears, *Together with Us: A Personal Glimpse of the Eureka Youth League and its Origins: 1920 to 1970* (Self published: Melbourne, 2002), pp. 111–12.

47 Pauline Armstrong, *Frank Hardy and the Making of Power Without Glory* (Melbourne: Melbourne University Press, 2000), pp. 97–8; Charles Lowe, *Report of Royal Commission Inquiring into the Origins, Aims, Objects and Funds of the Communist Party in Victoria and Other Related Matters* (Melbourne: Victorian Parliament, 1950), pp. 41–2.

48 Mendes, "From the Shtetl", pp. 59–60.

49 *Ibid.*, p. 61.

50 Peter Medding, *From Assimilation to Group Survival* (Melbourne: Cheshire, 1968), p. 238.

51 John Goldlust, *The Jews of Melbourne: A Community Profile* (Melbourne: Jewish Welfare Society, 1993), p. 142.

52 *Ibid.*, pp. 214–16.

53 Suzanne Rutland, *Edge of the Diaspora* (Rose Bay: Brandl & Schlesinger, 1997), pp. 310–13.

54 Dennis Shanahan, "Old friends, new tension", *The Australian*, 14 July 2003; Bernard Freedman, "Crean to address community", *Australian Jewish News*, Melbourne edn, 15 August 2003.

55 Rod Myer, *Israel and the ALP* (Melbourne: B'nai B'rith Anti-Defamation Commission, 2003).

56 Lyle Allan, "Ethnic Recruitment or Ethnic Branch Stacking? Factionalism and Ethnicity in the Victorian ALP", *People and Place* 8, 1 (2000): 28–38.

57 Philip Mendes, *The New Left*.
58 Ann Curthoys, *Freedom Ride* (Crows Nest: Allen & Unwin, 2002), pp. 23, 33, 36, 39, 66–7, 85–6.
59 Mendes, "From the Shtetl", pp. 67–9.
60 Statement by Peace Network member Sol Salbe at an Australian Jewish Democratic forum, 17 August 2003.
61 Hinde Ena Burstin, "Looking Out, Looking In: Anti-Semitism and Racism in Lesbian Communities", in Peter Jackson & Gerard Sullivan, eds., *Multicultural Queer: Australian Narratives* (New York: Haworth Press, 1999), pp. 143–57; Michael Schembri, "Ethnic Gay and Lesbian politics: A Taste of Things to Come", in Craig Johnston and Paul Van Reyk, eds., *Queer City: Gay and Lesbian Politics in Sydney* (Annandale: Pluto Press, 2001), pp. 221–4.
62 Peter Kohn, "Pro-Peace or pro-Palestinian?", *Australian Jewish News*, 20 June 2003.
63 The author was full-time coordinator of AJDS from January 1989–May 1990.
64 Philip Mendes, "Australian Jewish Dissent on Israel: A History of the Australian Jewish Democratic Society (Part 1)", *Australian Jewish Historical Society Journal* 15, 1 (1999): 117–38; Philip Mendes, "Australian Jewish Dissent on Israel: A History of the Australian Jewish Democratic Society (Part 2)", *Australian Jewish Historical Society Journal* 15, 3 (2000): 459–74.
65 Mark Briskin, "AJDS attacked for supporting Palestinians", *Australian Jewish News*, 11 May 2001; Grahame Leonard, "The right to protest has its limits", *Australian Jewish News*, 24 August 2001.
66 Philip Mendes, "Think the Jewish Left is politically bankrupt? Think again", *Australian Jewish News*, 20 December 2002.
67 Alana Rosenbaum, "Peace petition irks community leaders", *Australian Jewish News*, 7 June 2002.
68 Alana Rosenbaum, "JCCV blasts left-wing group over Israel motion", *Australian Jewish News*, 15 November 2002; Aviva Bard, "Sydney's deputies slam Melbourne group", *Australian Jewish* News, 29 November 2002.
69 Peter Kohn, "pro-peace"; Jewish Voices for Peace and Justice NSW, promotional leaflet (Sydney, 2003).
70 Information provided by Jews Against the Occupation convenor Vivienne Porzsolt via e-mail, 21 November 2003.
71 Staff Reporter, "New group to address anti-Semitism at conference", *Australian Jewish News*, 27 June 2003; Dawn Cohen, "Byron Bay blues", *Australian Jewish News*, 1 August 2003.
72 Mark Briskin, "A community mobilised", *Australian Jewish News*, 24 September 1999; Alana Rosenbaum, "Jews rally for Aborigines", *Australian Jewish News*, 14 April 2000; Samantha Baden, "It's our duty to speak out on refugees, say Jewish leaders", *Australian Jewish News*, 24 August 2001; Seamus Bradley, "Passover vigil at Maribyrnong", *The Age*, 1 April 2002.
73 Judith Berman, "Australian Jewry and the Lessons of the Holocaust" (Perth: Unpublished paper, 2002).
74 Philip Mendes, "Deconstructing the Left on Zionism and Israel", *Australian Jewish Democratic Society Newsletter*, June (2003): 8–9.

5 | Jews and the Liberal Party of Australia

PETER BAUME

The Liberal Party of Australia, as a separate entity, is young compared to other large Australian political parties. It was formed only in 1944 when Robert (later Sir Robert) Menzies brought together a number of non-Labor parties and groups in Albury and welded them into the Liberal Party of Australia.[1] As of the end of 2003, this Party has been in federal government for 41 of its 59 years of existence. So any Jewish service to parliaments in parties prior to 1944 might have been with an important non-Labor Party, but it was not with the Liberal Party of Australia.[2]

The search for names of Jews involved in the Liberal Party of Australia has been confined to the years since 1944. There are few such Jewish names, at least until very recently. That is probably because the Party has been seen as an Anglophile establishment party where Jews, as "outliers" and newcomers, "parvenus" almost, often felt unwelcome, or diffident about playing a significant role.[3] When I was at State Council meetings of the NSW Branch of the Liberal Party of Australia, it was usual to sing "God Save the Queen" at the start of meetings. The organization contained some very conservative elements as well as some very progressive thinkers. That it was a coalition of parties, "a broad church", was apparent to me each time that I met the two groups.

In both major Australian cities, Jews are residentially concentrated. In Sydney, more than half of the Jewish community lives in the state seats of Waverley and Vaucluse and in the federal seat of Wentworth. In Melbourne, Jews are found congregated particularly in the state seat of Caulfield (and previously the seat of St Kilda) and in the federal electorate of Melbourne Ports.[4] Not surprisingly, in view of this, more than half of the membership of one young Liberal branch (Vaucluse) was said, by the President, to be Jewish.[5]

Jews in the Liberal Party's Victorian Division include Walter Jona, who was state Member for Hawthorn and had Cabinet appointments as Parliamentary Secretary to Cabinet, Minister for Immigration and Ethnic Affairs, Assistant Minister of Health, and Minister of Community Welfare Services.[6] Louis Stuart Lieberman (his father was Jewish; he describes himself as "ecumenical") was Member for Benambra and federal Liberal MP for Indi (1993–2001).[7] Sir Archie Michaelis was Speaker in the Victorian Parliament (1950–2), and had been an MLA representing the seat of St Kilda for many years prior.[8] Baron David Snider was Liberal Member for St Kilda (1955–64) and MLC for Higinbotham (1964–6).

In New South Wales, Asher (later Sir Asher) Joel was elected to the Legislative Council as an independent, and later (he had extensive rural press interests) joined the Country Party. Leon Samuel Snider was a Legislative Councillor for many years as a Liberal (1944–59), and then until 1965 as a member of the Country Party. Barnett Morton Cohen was Liberal member for Bligh (1965–8), when he died. Dr Derek Freeman and Margaret Davis were also Liberal Party Legislative Councillors.

More recently, a significant number of Liberal Party political staffers have been Jewish. For example, Jews have served as senior advisers to Prime Minister Howard and to four Ministers in his governments: Alexander Downer, Brendan Nelson, Richard Alston and Bronwyn Bishop. This Jewish presence has also been mirrored in the ranks of state Liberal opposition leaders John Brogden (NSW) and Robert Doyle (Victoria), as well that of a number of former Kennett Government ministers in Victoria. Prominent current and ex-staffers in recent years include Andre Stein, Danny Rosen, Josh Frydenberg, Yuron Finkelstein, Nathalie Samia, Jonathon Epstein, Richard Shields, and Julian Sheezel.[9] In the recent New South Wales local council elections, the *Australian Jewish News* identified some thirty Jewish candidates, of whom four stood as Liberals.[10]

Overall, the difficulty in finding Jewish names is significant in itself, indicating that only a limited number of Jews has represented the Liberal Party, though many Jewish leaders, quite pragmatically, have worked with Liberal leaders on issues of concern to those leaders and their communities.

Some well known Liberal politicians have been of Jewish descent. Michael Baume, a Liberal MHR (1975–83) and Senator (1985–93), had a Jewish father, and was brought up as an Anglican. In the case of Nick Greiner – who was Premier of New South Wales (1988–92) – both his parents were Jewish, with his mother once being very religiously observant. However, like many Hungarian Jews, both converted to Catholicism after World War II and the Holocaust. Greiner is Catholic by upbringing, by schooling and by public identification. Former Victorian Premier, Jeff Kennett, who led that state from 1992 to 1999, also has Jewish ancestry, his maternal grandfather being Jewish.

A word is in order about Malcolm Fraser, who was Prime Minister and Leader of the Liberal Party between 1975 and 1983. His mother, Una Woolf, was an Anglican (and later a Presbyterian) by choice, but her father, Louis Arnold Woolf, was Jewish. On the Jewish law of matrilineal descent, then, neither Una Woolf nor her son were Jews.[11] One could add Malcolm Fraser to the list above only on a broadly ethnic (rather than religious) definition – but not with his concurrence, one suspects. He was, and is, of course, whatever his formal religious affiliations, very sympathetic to Israel and to Jewish causes. It also should not go unremarked that he appointed Sir Zelman Cowen as Governor General (1978–82), the second Jew to hold this high office.[12]

The difference between the general approach of the two major parties to matters Jewish is illustrated for me by a story about Labor MP Barry Cohen, one of the four Jews in federal Parliament between 1974 and 1991. The story is told that, on a swearing-in day, he was seen by Prime Minister Gough Whitlam to be depressed and sad. The reason was that he had no yarmulke, and he needed one for swearing in. It is said that Gough took him to his own desk, opened a drawer and said: "Which colour?"

Surveys have shown a strong, and increasing, conservative leaning among Jews, possibly a reaction to unfortunate personal experiences under Communist regimes in Central and Eastern Europe.[13] In addition, it is said that Australian Jews follow their socio-economic interests and vote conservative as they become more affluent.[14] As occupational status rose, so did support for parties other than Labor.[15] Further, a survey of Melbourne Jewry suggests that while Jews overall support the Liberal Party, age plays a part, with younger voters more likely to vote for the Liberal Party and older voters more likely to support Labor.[16] Support for the Liberal Party was found to be very strong among very religiously observant Jews and among recent arrivals. Put simply, Jews' votes have increasingly gone to the Liberal Party while Jewish political activism has not.[17]

The small number of Jews on the Liberal side in Parliament thus seems *not* to reflect voting patterns. The small numbers of Liberal Party MPs and Senators who are Jewish might indicate a concentration within that Party on mainstream persons, established values and accepted behavior, or it might reflect a disinclination of Jews in the Liberal Party to put themselves forward for Parliamentary selection. There was a time in the mid-1970s when Aboriginals, Jews, and people from non-English speaking backgrounds (NESB) were selected by the Liberal Party of Australia – possibly as deliberate policy. But if there are few candidates from any group, then few people from that group are likely to be chosen at contested preselections.

The "official" percentage of Jews in the population ranges from 0.44 to 0.56 percent.[18] Depending as it does on self-identification, it is likely to be an underestimate, and the true figure is probably closer to 1 percent.[19] If the Parliament is just under 230 people in total, then there might be times when that 1 percent is, and is not, represented. We should not read too much into the numbers at any one moment. But if the numbers are consistently disparate between the parties in the Parliament (as they seem to be), or if the totals are continually less than they theoretically should be (as they also seem to be), that is likely to be more significant. On either test, the Liberal Party of Australia has not included the Jewish community adequately in its parliamentary representation. It has certainly performed worse than the Australian Labor Party in this regard. In one sense, the Liberal Party of Australia has always spoken for the established and better off and, to that extent, has been a sectional party. Anyway, political parties are more interested in overall electoral success than they are in representation of each minority in the community; many decisions are brutal and vote driven.

I served seventeen years in the Australian Parliament as Senator for New South Wales (1974–91) and more years in the Liberal Party organization. At no time in the Parliament was any comment made by parliamentary colleagues about religion (although lots of comments were made about policy differences) and there were few, if any, comments in the Party about my religious affiliations. Two comments did come, one from an anti-Semitic Party opponent who had been a Nazi in Europe and with whom, not surprisingly, I did not get on at all. He was reported as referring to me as "the Judele" (little Jew). The other was a Liberal candidate in a strong Labor seat (it is hard sometimes to get acceptable candidates in "hard luck" seats) who made unwise remarks to me that were recognizably from "The Protocols of the Elders of Zion", a well-known anti-Semitic document.[20]

But these views and these remarks were exceptions. Some people I knew in the Party were Jewish and there was neither religious comment, nor was their religion a factor, in how they functioned or whether they prospered. They just did their job and were judged on how well the job was done. Of course, adverse comment might have existed and might have been kept from me deliberately.

Parliament began each day with Prayers. I wore a yarmulke for those prayers always. Sometimes the Parliament sat on Jewish holy days and I was always given leave for such days without question. For swearing in ceremonies, I asked for, and received, Hebrew Bibles. Some of my Bibles, and my Ministerial certificates, were signed by a Jewish Governor-General. For my last day in Parliament, as Honorary President, I wore my yarmulke, as usual, for prayers. After all, I was a publicly identifying Jew and, although my religious belief was not, and is not, strong, I was proud of being Jewish, and of so identifying. My religious beliefs are more questioning than ever today, but that is another story.

When I crossed the floor to support a "Jewish" matter (the War Crimes Legislation), there was complete understanding within the Liberal Party Room, and no criticism from parliamentary colleagues.

Few people, wherever they live, have thought-through political views based on a coherent ideology. Most people are "middle of the road", with no very strong views, and they seem to drift to whichever political party is in the majority in that area. They "go with the flow". So in strong Labor areas, many of the middle "moderates" vote for that party. Similarly, in strong Liberal areas, many middle "moderate" people support the Liberal Party. Many Jews live in Liberal voting areas and vote Liberal. That does not mean necessarily that all those people have a coherent or fixed political philosophy.

It is the same in the Coalition Party Room. There are a few people at either policy extreme of any contested issue. Those people at the extremes might have passionate views on matters as diverse as wheat marketing or Aboriginal land rights. Most people "float" in the middle with unfixed views on many matters; if one can "capture" them on an issue, one has a strong majority in that arena. One is likely to be regarded by colleagues as an "expert" on a limited number of issues (as I was on health and welfare matters, for instance). On such issues colleagues will listen and might follow you. On other matters they will ignore what you say. I have seen, in the Party Room, instances where numbers of people studiously read newspapers and avoided listening to the speaker.

In my case I was promoted regularly, ending up in the Cabinet of Malcolm Fraser who was a fine, loyal and supportive person to me. Many people are somewhat surprised by the Malcolm Fraser they have seen in the years since he left Parliament. Actually, he was always like that, though he came from a "noblesse oblige" position, rather than a "small-l" liberal position like mine.

Eventually my Party swung away from me, becoming more and more conservative. No more was it a "broad church". The philosophy of Conservatives, like that of early Liberals, might be decent enough, but it is not my philosophy. So a Conservative Party is not my party. Remember that Menzies is reported to have said: "We took the name 'Liberal' because we were determined to be a progressive Party, willing to make experiments, in no sense reactionary . . . "[21] That is not how the present Liberal Party seems to me.

Things came to a head over equal employment opportunity for women (I supported women against my Party), and Professor Marian Sawer has set out the events that overwhelmed me in 1987. As is recorded in her book, I left Parliament in 1991 to take up a Chair at the University of New South Wales.[22] I left the Party in 1996. Other writers have commented in detail on my beliefs and practices.[23] Suffice to say here that lack of compassion might be widespread and supported electorally today, but it is neither admirable nor pretty. I am not happy with a nation that shows very little compassion publicly or accepts widening inequality, as our nation seems to do.

After retirement, a dinner was held for me in the Parliament of NSW. Chris Puplick, then a Liberal Senator, spoke at the dinner and reminded people of the description of Jews as "stiff-necked" in several places in the Bible.[24] He said words to the effect that he had never appreciated that description fully until he worked with me (he was on my staff at one time)!

At the time of writing there is only one identifying Jew (Michael Danby) in the Australian Parliament and he is on the Labor side. In an interesting development, David Southwick, a young Jewish businessman, has recently won Liberal Party preselection to contest Danby's federal seat of Melbourne Ports in 2004.

It is worth recording that this seat is the one in Victoria where most Jewish voters are concentrated. Many of the Jews who came to Australia in the post-war period came from Central Europe. Suzanne Rutland cites the strong support of this group for Labor, and identifies several factors for it, including:

- traditional support of European Jews for social democratic parties which they brought with them,
- the Bundist (General Jewish Workers Movement) tradition, which was strong in Eastern Europe,
- the refugee policy of Australian Labor Governments between 1941 and 1949,
- the support of Labor (through Doctor Evatt) for the creation of the State of Israel.[25]

Rutland makes the point that Jewish political allegiances have fluctuated. Before 1920, she records that most politically active Jews were identified with liberal factions of non-Labor parties. She also quotes Encel and Buckley, who observe that "by the early 1970s, support for the Liberals had increased, reflecting the rise in socio-economic status of Sydney Jewry. Hungarian Jews tended to support the Liberal Party because of their experiences in communist Hungary".[26] So it appears that Jews, in increasing numbers, have supported the Liberal Party since the 1970s.[27]

Another important way in which the Jewish community influences the Liberal Party is by talking to its leaders and making them aware of Jewish wishes and views. This is referred to (usually pejoratively) as the "Jewish lobby". Sometimes such activity is associated with tokens of esteem – for instance, the Distinguished Public Service Award given by the American Jewish Committee to Prime Minister John Howard in 2002, and the honorary doctorate given to the same man by Bar-Ilan University in Israel in 2000.[28] At other times the Jewish community has been critical of the Liberal Party.[29] Jewish leaders talk, of course, to both political camps to make sure that their viewpoint is heard on both sides. Official Australian policy remains pro-Israel.[30] It has been pointed out that Jewish donors contributed to Party funds generously in 2001 and 2002 – but to both major political parties![31] Sam Lipski makes the point that Jewish leaders are particularly effective because they are well organized and articulate, they include a disproportionately large number of successful business leaders, and they serve as a singular model of what migrants to this country can achieve.[32]

Some recent events make it possible that more Jewish people will want to vote against Labor in the future. In 2003, Labor MP Tanya Plibersek called Israel "a rogue state" in the Parliament and described Israeli Prime Minister Ariel Sharon as "a war criminal".[33] Former MP Barry Cohen is reported to have written to then Leader Simon Crean: "At the moment I can't imagine any Jew with feelings toward the State of Israel supporting the Australian Labor Party".[34] And the *Australian Jewish News* editorialized that: "it is quite conceivable that some Australian Jews will shift their support from Labor to Liberal at the next federal election on one factor and that is Israel".[35] Only time will tell what will happen at the election due in 2004.

One of the more attractive features of the Constitution of Australia is the result of section 116, which reads:

> The Commonwealth shall not make any law for establishing any religion, or for imposing any religious observance, or for prohibiting the free exercise of any religion, and no religious test shall be required as a qualification for any office or public trust under the Commonwealth.[36]

Whatever else is required in Australia, there is no state religion, and all comers are welcome to take part in the running of the country. This makes it easier for minority groups to prosper in Australia than in some other countries such as England that has an established religion. After all, we have had Jewish Governors-General here and Jews have been state Premiers. The British have the unfortunate history of Lionel Rothschild, a Jew who was elected several times to the House of Commons by the City of London (1849 and 1852) but was not allowed to take his seat until 1858 because of the religious test then existing.[37]

So, in theory, there is no reason why any religion should not be seen in the Australian Parliament. But I cannot remember a Muslim MP in my time – certainly not at federal level and probably not at state or territory level either.

The preselectors tend not to vote on religion and would not, therefore, tend to support or reject any candidate on account of religion. Let us be clear on that. In the Liberal Party of Australia, in my experience, preselectors did not vote for or against Jews on account of religion. But I know that sometimes preselectors look at family formation, at easy identification with the mainstream, at past performance, at potential, and at things that might help them decide who might represent them well in Parliament.

This is how it should be in a nation with no state religion. Religious affiliation should play no part in whether or not one prospers in politics.

Long may it continue.

Notes

The editors are grateful to Walter Jona and Anton Hermann for their comments on an earlier version of this chapter, and to Jason Aldworth for supplying additional information.

1 Gerard Henderson, *Menzies Child: The Liberal Party of Australia* (Sydney: Harpers Collins, 1994), p. 81.

2 On Jewish political involvement in this earlier period, see Walter Jona, "Jews in Victorian Politics 1835–1985", *Australian Jewish Historical Society Journal* 10 (1986): 2–14; and the Appendix this volume.

3 Sol Encel describes the Liberal Party as a "middle class Protestant Party". Encel quoted in Vic Alhadeff, "The Jewish vote: a mixed response", *Australian Jewish News*, Sydney edn [hereafter *AJN*] 1 March 1996.

4 See Sol Encel, "Jewish vote", *AJN*, [letters] 14 March 1996; and Bernard Freedman, "First Jewish federal MP for seven years", *AJN*, 9 October 1998.

5 Yaron Finkelstein, "Jewish Liberals" [letters], *AJN*, 8 March 1996.

6 See Hilary L. Rubinstein, *The Jews in Victoria 1835–1985* (North Sydney: Allen and Unwin, 1986), p. 211; and Geoff Browne, *Biographical Register of the Victorian Parliament 1900–84* (Melbourne: Victorian Government Printing Office, 1985), p. 110.

7 *Parliamentary Handbook of the Commonwealth of Australia*, 29th edn (Canberra: Department of the Parliamentary Library, 1999), p. 160; and *About the House*, 19 Feb 1997, p. 3.

8 See Michael Blakeney, "The Australian Jewish Community and Post-War Mass Immigration from Europe", in W. D. Rubinstein, ed., *Jews in the Sixth Continent* (North Sydney: Allen and Unwin, 1987), p. 330; and www.parliament.vic.gov.au/speaker/former/michaelis.htm.

9 Information supplied by Jason Aldworth, Victorian Jewish Liberal Party activist and campaign manager for Melbourne Ports candidate David Southwick, 27 February 2004.

10 Aviva Bard, "NSW council elections: candidates, issues", *AJN*, 19 March 2004. The report did not claim to be comprehensive.

11 See Philip Ayres, *Malcolm Fraser: A Biography* (Richmond, Vic.: William Heinemann, 1987), p. 6; and www.nma.gov.au/primeministers/10.htm.

12 The first was, of course, Sir Isaac Isaacs, the first Australian-born Governor General (1931–6), and on whom Sir Zelman wrote as a biographer. See Zelman Cowen, *Isaac Isaacs* (Melbourne and New York: Oxford University Press, 1967).

13 John Goldlust, *The Jews of Melbourne: A Community Profile* (Melbourne: Jewish Welfare Society Inc, 1991).

14 See Daniel J. Elazar with Peter Medding, *Jewish Communities in Frontier Societies: Argentina, Australia and South Africa* (New York: Holmes and Meier, 1983), p. 297; and Philip Mendes and Geoffrey Brahm Levey, "The 'Jewish vote' will not be swayed over Labor's Middle East pangs": [www.onlineopinion.com.au/view.asp?article=758].

15 Peter Y. Medding, "Factors influencing the Voting Behaviour of Melbourne Jews", in Peter Y. Medding, ed., *Jews in Australian Society* (Melbourne: Macmillan, 1973), p. 154.

16 Goldlust, *The Jews of Melbourne*.

17 Alhadeff, "The Jewish vote".

18 See, for example, W. D. Rubinstein, *Judaism in Australia* (Canberra:

Australian Government Publishing Service, 1995), p. 23; John Goldlust, *The Melbourne Jewish Community: A Needs Assessment Study* (Canberra: Australian Government Publishing Service, 1993), p. xiv; and www.tau.ac.il/Anti-Semitism/asw2002–3/australia.htm.

19 See Suzanne D. Rutland, *Edge of the Diaspora: Two Centuries of Jewish Settlement in Australia*, 1st edn (Sydney: William Collins, 1988), p. 287; and Goldlust, *The Melbourne Jewish Community*, p. 5.

20 Konrad Heiden, *Der Fuehrer* (New York: Houghton Mifflin, 1944), pp. 1–18.

21 Robert G. Menzies quoted in Graeme Starr, *The Liberal Party of Australia: A Documentary History* (Melbourne: Drummond/Heinemann, 1980), p. 79.

22 Marian Sawer, *The Ethical State? Social Liberalism in Australia* (Melbourne: Melbourne University Press, 2003), p. 173.

23 See Don Harwin, *Peter Baume: Principle and Politics* (NSW Liberal Forum, 1998); and Patrick O'Brien, *Factions, Feuds and Fancies: The Liberals* (Melbourne: Penguin Australia, 1985).

24 *The Bible: The Old Testament* (Hebrew and English) (London: The British and Foreign Bible Society, 1978), for example, Deuteronomy, chap. 9, verse 6, and Exodus, chap. 33, verse 3.

25 Rutland, *Edge of the Diaspora*, p. 286.

26 *Ibid.*, pp. 286–7.

27 Alhadeff, "The Jewish vote".

28 See respectively Isi Liebler, "Few would speak out as Howard did", *AJN*, 19 May 2000; and www.ajc.org/InTheMedia/Publications.asp?did=432.

29 See, for example, Sam Lipski, "John Howard's friendship", *AJN*, 14 June 1996; Editorial, "Mr Howard's leadership", *AJN*, 27 September 1996.

30 See Michael Kapel and David Greason, "Howard's way – on Hanson, multi-culturalism, Israel", *AJN*, 15 May, 1998; and Liberal Party of Australia (Victorian Division), 132nd State Council Determinations, p. 23.

31 See Bernard Freedman, "Jewish donors back main political parties", *AJN*, 20 February 2003.

32 Lipski, "John Howard's Friendship".

33 See *AJN*, 20 February 2003.

34 Dan Goldberg, "Labor pains", *AJN*, 20 February 2003.

35 B'nai B'rith Anti-Defamation Commission, *Special Report* No. 13, June 2003.

36 Geoffrey Sawer, *The Australian Constitution* (Canberra: Australian Government Publishing Service, 1975), p. 61.

37 *The Modern World Encyclopedia*, volume 7 (Home Entertainment Library, 1935), p. 467.

6 | Political Conservatism and the Australian Jewish Community

WILLIAM D. RUBINSTEIN

Such survey evidence as exists suggests that Australian Jewry has been, for the last thirty years or so, mainly pro-conservative in its political preferences. Despite the evidence which exists to support this conclusion, many observers will probably be surprised at the finding. Australian Jewry is not generally perceived as an obviously pro-conservative community but, on the contrary, is regarded by outsiders (and by many members of the community itself) as left-liberal in its orientation. This essay explores some dimensions of this question, employing the existing evidence.[1]

Mainstream political conservatism in post-war Australia has mainly revolved around support for the Coalition, with a fairly typical Western post-war conservative platform of support for free enterprise and the American alliance. There are many Australian dimensions of political conservatism which are *sui generis*: for instance, right-wing parties in Australia until the 1970s supported high tariffs and a variety of semi-socialistic modes of government support for the public welfare, while the question of residual loyalty to Britain (and, more recently, to the monarchy) remain as issues. Australian conservatism has also, until recently, been supportive of high rates of immigration and, from the 1970s, for "multiculturalism". In recent years, the Coalition has become much more emphatic in supporting a Thatcherite program of limited government, and more critical of high rates of immigration and some aspects of "multiculturalism". Nevertheless, the Coalition has remained firmly in the centre-right, while the centre-left ALP has also moved to the right over issues such as privatization.

Only scattered survey data, limited in nature, exist about Jewish voting preferences in post-war or contemporary Australia – one of the greatest gaps in our understanding of the Australian Jewish community, and a contrast with the United States and Britain, where much more extensive electoral data exist. Peter Medding found a significant ALP majority among the 124 Melbourne Jews he surveyed in the 1958 federal election, with the ALP preferred to the Coalition by 57:31 percent. Medding concluded that about two-thirds of Melbourne Jews supported the ALP, if "don't knows" were removed.[2] ALP support was particularly strong among Eastern and Central European Jews, only about 20 percent of whom supported the Liberals in 1958 or at the 1961 general election.[3] Among Australian-born Jews, however, there was about a 50:50 split.[4] Among other factors, it seems likely that many recent immigrants would have been grateful to ALP leaders such as Arthur Calwell for letting them settle in Australia.

However, a later study by Medding of Melbourne Jews' voting preferences at the 1966 federal election found that the gap between the two parties had narrowed very considerably, with only a 41.9:39.5 percent lead for the ALP. Hungarian and Czech-born Jews preferred the Coalition.[5] Similarly, in a study of New South Wales Jews' voting preferences in the 1969 federal election, 55.3 percent of the 1,330 respondents voted Liberal and 39.1 percent Labor.[6] Since these studies, however, there has been only scattered and inadequate data, all of which suggest a right-wing drift in Australian Jewish voting behaviour. In 1991 the Jewish Welfare Society conducted an important survey of the Melbourne Jewish community, based upon a random sample of 640 Melbourne Jews. By 1991 there was a clear and dramatic preference for the Coalition, with 59 percent stating their intention "if a Federal election were held at the time of the interview" to vote for the Coalition, only 22 percent for the ALP, 7 percent for smaller parties, with 14 percent "don't knows".[7]

Very significantly, respondents who described themselves as "Strictly Orthodox" expressed a remarkable 83 percent level of support for the Coalition, as did an identical 82 percent of respondents who "arrived between 1976 and 1985", many of whom were ex-Soviet Jews.[8] Respondents who "arrived in Australia before 1946" – mainly German and Austrian refugees, older Anglo-Jews, and some Eastern Europeans – gave 49 percent support to the ALP. Thirty-two percent of Jews "aged 60 years or older" supported the ALP.[9] (In 1991, when the Melbourne survey was undertaken, Bob Hawke was about to be challenged, and was succeeded on 19 December 1991, as Prime Minister by his federal Treasurer Paul Keating, during a severe national recession.)

In 1995 the Australian Institute of Jewish Affairs (AIJA), a Melbourne-based organization, conducted a survey of the characteristics and beliefs of persons holding leadership positions in the Australian Jewish community, from lists provided by the Executive Council of Australian Jewry (ECAJ), the national representative body of the Jewish community. The nearly 1,000 questionnaires which were distributed were sent to a wide range of chairs and directors of organizations, executives, committee members, and rabbis. Of these, over 700 were completed and returned.[10]

A total of 706 Jewish leaders responded to the questions asking which party they were most likely to vote for at the next national election. Of these 455 (64 percent) stated "Liberal" (i.e., the principal component of the Coalition), 184 (26 percent) for the ALP, 23 (3 percent) for the Australian Democrats (a minor, somewhat left-of-centre party) and 46 (6 percent) for other parties.[11] There was thus a clear, indeed dramatic, preference among Jewish leaders in the mid-1990s for the conservative party. By states, the percentages for the Liberals and the ALP were as follows: Victoria 61:29; New South Wales 65:26; Other States 69:20.[12] At this time, Paul Keating's ALP was clinging to power with a narrow majority; it was ousted from office by the Coalition, led by John Howard, in March 1996. While there were no obvious issues of concern to the Jewish community where the ALP was notably weak, Keating was clearly less positive towards Israel than his predecessor Bob Hawke, while his abandonment of the possibility of war crimes trials for alleged Nazi war criminals in Australia might have been found disturbing by some. On the other hand, the Keating government's visibility on the Aboriginal land rights issue might have struck a positive chord with some Jews.

Since the mid-1990s, most regrettably, to the best of my knowledge there have been no surveys of any kind of Australian Jewish political preferences, a serious omission. There is, however, no reason to suppose that the basic pattern of a strong conservative voting preference has changed. Many left-liberal Jewish leaders, and much of the Jewish press, appeared to be disturbed over the phenomenon of Pauline Hanson's "One Nation" party when it was formed in 1996, and over the Howard government's handling of the *Tampa* asylum-seekers, although criticism, common early in 2001 when the issue surfaced, became distinctly muted after 11 September 2001, when the implications of Australia taking in significant numbers of Muslims at a time of terrorist threat arguably became very clear to most Jews. In 2002–3 a segment of the opposition ALP became vocally critical of Israeli policy *vis-à-vis* the Palestinians, in Parliament and in the media. As elsewhere in the Western world, the left in Australia contains a component of fiercely anti-Israel activists. Relatively muted in recent years, the violence of the so-called "second *Intifada*" of 2000–3 brought renewed criticism of Israel from these quarters. It is therefore difficult to believe that the basic pattern found here, of a strong pro-conservative voting preference by the Australian Jewish community, has altered since the mid-1990s.

All of the available evidence thus suggests that Australian Jewry is strongly right-wing in its voting preferences. Strikingly, no evidence – from an admittedly limited range of survey evidence – exists which contradicts this picture. Australian Jewry's voting behaviour is thus seemingly very close to that among British Jews and very different from that among American Jews. In Britain, a strongly pro-Conservative Jewish voting majority has existed at every general election since at least the 1970s.[13] In contrast, every discussion of the voting and political preferences among

American Jewry has stressed the continuing left-liberalism and large pro-Democratic majority of the community, ironically, given the fact that arguably the most visible and influential political activists and policy-makers among American Jewry since the 1970s have been its so-called "neo-conservatives".[14] The Jewish communities of Britain and Australia may thus comprise a distinctive "Commonwealth Jewry" with its own pathways and loyalties, these quite apart from predominant trends in the much larger Jewish community of the United States.

It is possible to go some distance – but only some – in demonstrating how Jewish voting trends are likely to work in practice in the case of the most heavily Jewish parliamentary seat in Australia, Melbourne Ports, which includes the densely Jewish areas of St Kilda East and Caulfield. About 29 percent of the seat officially declared itself to be Jewish at the 1996 census; assuming underreporting of Jewish identity, the actual figure is likely to be more like 35–40 percent.[15] What a careful examination of the voting patterns in Melbourne Ports at the 2001 federal election apparently shows is that Jews voted for Michael Danby, the local MHR, who is Labor and Jewish, but reverted to a much greater likelihood of voting Liberal for the federal Senate election, held at the same time. Although one cannot, of course, categorically draw any conclusions about Jewish voting behaviour, such a pattern seems likely. Danby (b. 1955) is the only Jew currently in the federal Parliament. He is a high-profile activist on behalf of pro-Israel and Jewish causes, and clearly regards the local Jewish community as his core support.[16] As a right-wing Laborite, he has been severely criticized by many on the often dominant left of the party, and has also, over the years, made his share of enemies in the Jewish community who, nevertheless, recognize his obvious value as the only current Jewish parliamentarian. Reports about Danby, usually supporting Israel or attending a Jewish function (illustrated with photographs), appear in virtually every issue of the *Australian Jewish News*, the Jewish community's weekly newspaper.

Since Australian elections are always held on a Saturday, Orthodox Jews cannot vote on that day, but must cast their ballot beforehand by the variety of types of ballot options which exist: "absent", "provisional", "pre-poll", or "postal" vote, especially the last.[17] Among votes cast on election day 2001, Danby received 39.43 percent of first preference votes compared to 39.42 percent for his Liberal opponent Andrew McLorinan. Among all absent voters, Danby received 38.05 percent compared with 39.58 for McLorinan. Among postal votes, the type probably cast by observant Jews, Danby received more votes than McLorinan, 2,524:2,409. (Danby won by 56:44 percent after the distribution of preferences.) However, the Senate election results in Melbourne Ports, held at the same time, showed very different results. There, the Liberal slate received 35.57 percent of the vote compared with 30.92 percent for the ALP slate among ordinary votes cast on election day. Among absentee votes of all kinds, however, the Liberal slate trounced the ALP by 7,816–5,308 votes (59.6:40.4 percent), or 2,508 more. This gap amounted to 3.05 percent of all Senate votes cast in Melbourne Ports. Obviously, not all of these were cast by Jews, but two inferences seem plausible: Danby has a personal following in the Jewish community of perhaps several thousand votes, while the Liberal Party (in the absence of a candidate such as Danby) probably has a significant majority among local Jewish voters.[18]

What factors have gone into creating this apparent strong conservative majority among Australian Jewry or, indeed, within some other Jewish communities? In this section I would like to identify a number of significant factors which are likely to influence whether a Jewish community will have a conservative electoral majority. So far as I am aware, insufficient comparative data exist to ascertain whether this list of factors is accurate or not, but it seems plausible to me that it is. It goes without saying that every Jewish community is *sui generis* and operates in a socio-economic, political, legal, and historical framework which is unique. Nevertheless, there are likely to be commonalities and common patterns, although one should bear in mind that these may well be less important than the differences.

1. In my opinion, probably the most important correlational factor in determining whether a Jewish community is likely to support right- or left-wing parties is the percentage of the Jewish community which regards itself as religiously Orthodox, rather than non-Orthodox (Reform, Liberal, Reconstructionist, etc.) or secular. There is some question here about the Conservative/Masorti strand (which did not exist in Australia until very recently). It seems that most Conservative Jews were formerly Orthodox, but broke away either because they could not fully engage in Orthodox practices such as *kashrut* ("keeping kosher"), or because they objected to the separation of the sexes in Orthodox worship. It is likely that their political stance continues to reflect their Orthodox backgrounds.

    The thesis advanced here is that the larger the component within a Jewish community who regard themselves as Orthodox Jews, and the smaller the percentage who regard themselves as Reform or Liberal or non-religious, the higher the vote for the major right-of-centre parties is likely to be, and this factor is the most important identifiable element in determining voting patterns among Jews. Caveats to this thesis are, of course, obvious. Not all (or, perhaps, many) Reform/Liberal Jews are necessarily supporters of left-of-centre parties. Orthodox adherents may well be poorer, and have a lower socio-economic status, than Reform/Liberal Jews, introducing a further significant element in determining voting behaviour. While secular, non-religious Jews are almost certain to vote for left-of-centre parties more frequently than religious Jews, right-wing Jewish secular nationalism also has a long tradition stemming from Vladimir Jabotinsky and his early supporters.

Within the Orthodox camp, it is also reasonable to assume that, by and large, Strictly Orthodox adherents (represented in Australia chiefly by the Lubavitchers and Adass) are more likely to be right-wing voters (in Australia generally supporting the Coalition) than are members of "moderate" Orthodox synagogues, generally the residual remnants of the old Anglo-Orthodoxy such as the Melbourne Hebrew Congregation and the Great Synagogue in Sydney, although here, once again, the fact that adherents of "moderate" Orthodoxy from "old families" are arguably likely to be wealthier than more right-wing Orthodox adherents, also affects their likely voting patterns. It is also reasonable to assume that adherents of Mizrachi (a denominational movement of modern Strictly Orthodox Zionists) are predominantly right-of-centre voters. As with almost any sociological argument, it is difficult to distinguish the direction of causality. Many secular Jews probably cease being religious because of their left-liberal reformist universalism: voting causality in such cases stems from a pre-existing ideological foundation which influences religious affiliation, not the other way around. Nevertheless, it is argued here that a strong associational pattern exists and will be found by sophisticated survey research.

These differences in religious affiliation constitute, in my opinion, the most important single factor in explaining the very different voting behaviour of American and British Jewry in the contemporary world. As noted, British Jews in recent decades have been far more likely to vote Conservative than American Jews are likely to vote Republican. While obviously there are a wide range of factors involved in these patterns, it is most significant that about 80 percent of British Jews are believed to be affiliated with an Orthodox synagogue, while less than 20 percent of American Jews, it seems, are affiliated with an Orthodox congregation.[19]

The situation in Australia plainly resembles that in Britain much more closely than America. About twenty percent of the Jews in Melbourne and Sydney affiliated to a synagogue appear to belong to the Reform movement, while the great majority of Jews appear to belong to an Orthodox synagogue. Strictly Orthodox synagogues are certainly more visible and powerful, especially in Melbourne, than ever before. Of the forty-two synagogues in Melbourne, all but five are Orthodox (although this in itself is no guide as to the size of the their congregations), and the situation in Sydney and elsewhere is similar. The importance of Orthodoxy in determining, or being strongly associated with, a dominant right-wing electoral majority, may be a relatively new phenomenon which was not present in Australia or Britain fifty years ago. Too little is known of this phenomenon definitively to suggest why this was so: possibly the working-class background of many Jews at the time provided a stronger pathway to voting behaviour; possibly today's voting trends are associated with highly visible, often triumphalist, Strict Orthodoxy which has become so strong a part of Diaspora Jewish life during the past thirty or forty years. The dynamics of this process, if it exists, remains to be explored.

In and of itself, this denominational breakdown can only be suggestive and indicative, but it seems a valuable tool in hinting at what the predominant political stance of most Australian Jews is likely to be. As has been seen, the limited survey evidence which exists suggests a very strong correlation indeed between religious identification as "Strictly Orthodox" and pro-Coalition voting intention. In Israel, it might be noted that the post-1977 strength of the political right shows at least as strong an association with the rise of visible Strict Orthodoxy.

2. A second important indicator of political affiliation is likely to be attendance at a Jewish day school, although here one must be very careful. There is a wide range of Jewish day schools reflecting many denominational and ideological viewpoints in the community, with (in Melbourne) The King David School (established by the Reform – called in Australia the Liberal or Progressive – movement) and Sholem Aleichem (the Yiddish School) being explicitly on the Jewish "left". All the Jewish day schools, including Sholem Aleichem (strongly affiliated with the Bund) are pro-Israel. Parents who send their children to Jewish day schools (or to any other type of school) already presumably adhere to a particular denominational or ideological perspective, and are attempting to inculcate this into their children.

Nevertheless, it seems arguable that education at most Jewish day schools moves students away from a broad universalistic left-liberal outlook to a more non-universalistic, inwardly Jewish, and hence conservative perspective. We simply do not know enough about the effects of school attendance, however, either at a Jewish or non-Jewish day school, to draw any more than rough conclusions, and nor do we know how years of schooling at a Jewish day school affects this picture. Nevertheless, at least one piece of interesting evidence exists. In November 1988 the Melbourne edition of the *Australian Jewish News* reported on a poll of 575 Jewish day school students from nine (unnamed) schools in years 9–11 as to their voting choice in the Israeli election held on 2 November 1988. The results were: Likud 34 percent, Labor 19.8 percent, religious parties 14.4 percent, right-wing parties 19.6 percent, left-wing parties 4.8 percent, Arab parties 1.0 percent, informal 6.4 percent. Right-wing and religious parties thus secured 68 percent of the vote, left-wing parties only 24.6 percent of the vote, among these presumably representative Jewish day school students.[20] It should be noted that the very high percentage of Jewish day school students in the Melbourne and Sydney communities contrasts with its mirror image in the United States, where, until recently, the overwhelming majority of Jewish students attended a secular state day school with no network of full-time Jewish education available except among the Strictly Orthodox.

3.   Closely associated with this may well be the importance of the Zionist movement in the Australian Jewish community and of Israel to Jewish identity and identification. While Israel is obviously central to virtually all contemporary modes of Jewish identity, the Australian Zionist movement is, it would seem, also notably strong. In Australia, too, there has been a near-complete absence of avowedly anti-Zionist Jewish movements of any kind, with the exception of tiny, obscure Marxist groups. Although letters by local Jews critical of Israeli actions *vis-à-vis* the Palestinians frequently appear in the Australian Jewish press, these overwhelmingly appear to be written by persons well-aware of their minority status and unpopularity, and are sure to be answered, often in strident terms, by subsequent correspondents.

4.   The political loyalties of Jewish communities are also likely to be influenced negatively by perceptions of anti-Semitic attitudes held by the mainstream parties, in particular by perceptions of religious or ethnic anti-Semitism by the right-wing party (or parties) and by anti-Zionism by the left-wing party (or parties). Plainly, perceptions of a welcoming attitude towards Jews and a sensitivity to Jewish issues is also likely to influence Jewish voting patterns in a positive way. In Australia, since the 1960s both major parties have generally gone out of their way to appear supportive of Jewish issues and Israel, with Malcolm Fraser, Bob Hawke, and John Howard notable for their visible support. Yet there have been perceptible differences. While in general the only sour note on the Coalition side has been the pro-Arabism (often for reasons of trade and export) of some parts of the National Party, the Jewish community's relations with the ALP have frequently been cooler. Gough Whitlam's undisguised opposition to Israeli policy as Prime Minister in 1972–5, the fierce anti-Zionism of part of the Victorian "socialist left", especially the wing around Bill Hartley (expelled from the ALP in the mid-1980s), and the recent vocal support given by a number of left-wing ALP parliamentarians to the Palestinians, especially in New South Wales, have almost certainly cost the ALP many Jewish votes, although as only one of many factors in voting preference.[21] Australia, too, has no real tradition of right-wing anti-Semitism (except of the alleged Melbourne Club "snob" social anti-Semitism sort), with some of its central heroes, above all Sir John Monash, being Jewish, although it does have a populist anti-"Rich Jew" tradition of the *Smith's Weekly* type which may persist in a disguised form among components of the ALP.

5.   Self-evidently, the socio-economic status of the Jewish community is also extremely important in determining electoral loyalties; normally

it is assessed as the single most important factor in accounting for voting behaviour. In Australia, it seems perfectly clear that this factor would advantage the Coalition, given the very high levels of upper middle-class status and occupation and high incomes shown in all recent studies of the Jewish community.[22] In Australia, too, Jews have predominantly entered the private managerial and professional sector rather than the state sector, where they are, almost certainly, less numerous in comparative terms than in the private sector. There are almost certainly, in comparative terms, fewer Jewish civil servants, university lecturers, and schoolteachers than doctors, lawyers, and business entrepreneurs, especially those who are self-employed or in small businesses rather than in corporate managerial structures, areas which are arguably more likely to be amenable to Coalition electoral appeals than to the ALP. While many observers would regard this as the key to explaining the strong lead among Jews for the Coalition, anyone familiar with the contemporary Jewish problematic will realise that it is almost certainly less important than any of the ensemble of specifically Jewish issues or perceived electoral cues. (In the United States the most notable and obvious fact of Jewish political behaviour is that there is a gross incongruity between the high socio-economic status of Jews and their left-liberal Democratic voting preference.) In Australia, however, this factor must perforce advantage the Coalition at most elections, although only in association with other issues.

6.   The patterns of immigration are also a factor. Most American Jews are the descendants of Yiddish-speaking immigrants from the Russian Pale of Settlement who arrived between 1881 and 1924, when stringent immigration barriers were erected by the American government. While there was a pre-existing Sephardi/German Ashkenazi American Jewish community, it was swamped by the vast size – over two million – of the great wave of Jewish migration to the United States during that period, and acted as a leadership elite for this wave in only a limited sense. Although perhaps 200,000 or more Holocaust refugees and survivors came to America between 1933 and the mid-1950s, this represented only a very small part of a community of over five million. The great wave of migrants was also largely self-selected, representing largely secular and urban as opposed to Orthodox and rural Jews. Many were socialists (although often capitalists as well) whose attitudes had been formed by Czarist oppression and pogroms.

Immigration patterns to Australia were quite different. A highly acculturated English-speaking elite element of Jews from Britain (or Germany) dominated the community until the 1940s, almost invariably providing its leadership element until the 1960s. Many were intensely loyal to Britain and the Empire, and were, it seems genuinely accepted as equals by the gentile majority, meeting few if any anti-

Semitic barriers. Between about 1937 and 1957 a very large (in comparative terms) wave of Holocaust survivors and refugees came to Australia, chiefly survivors from Poland and Hungary. Many had also lived under, and suffered from, Communist totalitarianism. Since the 1960s they have been joined by waves of Jewish immigrants from South Africa, the ex-Soviet Union, and perhaps Israel.

Strikingly absent was any real equivalent of the great wave of migrants from the Pale who came to the United States and other communities in the "New Diaspora" during the four decades or so after the 1881 pogroms. Some migrants of this type did, of course, come to Australia, but in relatively small, even insignificant numbers. The characteristic secular radicalism and hostility to authority of this group, so marked as features of the political and cultural face of American Jewry to this day, was thus scarcely a component of Australian Jewry. Instead, each of the waves of Jewish migrants – British, Holocaust survivors, recent arrivals from the Soviet Union and South Africa – was, in its way, markedly more conservative, religious, and "patriotic" (first to the Empire, then, arguably, to a dual concept of Australian/Israeli loyalty) than was the great wave of Jewish migrants to America. Only a limited number of left-Jewish groups emigrated to Australia in any numbers. These were very small pre-1939 pro-Communist groupings such as the Gezerd, and left-wing socialist groups such as the Bund, but, in the post-war period, most of these became increasingly de facto moderate or even right-wing in the wake of Soviet anti-Semitism and the unrelenting attack on Israel by the left and Third World forces. In fact, Australia's Jewish left has arguably been much smaller and more marginal than that in the United States or even Britain, where the Communist Party and leftist and left-liberal movements were strongly associated with immigrant Jews and their children. Australia has had many leftist Jews, but it has arguably not had an equivalent of the mass Jewish radicalism of London's East End or New York's Lower East Side or Brownsville.

7. A final element which is often overlooked is the relative geographical and residential stability of the Australian Jewish community. This is, again, in marked contrast to the American situation. In the United States, arguably the most important demographical fact of American Jewish life over the past fifty years has been, first, the shift of population away from New York and the northeast to the west and south, and, secondly, the movement away from established urban Jewish neighbourhoods to the suburbs, often driven (although seldom frankly admitted) by "white flight", the fear of black and Hispanic crime, drugs, and social disorganization as poor blacks and Hispanics moved to the northern urban slums. Nothing parallel has occurred with the Australian Jewish community, whose residential patterns have

remained remarkably stable for the past fifty years or more, and show little sign of altering. While many American Jews express astonishment at visiting their old neighbourhoods in Brooklyn or the Bronx from the 1940s or 1950s, now often hellish burned-out slums, similar returnees to Caulfield or Dover Heights would find that remarkably little has really changed. Nor have there been any fundamental Jewish residential shifts within Australia during the past fifty years, with the exception of the growth of a new community in the Gold Coast and the enlargement of the Perth community chiefly through overseas immigration.

Taken together, these factors probably go far towards explaining the predominant political conservatism of Australian Jewry. Yet many observers will surely be surprised by these findings, believing that Australian Jewry is predominantly left-of-centre. There are arguably two main reasons for this (apart from any generalized impression that Jews are normally on the left): while a certain number of Jewish activists are associated with the Australian left, fewer are associated with the political right; and, secondly, Jewish roof bodies have been notable, at least in recent years, for endorsing a range of left-liberal issues ranging from Aboriginal land rights to generosity towards refugees. One must, therefore, explain this apparent paradox. Probably the easiest way of doing so is to point to the fact that the largest element in Australian Jewry constitutes a "silent majority" in the literal sense, which is intensely non-universalistic and concerned primarily, indeed overwhelmingly, with Jewish issues, especially religious values, the maintenance of the day school system, and, above all, the security of Israel.[23] Since conservatism is therefore regularly expressed in, and mediated by, specifically Jewish concerns and values, it is less often expressed in overt support for more mainstream conservative issues.

On the other hand, "universalistically"-oriented left-liberal Jews are much more vocal in voicing a broader agenda which is not specifically Jewish. There are other specifically Australian factors at work, too, especially the very limited number of Jews of any orientation in high profile media positions, and the very small number of Jewish "public intellectuals" compared with America or Britain. Jews who regularly appear in the press and who might be described as right-of-centre, such as Colin Rubenstein and Sam Lipski, often comment on the Arab–Israeli conflict rather than on non-Jewish issues, while those Jews who comment more broadly, such as Peter Singer and Robert Manne, are clearly not on the political right (or, in Manne's case, once was but no longer is). In recent years, it has been the case that the representative bodies of the Jewish community have supported a number of civil rights issues, sometimes, quite possibly, against the wishes of the Jewish "silent majority", more visibly than in the past.

In some measure, this occasional willingness to endorse non-Jewish left-liberal positions may stem from the relegitimization of Jewish leftist groups within the Australian mainstream, post-Cold War, after decades of marginalization, especially in Victoria, where the Jewish Council to Combat Fascism and Anti-Semitism, Melbourne's main leftist body, was expelled from the Victorian Jewish Board of Deputies, the community's representative body, in 1952 as a Communist front group. In the early 1990s a left-liberal body (containing, occasionally, some of the surviving personnel of the Jewish Council), the Australian Jewish Democratic Society, was admitted to the Jewish Community Council of Victoria (as the Victorian Board of Deputies was then known). Its admission and consequent legitimation in the mainstream may have accounted for the greater willingness of the Jewish Community Council to endorse left-liberal positions on the occasions that it did.[24]

The logic of this support is plainly that broadly endorsing civil rights issues will benefit Jews, who have obviously suffered from the denial of these rights so often in the past; as well, there is the implicit or explicit hope that other minority groups, and the left generally, will come to sympathise with specifically Jewish concerns, especially support for Israel. Whether such a belief is anything more than a vain hope is, however, somewhat doubtful.

One might also question the extent to which Australian Jewry's representative bodies have moved towards a more universalistic agenda in recent years. A perusal of current (mid-2003) websites among Australian Jewry's leading representative bodies revealed only one component among any such body that could reasonably be described as endorsing a non-Jewish left-liberal issue, a pro-Aboriginal land rights page on the New South Wales Jewish Board of Deputy's website. (Significantly, no equivalent page exists on the website of Victoria's corresponding body, the Jewish Community Council of Victoria.) The overwhelming majority of the material on Australian Jewry's websites endorse or explain the mainstream Jewish position on a range of specifically Jewish issues, especially support for Israel. Smaller Jewish groups appear to be the main venue of support for non-Jewish left-liberal issues, with Australian Jewry's major representative bodies generally eschewing such issues.

Notes

1   For non-Australian readers: Australia has two main political groupings, the Coalition and the Australian Labor Party (ALP). The Coalition consists of the Liberal Party, an urban-based centre-right party, and the National (formerly Country) Party, a rural-based party generally to the right of the Liberals on social issues but often to its left on economic matters. The two right-wing parties have invariably held office as a Coalition, hence the term. The Coalition held national power in 1949–72 (under Sir Robert Menzies and his successors, the so-called "Ming Dynasty"), 1975–83 (under Malcolm Fraser) and since 1996 (under John Howard). The ALP is a typical social democratic party which has never been committed to socialism in a doctrinaire way. It was in power in 1941–9, 1972–5 (under Gough Whitlam), and in 1983–96 (under

Bob Hawke and Paul Keating). A number of minor parties also exist. Australia has never had a successful extreme right- or left-wing party, although the ALP's left wing has often been more extreme (and anti-Zionist) than its centre. Each of Australia's states and territories has an elected government representing the same party alliances.

2   Peter Medding, *From Assimilation to Group Survival* (Melbourne: Chesire, 1968), p. 238 – this (and other voting data cited here) is from "The Non-Universalistic Community" in W. D. Rubinstein, *The Jews in Australia: A Thematic History – Volume Two, 1945 to the Present* (Melbourne: Heinemann, 1991), pp. 34–5.

3   Medding, *From Assimilation to Group Survival*. This was at least slightly odd, since many East European Jews were staunchly anti-Communist and might have preferred Robert Menzies and the Liberals to the ALP.

4   *Ibid.* Table 11.3, p. 241.

5   Peter Y. Medding, "Factors Influencing the Voting Behaviour of Melbourne Jews", in Peter Y. Medding, ed., *Jews in Australian Society* (Melbourne: Macmillan, 1973), pp. 144–5.

6   S. Encel and B. S. Buckley, *The NSW Jewish Community: A Survey* (Sydney: NSW University Press, 1978), pp. 68–9. The figures cited represent the percent averages of the male and female respondents.

7   John Goldlust, *The Jews of Melbourne: A Community Profile – A Report of the Findings of the Jewish Community Survey, 1991* (Melbourne: Jewish Welfare Society, 1993), p. 142. This finding was contradicted by Irving Saulwick, the prominent pollster (who is Jewish) and who contributed to the 1991 Profile. In his introduction (p. ii) Saulwick states that "my own figures for the federal election on 13 March 1993, on an Australia-wide basis show the Labor vote higher than the Coalition vote". Saulwick does not elaborate on this comment and does not explain whence "his own figures" derive. If they are taken from a normal random sample of 2,000 or so voters used in public opinion surveys, only about 10 respondents would be Jewish, far too few to derive meaningful figures. The March 1993 federal election was won unexpectedly and narrowly by Paul Keating against John Hewson and his "Fight Back" program.

Jewish voting intentions (as revealed by the limited survey evidence which exists) appears to be distinctively more pro-Coalition in recent years than the Australian electorate as a whole. At the 1990 general election, for instance, the Coalition received 43.2 percent of first party preferences, the ALP 39.4 percent (the ALP won on minor party preferences). At the 1996 general election, the Coalition received 42.7 percent of first preferences, the ALP 37.8 percent. The ALP has always done better than this after the distribution of preferences, although since 1949 it has never received more than 53.2 percent of the vote after preference distribution at any general election (it received this total in 1983, when Bob Hawke swept to power). See Peter Wilson, ed., *The Australian Political Almanac* (South Yarra: Hardie Grant Books, 2002), pp. 440–3.

8   Goldlust, *The Jews of Melbourne*, p. 142.

9   *Ibid.*

10 Bernard Rechter, "Jewish Leadership Survey", *Australian Institute of Jewish Affairs Paper* [no date, c. 1996], p. 1.

11 *Ibid.*, p. 5. It is not clear how "Don't knows", etc., were classified.

12 *Ibid.* The relevant table wrongly gives the Liberal percentage in the "Other States" as 49 percent.

13 W. D. Rubinstein, *A History of the Jews in the English-Speaking World: Great Britain* (London: St. Martin's Press, 1996), pp. 393–5, citing the research of Geoffrey Alderman. Jewish support for the Labour Party reportedly rose at the 1997 and 2001 British general elections, but less survey evidence apparently exists than for previous elections.

14 See, for instance, the essays in the excellent collection edited by L. Sandy Maisel and Ira N. Forman, *Jews in American Politics* (Lanham, Maryland, 2001), which summarizes the substantial literature and describes recent trends, including an alleged shift to the political right in recent elections.

15 Wilson, ed., *Australian Political Almanac*, p. 262.

16 *Ibid.*, p. 263. Melbourne Ports also includes such inner Melbourne suburbs as Port Melbourne, South Melbourne, Middle Park, and St Kilda, where there is only a small Jewish vote.

17 Statistics derived from *Election 2001: Division Results, Volume 3* (Australian Electoral Commission, ACT, 2002), pp. 134–7. I am most grateful to the Australian Election Commission for providing me with this useful work.

18 Among postal votes (as opposed to other kinds of absent votes), the Liberal Senate slate outpolled the ALP 2,572:1,535, i.e. 62.6:37.4 percent.

19 *The World Almanac 2003* (p. 635) states that the total membership in the Union of American Hebrew Congregations (Reform) is 1,500,000; membership in the United Synagogue of Conservative Judaism is 1,500,000; while that in the Union of Orthodox Jewish Congregations of America is 1,075,000, with 65,000 affiliated to the Jewish Reconstructionist Federation. The round numbers of these figures strongly suggest that they are inaccurate (and probably exaggerated). It seems likely that Strictly Orthodox adherents are, on the other hand, undercounted. About two million American Jews do not appear to belong to any synagogue.

20 Rubinstein, *Jews in Australia*, p. 49 n. 83, citing the *Australian Jewish News* (Melbourne edn), 1 November 1988.

21 On the story to 1991, see Rubinstein, *Jews in Australia*, pp. 379–573.

22 *Ibid.*, pp.111–43. For results derived from the most recent census, see idem., "Australian Jews in the 2001 Census", *Journal of the Australian Jewish Historical Society*, November 2003.

23 The "non-universalistic community" was my description of post-war Australian Jewry, which I offered in Rubinstein, *Jews in Australia*, pp. 1–50. It has since been used by a number of other commentators such as Judith Berman and Philip Mendes, and is meant to contrast with the left-liberalism of American Jewry.

24 It must also be noted that there were very distinct limitations to this shift to the left: in the late 1990s the Jewish Community Council voted against admitting a Jewish homosexual group as a constituent member, after a fierce debate. The admission of the homosexual group was strongly opposed by Orthodox delegates. Also NSW Jewish Board of Deputies president Stephen Rothman has recently challenged the Australian Jewish Democratic Society's right to present itself as a "Jewish organization". See "Letters", *Australian Jewish News*, 18 June 2004.

7 | Anti-Semitism and Australian Jewry

ANDREW MARKUS

The purpose of this chapter is to analyze, in a historical context, Australian Jewish responses to anti-Semitism and the impact of anti-Semitism on Australian Jewry since World War II. There are a number of difficulties in approaching this topic in terms of both definition and concept.

First, what constitutes a "Jewish" response in the context of actions of individuals and groups who speak as members of the Jewish community, but are disowned by large numbers of that community? The problematic nature of labelling views as "Jewish" generally passes with little comprehension within the mainstream media.

Second, how is the field of study – responses to "anti-Semitism" – to be delimited? While core elements are readily identifiable, anti-Semitism has a number of facets. There are Christian, Muslim and secular variants, between which and within which are contained both overlapping and distinctive elements. The capacity to change or mutate, to take on different colourations, has been one of the characteristics of the history of anti-Semitism. In his book *Antisemitism: The Longest Hatred*, Robert Wistrich deals with "myths, . . . stereotypes, . . . fantasies and obsessions that have characterized the anti-Semitic discourse for more than two millennia".[1]

Generally, there is no difficulty in establishing the provenance of anti-Semitism – hatred of Jews as a group. Antisemitism may be defined by reference to three core elements: essentializing, the specification of character traits and modes of behaviour supposedly unique to people designated as "Jews"; ascription of permanence or fixity to "Jewish" behaviour, depicted as impervious to change, constant across time and historical context; and depiction of such behaviour as malevolent, designed to win control of other peoples.

In some cases, however, provenance may be disputed. With specific reference to the last half of the twentieth century, does the mutation

"Holocaust denial" constitute anti-Semitism? To my mind, the answer is beyond dispute. Holocaust denial rests on the premise that the category "Jews" are liars engaged in a massive conspiracy. Holocaust denial is not primarily about the Holocaust; it is not some disinterested debate about what happened during World War II. Rather, it is a present focused exercise with the objective of exposing Jewish activities and influence. Hence reacting to Holocaust denial is clearly a case of reacting to anti-Semitism.

More problematic are the criticisms of Zionism and Israeli government policies. At times, such criticism is justifiable political comment, at others little more than thinly veiled manifestation of anti-Semitism. In his studies of the Australian left Philip Mendes has noted the frequency of unbalanced criticism in discussion of Israel.[2] There is a tendency to adopt stereotypes applicable to all Jews; hostility to Jews and Judaism; recourse to anti-Semitic rhetoric; trivialization of Jewish historical experience, notably of the Holocaust, and the drawing of fatuous comparisons between Nazi and Israeli actions, described by some as the defining characteristic of the mutation labelled "new anti-Semitism".

It is one thing, however, to consider dispassionately whether criticism of Israel is reasonable and well grounded; another to consider the view taken of such criticism within sections of the Jewish community. There is often discordance between the way events in the Middle East are evaluated within mainstream Australian opinion and by many Australian Jews. As Professor Leon Mann has observed, "it can be said that Israel in a very real sense represents an extension of self for many Jews".[3] As this chapter deals with Jewish reactions, the subject's view of criticism of Israel is the central concern. Correctly or incorrectly, such criticism is often seen as unjustified, a function of prejudice, of anti-Semitism, and thus falls within the area covered in the following discussion.

A third definitional issue relates to means by which anti-Semitism is manifested. Anti-Semitism is expressed in word and deed. It is manifested in verbal attack, directed at an individual or the group. It may appear in written form, in letters, pamphlets, newspaper articles, books, on internet sites, distributed through e-mail, in graffiti painted on walls. It may also lead to harassment, various forms of discrimination, and acts of violence directed at a particular person or property.

The Impact of Anti-Semitism: An Overview

The central problem that this chapter seeks to resolve is relatively simply answered. What has been the impact of anti-Semitism on Australian Jewry? If the question is understood in terms of physical acts, violence against person and property, then the answer is that the impact has been minor. Violence has not been entirely absent, with a number of incidents in recent years, but judged in historical terms and by the standard of Jewish life in the Diaspora it is at the minimal end of the scale.

If the question is understood in terms of discrimination, whether formal or informal, representing exclusion from certain occupations, educational institutions or residential districts, or limitations on social interaction, then the answer again is that such discrimination has not had a major impact. While there has been discrimination, particularly before 1970, it has been possible for Jews to rise to the highest echelons of Australian society.

If, however, the question is understood in terms of perception, of fear, then the influence of anti-Semitism on Australian Jewry has been profound. Possibly more than any other factor, fear and concern for the future have been of fundamental importance in shaping the interaction of Jews with non-Jews.

The devastating impact of anti-Semitism has been imprinted on Jewish consciousness across the ages, but never more so than in the period of the Holocaust. When considering reactions since the 1940s, it is necessary to consider the subject from the perspective of a people traumatized and the legacy of that trauma: a greatly heightened sense of vulnerability and sensitivity to the dangers of anti-Semitism, a lack of what in other contexts might be described as moderation and balance. Contemporary events are refracted through the prism of the Holocaust.[4] Threats, whether domestic or to Israel, are accepted at face value, for experience has taught Jewish people to look after their own interests and to err heavily on the side of caution.

A qualification is, however, required. Level of concern varies across time and is uneven across age groups. Its impact was most marked in the immediate post-war years – on the generation that experienced the Holocaust, both directly and as powerless spectators – and since the mid-1990s. For later generations, anti-Semitism is of greatest concern for those who identify closely with the fate of Israel, who are involved in the community, parents whose children attend Jewish day schools, and the children whose schooling is undertaken from preschool onwards behind security fences protected by guards.

The cost of responding to anti-Semitism is to be measured by various indices, including the psychological and financial. The psychological cost varies according to the individual, at the extreme manifesting in behavioural dysfunction. The financial cost has been substantial, not least over the last decade, as millions of dollars have been expended on security. Terrorists have made it clear that all Jewish persons and institutions are legitimate targets. The consequent allocation of resources to security has shaped community development, foreclosing or limiting options, including those in the cultural and educational sphere.

The Late 1930s to 1952 and the Role of
the Jewish Council

The fear of anti-Semitism in twentieth-century Australia peaked during three periods: a rough approximation locates these periods from the late 1930s to 1952, 1975 to 1982, and from 1996 onwards.

At the beginning of the period under study, open expression of anti-Semitism and a degree of discrimination was a feature of Australian life. The Jewish immigrants who arrived in the inter-war period, particularly the larger numbers of the late 1930s, faced open hostility. This was manifest in newspapers, particularly *Smith's Weekly* and *The Bulletin,* and expressed by some members of federal and state parliaments. In the immediate pre- and post-war periods, openly racist comments could still be made and limitations were placed on economic and social interaction with Jews. Discrimination was entrenched in some of the professions, including the law; Jews were denied admittance to the Melbourne Stock Exchange and membership of the Melbourne Club, tennis and golf clubs.[5]

As Australia embarked upon the most ambitious immigration program in its history, announced in 1945 and implemented in 1947, Jews continued to be treated as a people apart. Between 1939 and 1953 immigrants were required to declare in writing whether they were "Jewish", from 1946 a numerical quota limited Jewish passengers on ships and airplanes travelling to Australia, and Jews were excluded from participation in the first stage of the Displaced Persons program. In contrast with this exclusion, there was lax screening of non-Jewish DPs, with the result that a number of war criminals gained admission.[6]

Prior to the Holocaust, communal representation had been structured to give voice to the Anglo-Australian Jewish establishment and was based on synagogue membership. Secular organizations, in most cases established by recent immigrants, were excluded. In the context of news reaching Australia of the massacre of European Jewry, Anglo-Australian Jews dropped their opposition to reform. A heightened sense of vulnerability led to acceptance by Jews of all persuasions of the argument that effective defence necessitated unity. It was now understood that wealth and social standing would not guarantee security – that anti-Semites made no distinction between the assimilated and the outsider, between leader and rank and file, between secular and orthodox.

Reforms were undertaken in the years 1942 and 1943, with the form of representation then adopted lasting with relatively little change to the present day. Discussing the New South Wales Jewish Board of Deputies, Professor Bill Rubinstein has written:

> By far the most important reason for the uncanny ease with which this change took place ... was the ever-growing awareness of the unprecedented cata-

strophe for Jewry which was then unfolding in Europe.... Over and over again,
Jewish powerlessness and helplessness, and the lack of a systematic, organized
Jewish mechanism to rescue Jews, were pinpointed as the root cause of the
unfolding catastrophe ... [7]

The New South Wales and Victorian Jewish Boards established public
relations committees and there was monitoring of press reports. Yet the
roof bodies preferred to err on the side of caution in challenging bigotry,
favouring behind-the-scenes negotiation. Rubinstein writes of the
"extreme reluctance of the Jewish community's [national] roof body [the
Executive Council of Australian Jewry (ECAJ)] to meet the anti-Semitic
outbursts of the late 1940s in a consistent or aggressive manner".[8]

The Jewish Council to Combat Fascism and Anti-Semitism, formed in
Melbourne in May 1942 and led by recent immigrants, stood in marked
contrast. The Council set a model for activism rarely matched in subsequent years and soon occupied the central position in combating
anti-Semitism, a position it held until the early 1950s.[9] It gained sufficient
financial support to employ a number of full-time staff, in the late 1940s
a director, research officer, financial organizer and secretary. The Council
engaged in a broad range of activities. It investigated complaints of anti-
Semitic incidents and took follow-up action where warranted; monitored
the mainstream press, radio broadcasts and anti-Semitic groups and established a research library; issued monthly media press releases; investigated
extremist groups; and convened public meetings.

The Council worked to counter misconceptions and anti-Semitic
stereotypes. For a time it sponsored a Friday evening radio program,
featuring talks by leading members of the Jewish community. It also staged
plays for radio and maintained close links with Brian Fitzpatrick, a prominent labour activist whose weekly broadcasts on 3XY and writings
"consistently championed the cause of democracy and racial tolerance".[10]

The Council issued a number of pamphlets, presenting carefully
reasoned, factually detailed accounts, including Len Fox's "Australia and
the Jews" and Ernest Platz's "New Australians". In response to the negative coverage of the struggle to establish the State of Israel, during 1947–8
the Council distributed 90,000 copies of Evelyn Rothfield's "Whither
Palestine". A newsletter was started in July 1948, with a print run of 25,000
and distribution to every parliamentarian, trade union leader, clergyman
and newspaper.

A third area of activity was the provision of speakers to the general
community. The Council's star was the Rev. Burgoyne Chapman, a
Christian minister who addressed some 186 meetings and 63 schools
during 1949–51. Other Council representatives gave talks to trade unions,
churches and youth groups.[11] Its legal committee prepared a draft Bill to
outlaw racial and anti-Semitic propaganda, in line with similar legislation
prepared in England, with little result.[12]

The Council thus utilized the full range of reactive and proactive strategies, which were to be the mainstay of anti-defamation activities in the years ahead:

1. monitoring of extremist organizations and the mainstream media;
2. provision of information to opinion makers, including lobbying for legislative change;
3. combating misconceptions and stereotypes in the public realm;
4. partnership with non-Jewish organizations to combat manifestations of prejudice and bigotry, whether directed against the Jews or other minorities.

After the Council's decline in the early 1950s, its professionalism was not to be matched for 25 years.

The heightened level of concern over anti-Semitism in the immediate post-war years was evident following the Menzies government's announcement that Germans would be recruited as part of the post-war immigration program. An annual intake of 25,000 Germans was envisaged over a period of five years, 100,000 in total.[13]

The campaign against German immigration was a watershed in the Jewish community's history, its first open conflict with government. While reasonable arguments could be mounted against this program, the way issues were presented mirrored the very extremism that the Jewish community had sought to combat. Prospective German immigrants were criticized in unmeasured terms, their entry to Australia depicted as leading inevitably to a fundamental shift in public life and values. The resort to crude stereotyping and unfounded allegations served to undermine informed and balanced debate and foster bigotry.

The Council presented the view that Australia could not afford to provide entry to those "educated and reared under Fascism"; while "anti-Nazis" would be welcome, other Germans represented a threat to the "economic and political security of all Australians". It could not be expected that "the migrating Germans . . . have thrown off the Nazi ideology or are even willing to do so". In material distributed to Australian Council of Trade Unions delegates, the Council alleged that "the Government is not concerned with bringing skilled German workers to this country, but in bringing here . . . German migrants selected for the sympathetic attitude with which they regarded the Nazi regime".[14]

The President of the ECAJ, Ben Green, declared in an address to the Victorian Jewish Board of Deputies that if the government plans were implemented,

> within a year or two, for every Jew in this country, there will be four trained Jew-haters . . . The introduction of large numbers of Germans . . . will destroy the Jewish community's existence as we know it today . . . The yellow badge that Jews wore in Europe, will be introduced into Australia.[15]

Indicative of the emotionalism engendered, a one-page flyer, authorized by the ECAJ, argued that German migrants would introduce Nazi ideas, undermine democracy and lower the standard of civic morality. It concluded:

For Australia's Sake! For your Children's Security! Do YOUR Share NOW TO KEEP NAZIS OUT OF AUSTRALIA.

The 1960s: Anti-Semitism at its Nadir

In the context of political divisions within the Jewish community and the defeat of the campaign against German immigration, the Council's influence and the range of its activities were curtailed, although it was not disbanded until 1970.

In part, the Council's work was taken over by the Jewish Boards of Deputies in Victoria and New South Wales, which maintained public affairs committees whose brief included monitoring and responding to anti-Semitic activities. The resources devoted to such work were greatly reduced from the heyday of the Council, and those undertaking it were part-time volunteers.

In the 1950s and much of the 1960s there were relatively few local episodes of anti-Semitism to trouble the local community, and little criticism of Israel which required response. The focus turned to fostering good will through contacts with leading politicians and the media.[16]

In the 1960s Jewish leaders and individual members of the community felt sufficiently confident of their role in Australian society to engage with issues of racial and ethnic discrimination and social justice. They did so as part of a broad social movement, which won acceptance for the principles of integration and then multiculturalism. Walter Lippmann of the Australian Jewish Welfare Society played a leading role in this movement.[17]

While there was this engagement with movements for social change, close vigilance of extremist organizations continued. Since 1945 small groups of anti-Semitic activists have been a constant irritant to the Jewish community. In the pantheon of the relatively weak Australian far right, the League of Rights was distinguished by its staying power. Unlike neo-Nazi groups, which were openly confrontational and espoused anti-democratic ideas, the League, under the leadership of Eric Butler, sought to maintain a veneer of respectability. In this quest, it enjoyed a measure of success, at times involving members of parliament in its activities and making inroads into the rural support base of the National and Liberal Parties. A few sympathizers in the media gave Butler the opportunity to present his views and he enjoyed a measure of community standing.[18]

Jewish organizations have sought repeatedly to expose the racism of his movement. While attempting to present itself as a defender of community interests against communism and other "anti-Australian" movements, the

League also purveyed the crudest forms of anti-Semitism through a range of publications, including its newsletter, the *New Times*. Butler's *The International Jew* presented the argument that "Hitler's policy was a Jewish policy".

The Research Services division of the Victorian Jewish Board of Deputies (VJBD) monitored League activities throughout the 1960s. Established in 1961 following alarm caused by a series of swastika daubings, Research Services was staffed by volunteers, mostly veterans of the armed services. They were able to maintain close links with the Victoria Police and other government agencies and over the decade prepared reports on extremist groups, including those operating within migrant communities. Antisemitic incidents brought to the attention of the VJBD were investigated and a numerical tally was compiled for presentation in its annual report.[19] In the early 1970s, several individual Jews were involved in physical confrontations with neo-Nazis, as well as with elements of the far left, an ominous pointer to the future.[20]

1975–1982: Responses to the "Seven Lean Years"

The late 1950s saw the emergence of Isi Leibler to a position of leadership. Leibler possessed a rare prescience in evaluating patterns of development in the contemporary world. He also had the ability to compile lucid and comprehensive reports, to establish effective strategies and to secure funding for implementation, in part from his own resources.

While serving as chairman of the VJBD's Public Relations Committee in the 1960s he supported the close surveillance of extremists, but also urged the importance of a broader focus. He wrote in 1960 that while "combating of anti-Semitism [is] . . . of vital importance, we nevertheless feel that the most important field of public relations activities to be developed is on the positive rather than defensive line".[21] Positive activities included the fostering of contact with the press, politicians and the churches. It also included support for the development of an open society. In his annual report for 1960 to the VJBD, Leibler stated:

> I believe that it is essential for Jews to join with other groups in Australia in promoting the philosophy of a pluralistic society which unlike totalitarianist regimes implies unity in a common end without uniformity in culture, religion or communal organisation . . . The Jewish community must be at the forefront and willing to co-operate with all elements from left and right who are dedicated to the concept of an open society without which pluralism and a full Jewish life in impossible.[22]

From the late 1960s, Leibler began to warn of a dramatic shift in attitudes to Israel, one which threatened the security and viability of Jewish life in the Diaspora. He was subsequently to characterize the period 1975–82 as the "seven lean years" – the period when the left and centre often turned against Israel.[23] In Leibler's analysis, three factors explained the shift in attitudes.

First, following the Six-Day War, the "Soviet propaganda industry" successfully propagated anti-Israel views within the trade union movement. Further, the New Left made support for the PLO their major political objective – and in doing so brought to the propaganda battle "well equipped, ideologically committed, . . . veterans of political warfare from the Vietnam days". Long established anti-Semitic groups capitalized on the growing hostility to Israel, but they were not the main problem: "in contrast to the radical right extremists who numbered tens or at the most hundreds we are now confronted with hostile mass movements which have potential support numbering tens of thousands".

The second factor was the passing of time since the Holocaust, which by the early 1970s had become an event little known and little acknowledged by the generation then coming to maturity.

> The protective shadow of Auschwitz which for nearly twenty years acted as a barrier against manifestations of open anti-Semitism from "respectable" quarters is no longer applicable. Jews are now openly defamed without engendering a sense of guilt or conjuring an association with Nazi genocide . . . It is as if Nazism never happened. It is this indifference to anti-Semitism even amongst "decent" people, which above all, paves the way for the growth of the new anti-Semitic forces throughout the world.

Third, there was the politicization of the large Arab communities in Australia, "backed by enormous funds from overseas oil wealthy Arab countries". This funding made possible significant improvements in the presentation of Arab views within the Australian mainstream.[24]

Indicative of the changing environment, in 1974 the national union of Australian university students passed a series of resolutions declaring support for the liberation forces of Palestine. Mendes comments that by this date support for Palestinian views "had become almost hegemonic on the Australian Left".[25] In 1975 anti-Israel sentiment was given international imprimatur by the United Nation's General Assembly resolution equating Zionism with racism.

The response within the Jewish community was a marked shift in the scale of action to combat anti-Semitism, including action to counter the application of double standards to the Middle East conflict.

The existing roof bodies took on a wider range of responsibilities. This was particularly the case in New South Wales where finance available to the Jewish Board of Deputies (NSWJBD) made possible the appointment of a full-time Public Relations Director in 1975 and a research officer in 1982. Those appointed to these positions, Robert Klarnet and Jeremy Jones, were to become long-standing leaders in the field of public relations.

By the mid-1980s, the NSWJBD Public Relations office was engaged in monitoring six major daily newspapers, over 60 magazines and the electronic media. In conjunction with B'nai B'rith a watch was kept on the ethnic media, especially the Arab press, and a speakers' service accepted engagements throughout the state. Separate Labor and Liberal "Friends of Israel" groups were established. In 1983, Jones visited organizations in New York and London to broaden his understanding of "best practice". He cemented close co-operation between organizations in Sydney (as the local representative of Australia-Israel Publications and Executive Vice-President, then President of ECAJ), bringing greater professionalism to anti-defamation activities, including maintenance of centralized records.[26]

The work of the roof bodies was supplemented by new institutions, their scale of activity for the first time exceeding those of the Jewish Council in the late 1940s. Three new organizations and a number of museums were established. Overseas models, the American Jewish Affairs Council, Anti-Defamation League, the London-based Institute of Jewish Affairs, and Israel's Holocaust Remembrance Authority, influenced their formation. The number of initiatives reflected the widespread perception of crisis.

The first new body was Australia-Israel Publications (AIP), established in 1974. In 1977, AIP introduced a fortnightly newsletter, the *Australia/Israel Review*, edited by Sam Lipski. Its subscriber list grew to 2,000 and it was distributed free to parliamentarians, trade unionists, church leaders, academics, senior journalists, and the media.[27] Although established to present the case for Israel, from the early 1980s AIP devoted considerable resources to monitoring Australian extremists, with regular reports from Jeremy Jones and others published in *The Review*. At times it drew on intelligence gained from investigative work and for much of the 1990s employed David Greason, one of the leading experts on the Australian far right, as *The Review*'s Melbourne correspondent. In 1995, AIP evolved into the Australia/Israel & Jewish Affairs Council (AIJAC), whose activities are examined in detail in chapter 12.

The second of the organizations formed in the 1970s was the Anti-Defamation Commission (ADC) of B'nai B'rith. Its formation was preceded by local anti-defamation committees formed by B'nai B'rith groups in Melbourne and Sydney.[28] The ADC was almost exclusively concerned with Australian developments. The organization was sustained by a levy paid by members of B'nai B'rith, a communal appeal begun in 1996 and revenue from public events. At times, it took over anti-defamation work on behalf of the cash-starved Jewish Community Council of Victoria, the successor body to the VJBD.

The ADC's major contribution lay in the careful culling of media reports, supplemented by its collection of extremist publications. It privately circulated an annual report detailing each organization. At the peak of its activism following the appointment of an Executive Director in 1997, the ADC also took on an advocacy role, interceding with government ministers and presenting research reports of substance in support, for example, of Victorian legislation to outlaw racial vilification.

Other organizations were formed during the 1980s. Two initiatives of a broader nature, directed to meeting long-term goals rather than providing a capacity for immediate response, were the establishment of museums, particularly Holocaust museums, and a Jewish "think-tank", the Australian Institute of Jewish Affairs (AIJA).

Public Holocaust commemoration in Australia dates from April 1944, the first anniversary of the Warsaw ghetto uprising.[29] Over the following years, survivors were engaged in a range of activities, including the establishment of memorials in cemeteries. In the 1970s, attention was directed outward. The fading memories of the Holocaust, as noted by Isi Leibler, and the growing boldness of Holocaust denial, were factors contributing to this process.

In 1980, a Holocaust exhibition was held in Melbourne, organized by B'nai B'rith. Some 7,500 attended. The following year the exhibition attracted more than 40,000 visitors when staged in the Sydney Town Hall. In the aftermath of the Melbourne exhibition, the Kadimah and Australian Federation of Polish Jews took the decision to establish a museum to serve as a site of commemoration and public education, and as a documentation centre. Melbourne's Holocaust Museum was opened in 1984, Sydney's in 1992, the delay explained in part by divisions amongst its proponents. Two years earlier, in 1990, a smaller Holocaust Institute was established in Perth.[30]

Judith Berman writes that "the founders . . . were spurred on in their tasks by the perception that the truth of the Holocaust needed to be told in detail, and supported with documentation, especially at a time when the Holocaust was being declared a hoax by some commentators, and neo-Nazi activity was increasing".[31] Indicative of such attitudes, in Melbourne Henia Liebman observed that it was impossible for survivors to remain silent while "nests of Neo-Nazis around the world, groups of 'revisionist historians' keep up the flames of anti-Semitism". One of the key Sydney proponents, Marika Weinberger, commented that "our responsibility . . . [was] not only to remember the dead but to warn the living that the unthinkable remains possible".[32]

There were also groups outside the Museums that worked for Holocaust education, notably B'nai B'rith's Raoul Wallenberg Unit which developed a highly successful touring exhibition, Courage to Care, to honour the "Righteous Gentiles", non-Jews who aided Jews during the Holocaust. The Courage to Care concept was taken up in Sydney, which also became the site of a successful initiative under the federal government's Living in Harmony Project, the "Fair Go Australia" education program. In keeping with these endeavours were the various initiatives to develop interfaith dialogue, including the establishment of the Victorian Council of Christians and Jews in 1985.[33]

The fourth of the new organizations was the Australian Institute of Jewish Affairs (AIJA), established in 1983 under the Chairmanship of Isi Leibler and with the support of co-Presidents Richard Pratt and Mark Besen.[34] The Institute, with private funding, aimed to sponsor and publish research on contemporary Jewish affairs of concern to the Australian (and Asia-Pacific) Jewish communities, establish a resource centre and conduct conferences and public lectures.

A high point in AIJA's development was reached relatively early, with the hosting in 1984 of an international conference on anti-Semitism. For this conference the Institute brought to Australia the Chief Rabbi of the Commonwealth, Sir Immanuel Jakobovits, Abraham Foxman of the American Anti-Defamation League, Allan Gerson, Special Counsel to the US Ambassador to the United Nations, and noted academics Dr Stephen Roth, Professor Itamar Rabinovich, Dr William Korey, and Professor Zwi Werblowsky. The attendance at the opening function, held on a Saturday evening, exceeded 1,000; more than 500 attended over the following two days.[35]

Achievement

With the transformation in scale of anti-defamation activity since the mid-1970s, the Jewish community has developed the most sophisticated structure of any Australian ethnic community to monitor its enemies, to provide information and briefings to journalists and politicians, and to work to influence opinion makers. In the context of the growing physical threat, the state roof bodies established security groups, in close co-operation with law enforcement authorities. This development, which necessitated the employment of professionals, contracting of private security firms and the training of volunteers, imposed a huge financial burden on institutions with the annual cost measured in the millions of dollars.

In contrast with the ad hoc responses by volunteers in the field of anti-defamation from the early 1950s to 1975, this later era was characterized by increasing professionalization, the employment of full-time staff and voluntary work of lawyers, academics and fundraisers.

The Australian organizations never matched the resources of lead overseas organizations, such as the Anti-Defamation League, based in New York, with 29 regional offices and an operation budget of US$52 million in 2002. Notwithstanding financial limitations, organizations with significant capacity were established. Research reports of substance were generated at short notice. Strong ties were developed with leading politicians. The Jewish community joined others in lobbying for the enactment of legislation to outlaw racial discrimination and then to extend its scope to cover racial vilification, and also to provide for the prosecution of war criminals who had gained residence in Australia. There was even an international impact, with the first significant progress towards repeal of the 1975 United Nations resolution being made in Australia.[36] In the development of interfaith dialogue, Australia provided a lesson for emulation. There was a proud record of achievement.

1996 to the Present: Reasons for Concern

The third peak of heightened community alarm occurred from 1996 to the present. At the beginning of this period, two independent candidates, Pauline Hanson and Graeme Campbell, were elected to federal parliament. They both ran on populist platforms, critical of multiculturalism, Asian immigration and Aboriginal rights. Hanson, the most successful Australian populist of the last half century, made no directly anti-Semitic statements, but the far right had no difficulty in recognising a kindred spirit and her movement as presenting the long-awaited opportunity to gain a place within the mainstream.[37]

Campbell, unlike Hanson, openly associated with the League of Rights, appearing on League platforms at public meetings. In the context of the power struggle to win the leadership of the so-called "nationalist" movement he won the League's endorsement, but One Nation remained in the ascendant. The Queensland election of June 1998 saw One Nation gain 23 percent of the vote and 11 parliamentary seats. It was a time of consternation within the Jewish community – mirroring levels of concern within the wider society.

Coverage of the Israeli–Palestinian struggle provided a second area of concern. There were rising levels of hostility to Israel as the peace process faltered and then came to a violent end in 2000 with the launch of the second intifada. The response of Israeli armed might to the murder of its citizens evoked hostile, unbalanced commentary, at times within the mainstream print media, government broadcasters (ABC, SBS), and from some backbench members of the major parties, as well as Australian Democrats and Green representatives. The extent of shift in public opinion was evidenced by the decision of the Sydney Peace Foundation to award its Peace Prize for 2003 to the Palestinian activist Dr Hanan Ashrawi and by attitudes to the Jewish community during the subsequent public controversy (see chapter 13 this volume).

A tangible indicator of change was the number of anti-Semitic incidents logged by Jewish organizations. ECAJ compilations showed incidents under 200 per annum from 1990–5; 250 between 1996 and 2000; and more than 500 in 2002 and 2003. Threats against individuals and organizations rose from 50 in 1992 to 450 in 2002, with by far the largest number recorded in Sydney.[38] In these turbulent times, the resources and professionalism of the organizations established in the 1970s proved to be of significance. Following the 1998 Queensland election, when preference deals with the Liberal and National Party facilitated the election of One Nation candidates, much use was made of research files. These files provided an immediate resource for those seeking to trace the background of individuals, including those who gained preselection. A number of neo-Nazi activists and other extremists were identified; the subsequent media attention was one of the factors that left One Nation in disarray prior to the federal poll.[39]

Politicians and journalists made extensive use of Jewish organizational records. Such was the call on resources that the ADC increased its staffing and spent more than its annual budget in three months.[40] Jewish leaders found their standing enhanced in the mainstream and they took a leading position in condemnation of One Nation and in bringing pressure on the Coalition parties.

Mark Leibler, in his capacity as national chair of AIJAC, wrote to Prime Minister Howard immediately after the Queensland election results were known with the demand that the Coalition disavow any preference deals with One Nation. This view was supported by ECAJ vice-president Jeremy Jones and the Queensland Jewish Board of Deputies president Laurie Rosenblum. ECAJ President Diane Shteinman, AIJAC national policy chairman Colin Rubenstein and ADC executive director Danny Ben-Moshe, voiced criticism of Howard's initial favourable reaction to the prospect of One Nation capturing the balance of power in the Senate.[41] During the previous year, Justice Marcus Einfeld had argued that "we must never allow society to forget that the train of racial and other forms of discrimination never stops at the first station. It may be indigenous black people and Australians of Asian origin today. It takes little to imagine who will not be far behind".[42]

Jewish organizations and leadership made an important contribution in the battle against One Nation. The community could take comfort from the party's rapid decline. There was, however, less success in efforts to influence the mainstream media to adopt a more balanced stance in the reporting of the Israeli–Palestinian conflict. In the second half of the 1970s, the VJBD fought a lengthy battle to change the virulently anti-Israeli programming of community radio station 3CR; it took years of effort to bring even minor change.[43] Over the last two decades the documentation of media bias, and lodging of complaints against government broadcasters SBS and ABC, individual journalists and cartoonists, entailed a huge commitment of time and resources and yielded only minor victories.[44] It remained possible for newspaper editors to publish openly anti-Semitic material in the context of opposition to Israeli policies.

Many Voices

While the above discussion has sought to identify the nature and scope of action to combat anti-Semitism since the 1940s, highlighting its major features, it would be wrong to leave an impression of a united, harmonious community, working for the attainment of agreed goals.

The Jewish community, like all communities, is divided within itself by political allegiance, regional interest and personality differences. Differing groupings compete for control and for acceptance of their own perspectives. Thus from the late 1940s to the early 1950s there was a bitter struggle in Melbourne over the direction pursued by the Jewish Council. Critics charged that the Council was under the influence of the Communist Party, as evidenced by its failure to respond to the growing evidence of anti-Semitism in communist Europe. The outcome was the expulsion of the Council from the VJBD.

Over the last three decades community discord has been sparked by organizations independent of the roof bodies involving themselves in domestic Australian politics, by the jockeying for position of rival organizations and by failure to agree on tactics. AIJAC was involved in fierce communal disputation following its decision in 1998 to publish a partial list of One Nation members and in 2003 over its role in the Ashrawi affair.[45]

Competition can limit the effectiveness of response; one evident cost is the direct duplication of effort, for example in research and documentation. There is also the problem of mixed messages delivered to political and media contacts, and the weakening of Jewish representation, when a lack of unity is evident. At times, the community has been embroiled in fierce disputation, resulting in calls for greater co-ordination and accountability. In 2003, in the aftermath of what was widely depicted as the Ashrawi debacle, Justice Marcus Einfeld and others suggested a public inquiry into how the affair had been mismanaged.[46]

Some seven years earlier Sam Lipski, at a time of public contestation between AIJAC and the ADC, had also suggested reappraisal. It was necessary, Lipski wrote, to determine who should speak on domestic issues on behalf of the Jewish community; how best to expend community resources; and the most effective tactics. Lipski highlighted problems with current strategies:

> the real Australia in which we live has not suddenly become a racist nightmare or an anti-Semitic, threatening and dangerous place for Jews. We, the most successful of the predominantly immigrant communities in the country and the one with most reason to be grateful to it, should not carry on as if our relating to the Australian public is to be dominated by the dark shadows of racial vilification, war crimes, and fringe extremists of the right or left . . . Keeping records and files on the nasties, even investigative "reporting" . . . are not the be-all or end-all of helping the development of this nation's tolerant society . . . Our collective interest . . . now require[s] far more positive, less defensive, more subtle, more muted and far more informed, long-range, well-funded, communally accountable structures . . . [47]

Lipski was writing before the crisis sparked by the 1998 Queensland election result and before the sharp spike in the level of anti-Semitism in
western culture. The history of anti-Semitism is replete with unexpected
turns. Analyses of developments at any specific moment can never be
made with surety. While calls for rationalization of scarce resources have
much to commend them, they should be seen as part of the process of political debate, made by protagonists holding positions within that debate –
not as truth statements beyond the field of politics.

Paradoxically, a great strength of Jewish communities has been division.
Division can produce waste, lack of co-ordination, short-term tactical
disaster. However, competition also maximizes activity, debate, and
commitment. Competition betokens dynamism. It provides scope for
different evaluations, different approaches. The institutions established
since the mid-1970s each developed a core of supporters, each determined
to contribute in their own way to a shared goal. Action to combat anti-
Semitism is necessarily an imperfect art whose outcome may be
determined by factors beyond local or national control. Sadly, anti-
Semitism will continue to challenge Jewish communities for the foreseeable
future.

Notes

I wish to acknowledge the assistance provided by Danielle Charak, Dr. Paul
Gardner, Jeremy Jones and Associate Professor Suzanne Rutland. The interpretations and conclusions reached are solely my own.

1   Robert Wistrich, *Antisemitism: The Longest Hatred* (London: Thames
     Methuen, 1991), p. xxvi
2   Philip Mendes, "Left Attitudes Towards Jews", *Australian Jewish Historical
     Society Journal* (henceforth *AJHSJ*), part 1, 13 (1995): 109–11, 117.
3   Leon Mann, "The Australian Jewish Community and Israel", ECAJ
     Symposium: "Australian Jewry in the Next Twenty-Five Years", 13–14 June
     1976, Victorian Jewish Board of Deputies papers, State Library of Victoria
     (henceforth VJBD), ms. 9532, box 22.
4   Lecture by Professor Yehuda Bauer on the impact of the Holocaust,
     Australian Centre for the Study of Jewish Civilisation, Monash University, 19
     March 2003: "tendency of Jewish communities all over the globe to see in
     every kind of slight . . . against them the spectre of the Holocaust again. If you
     go through large countries like the United States, you will find the Jewish
     community talks about a rise of anti-Semitism when it was actually declining.
     That's quite natural, you immediately react to the slightest provocation in a
     kind of overstated reaction".
5   "Annual Report of the Victorian Jewish Board of Deputies For the Year Ended
     1960", p. 18, VJBD, box 1; Melbourne *Truth*, 16 April 1960; Melbourne *Sun*,
     6 May 1960; Suzanne Rutland, *Edge of the Diaspora* (Sydney: Collins, 1988),
     pp. 230–1.
6   Rutland, *Edge of the Diaspora*, pp. 233–6; Andrew Markus, "Labour and

Immigration 1946–9", *Labour History* 47 (1984): pp. 73–90; Mark Aarons, *War Criminals Welcome* (Melbourne: Black Inc, 2001).

7   W. D. Rubinstein, "The Revolution of 1942–44: The Transformation of the Australian Jewish Community", *AJHSJ* 11, part 1 (1990): 146, 148; Hilary Rubinstein, *The Jews in Victoria* (Sydney: Allen & Unwin, 1986), chap. 11.

8   W. D. Rubinstein, *The Jews in Australia: A Thematic History*, vol. 2 (Melbourne: Heinemann, 1991), p. 399.

9   There is an extensive literature on the Council. Recent studies include a three-part study by Philip Mendes published in the *AJHSJ* 10, parts 6 & 7, and 11, part 1 (1989–90), and Rubinstein, *Thematic History*, esp. pp. 401–10.

10   See Council Annual Report 1949–50, sub-heading "Radio" (personal collection of Philip Mendes).

11   Annual Report 1950–1, "Publicity".

12   Annual Report 1947–8, "Legislation . . . ".

13   For a recent overview of this campaign, see Philip Mendes, "Jews, Nazis and Communists Down Under", *Australian Historical Studies* 119 (2002): 73–92.

14   *Keep Australia Free from Nazis*, p. 5 (pamphlet, n. d.); one page typescript, "To All ACTU Delegates: Stop the ratification of the Migration Agreement", n. d.

15   Address by Mr Ben Green to the Victorian Board of Deputies, 5 February 1951, typescript, VJBD, box 7.

16   Peter Y. Medding, *From Assimilation to Group Survival* (Melbourne: Cheshire, 1968), pp. 71–5; Rubinstein, *Thematic History*, pp. 416–17.

17   Mark Lopez, *The Origins of Multiculturalism in Australian Politics 1945–1975* (Carlton: University of Melbourne Press, 2000), esp. p. 112.

18   See, for example, K. D. Gott, *Voices of Hate* (Melbourne, Dissent Assoc. Publication, 1965); Andrew A. Campbell, *The Australian League of Rights* (Collingwood, Vic.: Outback Press, 1978); various Jewish community publications, including the ECAJ pamphlet *The League of Rights. An Evaluation of Australia's Foremost Organisation Promoting Racial and Religious Hatred*, 1985 (copy in the State Library of Victoria).

19   For activities of the Research Services group, see VJBD, boxes 35, 41.

20   Philip Mendes, *The New Left, The Jews and the Vietnam War 1965–1972* (North Caulfield: Lazare Press, 1993), pp. 128–30.

21   Report of the Chairman of the Public Relations Committee, Annual Report of the Victorian Jewish Board of Deputies 1960, p. 23, VJBD, box 1.

22   *Ibid*, p. 27.

23   Rubinstein, *Thematic History*, p. 459.

24   "The Escalation of Anti-Israeli and Anti-Semitic Agitation in Australia", ECAJ Conference Report (roneo copy), September 1974, VJBD, box 120.

25   Philip Mendes, "Australian Union of Students Middle East Debates 1974–75", *AJHSJ* 12, part 1 (1993): 189.

26   Suzanne Rutland and Sophie Caplan, *With One Voice* (Sydney: Australian Jewish Historical Society, 1998), pp. 293–309.

27   Hyams, Bernard, *The History of Australian Zionism* (S. Caulfield: Zionist Federation of Australia, 1998), pp. 136–8.

28   Paul Gardner, "The B'nai B'rith Anti-Defamation Commission in Australia and New Zealand: An Outline of its History", typescript, 2003.

29   Judith Berman, *Holocaust Remembrance in Australian Jewish Communities*,

1945–2000 (Crawley: University of Western Australia Press, 2001), p. 16.

30   *Ibid.*, pp. 105, 120, 122, 125, 130.

31   *Ibid.*, p. 104.

32   *Ibid.*

33   See the Courage to Care web sites, Victoria at: www.arts.monash.edu.au/affil-iates/hlc/courage/; and NSW at: www.aijac.org.au/resources/reports/sbs_report.html. For information on Fair Go Australia, see www.bnaibrith.org.au/index.asp?pRef=FairGo. *Gesher: The Official Journal of the Council of Christians & Jews*, has been published since 1990.

34   For AIJA's activities, see its newsletter, *AIJA Survey*, and its periodical *Without Prejudice*.

35   *Anti-Semitism and Human Rights. Proceedings of a Seminar* (North Melbourne: AIJA, 1985); ECAJ, "Annual Report 1984", p. 22, VJBD, box 120.

36   Hyams, *The History of Australian Zionism*, p. 141.

37   Andrew Markus, *Race: John Howard and the Remaking of Australia* (Crows Nest: Allen & Unwin, 2001), esp. chapter 6.

38   ECAJ, Jeremy Jones, "Report on Anti-Semitism in Australia, 1 Oct. 2002–30 Sept. 2003" (privately circulated).

39   See, for example, *The Australian*, 10 June 1998; *The Age* 18 and 21 June 1998; 11 August 1998.

40   Grahame Leonard in *Australian Jewish News*, Melbourne edn (henceforth *AJN*), 16 October 1998.

41   *AJN*, 19 and 26 June 1998.

42   Marcus Einfeld, speech delivered at a "Seminar on racism and the Jewish community", 10 August 1997, typescript, p. 31 (ADC files).

43   For the battle against 3CR see, for example, ECAJ, "Public Broadcasting in Australia", Annual Conference 1979 VJBD, box 21; "3CR: A Matter of Public Concern", Compiled by: Victorian Jewish Board of Deputies, n.d., VJBD, box 120; Philip Mendes, "Denying the Jewish Experience of Oppression . . . the 3CR controversy", *AJHSJ* 16, 3 (2002): pp. 368–82.

44   See, for example, AIJAC, "SBS-TV and the Middle East", October 2003: www.aijac.org.au/resources/reports/sbs_report.html.

45   See *AJN* (Melbourne and Sydney edns), 17 July 1998, 14 and 21 November 2003; and chapter 13 this volume.

46   *AJN*, 14 November 2003.

47   *AJN*, 8 and 15 November 1996.

8 | Pro-Israelism as a Factor in Australian Jewish Political Attitudes and Behaviour

DANNY BEN-MOSHE

This chapter examines the influence of support for the State of Israel on Australian Jewish voters and politics relative to local political concerns.

A review of the literature on Australian Jewish political preferences provides information on Jews' voting patterns, the policies of Jewish organizations on a range of political issues, and the attitudes of individual Jews on these issues. However, there are no data that link attitudes of Jews on specific issues, such as concern for Israel, with their electoral behaviour. Given the absence of such data, answers to our question need to be accessed from multiple sources. They include:

- The electoral campaigns of political parties aimed at the Jewish community: It is assumed that political parties base such campaigns on the issues they believe will resonate with the Jewish public.
- The extent of Israel-related activities by federal and state parliamentarians with a sizeable number of Jews in their electorates.
- Unrepresentative qualitative data of Jewish opinion on policy issues.
- Quantitative data from surveys of the Jewish community.
- Comparative Jewish political and philanthropic engagement with Israel-related and Australian political causes, such as participation in public demonstrations.
- The level of Jewish involvement in various political parties and the extent to which such involvement has been affected by Israel-related factors.
- The actions and opinions of representatives of Jewish organizations.

By examining the above sources, it is possible to draw at least some tentative conclusions about the extent to which, and the way in which, the "Israel" factor impacts on how Australian Jews vote and engage in politics.

For present purposes, I have limited the study to the period beginning with the first Howard Government in 1996 to early 2004. This period has seen a range of competing and important issues for the Jewish community – such as racism, reconciliation, economic reform and terrorism – at the top of the political agenda. I have also limited my analysis to the New South Wales and Victorian contexts, these being where the overwhelming majority of Australian Jews reside. Before answering our research question, it is necessary to understand the place of "Israel" in Australian Jewish life.

Australian Jewry and Israel

Israel is central to the identity of Australian Jews. This can best be explained by reference to several factors.

The Holocaust

Australian Jewry has the highest per capita number of Holocaust survivors of any country except Israel.[1] As a relatively young community which grew significantly through European immigration in the immediate periods both before and after World War II, the Holocaust shaped the world-view of generations of Australian Jews.

Up until the Holocaust, Zionism remained a minority idea amongst world Jewry, including in Australia where the pro-British environment limited Jewish support for the Zionists who were fighting the British in Palestine. However, as the enormity of the Holocaust became known, the Zionist case that Jews needed a home like everyone else with an army to protect itself like everyone else was accepted by the majority of world Jewry. This was all the more pronounced in Australia because of the arrival of refugees from Europe where many had been active in Zionist organizations, and which they subsequently established in Australia. In addition, while the Anglo-Jewish establishment of the 1930s was anti-Zionist, Australia never had a strong Liberal or Reform Judaism movement, with its core anti-Zionist belief as existed in America.[2]

With 50 percent of the current Australian Jewish community being either Holocaust survivors or their descendants, the Holocaust remains a driving factor behind the community's strong identification with the Jewish State.[3] The nexus between the Holocaust and support for Israel was clearly revealed by Victorian members of the United Israel Appeal's seniors group in a 2003 survey of their attitudes to Israel. Asked why they were Zionists, indicative responses were:

"I appreciate the fact that the Jewish people need a haven from persecution".

"The Jewish people have to have their own country".

"I am a Holocaust survivor. If we would have had a homeland before World War II we would have had somewhere to go".

"Experience of life before and during World War II taught me there is no other option for Jewish people but our own state".[4]

It was attitudes such as these, expressed by a generation now aged over seventy, that confirmed the importance and centrality of Israel for Australian Jewry.

Communal Structures

The centrality of Israel in Australian Jewish life also is reflected in communal structures. Zionist organizations have the same status as the official roof bodies. Indeed, Jewish community delegations to the Prime Minister consist of joint delegations from the Executive Council of Australian Jewry (ECAJ) and the Zionist Federation of Australia (ZFA). Pro-Israel fundraising bodies are amongst the community's largest, and there is a degree of competition between those who seek to raise money for local Jewish causes, such as welfare services, and those who raise money for Israel.

The embeddedness of "Israel" in Australian Jewish life is reinforced by and supported by the Jewish day-school system which, at 67 percent, has the highest communal enrolment among Jewish communities in the West.[5] The Zionist education they are given, which includes knowledge of, and love for, Israel and literacy in Hebrew, means ongoing generations of Australian Jews know about and identify with Israel.[6]

The cultural significance of Israel in the community, and its likely continuation, extends beyond the day-school system to Jewish youth activities. On a weekly basis, 1,500 eight to seventeen year olds meet under the auspices of the Zionist youth movements where they are led by 200–250 *bogrim* (graduate leaders) who have participated in year-long Israel programs.[7] By comparison, there are 200–250 members of Jewish Scouts and Guide groups Australia wide[8] and 30 participants aged eight to eighteen who meet on a weekly basis in Melbourne under the auspices of the non-Zionist Skif movement.[9]

Israel is also central to the experience of Jewish university students. Every year on campuses across Australia, the Australasian Union of Jewish Students (AUJS) promotes "Israel week", which consists of seven days of cultural and educational activities about Israel. Australian Jewish students' commitment to and identification with Israel was seen in AUJS's political activism following the outbreak of the "Al-Aqsa Intifada" in 2000. Their activities included a poster campaign across Australian universities about suicide bombings in Israel and a range of initiatives to counter anti-Israel and pro-Palestinian groups and activities.[10]

Geography

A factor that helps to explain Australian Jews' commitment to Israel is their geographic isolation. While before World War II distance limited the development of the Zionist idea in Australia,[11] since then it has led to a greater attachment to Israel.[12] Because Australia is (apart from the small New Zealand community) half a world away from other Jewish communities, it has closely identified with Israel as a Jewish centre for ongoing contact and inspiration.

Jewish Media

The importance of Israel is seen in the coverage extended to it in the *Australian Jewish News* (*AJN*), the main community newspaper, which claims a readership of 35,000 in NSW and 42,000 in Victoria.[13] According to Dan Goldberg, the Melbourne editor of the *AJN*, while the majority of front page stories are local, the "vast majority" of letters relate to the Middle East, with editorials divided 50:50 between local and international issues.[14] Similarly, Sydney *AJN* editor Vic Alhadef estimates that while 10 percent of lead stories and editorials are Israel related, fifty percent of letters to the editor are about Israel.[15]

Fundraising

With its establishment, the Jewish State was in need of financial assistance, and fundraising for Israel became and remains a core Jewish activity. The nature of this was evidenced by a 1993 survey of Melbourne Jewry, which asked respondents how they would divide $100 into charitable donations, with Israel receiving the majority share.

Table 8.1 Jewish Charitable Donations

Of $100 to donate would give (percent)	Local Jewish	Israel	Non-Jewish
None	11.7	11.8	33.0
1–49	55.3	40.1	58.2
50	18.8	20.6	5.3
51–99	10.6	19.7	1.7
100	3.6	7.9	1.8
TOTAL	100.0	100.0	100.0

Source: John Goldlust, *The Jews of Melbourne: A Community Profile. A Report of the Findings of the Jewish Community Survey 1991* (Melbourne: Jewish Welfare Society, 1993), p. 54.

This commitment to philanthropic giving to Israel extends across generations, with 77 percent of AUJS students surveyed in 1991 saying that they would see themselves making a regular financial contribution to Israel. Only 8 percent said that they would not.[16]

The depth of feeling for Israel and the way this is reflected in Australian Jewish communal structures become clearer when compared with developments overseas. Following the 1990 National Jewish Population survey in the United States, which established an assimilation rate of 52 percent, a major debate erupted about whether funds raised in the Diaspora should be directed towards Israel at the expense of the Diaspora community. In both the United States and Britain, the debate led to structural reforms so that funding could be jointly raised for Israel and the Diaspora, but such changes did not take place in Australia. For example, whereas in Britain the United Israel Appeal (UIA) became the United Jewish Israel Appeal (UJIA), which jointly raises money for Israel and British-based projects, in Australia it remains UIA, not UJIA, and is the preeminent fundraising body.[17]

Indicative of Israel's standing, it is relevant to note that in New South Wales there is a Jewish Communal Appeal for domestic Jewish causes (excluding synagogues and certain other causes) and separate appeals by pro-Israel organizations such as UIA and the Jewish National Fund. These Israel-oriented organizations raise more than twice as much as what the JCA sets as its appeal targets, which in 2001–2 was $7.8 million.[18]

Israel Visits and Emigration

One way Australian Jewish commitment to Israel is manifest is through the high number of visits to the Jewish State. A 1991 survey of Melbourne Jewry found 73 percent had visited Israel with 48 percent doing so two or more times.[19] A 1995 survey of Jewish community leaders, which included executive members of even the smallest Jewish organizations, found that nine out of ten had visited Israel, with many having done so on multiple occasions.[20] This pattern appears set to continue with participation in a youth or student program in Israel an Australian Jewish rite of passage. For example, AUJS report that 280 people will join their Israel programs in 2004, the highest number ever despite the ongoing violence between Israel and the Palestinians.[21]

Aliyah, emigrating to Israel, is the penultimate Zionist act, and although it is a minority phenomenon, Australia has the highest per capita rate of *aliyah* in the Western world. This indicates how deep Zionist feeling runs in the Australian Jewish community.[22]

The extent of Australian Jewish identification with Israel was most powerfully expressed during the Arab–Israeli wars of 1967 and 1973 when Australian Jewry felt extreme distress at the prospect of Israel's annihilation. This concern for Israel drives pro-Israel lobbying, which is another core aspect of Jewish communal life.

Whether the pro-Israel work is done well or not is beyond the scope of this chapter, but there is a clear grass roots demand for such organized public relations work. The 1995 survey of Jewish community leaders asked if they thought the Australian media was biased against Israel. Forty percent of Victorian Jewish leaders, 50 percent of those from New South Wales and 57 percent from all other states agreed that they were.[23] Evidence of a Jewish grass roots reaction to media bias was seen in mid 2003 when the *Sydney Morning Herald* published a cartoon comparing Israel's security fence on the West Bank with the Warsaw Ghetto behind which Nazis herded Jews in 1943. The paper was reportedly deluged by complaints,[24] with one member of the Jewish community lodging a complaint about the cartoon with the Australian Press Council.

The willingness to act in a political manner for Israel is evidenced by the solidarity rallies with Israel in 2002, the largest ever Jewish rallies in Australia. In Sydney 10,000 Jews, about a quarter of the Jewish community, rallied in Hyde Park,[25] while in Perth 2500 Jews, between a third and a half of the community demonstrated.[26]

The conclusion that can be drawn from the above discussion is that Israel dominates the Australian Jewish agenda. This is a result of its centrality to Australian Jewish identity. The depth of identification with Israel was illustrated in the 1991 survey of Melbourne Jewry. Asking respondents how they feel "when international events put Israel in danger", 28 percent replied their feeling would be "as strong as if danger was to self, 58 percent would feel "special alarm because it is Israel", 12 percent "more concerned than if it was another country" and 2 percent "the same as if any country was in danger".[27]

It is this depth of feeling that translated politically in 1975 to the Australian Jewish leadership taking the unprecedented step of calling for the community to vote for a particular party. This was a response to Labor Prime Minister Gough Whitlam shifting government policy from what had been previous Australian governments' pro-Israel stance to a perceived position of hostility towards Israel. As a result, Jewish community leaders called on Australian Jews to vote for the Coalition and Malcolm Fraser.[28]

The 1975 election saw the nadir of Jewish voting for the Labor Party. Jewish support for the ALP dropped from 75 percent in the 1940s – when Jews favoured the ALP probably because of its support for Israel and Jewish immigration, among other reasons – to 30 percent at the time of Whitlam's "even-handed" position on the Middle East. However, in his 1982 study, W. S. Logan argues that the reduced Jewish vote for the ALP reflected not only Israel-related factors, but also generational changes in the socio-economic circumstances of many Australian Jews as they became more established and integrated in the Australian community.[29]

Beyond Israel: Competing Issues and Factors

Although Israel is central to Australian Jewish identity and political and communal activities, it remains one of several factors that are of importance to the Jewish community. The range of issues on the communal agenda was illustrated during the 2001 federal election when the ECAJ asked both the Government and the Opposition for their policies on nine issues, including the Israeli–Palestinian conflict, Jewish day schools, communal security, complaints systems for the Special Broadcasting Service, immigration, war crimes and human rights.

The multiple demands on Australian Jewry are manifest during the traditional *Kol Nidre* appeal when it is customary to give a charitable donation on the occasion of the *Yom Kippur* (Day of Atonement) holiday. In many synagogues in Melbourne, for example, congregants are given donation forms for the United Israel Appeal, the Jewish Community Council of Victoria and the United Jewish Education Board.

The multiple communal concerns are also reflected in the nature of communal political engagement. For example, in 1996 when the New South Wales Jewish community honoured Premier Bob Carr through the establishment of the Bob Carr Forest, they did so based on his staunch friendship of the Jewish people, manifested through steadfast support for Israel, his active campaigning on behalf of Soviet Jewry and his vigorous promotion of anti-racism legislation.[30] Like "Israel", the importance of these other issues to the Jewish community is explained by historical and moral considerations. For some Jews it is based on the Jewish ethic of *Tikkun Olam*, of making the world a better place. For others, it is based on the Jewish historical experience of anti-Semitism that makes fighting racism obligatory, and still others are motivated by practical concerns for organized Jewish life in Australia.

Which issues dominate concern within the Jewish community unsurprisingly depend on perceptions of crisis at any particular time. For example, when a 1999 survey of young Jewish adults in Sydney found an assimilation rate of 50 percent, Jewish continuity, and the related issue of Jewish education, were confirmed at the top of the communal agenda.[31] Indeed, the 1995 survey of Jewish community leaders identified the three main issues of concern to be Jewish education, intermarriage and, to a lesser extent, anti-Semitism.[32]

A Jewish day-school education is regarded as an important barrier against assimilation and with Australian Jewry having the highest rate of Jewish day school attendance in the Diaspora, financial issues relating to private education have featured prominently in election campaigns.

In 1998 when the Coalition proposed introducing a 10 percent Goods and Service Tax, the potential impact of this tax on Jewish schools became a major issue in Melbourne Ports, the electorate with the highest concentration of Jews in Australia and a marginal seat where the Jewish vote could determine its outcome. Australian Labor Party candidate Michael Danby argued 10 percent would be added to school fees, with Liberal candidate Fiona Snedden responding that Jewish day schools would be exempt, and that a Labor government would close private schools. So significant was this debate that the then shadow Education Minister, Mark Latham, issued a statement to the *AJN* rejecting Snedden's claims.[33] This issue remained at the fore in the 2001 general elections, despite the "Al-Aqsa Intifada" and the war on terror. This issue featured prominently in the *AJN*'s election coverage.[34]

Australian Jews also share the concerns of other Australians on issues such as the environment and the economy. Thus, in 1998, while Danby's Melbourne Ports campaign referred to Pauline Hanson and her right wing One Nation Party and Prime Minister Howard's failure to deal with it, Liberal Party advertisements focused on tax and economic management, suggesting that it is the latter issues that the coalition thought would help sway Jewish voters to them.

Table 8.2 1991 Jewish Voting Preferences by Jewish Religious Orientation (in percentage)

	ALP	Coalition	Dems	Other
Strictly Orthodox	0	82.8	8.3	8.9
Traditional religious	23.6	67.2	2	7.1
Liberal/Reform	29	63	5.7	2.3
Jewish but not religious	26.8	62.3	4.5	6.4

Source: John Goldlust, The Jews of Melbourne: A Community Profile. A Report of the Findings of the Jewish Community Survey 1991 (Melbourne: Jewish Welfare Society, 1993), p. 154.

Table 8.3 Voting Intention of First Time Jewish Voters, 2001

Reason	Party
Best interest of Jews and university students	Liberal
For environment and refugees	Greens
For public education and reconciliation	Labor
Economic management	Liberal
Strong response to 9/11	Liberal
For Israel's interest in Australia	Don't know, but not Labor
Economic management	Liberal
Women's issues such as equal pay and maternity leave	Don't know: Greens, Democrats or communists
Not interested	Don't Know

Source: Australian Jewish News, Sydney edn, 9 November 2001.

On the broad range of issues, there would appear to be, as one might expect, a relationship between Jewish religious orientation and general political preference, the less religious being the more left wing generally, and vice versa. This was shown in the 1991 study of Melbourne Jewry which asked respondents to state their voting preferences. They responded as detailed in table 8.2.

The diversity of considerations and how these are manifest at the ballot box were evident when the *AJN* asked ten Jewish first-time voters how they would vote in the 2001 federal election (table 8.3).

It is clear, then, that Israel is but one of several issues of importance to Australian Jews. However, its potential impact on the electoral process can be explored by examining the significance of Israel in the political activity of the federal and state MPs representing the areas with the highest concentrations of Jews.

Party Campaigns, MPs and Israel

Jews are residentially concentrated in two main areas that overlap particular electorates in New South Wales and Victoria. In the former, it is the Sydney state seat of Vaucluse and the federal seat of Wentworth, and in the latter it is the Melbourne state seat of Caulfield and the federal seat of Melbourne Ports. The percentages of Jews in these electorates are: Vaucluse 19 percent, Wentworth 13 percent, Caulfield 29 percent, and Melbourne Ports 30 percent. Members of Parliament for these seats are leading advocates for Israel, a fact which strongly suggests their awareness of the importance of Israel to their constituents.

Both the Labor and Liberal parties also emphasize support for Israel in their electoral campaigns in these seats. In the 2001 election, for example, the incumbent (Jewish) Labor MP for Melbourne Ports, Michael Danby, included an advertisement in the *AJN* which stated "Support Israel, Vote 1 Danby",[35] while in the 1998 federal election Danby's Liberal opponent, Fiona Snedden, emphasized her commitment to the Jewish people and Israel.[36] A similar pattern is evidenced in Wentworth where, for example, in the 2001 federal election both Liberal and Labor candidates condemned a controversial resolution of the NSW Teachers Federation that was critical of Israel.[37] So great is the concern of these parties about how "Israel" affects the way their Jewish constituents vote that Israel becomes a rare policy area of ongoing bipartisan support.

This same process occurs at the state level, where Israel regularly features on the agenda of the members for Vaucluse and Caulfield even though state parliamentarians are not directly concerned with foreign affairs. In Vaucluse, for example, local member Peter Debnam, who regularly attends Israel-related and other Jewish community functions, spoke in parliament in 2002 against media bias against Israel[38] and the need to support the war on terror, for which he quoted former Israeli Prime Minister Bibi Netanyahu.[39] The same is true for the member for Caulfield, Helen Shardey, who also regularly attends Israel-related and other Jewish community functions, and is the convener of the Victorian Liberal Friends of Israel. In 2003, when a Liberal Party branch president banned Israelis and Americans from his business in protest at the Iraq War, Shardey was at the forefront of efforts to remove him from the party.[40] As with their federal parliamentary colleagues, the actions of Debnam and Shardey reflect what they believe are the concerns of their electorate.

The fact that the MPs in these four constituencies are such strong supporters of Israel can actually pose an electoral dilemma for Jewish voters on occasion. In 2003, for example, when the Labor Party was embroiled in controversy over backbench attitudes towards Israel following anti-Israel remarks by federal MP Julia Irwin, former Jewish Labor federal Minister Barry Cohen wrote to the then Labor Party leader Simon Crean that he could not imagine "any Jew with feelings towards the state of Israel supporting the Australian Labor Party".[41] Indeed, this issue led to extensive media coverage about the Jewish community falling out with the ALP. In an attempt to allay these concerns, Simon Crean addressed a specially convened Jewish community meeting to affirm his support for Israel.[42] Three hundred and fifty members of the Jewish community attended the meeting in the Jewish community centre, located in Melbourne Ports. However, if they wanted to punish Crean or the ALP at the ballot box they had limited options, since for the residents of Melbourne Ports, voting against Crean would mean voting against Danby. This would be a quixotic move because voting against Danby to punish Irwin/Crean would be voting against the one Jewish member of federal Parliament, and one of Israel's strongest friends in both the parliamentary Labor Party and parliament as a whole.

What, however, happens if there is an alternative Jewish candidate who is equally pro-Israel? All the candidates the Liberal Party have hitherto run against Danby have emphasized their pro-Israel credentials, but they haven't been Jewish. At the next election, Danby will compete against the Liberals' Jewish candidate, David Southwick.[43] Responding to the suggestion that some people may think it is a shame two Jewish candidates are standing against each other, Southwick opined "at least people will know that, whatever the result, there will be a Jewish person representing them in Melbourne Ports after the election". He added that the main issue is that the Liberals were more supportive of Israel and its security barrier. Further indicating the significance of Israel in his campaign, Foreign Minister Alexander Downer briefed Southwick on his recent visit to Israel and Southwick thanked Downer for the Government's military commitment to the war in Iraq which involved destroying missiles capable of hitting Israel. A photo of Southwick being briefed with Downer appeared in the *AJN*, suggesting Downer appreciates the significance of this issue in the

electorate of Melbourne Ports.[44] The next election will provide some indication of whether Jews who voted for Danby, either as a coreligionist
and/or an advocate for Israel, will now feel free to vote for the Liberal Party
candidate for much the same reasons.

The MPs in Melbourne Ports and Wentworth clearly appreciate the
significance of Israel to the local Jewish community. When Mark Latham
was elected Leader of the Labor Party in 2003, the first question the ECAJ
asked on behalf of the Jewish community was about his policies on Israel.[45]
Similarly, in February 2004, when Malcolm Turnbull successfully challenged Peter King to represent the Liberal Party in contesting the electorate
of Wentworth at the next general election, he emphasized his support for
Israel. The fact that local members are so supportive of Israel suggests that
there would be an electoral backlash if they weren't. The MPs themselves,
however, must be aware that support for Israel is no *guarantee* of the Jewish
vote. In response to Danby's "Support Israel , Vote 1 Danby" advertisement, the *AJN* reported getting letters of complaint rejecting the equation
that supporting Israel meant supporting Danby.[46] This underscores that
the Jewish community is not monolithic in its views or driven by a single
issue. Israel remains one issue, albeit clearly an important one, to the
community. Jews have multiple identities and voting values, they are
parents, teachers, small business people etc. When an *AJN* vox pop asked
seven Jews how they would vote and why in 2001, one said they would vote
for the Liberal Party because it is more friendly to Israel and because of
the need for stability after 9/11, but the other six all cited domestic issues,
from the GST to the environment.[47]

The concern for Israel is clearly a strong factor in Australian Jewish life
and it does affect the ways Jews cast their votes. However, while Israel is
an issue of emotional and symbolic importance to Australian Jews, what
Australia does or does not do in relation to the Arab–Israeli conflict impacts
little on Australians' own lives. In contrast, policies in other areas of
concern to the Jewish community do impact on their day-to-day lives, a
fact that is reflected in party campaigns aimed at the Jewish community.
For example, in the 2001 federal election, a Liberal Party advertisement in
the Sydney *AJN* focused on one issue – economic management.[48]
Ultimately, with the high cost of Jewish education being a major communal
issue, the direct impact of government policies on the hip pockets of Jewish
families may be more of a consideration than government policy on the
Middle East. However, the President of the Western Australian Jewish
community, Joe Berinson, said: "Israel would be the major concern for
Perth Jewry, there are intensive feelings about that. The other issue of
major importance is Jewish education but far fewer people have given
consideration to the policy implications of policies on Jewish education
compared with Israel".[49] As concern about the cost of Jewish day-school
education grows, this may change.

When Australians go to the ballot booth on federal election day they can split their vote for House of Representatives and Senate candidates. The main beneficiaries of the Senate's system of proportional representation are the smaller left-liberal parties, such as the Greens and the Australian Democrats, whose policies on issues such as reconciliation and refugees are arguably closer to the social justice orientation of the Jewish community than those of either of the major parties.

It follows that Jews involved in these parties explain their involvement by the consistency between their party platform and Jewish values. For example, Janine Zimbler, a Jewish Greens candidate in the 2000 Randwick (local) Council elections in Sydney, explained that "The Greens ideology fits in well with the concerns of the Jewish community because of its focus on issues of social justice, democracy and environmentalism".[50] And Victorian Australian Democrats candidate, Ari Sharp, explained that his position on refugees and reconciliation was based on his synthesized views as a Democrat and as a Jew.[51]

The key question is what happens to this Jewish support when these parties take hostile positions towards Israel? In 2002, the NSW state leader of the Australian Democrats, Dr Arthur Chesterfield-Evans, cited American policy towards Israel as the cause for the "9/11" attacks on the World Trade Centre[52], and Jewish organizations condemned the Democrats when their foreign affairs spokesperson, Senator Vicki Bourne, called on Prime Minister Howard to take a harder line against "Israeli aggression in Palestine".[53] However, the primacy of these issues for the Jewish voter would depend on the political context. In 2001, Israel may have been paramount, but in 1998 it was the showdown in the Senate between the xenophobic One Nation party and the Australian Democrats. Jewish voters also consider the particular party candidate. For example, in NSW, federal Australian Democrats Senator Aden Ridgeway – the Australian Parliament's only sitting Aboriginal member – is considered a good friend of the Jewish community.[54]

How changing Jewish priorities over Israel affect their party involvement and support may be seen in relation to the Greens. In 2002, for example, after two years of the Al Aqsa Intifada, the NSW Greens State Delegates Council passed a one sided resolution on the Israeli–Palestinian conflict that included a proposal for suspending diplomatic relations with Israel. In response, three Jews resigned from the party, including former Greens candidate Arthur Hurwitz. This followed a resignation from the Greens earlier in the year of Hurwitz's campaign manager and Randwick-Botany representative to the Council, Robert Berman. Berman became "very disillusioned by the anti-Israel feelings". He explained, "I realized they would never come out in support of Israel. It was a big sticking point for me". Similar concerns were expressed by Randwick-Botany Green and NSW Jewish Board of Deputies member, Irving Wallach. These examples suggest that some Jews are prepared to dump the party that they consider best represents their domestic political concerns out of loyalty to Israel.[55]

The Hurwitz and Berman episodes were followed in 2003 with the Greens proposing a Senate motion to establish a Palestinian state.[56] Extrapolating from these cases, it can be expected that many Jews who voted for the Greens because of the refugee issue in 2001 will not vote for them at the next general election because of their negative attitudes towards Israel.

The impact of the Jewish vote is limited by the smallness of the Jewish population and its concentration in just a few electorates. Indeed, given that Wentworth is a safe Liberal seat, it is really only in Melbourne Ports where the Jewish vote could decide the seat's outcome. As the West Australian Jewish community grows, this could also conceivably occur in the marginal seat of Stirling, which presently has 1,832 Jews or 1.5 percent of the constituency total.

However, it is also true that Jews' influence in Australian politics extends well beyond the ballot box. Jewish political involvement includes:

- *Involvement in political parties:* For example, 30 percent of the Vaucluse Liberal party branch and 50 percent of the executive are reputed to be Jewish.[57]
- *Financial donations to political parties:* For example, in 2001, Jewish communal identity Frank Lowy gave $300,000 each to the Labor and Liberal parties, Richard Pratt gave $218,000 to the coalition and $125,000 to Labor, and Harry Triguboff gave $278,000 to the coalition and $107,000 to Labor. The donations of these individuals arguably carry more weight than the votes of many thousands of Jews.[58]
- *Moral authority:* At a 1997 anti-One Nation rally, NSW MP Franca Arena singled out the "large number of Jewish people present" and said "If there is one group that understands the dangers of Pauline Hanson, it's the Jewish community. They have seen the rise of Nazism in Europe and elsewhere, and we don't want to see neo-Nazism in Australia".[59]
- *Sector-based political activism:* Politics is not limited to political parties and Jews have been politically active for Israel in a range of other forums. For example Jewish teachers were active in the NSW Teachers Federation in relation to an anti-Israel motion,[60] with the Eastern Suburbs Teachers Association calling on the NSW Teachers Federation to withdraw its critical resolution on Israel.[61] Similarly, Jewish academics established a counter petition to one by academics boycotting Israel.[62]
- *Media:* Given that politicians and the wider community form their view of Israel from media coverage, lobbying work in this area is a crucial aspect of political work that affects the standing of Israel.
- *Local activism and good leadership:* One of Israel's greatest federal parliamentary friends is Chris Pyne from the Adelaide seat of Sturt. Jews constitute only 0.002696 percent of his constituency, but strategic leadership and activism by the local Jewish community have con-

tributed to developing and consolidating Pyne's position as a great friend of Israel, manifest in his position as Chairman of the Parliamentary Friends of Israel.

Conclusion

Jewish voting has evolved over the twentieth century and is likely to continue to change in the twenty-first. "Israel" will remain an important factor in the way Jews vote in countries such as Australia, but the extent of its importance will depend on three main factors. First, the question of whether Israel is at war or peace. If it is the former, Diaspora Jews will feel an onus to stand by it and prioritize their actions accordingly, whereas if it is the latter, they will have the latitude to focus on local and general concerns. Second, the "Israel" factor on Jewish voters will obviously depend on the strength of the connection between future generations of Australian Jews and Israel. If the trend from overseas is repeated here, then this connection will weaken.[63] Third, and concomitantly, as Jews become more integrated into Australian society, and assimilated to the extent that they opt out of Judaism, they will vote more according to their general political concerns. Those who are concerned about maintaining a strong local Jewish vote for Israel must address all these factors.

Notes

The author is grateful to an anonymous referee for their suggestions and to the editors for their substantial editorial assistance.

1   W. D. Rubinstein, *The Jews in Australia: A Thematic History – Volume Two, 1945 to the Present* (Melbourne: Heinemann, 1991), p. 69.

2   See, for example, the history of the anti-Zionist American Council for Judaism in Thomas Kolsky, *Jews Against Zionism: The American Council for Judaism, 1942–48* (Philadelphia: Temple University Press, 1990).

3   www.join.org.au/community.htm accessed 30 September 2003.

4   Danny Ben-Moshe, "Intergenerational Australian Jewish Attitudes to Israel", A Research Report for the United Israel Appeal Victoria (forthcoming).

5   *Australian Jewish News* [henceforth *AJN*] 30 January 2004. All references to the *AJN* are to the Melbourne edition unless otherwise indicated.

6   The implication of the declining Jewish day-school enrolment because of high fees is not something that the community appears to have considered.

7   Maya Zerman, Australian Zionist Youth Council President, interview with author, 10 December 2003.

8   Beverley Rosenberg, Jewish scout coordinator, author correspondence with Danny Ben-Moshe, 25 December 2003.

9   Chana Kopel, Skif leader, interview with author, 10 December 2003.

10   It must be noted, however, that many Jewish students do not affiliate with AUJS.

11   Suzanne D. Rutland, *Edge of the Diaspora: Two Centuries of Jewish Settlement in Australia*, 2nd edn (Sydney: Brandl and Schlesinger, 1997), p. 295.

12   Rubinstein, *The Jews in Australia*, p. 523.

13   Information provided to author by *Australian Jewish News*.

14   Dan Goldberg, correspondence with author, 23 December 2003.

15   Vic Alhadeff, correspondence with author, 18 December 2003.

16   William Rubinstein, *Attitudes of Australian Jewish Tertiary Students to Their Jewish Identity*, Research Report No.4 (Australian Institute of Jewish Affairs, 1991), p. 11. The attitudes of current twenty somethings to Israel is being conducted by the author as part of his intergenerational study of Jewish attitudes to Israel.

17   The implications of this for communal planning are not seriously addressed with any urgency.

18   Investing in domestic causes can also be pro-Israel, such as Zionist education. Research also shows that the more strongly people identify as Jews, the more strongly they identify with Israel. Data on organizational income and appeal targets were provided by JCA, UIA and UIA (NSW), but they did not all want this information disclosed.

19   Goldlust, *The Jews of Melbourne*, p. 158.

20   Bernard Rechter, *Jewish Leadership Survey* (Australian Institute of Jewish Affairs, 1996).

21   *AJN*, 31 October 2003.

22   According to Rutland by 1987 over 700 Australians had settled in Israel, the highest per capita rate in the Western world, *Edge of the Diaspora*, p. 322.

23   Rechter, *Jewish Leadership Survey*.

24   *AJN*, 15 August 2003.

25   *AJN*, 19 April 2002.

26   *AJN*, 5 September 2003.

27   Goldlust, *The Jews of Melbourne*, p. 155.

28   Rubinstein, *The Jews in Australia*, p. 545.

29   W. S. Logan, "Australian Government Middle East Policy and the Domestic Jewish Vote: An Exercise in Electoral Geography", *Australian Journal of Politics and History*, 28, 2 (1982): 209–17.

30   *AJN* Sydney edn, 29 Nov 1996.

31   *AJN* Sydney edn, 18 June 1999.

32   Rechter, *Jewish Leadership Survey*.

33   *AJN*, 25 September 1998.

34   *AJN* Sydney edn, 19 October 2001.

35   *AJN* Sydney edn, 9 November 2001.

36   *AJN*, 26 June 1998.

37   *AJN* Sydney edn, 2 November 2001.

38   See Rechter, *Jewish Leadership Survey*, and the *AJN*, 15 August 2003.

39   *AJN*, 17 May 2002, p. 8.

40   *AJN*, 20 June 2003.

41   B'nai B'rith Anti-Defamation Commission *Special Report* No. 13, June 2003.

42   *AJN*, 5 September 2003.

43   *AJN*, 19 December 2003.

44 *AJN*, 13 February 2004.

45 *AJN*, 5 December 2003.

46 *AJN* Sydney edn, 9 November 2001.

47 *AJN* Sydney edn, 9 November 2001.

48 *AJN* Sydney edn, 9 November 2001.

49 Joe Berinson, interview with author, 20 December 2003.

50 *AJN*, 23 June 2000.

51 *AJN*, 26 October 2001.

52 *AJN*, 24 May 2002.

53 *AJN*, 26 April 2002.

54 See, for example, Senator Ridgeway's speech joining the Senate motion condemning anti-Semitism, 22 March 2004: http://parlinfoweb.aph.gov.au/piweb/view_document.aspx?ID=953833&TABLE=HANSARDS

55 *AJN*, 3 May 2002.

56 *AJN*, 4 April 2003.

57 *AJN*, Sydney edn, 20 September 1996.

58 *AJN* Sydney edn, 16 November 2001,

59 *AJN*, 23 May 1997.

60 *AJN* Sydney edn, 2 November 2001.

61 *AJN* Sydney edn, 23 November 2001.

62 *AJN*, 31 May 2002.

63 See for example Barry Kosmin, Antony Lerman, and Jacqueline Goldberg, *The Attachment of British Jews to Israel* (London: Institute of Jewish Policy Research Report No. 5, 1997).

Issues and
Controversies

9 | Mending the World from the Margins: Jewish Women and Australian Feminism

BARBARA BLOCH AND EVA COX

This chapter seeks to explore some connections between feminist activism and Jewish identity in Australia. In the space available, we have focused mainly on the generations of women who became politically active before and during the 1970s, eighties and to a lesser extent, the nineties. This activity became clearly identified with a political/social movement, also known as "second wave feminism" or "the women's movement".

The history of feminism abounds with Jewish women, from Rosa Luxemburg and Emma Goldman through Betty Friedan, Shulamith Firestone, Gloria Steinem, Robin Morgan, Letty Cottin Pogrebin, Andrea Dworkin, Susan Faludi and Naomi Wolf, most of whom have been particularly visible in American feminism. Philip Mendes notes that compared to America and Britain, there has been little research conducted on Australian Jewish involvement in "newer social movements" such as the women's movement, gay rights, the environment and so on. Our aim is not to define a "distinctive Jewish contribution"[1] to second wave feminism through recounting the activities of individual women. Rather, it is to provide some insights into the connections (if any) that can be made between Australian Jewish feminists' sense of their Jewish heritage, and their motivations for feminist action. Our investigations are *not* prompted by a desire to demonstrate that there is, within Judaism, a belief system more inherently predisposed to the notion of fixing the world, than those from other faiths and cultures. However, we do want to explore the kinds of explicit and implicit lessons that many feminist Jewish women from both religious and secular families have learnt.

In this chapter, our focus is on those women involved in broader feminist politics, the women's movement, rather than those who have directed their feminism to working within the Jewish community. To do so we have drawn on our own experiences as activists, some limited written material and a small e-mail survey using the snowballing method, to elicit thoughts and ideas on the connections between Judaism, feminism and activism. As far as we know, no other survey of this type exists as Jewish studies appear to mirror many others in not paying enough attention to women, and feminist studies tend to overlook the relation between Jews and feminism. We have focused on those women whose activities are conventionally described as political (for example, orientated to changing social institutions) and feminist.

Our definition of Jewish-ness is deliberately broad and inclusive. It is based on self-identification. We sent out seventy-five e-mails to individuals we knew were Jewish and to e-mail networks and lists to start the process, and others subsequently contacted us defining themselves within our category. We received forty-four responses from women around Australia. There has been a wealth of interesting responses, exceeding our capacity to fully utilize them in this chapter. Our respondents' ages ranged from one woman born in 1919 to a few born in the 1960s and 1970s, with an almost equal divide between those born before 1946 and those after. Birthplaces were spread around the world, although almost all women came from Ashkenazi backgrounds, and religious commitments were very diverse. Not surprisingly, perhaps, many women identified, either in their upbringings and/or in their practices as adults, as "culturally Jewish" and "secular". Interestingly, the diversity in ages, birthplaces, and religious involvement among those who responded was not clearly reflected in their responses, nor were there clear differences between the first and the second/third generations. Age, for example, did not seem to make much difference except for some variation in preferred structures and issues. Place of birth and upbringing were very varied and yet the responses were similar, or at least not obviously different in these regards.

Most respondents saw themselves as "outsiders" and few seemed to belong to any particular part of the feminist movement. Many of the responses were from women who identified with the traditions within Judaism that focus on the notion of *Tikkun Olam*, healing the world. Our reading of these data is not to essentialize the relationship of change agent and Judaism, but to explore our histories and present experiences with a view to seeing what may contribute to a significant minority of us becoming political activists, whereas others have made different choices.

Feminist Footprints

This section very briefly acknowledges early Jewish activism for, as Marlo Newton states in her history of the National Council of Jewish Women (NCJW) of Australia, "[t]he 1970s women's movement did not invent feminism".[2] A cursory glance over twentieth-century Australian history reveals the interrelationship between women's activities within the Jewish community, focused on fellow Jews, and those oriented towards the betterment and welfare of women's lives more generally.[3]

Most Australian Jewish histories make mention of individual women who have made contributions to the community, although none of the general histories utilize the terms "feminist" or "feminism". According to Suzanne Rutland, Jewish women were not particularly involved in the suffragist movement, "and no individual Jewish woman stands out".[4] Rutland suggests this was partly due to Australian Jewry's conservatism at that time, the end of the nineteenth century, and partly because of the suffragist movement's close connections with the Women's Christian Temperance Union.[5] However this analysis ignores possible Jewish influences on Vida Goldstein and Dora Montefiore because they were not defined as formally Jewish.

It was during the interwar years that the (to this day) most significant Australian Jewish women's organizations were formed, namely the National Council of Jewish Women (NCJW) and the Women's International Zionist Organization (WIZO). The NCJW was formed in Sydney in 1923 by the renowned Dr Fanny Reading. The original aims of the organization were partly religious,[6] partly to act as a philanthropic organization for the needs of Jewish and non-Jewish women, and in part social.[7] WIZO, the other major Jewish women's organization in Australia, had, by 1939, formed branches in all mainland Australian states.[8] The Australian Jewish feminist, Ruby Rich-Schalit, became its first federal president. Rutland argues that "Jewish women played a key role in changing the status of Zionism in Australia".[9] Hyams acknowledges that not only had WIZO become, by the mid-twentieth century, "the closest in Australia to being a mass Jewish organization",[10] it had also become a vehicle for Jewish women to emerge as "strong and forceful community leaders".[11] WIZO became a communal forum for women to be active "outside the entrenched, patriarchal Anglo-Jewish establishment".[12]

By the early 1970s and the emergence of "second wave feminism" in Australia and other Western countries, Newton reports on the "central conflict" for Jewish women concerning feminism. Judaism's fundamental focus on the family did not rest easily with feminism's emphasis on the patriarchal nuclear family as being one key source of women's oppression.[13] She states that the NCJW "pursued a form of feminism which stressed the importance of women achieving within the context of the family and communal life . . . while opposing radical challenges to Judaism or the structure of the Jewish community".[14] Rutland makes a similar point and also states that she did not find much evidence that Jewish women played key roles in the post-1970s feminist movement.[15] However, both our experience and that of some well-known activists who answered the questionnaire suggest that there were substantial contributions by many Jewish women to the feminist movement of the seventies. As the Australian movement was less focussed on individual tall poppies, this was often not visible.

Women Repairing the World?

Indeed if *Tikkun Olam* – healing or repairing the world – is an assignment the Jews are supposed to take seriously, Jewish feminists add to the repair kit not just the tools of Jewish ethics but the equity blueprints of feminism. We start with Judaism's core mandate to do *tsedakah* – the Hebrew word meaning charity, caring and the "right action" whose linguistic root means justice – and we apply that mandate to gender.[16]

> *Tsedakah* . . . the sacred obligation of every Jew to make the world a better place by ensuring justice for all.[17]

Is there something about Jewish-ness that triggers political activist, dissident and feminist involvement? This raises questions of whether one should expect to be able to find a singular explanation for the minority of identifying Jews who involve themselves in very diverse forms of political activism in a range of different settings over an extended time frame. It would seem more appropriate to look for commonalities of experiences which may have predisposed some to make decisions to become activists but left others responding in different ways.

In much of the literature, "feminist" is subsumed under the general categories of "leftist", "Jewish", or "radical". Stephen Whitfield rightly observes that "it is much easier to tabulate the impact of the Jews on radical movements and ideas *than to account for such influence*".[18] Whitfield identifies four discrete theories, whilst acknowledging "none has the compass or ingenuity to compel unmodulated assent".[19] They include *Tikkun Olam*, a sense of justice; the "sting of bigotry" through experiences of anti-Semitism; a rejection by conservative forces that pushed post-emancipation Jews to the left; and influences of the family. He offers another possibility – the Jewish intellectual traditions of questioning. He does not canvass the possibility that all of these plus more might be part of a shared history and "community" culture. So we have explored Hannah Arendt's concept of the "conscious pariah" as a basis for understanding our own and respondents' standpoints as an alternative model.

Whitfield is not alone in suggesting that certain Jewish traditions have played a role in directing some Jews towards seeking to act for a better, more just world. Pogrebin suggests that a commitment to feminism only adds to the Jewish concept of *tsedakah*, as described above.[20] And Newton, in her account of the history of the NCJW notes that one of the aims of the newly formed organization was concerned with "both Jewish and non-Jewish philanthropic work . . . This charge, to heal the world, is evident in every charitable endeavour undertaken by the Council of Jewish Women".[21] Six decades on, an American Jewish feminist, Sylvia Barack Fishman, explores the synergies and contradictions between feminism and Judaism. She also claims that many Jewish feminists have been "animated" by a "utopian agenda, a commitment to *tikkun olam*, repairing the world".[22]

Most of our respondents came from Ashkenazi backgrounds, were brought up within a religious framework, and were far more likely to be Reform than Orthodox. In terms of family backgrounds, about half stated (from options we provided) that their identification with Judaism was "family/cultural/not really religious at any time". As one respondent expressed it: "I am not observant but have a very strong Jewish identity". Such responses raise the interesting issue of what it means to be a secular Jew. Another respondent explained:

> I came from a secular lefty family, where questioning was encouraged. There was to a certain extent room for me to be myself. Being Jewish and of a non-dominant religion/culture/ethnicity gave me a picture of the world that set me up for activism. I must say I was also a daughter of the times being a teenager and young adult in the '70s.

Paul Mendes-Flohr points out that modernity brought with it for Jews the construction of a Jewish identity "without a belief in God; indeed much of modern Jewish thought has been devoted to devising strategies to foster a Jewish identity simply as membership in the Jewish people and a *Schicksalgemeinschaft* [a community of a shared fate] the latter of which may include a secular affiliation such as Zionism, Bundism, Diaspora Nationalism".[23]

Katya Gibel Azoulay, who explores interracial (Jewish and black) identity, suggests that radical Jewish activists in the decade from the mid-1960s to the mid-1970s in America "advocated and represented the Jewish commitment to social justice *without* necessarily an adherence or allegiance to religious expression".[24] The question of what it means to "have" a secular Jewish identity has been, as Azoulay puts it, "an intractable existential and intellectual problem since the Emancipation", and is one that cannot be fully pursued in this chapter.[25] As will be seen, many of our feminist respondents grappled with this issue in rejecting formal involvement in a Jewish community, directing their energies elsewhere, yet often having a strong sense of what it means to them "to be Jewish".

We are not suggesting a connection here that is unique to Judaism or Jews[26] and share Hannah Arendt's concern with what she has termed "Jewish chauvinism . . . From now on, the old religious concept of chosenness was no longer the essence of *Judaism*; it became instead the essence of *Jewishness*".[27] Arendt was referring to a secular Jewish intelligentsia of nineteenth-century Western Europe. Yet, as this section has briefly demonstrated, in exploring our theme, we need to be vigilant as Jewish women and as feminists that our legacy does not produce what one might call an uncritical cultural memory. Instead, we need "to give salience to

[our] Jewish identity [and where that leads us] without forfeiting a dedicated membership in other communities of identity".[28] As one of our respondents puts it:

> It's not that there is or isn't a concordance or affinity of the precepts and practices of Judaism with feminism – this can and has been argued either way . . . [To] put it broadly, it's in the context of being Jewish in an anti–Semitic culture and of being female in a patriarchal culture, that these identities are produced and lived and gain their particular meanings.

Turning to Arendt's analysis and her theories of political action may offer some useful categories to consider for analysing the women in this study. In her study of Jews living in German society, Arendt drew on Bernard Lazare's concept of the pariah by distinguishing between three models of action/inaction: the "conscious pariah" "who rebel[ed] and transform[ed] the outcast status thrust upon the Jew into a challenge to fight for one's rights";[29] the "social pariah" who recognized their outsider status but clung to the group and stayed within its conformity demands; and the "parvenu" who sought to assimilate in order to be acceptable to the dominant group.

Arendt saw the parvenu as what one might call "selling out" insofar as they abrogate their power to think for themselves and act politically by allowing the dominant group to define what they should do. Her later work developed this further with her emphasis on independence of mind, which took her through the unthinking banality of evil to the concept of thinking as dialogue with self in *Life of the Mind* (1977–8). She saw as core to some form of political action a rejection of compliance. Melissa Orlie states that the conscious pariah politicizes what she appears to be and thereby creates a space of freedom where she can reveal who she is (and can act/think?), creating a self by flouting the rules.[30] While this is the early Arendt, the basic concept of the conscious pariah can be seen in her later definitions of political action in *The Human Condition* (1958) and her ongoing interest in thinking and judging that she developed further after *Eichmann in Jerusalem* (1964). The responses from the questionnaires, as we will see, show many of the characteristics that Arendt valued in her politically active conscious pariahs. Even her expressed doubts about feminism *qua* movement should not be assumed to extend to criticisms of outsider activism as described below. Her problem was with the "homogenizing effect of an identity-based politics".[31]

Second Wave Feminism in Australia

The 1960s is now the legendary decade of activism, with many young people involved in the anti-war movements, human rights (particularly indigenous rights in Australia) and a more general youth-quake of rebellion against what many saw as the dull post-war period of conservatism. Australia was moving in the wake of many overseas movements, picking up on anti-Vietnam movements from the USA as well as freedom rides in support of indigenous rights, the counter culture and other political activities. While there were many women involved, the general leadership was male and much of the radical activity was spelt out in terms of individual liberation but with little awareness that such campaigns were deeply gendered.

The second wave feminist movement took off in the USA early in the sixties, with Friedan's *The Feminine Mystique* signalling a broadly popular political movement which looked at everyday lives and not only the more abstracted issues of left-wing politics.[32] Australia was later starting and was influenced by the USA and UK movements. Many women became politicized by the anti-war and counter-culture movements and began to become active on what could now be defined as "their" issues. Areas such as abortion rights and contraception were not on the wider political agenda at that time, and many women wanted to put them there.

Australia had been a very male oriented country, a settler society, once described as "the working man's welfare state".[33] Women were paid less than men, abortions were illegal, contraception hard to get, childcare nonexistent and female workforce and education participation rates well below male ones. We had acquired the vote fairly early, in 1902, except for indigenous women, but had made little use of it. The early suffragist movement seemed to dissipate after World War I, with some exceptions such as Jessie Street and early Jewish activists like Fanny Reading and Ruby Rich. These continued the battles on contraception and equal pay amongst other political issues. Generally, by the end of World War II, married women were back in their homes to free the jobs for men, and expected to breed the next generation. Inequality was deeply entrenched and sanctioned in ways which did not reflect the American experience of constitutionally protected individual rights. One of the major differences was that we saw government as both the discriminator – for example, in setting wages and making laws – and the perceived source of possible moves to greater equality through legislative reform.

Australian women were more than ready to take on the new feminism, when it emerged in the late 1960s. Some of these women had come from other left movements, others were attracted to feminism but had not been part of other political movements. A chronology, compiled by the feminist journal *Refractory Girl* in the 1990s, gives December 1969 as the first meeting of Sydney Women's Liberation.[34] The big issue for the next year in New South Wales, at least, was abortion, then illegal in most cases. The end of 23 years of Conservative rule nationally was obviously coming and political change was on the agenda. In 1972 the Women's Electoral Lobby was formed. The WEL website describes the next few years:

The period between 1972 and 1975 was one of rapid and major change in Australia, with the election of the Whitlam government. Elizabeth Reid was appointed as the assistant to the Prime Minister on Women's Issues in 1973. There was also a Women's Affairs section introduced in the Department of Prime Minister and Cabinet. The government contributed money to the United Nations International Women's Year, 1975. This funding went towards rape crisis and health centres. There were also a number of conferences looking at women's issues. The government also contributed funding to support non-profit childcare centres.

Other significant gains at this time included equal pay for women which had been a long-term problem as the concept of a family wage for the male breadwinner, introduced in 1908, had meant women working alongside males were paid much less for the same jobs. However, this was a limited legalistic entitlement that still left women earning much less than men because of the gender segregated workforce, and much more was done and remains to be done to value jobs where women predominate. While many outsiders claim that there is no need for continued feminist actions now, this was not a view held then by much of the media and political institutions, or, as shown below, by many continuing activists now.

There were many obvious reasons for Australian women to be ready to take on political activism to promote greater recognition of the issues important to us. We asked respondents what their first feminist involvement was. Most became involved in the 1970s, with most being attracted to groups like WEL and Women's Liberation, as well as campus women's groups. Those who identified specific issues named setting up refuges, contraception and health issues. A number also mentioned equal pay, working conditions and sexuality as key concerns. Some of the women who responded were well-known leaders and activists, others were equally involved but are not recorded elsewhere; many in both categories named themselves as early joiners and/or initiators. There is no doubt that they and other Jewish women were highly significant in almost all areas of the movement.

We asked what their current involvements were. Only a few have disconnected politically; many were still involved in some forms of general activism, and said they carried their feminism into these areas. Many were still actively involved in feminism, quite a few through the paid work they do, which was probably understated as someone was worried it didn't count because it was not voluntary! More generally, involvement was issue-based rather than organization-based and quite diverse, echoing the general state of activism today, for example, in gay and lesbian areas, in peace groups, in environmental issues and regarding asylum seekers. One younger woman active in the 1990s to the present showed a different attitude towards feminism. For example:

> Not sure that I can identify any specific feminist activism as I've always taken feminism for granted given the way I was brought up. I've never really felt the need to get involved with a specifically feminist activist group.

What emerged from the responses to these and related questions on their political and social involvement was repeated mention of involvement with groups that were suffering injustice. A few women made explicit connections between anti-Semitism and their awareness of questions of Palestinian oppression. There were quite a few involved in indigenous issues, in anti-racism, in general peace and refugee issues, local community politics and other broad political involvement which seemed to resonate with some of their responses on how they saw Jewish influences activating their political sense.

It is interesting to note the differences between Australian feminism and the American version. One Jewish immigrant, now returned to the USA, Hester Eisenstein, arrived in 1980 and compared the two in a 1991 set of essays. She commented in the second chapter, "Learning to speak Australian", on how feminism here was unfamiliar because of both different political and ideological elements. She noted both the cultural cringe that made us very aware of both European/British feminism and the USA version and our interest in moving into "public positions of influence" in the bureaucracy and political structures. She commented also on the pragmatic approaches by which we worked out tactics, which she ascribed to the Irish Catholic childhoods of many local feminists. She saw these as experiencing difference from the majority, which made them more likely to be prepared to plot and to strategize forward planning. It is interesting that an outsider to Australia saw that these mostly then ex-Catholics showed some residual effects from the sectarianism of the dominant Protestants which made them partial outsiders and fuelled their involvement in change politics as well.[35]

These differences partly explain why this chapter is not a record of Jewish-identified feminist activists. As Eisenstein has suggested, Australian feminists have had a stronger collective sense of our history, which has avoided too much emphasis on tall poppies. In practical terms, there are also problems. Many feminist activists have not identified themselves as Jewish in circles where it is not seen as relevant. Additionally, there are problems defining what is feminist activism. For the purposes of the discussion here, it is not necessary to distinguish between those women who have been identified as "leaders" and the many lesser-known women activists. We have been surprised at how many women have identified themselves in response to our limited search and the numbers confirm that there are many who have been involved, compared with the tiny proportion of Jews in the Australian population (0.44 percent at the 2001 Australian Census[36]).

Jewish Feminists in Australia – Conscious Pariahs?

While the material we have collected from our small questionnaire does not offer the possibility of statistical analysis, it does offer a rich array of points of view of self-defined Jewish-connected feminists. The responses given to two questions about connections between their Jewish experiences and feminism and other activism brought out all of the aforementioned "theories" noted by Whitfield and more. Family influences, family histories, personal experiences of being an outsider, an early encouragement to question, passions for justice which related to what they saw as Jewish teaching, and the contrast between those teachings and religious and other cultural practices on gender issues were all raised as explanations by respondents.

Our data suggest that being an outsider in all its varied possibilities was obviously a strong motive for wanting to make changes. These were not only defined as changes that benefited the respondents themselves and others like them, but also involved a commitment to justice for others that were also outsiders. One possible explanatory model that seemed to fit these women, and which also might be used to explain why many women with similar experiences were not moved to be change agents, is Arendt's typology of pariahs, as outlined above. It is the first of these types, the conscious pariah, which fits most of the women in our survey. Many expressed their sense of being outsiders both in feminism and in the Jewish community, of their long-time commitment to being change agents and to speaking out against any forms of injustice, particularly on gender issues. Some claimed long-term, so far back as to be not remembered, awareness of gender issues, others told of later awareness, but many were aware that becoming feminists set themselves in conflict with more conservative views of the family and women in some forms of Judaism.

We make no comment on the other forms of pariah-dom – the social pariah and the parvenu – but wanted to mention them here as ways of possibly explaining why so many other Jewish women, whose experiences mirror the ones in this survey, preferred to stay within the community mores or try for acceptance on the terms of the wider society.

Most respondents felt that there was a possible link between being Jewish and a feminist with about half giving an unqualified "yes" and a third saying "maybe" and all giving reasons. There were a few "don't know" and "no" responses, often from older, left-wing feminists who had been involved with the Communist Party and moved away from religion and its influence with fervour. Asked what they thought the links might be, open-ended multiple responses were coded to produce the following three main categories:

- Jewish traditions/*tikkun olam*/equity/social justice/ask questions;
- Traditional patriarchal Judaism, gender inequalities but strong women;
- Anti-Semitism/outsiders/holocaust.

These responses relate to Whitfield's explanatory categories. This suggests that these experiences/perceptions are interlinked in ways that cannot be as easily separated as the above coding suggests. To a later question on Judaism and political activism in general, a similar range of responses emerged. Even though this question included some suggested influences, making it a more prompted response, responses often echoed the points raised by the first question and were expressed in some detail, suggesting strong feelings rather than just prompted replies. The multiple responses were as follows:

Holocaust/anti-Semitism
Being Other/outsider/refugee
Jewish Sexism
Tikkun Olam/social justice/family politically active

Other frequently expressed political concerns included:

Jewish racism/Palestine
Feminist anti-Semitism
Sexuality

The verbatim quotes from our respondents below illustrate the range of responses to both questions on the origins of, and influences on, their feminist and political involvements:

High consciousness of group vs. more individual issues.

The experience of being other, the holocaust, directly experiencing anti-Semitism, patriarchal behaviour that disadvantaged me, the racism I witnessed being practised by Jews.

The *tikkun olam* tradition persists even when formal religion is no longer a significant factor. And my grandmother's story which became my mother's story, was one of gender discrimination, supported by orthodox Jewish law and culture. Antisemitism made me conscious of all discrimination.

Looking back still further, the Jewish concept of *tsedeka*, of righteousness or justice, has been a strong influence on Jewish thought and action through the centuries and it would not be too surprising, therefore, that women embraced by this tradition would see the contradictions between the justice sought for others and our subordinate position.

Pesach [Passover] as a political story about anti-slavery and freedom always appealed and Yom Kippur [Day of Atonement] as self-evaluation and reflection about a moral role in the world – the personal is political.

I think there is something about being raised Jewish in a Christian world that makes you feel like an outsider/other. One sort of otherness is obviously the basis for understanding other sorts: like the place of women in a man's world.

From a sociological perspective, the most important link has to be pariah status (I used to say that women are the Jews of gender). Jewish women get the double whammy, so to speak, being marginalized as women and as Jews.

Very briefly and broadly, being part of a minority culture with a history of perse-cution and survival against the odds made me sympathetic to other minority groups with a history of oppression, Aborigines, refugees. As a Jewish woman I feel obligated to fight against inequality and injustice (It is – or should be – in the genes?)

And later:

On my occasional visits to the synagogue, women's galleries and the rantings of conservative rabbis still make my blood boil. I once hissed a rabbi ranting against the ordination of women as Rabbis and found to my surprise that many other women in the women's gallery joined in.

Noticing the effects of oppression being from a culture and family that ques-tioned, and where there was room for me to think as a female. Being from a culture concerned with making things right (tikkun).

As I began forming my feminist views as a young woman I felt alienated from Judaism but I am now a believer and occasionally attend Shul [synagogue], I am lucky enough to have a woman Rabbi and go to a congregation where women are very much included.

Despite a lack of religious education I was brought up in an ethical Jewish frame-work and was made to understand that tolerance and respect were part of a Jewish worldview. (Parent politically active!)

However, one woman sounded a note of warning:

Being wronged and marginalized, whether one is a woman, or a Jew or a Palestinian or poor is not enough and does not make one more virtuous or morally superior. Bad faith can reside anywhere and everywhere.

Others raised concerns that this survey should not assume that what was said was specifically or solely due to Jewish traditions. That question needs to be considered in this analysis. Are there aspects of the Jewish-ness expe-rience that are "different" or do our experiences, as recorded above signal that there are possibilities of making radicals, as there are of making conformists and conservatives? Arendt's own model was intended to be wider than Jewish examples, although she used the Jewish experience to explore the more generalizable possibilities. Similarly, we suggest that it is the experiences, history and interpretations which create who we are and how we act. We are not passive products of these but choose within some limits to act or perhaps to accept the status quo, in Arendtian terms.

In this we are not unique. As mentioned above, the Australian women's movement also contains many Irish Catholics whose own history and experiences in those generations have created similar rebels. Exploring the website of a Muslim feminist, Irshad Manji, shows many similar viewpoints both from her and her correspondents, which confirm the idea that similar experiences create these types of radicalism.[37]As one of her readers says:

> Being raised Muslim myself (Pakistani parents) and later turning out lesbian (grown up in Sweden), I think people like us have a unique understanding of the worlds around us. I support you and wish you the best in your efforts" – Z.

Final Thoughts

The above quotes echo experiences and suggest that the intersection of some concept of justice as an obligation, experiences of being a "pariah", and some personal/social capacity for thinking and action may make the radical/activist. For women within patriarchal religions, there are many opportunities for this sense of "being created second" which brings an entry point to feminist activism. The concept of *Tikkun Olam*, the mending of the world, can be applied to much political activism, just as other religions may claim social justice/charity as their drivers. As in most religions, the texts and concepts are as often used to justify conservatism and traditionalism as radicalism. However, the particular combination of these plus the histories, experiences and perceptions suggest that there may be something specific to be said about Jewish activism.

One point to look at in conclusion is that for some of the women who responded, the role of outsider as feminist Jew or Jewish feminist may still carry discomfort as some feel an outsider within both these groups. These experiences of not being fully accepted, because of dissenting from some accepted views or failing to share some characteristics, reflect what Arendt sees as losing the freedom to think and comment. It is this rejection of "ideology" (in her terms) as the price of belonging within groups that makes the real conscious pariah.

This chapter suggests that being both female and Jewish often add up to a mix of experiences that push political buttons in those who have passions for justice. The Australian women's movement has benefited strongly from the activities of the many women with Jewish connections who have been part of it, and will undoubtedly continue to do so.

Notes

1 Philip Mendes, "From the Shtetl to the Monash Soviet: An Overview of the Historiography of Jewish Radicalism in Australia", *Australian Journal of Jewish Studies* 14 (2000): 54–77.

2 Marla Newton, *Making a Difference: A History of the National Council of Jewish Women of Australia* (Melbourne: Hybrid Publishers, 2000), p. 48.

3 There are a number of books and articles written by and about Jewish women in Australia. See Suzanne Rutland, "Perspectives from the Australian Jewish Community", *Lilith* 11 (2002): 87–101.

4 Rutland, "Perspectives from the Australian Jewish Community", p. 16.

5 *Ibid.*, p. 16.

6 This was significant since in the early part of the twentieth century, there was concern about increasing assimilation within Australian Jewry.

7 See Newton, *Making a Difference*, pp. 6–7.

8 Bernard Hyams, "Women in Early Australian Zionism", *Australian Jewish Historical Society Journal* 15, 3 (2000): p. 443.

9 Such as Dr Fanny Reading, Rieke Cohen, Ruby Rich-Schalit, Faye Schenk and Ida Bension (Wynn). See Suzanne Rutland, *Edge of the Diaspora*, 2nd edn (Sydney: Brandl and Schlesinger, 1997), p. 305.

10 Hyams, "Women in Early Australian Zionism", p. 448.

11 *Ibid.*

12 Rutland, *Edge of the Diaspora*, p. 305.

13 Newton, *Making a Difference*, p. 51.

14 *Ibid.*, p. 55. In contrast, Jewish women in North America have a proud history of issuing challenges to contemporary western Judaism, at least since the feminist movement of the early 1970s. There is a large literature on this subject. For a comprehensive bibliography and discussion of the controversies, see Judith Baskin, "Women in Contemporary Judaism", in Jacob Neusner and Alan J. Avery-Peck, eds, *The Blackwell Companion to Judaism* (Oxford: Blackwell Publishing, 2003), pp. 393–414.

15 Rutland, "Perspectives from the Australian Jewish Community", p. 15.

16 Letty Cottin Pogrebin, *Deborah, Golda and Me. Being Female and Jewish in America* (New York: Anchor Books, 1991), p. 236.

17 Newton, *Making a Difference*, p. 6.

18 Stephen J. Whitfield, "Famished for Justice. The Jew as Radical", in L. Sandy Maisel and Ira N. Forman, eds, *Jews in American Politics* (New York: Rowman and Littlefield, 2001), p. 233. Emphasis added.

19 *Ibid.*, p. 223.

20 Pogrebin, *Deborah, Golda and Me.*

21 Newton, *Making a Difference*, p. 6.

22 Sylvia Barack Fishman, *A Breath of Life: Feminism in the American Jewish Community* (Hanover: Brandeis University Press, 1995), p. 242.

23 Paul Mendes-Flohr, "Secular Forms of Jewishness", in Neusner and Avery-Peck, eds, *Blackwell Companion to Judaism*, p. 463.

24 Katya Azoulay, *Black, Jewish and Interracial. It's Not the Colour of Your Skin, but the Race of Your Kin and Other Myths of Identity* (Durham and London: Duke University Press, 1997), p. 60. Emphasis in original.

25 *Ibid.*, p. 134.

26 See, for example, the Encounter Program, "The Prophets Mantle", Radio

National, 15 February 2004, on how churches in Australia are grooming the next generation of Christian social activists.

27 Hannah Arendt, *The Origins of Totalitarianism* (New York: Harvest, 1966), p. 74. Emphasis added.

28 Mendes-Flohr, "Secular Forms of Judaism", p. 471.

29 Richard Bernstein, *Hannah Arendt and the Jewish Question* (Cambridge, MA: MIT Press, 1996), p. 16.

30 Melissa Orlie, "Forgiving Trespasses, Promising Futures", in Bonnie Honig, ed., *Feminist Interpretations of Hannah Arendt* (University Park: Pennsylvania State Press, 1995), p. 347.

31 Bonnie Honig, "Introduction: The Arendt Question in Feminism", in Honig, ed., *Feminist Interpretations of Hannah Arendt*, p. 7.

32 In a 1976 interview in the premier issue of the American feminist journal *Lilith*, Betty Friedan claimed that her passion for equality for women "was really a passion against injustice, which originated from my feelings of the injustice of anti-Semitism". Thanks to one of our respondents for pointing this out to us.

33 Lois Bryson, *Welfare and the State* (London: Macmillan, 1992), pp. 159–89.

34 n.a., *Refractory Girl and Women's Liberation* (Sydney: Refractory Girl Feminist Journal, 1993), pp. 12–16.

35 Hester Eisenstein, *Gender Shock: Practising Feminism in Two Countries* (Sydney: Allen and Unwin, 1991), pp. 11–12.

36 See *Australian Jewish News*, Sydney edn, 28 June 2002 for a breakdown of this figure.

37 http://www.muslim-refusenik.com.

10 | Jews and Aborigines

COLIN TATZ

Two small but significant minorities in Australia life – the Jews, a half percent of the population, generally envied for their seeming success; the Aborigines, at two percent, generally unenviable in their myriad problems. Appalling history is their connection, says Andrea Goldsmith, the Australian Jewish writer: "Expulsion, massacre, genocide, eternal scape-goats: Jews and black Australians are equally experienced".[1]

But metaphors and parallels don't necessarily make for ties between the two. We need to see whether there is a Jewish-Aboriginal association that merits the term "relationship"? If there is, can one locate a political, legal, economic, cultural, academic, or even a social connection worth reporting? Which Jews, what kind of Jews, have been involved, in a serious and substantial way, and over a reasonable measure of time, in the affairs of Aborigines and Islanders? With which of the many different Aboriginal societies have they been involved?

Since the record is, indeed, thin – and let me say, at the outset, that it has been anorexic – there must be some explanation, particularly when the Australian Jewish record is compared with Jewish participation in the American civil rights movement and in the anti-apartheid struggle in South Africa. Can this be explained simply by their markedly differing geogra-phies and demographies? In America and in South Africa, Jews and blacks are juxtaposed, interwoven, interconnected, while most Australian Jews have been able to live a lifetime without encountering an Aborigine or Islander in the flesh. Or is it more a matter of attitudes rather than prox-imity?

Decades of Empathy, Sympathy – and Despair

A characteristic of many Jewish communities is a need to be "expedien-tial", to ascertain just what is or isn't good for Jews and to act accordingly. Their very marginality, which makes for this kind of protective behaviour, in turn makes for an empathy with other marginalized peoples, as shown in some strong Jewish activism in the United States and South Africa. The record of "official" Australian Jewry, apart from a very small group of diverse individuals, shows a sustained expedience, a reluctance to get involved in contentious issues generally, let alone those affecting other marginalized peoples.

Early in the twentieth century there was great empathy and sympathy between Jews and Afro-Americans, and shared metaphors: Jews in bondage, blacks on plantations as slaves, the ghettoes, each group long-ing for their freedom, for liberation from discrimination, preferably in their own Zion. Julius Rosenthal, Emil Hirsch, Stephen Wise and, in par-ticular, Lilian Wald and Henry Moskowitz were present at the birth of the National Association for the Advancement of Colored People (NAACP) in 1909, joining W. E. B. du Bois in this significant enterprise. Jews were engaged in the National Urban League in 1910, the Anti-Defamation League of B'nai B'rith (ADL) in 1913, the founding of the National Conference of Christians and Jews in the mid-1920s, the Congress of Racial Equality (CORE) in 1942, the Leadership Conference on Civil Rights in 1950 and the Student Non-Violent Coordinating Committee (SNCC) in 1960. Jewish involvement in black affairs increased as the movement for civil rights strengthened. Jews have always been involved in ADL activity on behalf of black Americans, and even in today's poi-sonous race relations, the ADL persists with a "Blacks and Jews Conversation" program. Mutuality ended dramatically, and badly, in Crown Heights in 1991.

Several Jews were seriously injured in the Montgomery civil rights movement between 1954 and 1960 and two Jews were killed by the Ku Klux Klan in Mississippi in 1964. The involvement of Jewish students in so-called New Left (race) politics was remarkable.[2] From initial member-ship of Students for a Democratic Society (SDS), many Jewish students formed groups which expressed their own values, for example, Jews for Urban Justice, whereby the term "Radical Jew" became popular. About one-third of the students who went to Mississippi as civil rights workers in 1964 were Jews; in 1969, between one-third and one-half of 3,000 American campus radical activists were Jews. As Jews comprised some 5 percent of American students at that time, their over-representation was notable.

Why this extraordinary attention to the plight of black Americans? Percy Cohen argued that white supremacy policies and practices "aroused a moral sense of obligation which some of these students had acquired from their parents and/or their teachers; and it gave their search for a moral commitment a direction to follow".[3] There were contextual factors that influenced both Jewish and non-Jewish student involvement: the use of illegitimate violence against blacks in the southern states; guilt and sympathy arising from the conditions that led to black revolts in the north; the escalation of campus protests and the matter of free speech; increasing knowledge of the pervasive poverty in most of black America; the escalation of the war in Vietnam and the concomitant growth of the Peace Movement.[4]

The breakdown between Jews and Afro-Americans began in the 1960s. In 1965, author James Baldwin foresaw an emerging anti-Semitism from the Black Power movement in general, and it wasn't long before a serious anti-Semitism and an equally serious Jewish racism emerged.[5] Some of it was ideological and political; much of it was plain economics. For example, pre-World War II Jews had difficulty getting university appointments in cities like New York, so they became teachers, and rose to positions of school inspectors and superintendents (post-war). By then Afro-American teachers were in the system, only to find promotional paths filled by Jews, now seen as part of the oppressing class. And Black Islam turned out to be a form of Radical Islam, preaching all manner of dire treatments of Jews.

The final turning point, from which there hasn't been a return, was the Crown Heights murder, in 1991, of a Melbourne *yeshiva bocher*, Yankel Rosenbaum. A car in a Lubavitch motorcade accidentally knocked over two black children, killing one. A private Hassidic ambulance took the by now endangered driver away, an act that left local Afro-Americans furious at this seeming "racial" preference. A cry of "Get the Jew!" led to the stabbing of Yankel, the rabbinical student, who happened to be in the vicinity. With this murder and the ensuing three-day riot, Jewish-black relations disintegrated.

Freedom Fighters, Apostates and a Jewish Imperative

Following black government in 1994, many South African Jews, at home and abroad – in common with many of their fellow white South Africans – gave expression to the outrageous claim that they were either always opposed to apartheid or were closet freedom fighters. Even though Nelson Mandela "found Jews to be more broad-minded than most whites on issues of race, perhaps because they themselves have historically been victims of prejudice",[6] the majority of South African Jews went along with the apartheid system, prospered by it, voted for it, and condemned those of their sons and daughters who opposed it.

Prior to 1948, a handful of Jews, mostly Communist Party members, had opposed racial supremacy and the gross discrimination enforced in every sphere of life. Emil (Solly) Sachs, the trade unionist, and parliamentarians Hymie Basner and Sam Kahn were sharp voices long before post-war activism, before centuries-old apartheid was transformed into an official state ideology that brooked no deviation.

The Jewish Board of Deputies in Johannesburg was the last of the denominational institutions to condemn apartheid. Prominent Methodists attacked the system even before World War II. By the 1950s, individual Anglicans, like Father Trevor Huddelston and later, Bishop Ambrose Reeves, had become vociferous. Catholics, a small minority in South Africa and much discriminated against in the land of the Dutch Reformed Church (DRC), were articulate. Even senior figures in the DRC were charged with heresy for denying the biblical validity of apartheid, and great theologians like Dr Beyers Naude and Professor Albert Geyser, and the historian F. A. van Jaarsveld, were vilified, pilloried – tarred and feathered in the latter's case – before dismissal from their posts. It was not until the early 1990s that "organizational" Jews voiced an opinion on apartheid. (There were, perhaps, only six or seven critical rabbinical voices heard from pulpits until then; one, a Hungarian Reform rabbi, Dr André Ungar, was deported for his views.[7])

The "Treason Trial" began in the old Pretoria Synagogue in December 1956 with the indictment of 156 people. After many withdrawals of charges, the trial ended in March 1961 with the (unanimous) acquittal of the remaining 28 accused. Twenty-three whites were accused initially; fourteen were Jews. (Eight of the nine defence team were Jews.) The "Rivonia Trial" of 1964 led to the conviction of Denis Goldberg, the discharge of James Kantor, the acquittal of Rusty Bernstein, Bob Hepple giving evidence for the State, and to the dramatic escape from custody of Arthur Goldreich and Harold Wolpe before the trial.

Dozens of Jews had been involved in opposition to that nightmare world of "the South African way of life". A number had fought within the system, as members of parliament, jurists, journalists, unionists, medical practitioners, academics, rabbis. Others joined what came to be banned organizations, whether socialist or communist or simply groups of men and women who sought some form of social justice. Did they engage as Jews, or simply as South African communists, trade unionists, internationalists, liberals, as people with "a capacity for imaginative empathy with those most directly oppressed", or both? Even Nobel Laureate Nadine Gordimer, while denying that "Judaic values" influenced her writings, conceded that "as Jews, we must be sensitive to race".[8]

At the height of these political trials, the Jewish Board of Deputies and the editors of Jewish newspapers denounced those Jews as "not being representative" of the Jewish community, of not belonging. They were branded as apostates. People like Joe Slovo, Julius First, Ruth First, Baruch Hirson and Rowley Arenstein were seen as traitors to both a revered South

Africanism and to an ethical, upright Jewishness. The (outwardly) devout Jewish state prosecutor, Dr Percy Yutar, went after these "apostates" with as much zealotry as zeal.

Unsurprisingly, in the new "Rainbow Country", Jewish organizations, writers and journalists now proclaim the quintessential Jewishness of these traitors-turned-folk-heroes. In Immanuel Suttner's interviews with South African Jewish activists,[9] his book welcomes back "these worthy South Africans, socialists, communists or liberals", and yes, "these worthy Jews".

Different forces, factors and motivations led to such activism and such bravery. First, there was the gross, the blatant and the hypocritical in South African life, in Jewish South African life, that cried out for some change. Second, there was an obvious dissonance between Jewish ideals and Jewish behaviour. Third, there was the haunting feeling that Jews were only just white enough to enjoy legal, political, economic and occasionally, social privilege in that most anti-Semitic of societies. Fourth, there was an unconscious or subconscious realization that Jews never really belonged in that racial milieu.[10] Among historians of Jewish South Africa, only Milton Shain has been willing to state that obvious point, as evident from the titles of some of the chapters in his *The Roots of Antisemitism in South Africa* – "From Pariah to Parvenu", "Shirkers and Subversives" and, significantly, "Outsiders and Intruders".[11] Their whiteness was just barely salvation or redemption in that society, so suffused by hate.

In a real sense, those radicals were fighting as much for their Jewish survival, for some Jewish moral commitment, as for African, Indian and Cape Coloured liberation. Perhaps, for all their high profile and overt Jewishness, South African Jews *had* to prove points about themselves – in contrast to an Australian Jewry that was certainly less visible, much less "noisy", but more secure, more certain, about its place and future?

Gideon Shimoni's brilliant analysis of the Jews in apartheid South Africa concludes with this judgement:[12]

> Most detached and objective observers would agree: although there is nothing in this record deserving of moral pride, neither does it warrant utter self-reproach. From a coldly objective historical perspective, this was characteristic minority-group behaviour – a phenomenon of self-preservation, performed at the cost of moral righteousness.

In the new South Africa, paralleling the anti-Jewish sentiments of many Afro-Americans, there is now a rampant anti-Zionism/anti-Semitism from the African National Congress, some less than flattering comments from Nelson Mandela, and a variety of radical Islamic movements among the Cape Coloured people. Jews are portrayed as members of the oppressing class, a people of wealth and privilege, both there and in Israel.

The Jewish "Tradition" in Australia – Painters and Writers

The universality of experiencing one's own discrimination, and/or observing the suffering of others, has produced many Jewish activists, especially among intellectuals, in the United States and South Africa. Australian Jews are less moved by the black experience, and that is troublesome. Jews can be guilty of self-delusion and distorting reality. In 1992, Evan Zuesse contended that "Jews have *continually* been involved in efforts to understand and to aid in the Aboriginal struggle, far out of proportion to their overall numbers. Any significant Jewish presence at all in Aboriginal matters, of course, is already a disproportionate involvement, considering that Jews form only 0.5 percent of the total Australian population".[13] On Tuesday evening, 27 May 1997, thirteen Jewish leaders, mainly lawyers, met with six Aboriginal leaders during the Aboriginal Reconciliation Conference in Melbourne. All present wanted to foster continuing cooperation between the two communities. An ensuing press release declared that "the stolen generation was deprived of its precious gift of inheritance"; that not to accord the Stolen Children inquiry[14] serious consideration was "a blatant abrogation of moral responsibility"; that the "removal of children comes within the international legal definition of genocide"; and that the Jewish community "is concerned for the moral welfare of Australia". Several of the Jewish team talked about the *tradition* of Jewish concerns for Aboriginal Australians.[15]

Tradition implies a strong historical foundation. And linkage. We need to examine such claims against the realities, not to mount a case for or against Jews but to understand why their contribution to Aboriginal affairs has been so disproportionately *low*, especially from 1900 to the 1980s, when compared with Jews in the United States and South Africa.

One Jewish-Aboriginal connection dates back to the noted English writer on London Jewry, Israel Zangwill, who broke with Zionism in the 1920s and founded the Jewish Territorial Organization – to create a Jewish homeland, wherever possible, outside of Palestine (a place deemed too difficult and too bitter to contemplate). In the 1930s, the Melbourne philanthropist, Isaac Jacobs, espoused the Territorial cause, seeking approval for a *kibbutz* of 800 German and Austrian Jewish refugees in South Australia, an idea supported by the state premier but vetoed by the federal government. However, there was no consultation with, or discussion about, Aborigines. It was, after all, "their land" (the land they occupied) that was in question.

The London-based Freeland League, established in 1935, wanted to buy 7 million acres in the East Kimberleys, to support at least 50,000 Jews. Dr Itzhak Nahman Steinberg – the first People's Commissar for Justice after the Russian Revolution, but soon after a refugee from Lenin – arrived in Australia in 1936 to pursue this dream. The Kimberley scheme was well supported by the Australian Council of Trade Unions, the NSW Labour Council and the Perth unions. Churches offered support, as did the Western Australian premier. The *Canberra Times*, the *Age* and the *Sydney Morning Herald* opposed what the *Australian Worker* supported, namely, "a generous working class contribution toward the solution of the terrible refugee problem", a "haven for the victims of fascist ferocity".[16] Again, there was no concern for the lands occupied by Aborigines or for Aboriginal viewpoints – only the usual stereotyping and their diminution as a worthy people.

In 1933, another Jew arrived to promote a Jewish resettlement scheme in the Northern Territory. Melech Ravitch, renowned Yiddish poet, writer and critic, was the father of the artist Yosl Bergner. In 1937, JNL Kadimah published Melech's essay "Northern Territory Journey, 1933".[17] "The blacks in Australia cannot be regarded as the owners of the land", he wrote, because "they belong to the very lowest level of civilization". Amid much talk of wild, unmusical, frightening, opium-loving, and prostituting people, their future lay in being allotted "several thousand square miles of land" where they could be taught "to plough and sow, and thus the Aboriginal issue would be solved".

Yosl Bergner, born in Vienna but raised in Warsaw, came with his family to Melbourne as a 17-year-old in 1937. Melech had earlier brought photos of Aborigines from his Territory visit. To Yosl, "they looked exactly like Jews, dispossessed people". Yosl lived and worked in Melbourne, in textiles, at the markets, and in that Melbourne Depression he "saw Warsaw with its poverty". He befriended Judah Waten, the novelist and short story writer who had come to Perth from Odessa in 1914. "Everything I paint", said Yosl, "has an element of displacement".[18] Yosl and his artistic colleagues were intent not only on social realism but "with a concern for social injustice, with a fight for liberty and life against tyranny and reaction". And so he painted Aboriginal scenes against a background "with what I imagined was happening in Poland". His canvases carried titles such as "Village on Fire", "Looking Over the Ghetto Wall", "Fathers and Sons", the latter a portrait of depressed loneliness, of the Jewish/Aboriginal father who can't protect his sons.

Yosl joined the Australian Labour Company because, being an alien, he was ineligible for the regular army. He was stationed at Tocumwal, on the NSW-Victoria border of the River Murray. There he painted "Tocumwal Camp", and later, at the significant Anti-Fascist Art Exhibition in Melbourne in 1942, he presented poignant and powerful works titled "Aboriginal Man" and "Two Women". A later painting, "Aborigines" created a stir: it showed Aboriginal station workers, striking for higher wages, chained to a tree. It was based on a photograph he had seen of a Western Australian arrest (doubtless a reference to police harassment of the Pindan Group, the Pilbara Aborigines who went on strike for an adequate wage between 1946 and 1949). Another powerful image was "Aborigines are Coming to Town", town being Melbourne, a place out of bounds to most rural black people at that time. "Attitudes were very, very rough, unjust, you know", he said. At this point, he believed that he beheld two people of two very different cultures now unified; he kept comparing Polish ghetto Jews to the Aborigines he was seeing in country Victoria and New South Wales.

One vociferous critic of the Kimberley/Northern Territory proposal was A. P. Elkin, then professor of anthropology at Sydney University. He objected strongly to this potential Jewish presence, fearing its impact on Aboriginal life and culture. Curtin's Labor government vetoed the scheme in 1944.

Judah Waten, the indomitable communist, was a poet, novelist and short-story writer. His story collection, *Alien Son*, has become a classic in Australian literature.[19] Waten influenced Bergner on many issues, possibly on Aboriginal matters, but his stories are essentially the experiences of Jewish migrant families in Australia. "Black Girl" is his story of Lily Samuels (the choice of surname was no doubt deliberate) who lived in "a derelict place because they were unable to find accommodation in any other part of the city and because they were aborigines". It is a poignant and compelling story of black-white relationships, and of white sexual attitudes to "girls of colour".

Born in Hungary in 1915, David Martin was a successful and admired poet and novelist who came to Australia as late as 1949. For a while he lived in a bush town where his wife was the schoolteacher. His children's novel, *Hughie*, told the story of an Aboriginal boy in such a place. I have found only one poem on an Aboriginal theme, "Mission Station, North Queensland", written between 1953 and 1955. It captures in an instant the appalling attitudes and conditions prevailing then.[20]

> Yes, they mean well. They love the Simple Black.
> (I love my cat, that wayward little creature!)
> With humble pride they point to every feature:
> Drainage is good. We're pulling down the shack.
> We've stamped out hook-worm, promiscuity,
> And would do more, but . . . such a shiftless pack.

But that was all. I haven't scoured *all* of Australian literature for Jewish writers on Aboriginal themes, but none even peep, let alone leap, out of several anthologies.[21] In editing *Shalom*, Nancy Keesing pointed out "that there are not, and never have been, many Australian Jewish writers of fiction". (Where Jews and Aborigines do interact in a compelling way is in the works of two non-Jewish writers, Patrick White's *Riders in the Chariot* (1961) and Xavier Herbert's *Poor Fellow My Country* (1975).[22])

Fay Zwicky, noted poet, teacher and critic, comes closest to explaining the silence of the Australian-born Jewish writer.[23] She talks of "democratic repression", the bland Anglo-Saxon context, "the babble of speech masking a dumb void", "a landscape without a human being in it". It was reading the confident, assertive Jewish-American novelists like Bernard Malamud, Saul Bellow and Phillip Roth, that helped her articulate an awareness of self, and helped her overcome uncertainty about her own Jewish identity and its meanings. "To have compulsions in the Anglo-Saxon world . . . is to be marked out as a freak, an alien and unwanted voice". It was the "probing Quixotic honesty" of the American Jewish writer that enabled her to find her own voice "and the courage to speak".

Of the eighty authors[24] presented in three Australian-Jewish writer anthologies, only Andrea Goldsmith addresses Aborigines in general and my questions in particular. This fifth-generation Australian describes her search not so much for identity as for certainty.[25] In this journey, she finds Jewishness in books and in texts rather than in people or prayer: "My Jewishness I have found in books, my Australian-ness, when it existed at all, was little more than a whiff of eucalyptus". But she seems never to have been moved by the daily doses of Aboriginal highs and lows in the major newspapers, on radio or television, by the often appalling events in local Fitzroy, Framlingham or Lake Tyers. Only when she visited Uluru, Kata Tjuta and Kings Canyon in the Northern Territory – the great symbols of traditional Aborigines – was she able to ask the key question:

> I've never before felt my white Australianness so strenuously and I've never wanted it less. Why, I wonder, when I have identified so closely with other outsiders, have I not with Aboriginal Australians?

Goldsmith doesn't answer her question, but at least she wonders.

The Jewish "Tradition" – Students, Lawyers and Academics

On 20 December 2002, the *Australian Jewish News* published two important items. The first was a front-page headline, "Aborigines' Nazi protest honoured". The Australian Aborigines' League (AAL)[26] had passed a resolution in December 1938 protesting against Germany's treatment of Jews, especially after *"Kristallnacht"*, and had taken the protest statement to the German consulate in Melbourne, where their entry was denied.[27] A plaque was erected to commemorate this Aboriginal courage to care. The 1938 AAL protest was, of course, quite remarkable, if not astonishing, given that there wasn't a single Jew involved in the AAL in those days, or in any form of pro-Aboriginal advocacy.

The second feature – "Jews and Aboriginal Reconciliation" – depicted Jews "at the *forefront* of the battle for Aboriginal reconciliation, particularly in the legal field". Much was said about Jewish empathy, about not having "to tell Jews about human rights"; the role of Jewish lawyers, especially the late and celebrated Ron Castan QC, in Aboriginal land rights cases; Jews helping in the early days of the Aboriginal Legal Service in Fitzroy; the role of the [now] NSW Chief Justice Jim Spigelman in the 1965 Freedom Rides led by the late Charles Perkins; and the pro-Aboriginal advocacy of Justice Marcus Einfeld. In one scoop, so to speak, this edition was, in miniature, a laudation of the Jewish-Aboriginal relationship.

Can one talk of a Jewish "tradition" and "a continuity" in Aboriginal affairs, a relationship of help over a considerable length of time, something handed down orally from generation to generation, or set down on canvas or paper or film, or in some form of professional practice?

First, we need to look, however briefly, at some of the major issues in Aboriginal history since federation.

Establishing missions in remote parts of the continent, isolating Aborigines and Islanders both legally and geographically, was the focus of the 1900s. The 1910s continued a tradition of ambiguity from the colonies: assimilation as one answer, through the establishment of "assimilation homes" like Cootamundra Girls' Home in New South Wales, and extreme segregation as another response, such as the penal settlement of Palm Island in Queensland. In the 1920s, assimilation "havens" were established at Colebrook Girls' Home in South Australia and Kinchela Boy's Home in New South Wales, while massacres occurred at Forrest River Mission (WA) and Coniston Station in the Northern Territory.

By the 1930s, some public concern resulted in the formation of the Australian Aborigines League (AAL) in Victoria in 1932, followed by the Aborigines Progress Association (APA) in 1937. But it was in this decade that the eugenicist fantasies of O. A. Neville (WA), J. W. Bleakley (Q'land) and Dr Cecil Cook (NT) flourished. These were the bureaucrats who, together with Professor Baldwin Spencer a decade earlier, saw the solution in letting the "full-bloods" die out in inviolable reserves, pushing nice-looking half- and quarter-caste girls into marriage with white men (so that the colour gene would quickly disappear), and removing "mixed-blood" children from natural parents to be raised in assimilation homes, to the point where, said Neville, it "would be possible to *eventually forget that there were ever any Aborigines in Australia*".[28] The Australia Day Protest in Sydney on 26 January 1938 was a significant event, a day of mourning and a day on which the first major all-Aboriginal conference was held while mainstream society celebrated the landing of Captain Cook in 1788. War preoccupied the 1940s, but significant black reactions were occurring in the west with the Pindan Movement, referred to earlier.

Not a single Jew was involved in any of the events, protest actions, establishments, statutes, judicial or parliamentary enquiries.

An embryonic public consciousness of Aboriginal conditions was just visible in the 1950s. The National Aborigines Day Observance Committee (NADOC) was founded in 1957 to promote a day and a way of focusing mainstream attention on Aboriginal communities.[29] In the same year, the

Aborigines Advancement League (AAL) began operating in Melbourne as both a welfare service and a political lobby group, with Pastor Doug Nicholls as the key Aboriginal figure in the movement. Within a year, the AAL persuaded other advancement organizations, churches and trade unions to affiliate under a federal banner, in a national body originally known as the Federal Council for Aboriginal Advancement (FCAA), later amended to include Torres Strait Islanders, hence FCAATSI. For 21 years this body engaged in politicking for a better deal for Aborigines, which included federal voting rights for Aborigines and Islanders in the early 1960s, equal wages for equal work in the Northern Territory cattle industry in 1966, a referendum in 1967 to have Aborigines included in the national census and for the federal government to have legislative power on Aboriginal affairs (a state power in the constitution), some restitution for Aborigines caught in the Maralinga atomic testing site, better education and health, the return of the Mapoon people to the land from which they had been moved at gunpoint in 1963, and so on. There was a great deal of overlap between AAL and FCAATSI executive office-holders between 1958 and 1970, the "golden years" of this kind of pressure group politics when more battles were won than lost.

Only one Jew was *active* in both the AAL and FCAATSI – Lorna Lippmann. Other Jewish members of FCAATSI were Hans Bandler – always supportive of his wife, Faith – Emil and Hannah Witton, and Len Fox. This was the era of Aboriginal activists Joe McGinness, Faith Bandler, Charlie Perkins, Stuart Murray, Kath Walker (Oodgeroo Noonuccal), Bill Onus, Doug Nicholls, Mick Miller, Chicka Dixon; it was also the heyday of white colleagues like Don Dunstan, Gordon Bryant, Stan Davey, Barry Pittock, Jack Horner, Alick Jackomos, Lorna Lippman, Barry Christopher and Doris Blackburn.

The Queensland government promoted a tame citizens group in 1961, One People of Australia (OPAL), as an antidote to FCAATSI. In 1963, Sydney Aborigines, tiring of some of this white-dominated advancement activity, established a self-help and service body, the Foundation for Aboriginal Affairs (FAA). No Jews were involved in either organization. In 1964, the federal government established the Australian Institute for Aboriginal Studies (AIAS, later AIATSIS), a statutory body of one hundred academics charged with "recording the disappearing aspects of Aboriginal life before it is too late". Of the original founding and specially appointed members, only Ruth Fink and I were Jews.

Meanwhile, in 1961, a movement known as ABSCHOL (Aboriginal Scholarships) had begun in all universities. It started as a small Christian unit of the Australian Union of Students who collected funds to enable Aboriginal university attendance. Realising that teenagers were not finishing school, ABSCHOL sought funds to keep them there for as long as possible, usually by giving cash incentives to parents. The organization soon became "political", involving students in protests about land rights and similar issues. Federal initiatives under Labor led them to believe that they were redundant, and in 1972 the movement ended. A handful of Jewish students were involved, with two Victorian (Jewish) social workers, Phillip Boas and Colin Benjamin, as key directors.

In 1965, with the help of the Reverend Ted Noffs of the Wayside Chapel, some 30 Sydney University students, led by Charlie Perkins and Jim Spigelman (Perkins's right-hand man), undertook a 3,200 km bus tour of northern New South Wales towns. They "sat-in" in protest at racial discrimination in cinemas, bars and swimming baths. These Freedom Riders – including Wendy Golding, Judith Rich and four other Jewish students – clashed, on occasion violently, with local residents, but in the longer term this remarkable event ended apartheid in the arena of social facilities.

The mid-1960s to the early 1970s were important in Jewish community life. Dozens of Jewish students were (disproportionately) involved in New Left politics, especially at Melbourne and Monash Universities. Philip Mendes has chronicled this political activity, especially its opposition to the Vietnam War.[30] I taught some of the leaders and was acquainted with several of the vibrant group who opposed not only that war but also the 1971 Springbok rugby union tour of Australia; who engaged the anti-Israeli and anti-Semitic stances that arose with the Arab-Israeli war; and who founded *Survival* magazine to combat those sentiments and to fight anti-Semitism on various fronts.[31] *Tikkun olam* – the Jewish imperative to try to make the world more humane, to improve, heal, perhaps mend a flawed world – was present in their universalism, in their rebellion against the internal Jewish community "principle" of not getting involved "in a form of ethnic politics completely unacceptable to and alien to Australian political culture". Yet in all this mending of the world these young people could find no place or space for Aborigines, north or south, remote, rural or urban.

Why were all these Jewish boys and girls not involved in Aboriginal matters then? Where are they now? Only two are active: Robert Manne is very much with Aborigines in his work about the stolen generations, and Ron Brunton appears to do his utmost to disparage significant Aboriginal issues such as land rights and the forcible removal of children.

In 1966, the North Australian Workers Union (NAWU) sought to have Aborigines included in the Northern Territory (Cattle Station) Award, an agreement which left all Territory Aborigines working for about one-tenth of a white pastoral worker's wage. Following intensive fieldwork, (the late) Fred Gruen – a *Dunera* boy – and I supplied research information to the NAWU on cattle station awards and conditions.[32]

The 1967 referendum, falsely presented and touted by the federal government and much of the media as a "new deal" and as "citizenship rights" for Aborigines, was won overwhelmingly, partly because radical FCAATSI and the conservative government joined hands in promoting a yes vote.[33] Lorna Lippman and I were "celebrated" at the National Reconciliation Conference in Melbourne in 1997 as "referendum fighters".

In the late 1960s, a Methodist missionary from Yirrkala (NT), Ron Croxford, came to the Centre for Research into Aboriginal Affairs (CRAA) at Monash University to consult with the late Elizabeth Eggleston, Professor Louis Waller and me about the possibilities of pursuing Aboriginal land claims in civil court. Partly out of that advice to the group Croxford represented, came the first land claims in court, *Mathaman and Others* in 1969 and *Milirrpum v Nabalco* in 1971. In 1964, I had founded and was director of CRAA as a "balance" (or complement) to the AIAS, which had been created solely to retrieve the past and to eschew research into any "matters affecting the contemporary life of Aborigines". CRAA began as an applied research and action unit. Today it operates more as a student service and race relations education body, re-named the Centre for Australian Indigenous Studies (CAIS).

Aborigines erected a Tent Embassy on the lawns outside (old) Parliament House in Canberra in 1972. (It remains in place, despite repeated political and regular police batterings.) A stroke of genius, its message was too clever, with the great majority of Australians then (and now) not reading the message – that Aborigines were foreigners in Australia and were as much entitled to an embassy in the capital as any other nation. The founders were essentially the Aborigines from Sydney's FAA. No Jews were involved.

The land rights era began with the significant cases mentioned above, with Justice Woodward's commission on inquiry into land rights, and with the enactment of the *Aboriginal Land Rights (Northern Territory) Act* in 1976. Soon after, a notorious event in Western Australia became international news when the WA government, under Sir Charles Court, sent in a military-style armed convoy to ensure compliance with an order that a petroleum mining company, Amax, be permitted to drill on a known sacred site (known to contain no oil) situated on Noonkanbah, the Aboriginal-owned cattle station. In 1977, the Liberal Party did its damndest to disfranchise illiterate Aborigines in the West.[34] Jews were not involved, nor in protest against the 1975 decision to mine uranium in Arnhem Land, nor in the attempt by a small group of prominent Australians to lobby for a treaty with Aboriginal people.[35]

In the 1980s, no Jewish involvement was apparent in the Aboriginal movement to link up with children removed in earlier decades, nor in the Gurindji struggle for equal wages and land in the Territory, nor in the 1988 protests at the bicentenary celebrations.

In the twentieth century, only three Jews were involved in parliamentary or judicial enquiries on Aboriginal matters: Peter Baume, as a sympathetic federal Minister for Aboriginal Affairs (1980–2) and later, in 1989, as a dissenting member on a parliamentary select committee; Justice Marcus

Einfeld, who delivered a scathing report in 1988 on Aboriginal conditions in the border towns of Goondiwindi, Boggabilla and Toomelah;[36] and my directing a project that examined the social impact of uranium mining on Aborigines in Arnhem Land between 1978 and 1984.[37]

Certainly, Ron Castan and Jack Fajgenbaum were involved in several of the many land rights cases from the early 1990s. Justice Michael Kirby's oration for Castan in 1999 was a magnificent tribute to his work on the *Mabo* and *Wik* cases. Certainly, several lawyers, including Phillip Segal, have been involved for at least two decades in Aboriginal legal service work. But there is simply no evidence to claim a "tradition" and a "continuity" of Jewish *engagement*, and certainly none at the Jewish institutional level.

Anthropologists André Rosenfeld, John Bern, Ruth Fink, and David Trigger have long been associated with Aboriginal work, as "reconstructionists" and (most of them) as activists assisting in mapping for land claims. Warren Shapiro, Fred Myers and Faye Ginsberg, all American, have done notable work as anthropologists. Peter Ucko and Carmel (White) Schrire (South African) are noted prehistorians; and Ucko, a London Jew, took AIATSIS by the scruff of its conservative neck when, as principal in the 1970s and 1980s, he turned that body's attention fully to contemporary health, education, social history and uranium issues. Among the social psychologists, Ron Taft co-authored a book on race attitudes in the 1970s.[38] Medical scholars have been surprisingly few, with Max Kamien's work on *The Dark People of Bourke* the one significant analysis. Anthropologist Jon Altman (Israeli born, New Zealand educated) has made Aborigines in the economy his special field.

The lawyers of which the *Australian Jewish News* boasts came later in the day, almost a decade after land rights became the premier black agenda item. Louis Waller was there at the start of providing land rights advice, and in the formation of the first Aboriginal legal service in the mid-1960s.[39] The educators, A. and R. Doobov, were on the scene for a short period. The historians and social scientists – Lorna Lippmann, Colin Tatz, Robert Manne, Andrew Markus, Paul Bartrop, Peter Biskup, Roslyn Poignant, and Linda Briskman – have made Aboriginal issues central to their work, their involvement starting from between forty and ten years ago. As senior journalists, Michael Gawenda, Sam Lipski and Vic Alhadeff have always been ready to editorialize. Most of these contributions, important as they were for their time and context, have been sporadic, or episodic. Perhaps a handful have produced broad spectrum work, philosophical, reflective and judgmental work, while four or five Jews, at most, have devoted their careers to both research *and* political or legal activism in the Aboriginal field.

Why the Dearth?

First, Jewish settlement from 1788 never impinged on, nor was juxtaposed physically with, Aborigines.[40] Second, the Jewish struggle for recognition of religion, which came readily enough, was not comparable to the black experience of seeking "human-ness" and freedom from physical fear. Third, there was no physical interaction, except the chance meeting. (Post-war immigrant Jews, often enough allowed entry on condition they went to country towns, had more probability of encounter than Melbourne and Sydney Jews.) Finally, there was never any labour or occupational conflict, let alone business competition.

Pre-war Australians had no demonstrable interest in anything Aboriginal. Dying out, or extreme segregation, or social and economic assimilation for "half-castes" in urban areas was their destiny. Apart from a handful of bureaucratic eugenicists, a squadron of remote missionaries, three or four anthropologists, perhaps two journalists, one or two literary voices and a small clutch of painters, no one expressed any interest in Aborigines, and certainly not in Islanders.

Compared with the United States and South Africa, no raging social or political dynamic cried out for change. There were no *observable* strikes on cattle or sheep properties. (There were, but since these disruptions didn't take the traditional form of strike, with slogans and placards, no one recognized them for what they were.) No unions, militant or otherwise, worked on behalf of Aborigines. *Au contraire*, the unions opposed Aboriginal economic or wage progress at every turn. The left wing of politics, socialist or communist, was virtually mute on Aborigines. Why, then, should Jews have been visible or audible?

But, unlike South Africa and the United States, there has been no violent race politics in Australia. Activists and supporters have had no need to fear a Mayor Daley and cracked skulls or a terroristic secret police force as in South Africa. There was never a life and death struggle, a life and detention struggle, as with Ruth First and her 117 days in solitary confinement, her death by postal bomb. In a climate of peaceful politics, there could, and should, have been more activism by Australian Jews, not less.

One suggestion is that perhaps Jews relate only to minorities who share an experiential struggle for civil rights, as with black South Africans and Americans, that Jews somehow haven't, or don't, relate to hunter-gatherer societies. There is, indeed, a veritable galaxy of Jewish anthropologists concerned in, and with, San Bushmen, Canadian and American First Nations people, and the Inuit.[41] These scholars have had to battle more than vicious Jim Crow laws in American and South African legislatures. They have struggled in the more difficult ideological ring, fighting against the "scientific racists" who constantly seek out the ineradicable racial gene that justifies the hierarchy of the races, the superior "white race", the corrupting "Jewish race", the inferior "black race".

Jews in Australian academe are no longer a rare species, but they were thin on the ground in the first three decades after World War II. Those in university life tend to be in the professional fields of law, medicine, engineering and architecture. Those few Jews who have entered the arts and social sciences and who have had "compulsions" (as Zwicky calls them), who have cared, or cared enough, to work in what "tradition" calls "the struggle", are few in number.

In the 1950s, the Jewish Council to Combat Fascism and Anti-Semitism passed supportive resolutions, as did the Jewish Democratic Society and the Sydney Jewish Left in the 1980s. My contention about dearth rests on the absence of *any sustained engagement and action*, not on the presence of resolutions, of gestures or symbols of support, however well meant. To my knowledge, not one of these organizations provided money or manpower.[42]

Changes have occurred on many fronts these past two decades and more Jewish interest has surfaced. Some of it is in the form of anti-racism programs, such as those established by the Albert Dreyfus unit of B'nai B'rith, the Anti-Defamation Commission of B'nai B'rith, and the Jewish Holocaust Museum in Melbourne. Well-intentioned, they have yet to be tried, tested, evaluated. Much of present community action remains at the level of "multicultural" events, somewhat shy and hesitant "matzo-ball-bush-tucker" lunch meetings of the cultures. Several symposia have been organized by Jews anxious to know "what can we do?" and "how can we contribute?"

A few Aboriginal scholars have shown an interest in Jewish life and history, one or two in a hostile way, seeing the Palestinian plight as their more appropriate metaphor. The alleged similarities and empathic aspects of Jewish-Aboriginal religio-history have not attracted scholars from either side.[43]

Most of the many Jewish audiences I address still react in the manner of non-Jewish audiences. They are usually hostile as they question expenditure on Aborigines, when they disparage all land rights claims, when they blame Aborigines alone for all the physical, social, health and economic ills that beset them. I always hope that Jews will have moral insight and outlook; the fact that they don't continues to disappoint.

Unlike the United States and South Africa, there is, as yet, no Islamic movement that interests diverse Aboriginal communities and, happily, there is no vicious anti-Israel and anti-Jewish rhetoric, let alone physical abuse of Jews or their property. There is no reason for Aborigines to have any hostility towards a people they almost never meet, nor work with, nor visit socially, nor play games with, nor borrow money from, nor whose apartments they rent. Aborigines are rarely Christians and have no millennium-long baggage of contempt for Jews.

Some Jews, sometimes many Jews, have opposed racial injustice in the United States and South Africa. Some have raged against it, fought it, gone to jail for it, even died for it. They have been both revered and excoriated by fellow Jews for their value stance. What little passion or commitment there has been in Aboriginal affairs has come largely from those born outside of Australia, from those like Yosl Bergner, who were sensitized to insight by the experiences of their own immediate environs at their point of emigration. When Bergner saw Fitzroy and Tocumwal, he saw Warsaw.

Notes

1 "Only Connect: Musings of an Australian Jew", in Alan Jacobs, ed., *Enough Already: an Anthology of Australian-Jewish Writing* (Sydney: Allen & Unwin, 1999), p. 13.

2 Percy Cohen, *Jewish Radicals and Radical Jews* (London: Institute of Jewish Affairs and Academic Press, 1980), pp. 16–35.

3 *Ibid.*, p. 21.

4 See, among others, Debra Schultz, *Going South: Jewish Women in the Civil Rights Movement* (New York: New York University Press, 2001) and Michael Staub, *Torn at the Roots: The Crisis of Jewish Liberalism in Postwar America* (New York: Columbia University Press, 2002).

5 Shlomo Katz, ed., *Negro and Jew: An Encounter in America* (Toronto: Macmillan, 1969).

6 Nelson Mandela, *Long Walk to Freedom*, vol. 1 (London: Abacus, 2002), p. 101.

7 Gideon Shimoni, *Community and Conscience: The Jews in Apartheid South Africa* (Hanover: University Press of New England, 2003), pp. 140–8.

8 *Ibid.*, pp. 96–7.

9 Immanuel Suttner, *Cutting Through the Mountain: Interviews with South African Jewish Activists* (London: Viking, 1997).

10 See my *With Intent to Destroy: Reflecting on Genocide* (London: Verso, 2003), esp. p. 4.

11 Milton Shain, *The Roots of Antisemitism in South Africa* (Johannesburg: Witwatersrand University Press, 1994).

12 Shimoni, *Community and Conscience*, p. 276.

13 "Jews and Aborigines: A Shared Universe" in *Generation* 1 (1992): 11–16.

14 Formally known as Human Rights and Equal Opportunity Commission, *Bringing Them Home: Report of the National Inquiry into the Separation of Aboriginal and Torres Strait Islander Children from their Families* (Sydney, 1997).

15 Colin Tatz in the *Australian Jewish News*, May 1997. I was present at that meeting.

16 Workers OnLine International, 2002, issue 136, article by Andrew Casey, "The Un-Promised Land": http://workers.labor.net.au.

17 Reprinted in *Generation* 3, 1 (1992): 33–7.

18 "Painting the Town: The Story of Yosl Bergner", video, Ronin Films, Victoria (no date).

19 Judah Waten, *Alien Son* (North Ryde: Angus & Robertson, 1952).

20 David Martin, *Poems of David Martin 1938–1958* (Sydney: Edwards and Shaw, no date).

21 Nancy Keesing, ed., *Shalom: Australian Jewish Stories* (Sydney: Collins, 1978); Gael Hammer, ed., *Pomegranates: a Century of Jewish Australian Writing* (Sydney: Millennium, 1988); Alan Jacobs, ed., *Enough Already: an Anthology of Australian-Jewish Writing* (Sydney: Allen & Unwin, 1999).

22 J. J. Healy, *Literature and the Aborigine in Australia* (Brisbane: University of Queensland Press, 1989), pp. 273–9.

23 Fay Zwicky, "Democratic Repression: The Ethnic Strain", in *The Lyre in the Pawnshop: Essays on Literature and Survival 1974–1984* (Perth: University of Western Australia Press, 1986), pp. 91–102.

24 The *Pomegranates* book has inflated the number of writers by collecting just about anything and everything written by Jews, even by non-Jews on Jewish themes. The *Shalom* and *Enough Already* books at least present accomplished and recognized authors.

25 Jacobs, ed. *Enough Already*, pp. 3–17 at p. 13.

26 Not to be confused with the Aborigines Advancement League (AAL, Vic), which was formally established in 1957.

27 20 December 2002. The item was originally reported in the (now defunct) Melbourne *Argus* and in the *Age* on 3 December 1938. A plaque commemorating the "AAL's courageous stand was unveiled at the Jewish Holocaust Museum" on 15 December 2002.

28 Colin Tatz, *With Intent to Destroy*, pp. 89–92.

29 Now known as NAIDOC, celebrated for a week each July.

30 Philip Mendes, *The New Left, the Jews and the Vietnam War 1965–1972* (Melbourne: Lazare Press, 1993).

31 *Ibid.*, p. 143.

32 Fred Gruen, "Aborigines in the Northern Territory Cattle Industry – an Economist's View" in Ian Sharp and Colin Tatz, eds, *Aborigines in the Economy* (Brisbane: Jacaranda Press, 1966), pp. 197–215.

33 It was in fact a clumsy attempt by Prime Minister Harold Holt to have a "popular" question placed alongside one likely to be defeated, in this case, a question seeking approval to increase the number of House of Representatives members without a corresponding increase in the number of Senators. The Aboriginal question was heavily marketed as "a new deal" and won a resounding 90 percent of the national vote. The unpopular nexus question was badly defeated.

34 See Colin Tatz, *Race Politics in Australia* (Armidale: University of New England), pp. 24–40.

35 The original Aboriginal Treaty Committee comprised Dr H. C. "Nuggett" Coombs, Dymphna Clark, Judith Wright McKinney, Professor C. D. Rowley, Eva Hancock, Professor W. E. H. Stanner, Hugh Littlewood and Stewart Harris.

36 *Inquiry into the Social and Material Needs of the New South Wales-Queensland Border Towns of Goondiwindi, Boggabilla and Toomelah*, Human Rights and Equal Opportunity Commission, 1987–8.

37 *Social Impact of Uranium Mining*, Report for Minister of Aboriginal Affairs, Australian Institute for Aboriginal and Torres Strait Islander Studies, 1978–84.

38 Ronald Taft, John Lawson & Pamela Beasley, *Aborigines in Australian Society: Attitudes and Social Conditions* (Canberra: Australian National University Press, 1970).

39 The founders of the unofficial but effective Aboriginal legal aid service in Melbourne were Louis Waller, Elizabeth Eggleston, Colin Tatz (all at Monash University) and Colin Campbell, a practising barrister in Oakleigh. That was in 1964. After Labor won the federal election in 1972, government-sponsored services began. It was then that Ron Castan, among others, began a remarkable career of legal engagement on the Aboriginal behalf.

40 Paul Bartrop, "Divergent Experiences on the Frontier: Jews and Aborigines in Early Colonial Australia", *Australian Jewish Historical Society Journal* 14 (1997): 23–37.

41 One can begin with the illustrious German, Franz Boas, the legendary Belgian, Claude Levi-Strauss, and continue with Sol Tax, Max Gluckman, Meyer Fortes, through to Richard Lee, Harvey Feit, Michael Asch, Phillip Tobias, among many others, and end with the incomparable Hugh Brody.

42 I was an adviser to the AAL and FCAATSI from 1961 until 1971, and in that time saw no visible sign of support from Jewish organizations, official or left-inclined. Faith Bandler has several tales to tell about the absence of Jewish support.

43 See the opposing views of two Aboriginal writers, "Through Similar Journeys Comes Revelation" by Djiniyini Gondarra and "Aborigines and Jews: A False Analogy" by Gordon Briscoe in *Generation* 3, 1 (1992).

11 | Jews and Australian Multiculturalism

GEOFFREY BRAHM LEVEY

In late 1997, Prime Minister John Howard launched an issues paper, *Multicultural Australia: The Way Forward*, prepared by his newly formed National Multicultural Advisory Council. Before a gathering of religious and community leaders at Melbourne Town Hall, the Prime Minister introduced the document by speaking feelingly about the example of Eastern European Jewish migrants to Australia. "They came to Australia, in almost all cases, without any capacity to speak English. Within a generation they left their mark not only in commerce and business but, very importantly, in community charitable endeavours". And, he added, "they became forever Australian".[1] Howard had come to office with a reputation for being uncomfortable about the word and concept of multiculturalism, and his first twenty months in government, including his equivocation over the rise of Pauline Hanson's xenophobic politics, only confirmed that impression.[2] Thus his reference to Jewish migrants in launching the *Multicultural Australia* paper seemed redolent with meaning. Here was a group that arrived with nothing and could not speak English, but through hard work, self-reliance, and enterprise quickly succeeded not only in establishing itself, but also in integrating to the Australian way of life and in helping the country prosper. What better example could there be to other migrant groups arriving on these shores? What bigger contrast could there be to the idea of cultural communities parading their difference and demanding state recognition and support in the name of multiculturalism?

Howard's sense of the attitude of Jewish migrants and the already established Jewish community to life in Australia was, in some ways, historically astute. The willingness to integrate into Australian society *has* been a feature of the Australian Jewish experience. Yet, this has always been accompanied by another pattern quite at odds with any notion of national monoculturalism. As a strongly self-identifying community, the Jews have sought to maintain and reproduce their distinct traditions and identity. Moreover, they have long established a network of communal institutions that at once reflect and serve these interests. The advent of multicultural policy in Australia in the 1970s forced Jews to renegotiate the "integrationist" and "separationist" aspects of their identities. It forced them, that is, to rethink their status as a religious minority in an overwhelmingly Christian society and the way they ought to interact in a liberal democracy.

Between Integration and Separation

The question of the place of cultural minorities within modern states – to which "multiculturalism" is a recent answer – is a very Jewish one. It is, indeed, a version of the so-called "Jewish question" that so animated the intellectual and political classes in late eighteenth- and nineteenth-century Europe. Put simply, then the question was whether or on what conditions Jews should be granted civil equality. In their general and specifically Jewish formulations, such questions go to the foundations of the two dominant institutions of modern politics – liberalism and the nation-state. Jews' relation to multiculturalism as state policy in the late twentieth century needs to be understood in this context.

Liberal institutions – limited government, rule of law, individual rights, and significant church-state separation – turned previously corporate entities and groups into voluntary associations and consigned their particularistic attachments to a private sphere. Somewhat contradictorily, political entities aspiring to be "nation states" assumed that political unity required a culturally homogeneous citizenry, and thus assimilation to dominant norms often in the private as well as public spheres. These conflicting conditions marked the terms upon which Jews (and others) were admitted as citizens in modern Europe. "The Jews should be denied everything as a nation, but granted everything as individuals. They must be citizens", declared a deputy to the French National Assembly in 1789.[3] And so it was that in return for admission to citizenship, the Jews were expected to forgo their corporate existence, reform their traditions and behaviour in accord with local customs, and confine their religious and cultural distinctiveness to the private sphere.

There were national differences in how these expectations were institutionalized. And there was often residual reluctance by states or their societies to fulfil the promise of social integration and legal equality of Jews, which often reflected anti-Jewish prejudice.[4] Such prejudice also made the journey to Australia with European settlement, although the Australian case is unusual in some respects. First, a Jewish minority had been present in Australia since the "First Fleet", when a handful of Jews disembarked among the first consignment of convicts, thus giving the Jewish presence in Australia a certain historical authenticity.[5] Second, as historian Israel

Getzler notes, in the "Australian colonies Jews appear from the beginning to have enjoyed full civil and political rights: they acquired British nationality, voted at elections, held commissions in the local militia, were elected to municipal offices and were appointed justices of the peace".[6] As early as the mid-nineteenth century, a number were also elected to legislatures in New South Wales, Western Australia, and South Australia (see the Appendix). Yet, none of these "rights" of political participation enjoyed by colonial Jews was enshrined in law. It was simply that as a matter of political practice and, one surmises, of an already informal political culture, Jews were able to hold political office in Australia years before English Jews were so entitled in the House of Commons or American Jews were in some states of the Union.[7]

In general, Jews negotiated life in Australia by downplaying their Jewish distinctiveness and stressing their equal status as British subjects and Australian loyalty. They accepted the dominant Anglo Protestant ethos. "Their philosophy", as Suzanne Rutland notes, "was to eliminate any differences between Jew and non-Jew except in the very narrow religious sense".[8] They were Australians who happened to be of the Mosaic faith. It was the liberal formula that Jews had adopted in Britain and most other Western countries. Despite intermittent episodes of anti-Semitic prejudice and discrimination – culminating catastrophically in mid-twentieth-century Europe – it was also one that worked exceedingly well for a great many of them. Jews welcomed the opportunities, stability, and security afforded by liberal societies and flourished there like nowhere else. In a pattern repeated in virtually every Western country, including Australia, and often despite humble immigrant beginnings, Jews, as a group, rose rapidly into the middle and upper middle classes to become, within a few generations, one of the best educated, most professionalized, and most affluent groups in their societies.[9] The liberal state was, it seemed, "good for the Jews". Not even the Nazi Holocaust, which tragically exposed the precariousness of the entire Enlightenment project, could shake most Western Jews' faith in the liberal nationalist solution to the Jewish question.

The opportunity to participate and prosper in their society, however, only partly explains Jews' embrace of liberal conditions. Another major reason is that these conditions allowed them to maintain their Jewish identity. A liberal order, even one as begrudging in its toleration of cultural difference as was the Commonwealth of Australia for most of its first century, allowed both freedom of worship and a space for voluntary association in civil society. As a group, the Jews integrated and acculturated to Australian ways of life, but have resisted state and societal pressures to assimilate. Or if one prefers, they accepted assimilation in the sense of "taking in" Australian norms – becoming Australianized – but have rejected assimilation in the sense of "being absorbed" by Australian society.[10] Just what this residual Jewish identity consists in is a complex issue. What is clear is that it is not primarily a matter of formal religious commitment. As with world Jewry in general, most Australian Jews are religiously non-observant or minimally observant.[11] Yet, in a manner that many non-Jews especially find puzzling, it happens that even most secular Jews strongly self-identify as Jews and with Jewish peoplehood. At a structural level, Jews have established a vast array of communal institutions covering the gamut of religious, social, political, educational, welfare, health, media, and recreational needs.[12] Moreover, for over fifty years, through its Boards of Deputies and like roof bodies, the organized Jewish community has even operated a form of elected self-government. In a sense, the Jews have simply refashioned their traditional corporate existence in accord with the parameters permitted by liberal democracy.[13]

Being a minority has led some Jews to imagine a reordering of liberal politics and society. Perhaps the best-known example is the English playwright Israel Zangwill, whose play, *The Melting-Pot* (1909), popularized the now famous metaphor for depicting unity from diversity. Although an image of assimilation, Zangwill intended the melting pot concept as a challenge to Anglo-conformity in the United States. The "melting pot" stood for a more democratic form of assimilation in which all European immigrant cultures would merge to produce a "new American".[14] A few years later, a German immigrant, Horace Kallen, advanced the idea of "cultural pluralism". In his view, the United States was really a "democracy of nationalities", whose political order should aim for "harmony" rather than "unison". Then in the 1950s, theologian Will Herberg dared to suggest that the "three great democratic faiths" – Protestantism, Catholicism, and Judaism – constituted a "triple melting pot" that properly defined the contours of American society and politics.[15]

Such ideas had some influence in the academy and in broader debates over social policy. But at the time and until the civil rights movement and black consciousness in the 1960s, these ideas fell mainly on deaf ears in the Jewish community. Most American Jews remained steadfastly committed to the classical liberal emphasis on individual rights and liberties as the best protection of their religious and associational lives. And albeit in a polity without a bill of rights, quietly living within the limits of Australian liberal democracy as they found them was the preferred approach of Australian Jews as well.

The Challenges of Multiculturalism

From Federation in 1901 until World War II, Australia dealt with cultural diversity fundamentally through exclusion. The first act of the newly established Australian Commonwealth was the Immigration Restriction Act (1901) or "White Australia" policy, which defined the country as an outpost of the "British race". Under economic imperatives to "populate or perish", these restrictive categories were progressively loosened until

1973, when the Whitlam Labor Government ended all remaining vestiges of a racially discriminatory immigration policy.[16] The ensuing transformation of Australian society has been remarkable. By 1999, almost one in four Australians (23.6 percent) was born overseas, coming from more than 150 countries.[17]

Like Canada and the United States, Australia managed its cultural diversity up until the mid-1960s through assimilationist policies of "Anglo-conformity". Government documents suggest a new period of "integration" followed, where the settling and servicing of large numbers of migrants were emphasized, rather than the loss of their original language, culture and identity. The policy of multiculturalism is said to operate from 1973.[18] Initially focused on migrant settlement and welfare support for people from non-English speaking backgrounds ("NESBs"),[19] from the late 1970s, multiculturalism was increasingly framed in terms of addressing "all Australians" and had crystallized around the themes of social cohesion, cultural identity, and equality of opportunity and access. By the end of the 1980s the policy identified four planks that have more or less endured: the right of all Australians to equal opportunities without fear of group-based discrimination; the right of all Australians to maintain their cultural identities within certain limits; the economic and national benefits of a culturally diverse society; and respect for core Australian values and institutions – reciprocity, tolerance and equality (including of the sexes), freedom of speech and religion, the rule of law, the Constitution, parliamentary democracy, and English as the national language.[20]

Although the term "multiculturalism" was borrowed from Canada – where it concerned bilingualism and long established cultural communities – Australian multiculturalism dovetailed more with developments in the United States.[21] First, by the 1960s it had become clear that assimilatory and integrationist pressures weren't going to erase ethnic and racial group differences within a few generations as had been expected. As Nathan Glazer and Daniel Patrick Moynihan famously concluded after surveying the scene in New York City, "The point about the melting pot is that it did not happen".[22] The rise of the civil rights movement and black consciousness in the sixties also helped to ferment ethnic revivalism and identity politics more generally. Second, there was the earlier American experience with mass migration, including a body of social theory on the problem of immigrant absorption. Milton Gordon's work on types of assimilation and Horace Kallen's phrase, if not quite his idea, of cultural pluralism, in particular, influenced Australian thinking.[23] And yet multiculturalism played out very differently in Australia and the United States, with radically different consequences for their respective Jewish communities.

Where American social policy switched from an ethnic to a racial focus over the course of the twentieth century, Australian immigration and social policy exchanged a racial for an ethnic emphasis.[24] The mass European migrations to the United States from the late nineteenth century until the 1920s established migrant absorption, acculturation and assimilation as the chief social challenges of the day. These challenges were considered manageable because the newcomers or "ethnics" and the American-born were thought to share a common European cultural and moral heritage. In contrast, "race" defined those who were thought to be alien and unassimilable. The brunt of this marginalization fell disproportionately on blacks, Native Americans, and other people of "colour". Thus, despite arriving *en masse* as impoverished, non-English-speaking migrants at the turn of the twentieth century, the Jews were seen as "white" and quickly came to be included among the privileged majority.[25] From the late 1960s, as blacks became disenchanted with the results of the civil rights movement and dismissive of the idea that the liberal state could ever truly be inclusive and non-discriminatory, race rather than ethnicity increasingly defined the centre of political action and response in the United States. American multiculturalism emerged in the 1980s not as state policy, as it had a decade or so earlier in Canada and Australia, but rather from "below", as a critique both of the "colour-blind" liberal state and of models of cultural pluralism for ignoring race. In this societal struggle over identity, the Jews are viewed not as another minority patch in the multicultural quilt, but rather as members of the oppressive white majority, that is, part of the target of multicultural politics. Not surprisingly, American Jews tend to register ambivalence, if not hostility, toward multiculturalism. As Michael Galchinsky puts it:

> Jews are caught betwixt and between the liberal white dominant culture and the multicultural minority world. If we attempt to follow the old liberal model we need to continue to "mainstream" ourselves, to pass, to lead a double life. On the other hand, since we *can* pass, Jews cannot be included in the emerging culture of diversity.[26]

In Australia, the political ground shifted from race to ethnicity. As noted, the country defined itself in racial terms for its first half-century or so via the "White Australia" policy. Under this policy, Jews in Australia were originally considered to be "white". From the 1930s, however, Jewish refugees from Nazism were increasingly racialized to the point of exclusion. Indeed, as late as 1952, Australian immigration forms were still asking applicants to indicate whether or not they were Jewish. But with the demise of the "White Australia" policy, and under Australian multicultural policy, groups were defined in ethnic rather than in racial terms. Multiculturalism thus challenged Australian Jews differently from American Jews.

First, by sanctioning the acceptability and even the public support and celebration of cultural difference, Australian multiculturalism invited Jews to discard their time-honoured mode of political quietism and of publicly downplaying their Jewish distinctiveness as much as possible. It held out an opportunity to exchange their traditional quest for "invisibility" before the law for group visibility and a public profile, which, in Jewish historical experience, had been associated with persecution and invidious discrimination. American Jews had faced and adjusted to a similar challenge as part of the post-1960s emphasis on identity and pluralist politics, that is, *before* multiculturalism arrived on the American scene in the late 1980s and 1990s.[27] But in Australia, cultural pluralist politics arrived with multiculturalism and was integral to it. Second, the original emphasis of multicultural policy on ethnic groups defined in terms of national origin and "non-English speaking background" pressed Australian Jews to confront and others to consider the unsettling question of what kind of group the Jews are. Whereas in the United States the main agitators of multiculturalism were to exclude Jews as part of the dominant white majority, Australian multicultural policy left open the question of its relevance to Jews.

Perhaps because of the challenges it posed, there was little Jewish involvement or even discernible interest in the early theoretical and policy development of Australian multiculturalism. The handful or so of Jews who did have some involvement served in their individual professional capacities rather than at the behest of Jewish organizations. The standout exception was Walter Lippmann, President of the Australian Jewish Welfare Society from 1960–77. A German-Jewish refugee who had settled in Melbourne in 1938, Lippmann was concerned about Australia's attitude to migrants and about the ability of the Jewish community to reproduce itself in the Australian setting.[28] After Professor Jerzy Zubrzycki, one of the architects of Australian multiculturalism, he has been called the "leading activist" supporting the cultural pluralism model for Australian multiculturalism, who provided "significant secondary contributions in facilitating [the model's] ideological development".[29] Walter Jona served as Minister for Immigration and Ethnic Affairs in the Victorian government from 1976–9. Two Jewish Labor MPs chaired their respective state's advisory Migrant Task Force Committee (established by the colourful Minister for Immigration, Al Grasby) in 1973: namely, Richard Klugman in New South Wales, and Joseph Berinson in Western Australia. Sociologist Andrew Jakubowicz, who would soon produce significant research on ethnic issues, was also appointed to the NSW Committee. Prominent Melbourne journalist and broadcaster Sam Lipski was appointed to two government multicultural advisory bodies, the Australian Ethnic Affairs Council and the Ethnic Affairs Policy Task Force, in 1980–1. Also in this early period, then academic Colin Rubenstein was a consultant to the Australian Institute of Multicultural Affairs from 1980–5; Moss Cass, who had been Labor's shadow Minister for Health, Immigration and Ethnic Affairs (1975–83), chaired the Committee of Review of the Australian Institute of Multicultural Affairs in 1983; and Jakubowicz sat on the Board of Directors of the Special Broadcasting Service (SBS) from 1983–6.

Few Jewish academics had, by this stage, joined the debate over multiculturalism; most notably, Lippmann associates education professor Ronald Taft and sociology professor Sol Encel, who generally endorsed the multicultural measures being taken; Jakubowicz – now founder and director of the Centre for Multicultural Studies at the University of Wollongong – who viewed them as capitalist co-option; and psychology professor and arch conservative Frank Knopfelmacher, who contended that multiculturalism undermined the unity and character of the nation.[30]

Jewish communal bodies were generally diffident toward the new multicultural regime. One measure of this is the response to government consultative committees on developing the national multicultural policy. In a 1981–2 round of consultations, for example, only one Jewish organization in the country made a written submission, the ACT Jewish Community, Inc.[31] Yet, the Armenian Association of Western Australia, the Australian Arab Women's Association, the Byelorussian Association of Australia, the Catholic Education Office, the Greek Community of Albury-Wodonga, the Serbian Orthodox Church, the Uniting Church in Australia, and a host of other community groups around Australia saw fit to be heard. In another inquiry, in 1984, only Lippmann's Federation of Australian Jewish Welfare Societies made a written submission, and no Jewish organization in any state met with the committee.[32]

The question of how Jews might fit within the categories of Australian multiculturalism played out interestingly in the 1970s over membership in the new Ethnic Communities' Councils (ECC). The Councils were among the first non-government institutions established to advance the multicultural agenda in Australia. The Victorian ECC was the first to be set up, in 1974; the ECC of NSW followed in 1975. With their own long established elected councils, the Boards of Deputies, the Jewish communities in each state had a structural affinity with this new layer of voluntary political representation. Yet, as Jon Stratton has observed, Jews in Australia possessed neither of the two attributes marking ethnicity under Australian multiculturalism: common national origin and common language.[33] In the event, the Victorian Jewish Board of Deputies (VJBD) joined the ECC immediately, and the New South Wales Jewish Board of Deputies (NSWJBD) declined to affiliate.

According to Sol Encel, the NSWJBD's reluctance "was influenced by the attitude of the rabbinate, who were opposed to the idea that the Jews were an ethnic group".[34] Contemporary reports of the NSWJBD deliberations suggest the local opposition was more widespread. John Einfeld, then President of Moriah College, an Orthodox Jewish day school, discounted claims that Yiddish is a Jewish language and argued "Jews have everything to lose and nothing to gain by declaring themselves an ethnic group". Another communal member recalled that minorities were given recognition with the Treaty of Versailles only to have this turn into official discrimination and quotas against Jews.[35] The contrasting enthusiasm of the VJBD for the ECC may have reflected the personal influence of Walter Lippmann, who also was the founding president of the Victorian ECC.[36] However, a further clue is given in Lippmann's attempt to persuade his NSW colleagues to join the local ECC. The *Australian Jewish Times* reports him seeking to "dispel the apprehensions of members of the community who have local backgrounds stretching back generations".[37] The different attitudes of the VJBD and the NSWJBD likely reflected the different origins of their respective Jewish constituencies. The Melbourne community was steeped more in the *Yiddishkeit* of the pre-War and post-War European Jewish migrants. The Sydney community had a greater Anglo-Jewish presence and cultural integration with Anglo-Australian life.[38] Melbourne Jewry could accept the ethnic tag; Sydney Jews found it a threat to their status.

Although the NSWJBD eventually affiliated with the NSW ECC in 1988, the ambivalence over ethnic identification persisted.[39] During the 1990s, a number of state governments dropped the word "ethnic" from their agencies dealing with cultural diversity.[40] In 1999, the NSW Premier Bob Carr announced that his government would follow suit by replacing its 22-year-old Ethnic Affairs Commission with a Community Relations Commission and that henceforth he would be Minister for Citizenship instead of Minister for Ethnic Affairs. "'Ethnic' is an outdated term", he explained. "Children don't want to be identified as ethnic Australians; they are Australians pure and simple. They feel the term is divisive".[41] Some ethnic communities in NSW welcomed the announcement, while others expressed dismay. Some Jewish individuals also protested that dropping the "e" word felt like a denial of part of their identities.[42] The *Sydney Morning Herald* applauded Carr's initiatives on the grounds that Australian multiculturalism should mean an "Australian nation 'woven together' by the people who have arrived here over a period of 40,000 years"; it should not mean the Canadian model of cultural maintenance.[43]

The NSWJBD, in contrast, supported Carr's initiatives once the issue of the recognition and rights of cultural minorities was clarified. It lobbied for and indeed helped draft a preamble affirming the "principles of multiculturalism", which was added to the Act establishing the new Community Relations Commission. The preamble "recognises that the people of New South Wales are of different linguistic, religious, racial and ethnic backgrounds, who...are free to profess, practise and maintain their own linguistic, religious, racial and ethnic heritage".[44] The preamble thus confirms the importance of ethnic identity. The NSWJBD believed that "ethnic" was simply an unnecessary marker of cultural minorities.[45] By retaining cultural rights without being defined as ethnic, one's minority status would, in a sense, be mainstreamed. Jews in New South Wales could have the best of both worlds.

Carr's "Australians pure and simple" does not exactly capture, then, the complexity of Australian Jewish identity. The twin worlds that Jews occupy are reflected in how they choose to call themselves. Non-Jews will often write or speak about "Jewish Australians". But Jewish institutions and individuals in this country typically refer to themselves as "Australian Jews". The English language here is revealing. The noun "Jews" signifies the presumed primary identity; the adjective "Australian" is the qualifier. It's as if to say, "Jewish people, Australian branch". The same pattern is observed in most other diasporic Jewish communities. Australian Jews do tend to be "Jewish Australians", however, when they are appealing to their common citizenship with other Australians or else when they sense this commonality is expected in certain public contexts. When, for example, an editor of the *Australian Jewish News* called in to talkback radio it was, he said, as a "concerned Jewish Australian".[46] Similarly, when the Executive Council of Australian Jewry (ECAJ) seeks "to convey the concerns of the Australian Jewish Community" to the wider society, it refers "to the way in which Jewish Australians" have been affected.[47]

Another key marker of the dualism in Australian Jewish identity is the Jewish emphasis on endogamy. The overall Jewish intermarriage rate in Australia is estimated at 15–20 percent.[48] Although the rate is now over 50 percent in some parts of the United States and Britain and perhaps approaching this figure among younger cohorts of Australian Jews, in-marriage is still a comparatively strong value in Jewish life.[49] Former Prime Minister Bob Hawke discovered this rather emphatically when addressing an audience at Melbourne's St. Kilda Synagogue in 1999. Taking as his topic Australia's national identity in the twenty-first century, Hawke, a notable friend of the Jewish community, suggested that the success of Australia's multicultural society is evidenced by the high intermarriage rate between members of the different ethnic communities. The upset in the Jewish community was immediate and ongoing, and within a week Hawke felt obliged to clarify his remarks.[50] Still, demographically, Hawke's point about the integrative nature of Australian multiculturalism also applies to Jews, as the sharp increase in the acceptance of intermarriage as a personal option among younger Jews – as noted above – testifies. The irony is that this trend has occurred in an era when governments *abandoned* the pressure on minorities to assimilate and lose their distinctive identities.

Jews and Multiculturalism in Action

From the late 1980s, Jews became more involved in the formal institutions of Australian multiculturalism. Justice Marcus Einfeld was appointed foundation President of the Human Rights and Equal Opportunity Commission (HREOC) in 1986. In 1987, Uri Themal, a child Holocaust survivor and ordained rabbi, was appointed Deputy Chairperson of the NSW Ethnic Affairs Commission (EAC), and went on, in the 1990s, to direct Queensland's Bureau of Ethnic Affairs and its successor, Multicultural Affairs Queensland, within the Department of the Premier and Cabinet. Susan Bures, then editor of the *Australian Jewish Times*, assumed the NSW EAC Deputy Chair vacated by Themal. Dr Joachim Schneeweiss, one-time ECAJ president, was a member of the NSW Anti-Discrimination Board, and served on Prime Minister Hawke's Advisory Council on Multicultural Affairs (ACMA) that recommended the *National Agenda for a Multicultural Australia* in 1989. The successor bodies to the ACMA also have had Jewish representation. Michael Marx, a former NSWJBD president, has been Deputy Chairperson of the Community Relations Commission for a Multicultural NSW since 1999.

In recent years, numerous cases and controversies have occurred that throw light on Jews' relation to multicultural Australia and, indeed, on how multicultural Australia responds to cultural claims. In the space available, I will limit myself to a small, but instructive range of cases that include church-state separation, racial vilification, anti-discrimination, religious practices, and symbolic recognition.

Church-State Separation

Curiously, the advent of multiculturalism has not fundamentally eroded Jews' traditional acceptance of the dominant Anglo-Protestant ethos in Australia. Some Jewish leaders have shown concern where the entanglement between the dominant religion and state has appeared too brazen, as in the case of the Anglican Archbishop of Brisbane, Dr Peter Hollingworth, being appointed Governor General of Australia in 2001.[51] But by and large, Australian Jews continue to accept not only the Christian character of Australian society, but also that Christianity will likely – and perhaps even rightly – be reflected in state institutions at some level.

A case in point is the Jewish community's response to the annual "December dilemma" over the singing of Christmas carols and other Christmas cheer in state schools and kindergartens. In the lead up to Christmas 1998, a Jewish father sought to have the NSW Equal Opportunity Tribunal intervene to prevent Santa Claus from visiting his daughter's state school end-of-year party and Christmas carols from being sung there on the grounds that this discriminated against her Jewish faith and made her feel isolated. The Tribunal rejected the application. NSWJBD president at the time, Peter Wertheim, agreed: "Although it is fair to say minority groups should be protected from being pressured into conforming with the religious and cultural practices of the majority, the answer is certainly not trying to prevent the majority from engaging in their religion and culture".[52] Similarly, the *Australian Jewish News* called the Tribunal's determination "fair and sensible".[53] The multiculturalist idea that state schools should perhaps be sites of equality and shared experiences, much less the older, liberal idea that they should be sites of equality and common citizenship, was not an issue for the Jewish community.[54]

Racial Vilification

The Jewish community's commitment to multiculturalism became demonstrably clear from 1996 when the policy suddenly appeared threatened by the rise of maverick politician Pauline Hanson and her One Nation party. Jewish leaders spoke out frequently and as one against her brand of populism and xenophobic politics, and the rank and file of the Jewish community publicly rallied in support of Australian multiculturalism.[55] Jewish individuals were also prominent in establishing new organizations to combat the One Nation threat and promote multiculturalism, such as the Ethnic Coalition Mark II and the Unity Party, which fielded candidates in the 1998 federal election and the 1999 NSW state election.[56]

Well before Hanson arrived on the scene, Jews had led the effort to have laws prohibiting racial vilification at the state and federal levels in Australia.[57] Two landmark cases concerning the federal provisions bear mentioning. One is the first human rights case alleging racial vilification on the internet both to be heard and won in Australia. Jeremy Jones of the ECAJ submitted the complaint to HREOC in 1996 against the Adelaide Institute website of Holocaust denier Dr Fredrick Töben. Under the 1995 racial hatred provisions of the *Racial Discrimination Act 1975* (Cth), it is unlawful to "offend, insult, humiliate or intimidate another person or a group of people because of their race, colour, or national or ethnic origin". After a protracted legal process, the Federal Court of Australia upheld Jones's complaint in September 2002, with the Full Federal Court rejecting Töben's appeal in June 2003, and ordering him to remove the offending material from his website.[58]

The second case involves a complaint submitted jointly by the ECAJ and Jones in 1996 under the racial hatred provisions, this time against a Tasmanian woman, Olga Scully, for distributing anti-Semitic material in Launceston. In 1997, a HREOC commissioner found that the ECAJ was not a person in the eyes of the law and did not have legal standing to bring a complaint against activities by a person in Tasmania. Similarly, Jones was denied standing because, living in Sydney, he was too remote from the actions of Scully to be a "person aggrieved" in relation to them. In 1998, a Federal Court judge set aside the HREOC decision. He found that the ECAJ did have legal standing to bring such complaints because one of its constituent organizations, the Hobart Hebrew Congregation, represented the Jewish community in Tasmania and had a special interest and standing to bring such complaints. Jones was also found to have standing in his then capacity as Executive Vice President of the ECAJ, which represented the interests of 85 percent of the Jewish population of Australia.[59] Jones called the decision "historic", and indeed it is.[60] In multicultural Australia, national community bodies now appear to have a new level of legal recognition to act in behalf of their community's interests.

Anti-Discrimination

As with their approach to racial vilification, Australian Jews have been leading advocates of anti-discrimination legislation. As a group that has historically endured significant invidious discrimination or worse, and with a preponderance of lawyers today as members, this is unsurprising. An unusual case that enjoyed considerable public interest concerned a Melbourne Jewish woman's wish to establish a dating agency exclusively for Jews so that they might find eligible marriage partners within their community. Ms Ann Ivamy-Phillips secured an exemption from the Victorian Anti-Discrimination Tribunal in August 1998 after her initial application failed because of insufficient evidence supporting the need for such an agency.[61] Rabbis, Jewish academics, and the ECAJ testified that the problem of Jews finding an eligible Jewish partner given the small size of the local Jewish community was real, and threatened its survival. The President of the Tribunal, Cate McKenzie, concluded: "Other agencies . . . cater for the population as a whole . . . This service will cater only for Jews and give them the same equality of access".[62]

Speaking afterwards, Ivamy-Phillips said the pleasing result "illustrates the true multicultural atmosphere that people of different cultures and backgrounds can enjoy in Australia".[63] Although the Tribunal warned that other groups should not view its conclusion as a precedent, the decision effectively took sides in the philosophical argument over what kind of multiculturalism should prevail in Australia. It was another victory for the so-called "salad bowl" model of society – where groups retain their distinct identities – over the melting pot or mélange.

Religious Practices

Various Jewish religious practices have tested the terms of Australian multiculturalism. One that has raised questions about the limits of liberal and multicultural toleration is Jewish ritual slaughtering or *shechita*.[64] Jewish law requires that animals to be eaten not be damaged in any way and regards the standard slaughtering practice of prestunning the animal as damaging the animal. Jews have long enjoyed an exemption from Australian laws requiring all animals be stunned before slaughter. However, in a submission to the Australian Law Reform Commission's inquiry into multiculturalism and the law in the early 1990s, the Royal Society for the Protection from Cruelty to Animals called for "vigorous action" against Jewish ritual slaughter, which it described as barbaric and unacceptable.[65] Similar campaigns against kosher slaughtering have taken place in European countries, some successfully.[66] In 1993, a NSW government paper reviewing the cruelty-to-animal laws recommended that animal slaughter without prestunning be prohibited. The NSWJBD made it clear they would regard any such move as "religious discrimination".[67] No prohibition was enacted.

Other cases test less the readiness of authorities to accommodate Jewish religious practices than Australians' sense of society or toleration of cultural difference. An example is the establishment of an *eruv* or token fence (mostly, an almost invisible fishing line) around districts in which religious Jews reside. The *eruv* allows observant Jews to carry items and to push prams on the Sabbath and Jewish holy days. Many major cities around the world have an *eruv*; Melbourne had one erected in 1997, Sydney's 26-kilometre long *eruv* in the eastern suburbs was completed in 2001, although not without controversy. One local resident, a barrister, complained, "the very large area proposed to be enclosed would become a minority enclave". Another resident, who described herself as a fifth generation Australian, objected because the *eruv* was a sign of "separateness" and thus "divisive" in the community.[68]

Symbolic Recognition

Flags, anthems, insignia and public holidays are some of the ways that states officially represent their history and people. In general, and consistent with their position on church-state matters, Jews have not sought to have traditional Australian symbols and holidays changed to reflect the country's cultural diversity. In 1993, Rabbi Jeffrey Kamins of the Progressive Judaism movement called for three floating public holidays each year that "would allow Jews, Muslims, Hindus and others to nominate their special days". The Sydney rabbi, who hails from California, added: "It does seem that when the Christian holidays are our national holidays we are moving away from multiculturalism".[69] The idea failed to ignite broader support within the Jewish community.

Australian Jewry has taken two alternative approaches. One is the expectation that Jews will be included through their rabbinic or elected communal representatives at official state functions and ceremonies, where appropriate. The second approach has been to complement, where possible, Australian traditions with Jewish ones. In recent years, for example, some community groups have staged open public celebrations of *Chanukah* – the Jewish festival of lights that occurs around Christmas time – in city parks. There is an effort to make these carnivals accessible to all Australians, not just to Jews, with Australian celebrities in recent years participating. Sometimes the cultural cues get a bit confused, as when a newly arrived New York rabbi had twenty tons of snow pumped into Sydney's Hyde Park *Chanukah* fair on a summer's day.[70] Nevertheless, the Australian Jewish attitude to symbolic recognition is clear: namely, asking the dominant culture to make room for minorities, rather than expecting it to make itself over for them.

Conclusion

Like their co-religionists in other liberal democracies, Australian Jews were mostly followers in the transition to identity politics and multiculturalism, not leaders. At first, identity politics lay beyond the Jewish comfort zone, seeming to overturn the familiar liberal public/private regime that they had long accepted and prospered under. However, by the time of Prime Minister Howard's address in Melbourne Town Hall in late 1997 – with which this chapter began – the Jewish scene, like much else in Australia from decades past, had changed considerably. After some initial hesitancy, the organized Jewish community grew accustomed to identity politics and came to embrace multiculturalism as a vital national policy that best served its own and, indeed, all Australians' interests.

On the centenary of Australian federation in 2001, the *Australian Jewish News* celebrated how multicultural Australia had "evolved harmoniously into a nation of nations".[71] While this "salad bowl" image of Australian multiculturalism remains hotly contested both by advocates of Anglo-conformity and an Australian melting pot, there is little doubt where the sympathies of most of Australia's Jews lie. With Australian multiculturalism, however, has come a recasting of the traditional dualism in modern Jewish identity. In the aftermath of the liberal French Revolution, the catch cry of Jewish emancipation was "Be a Jew in the home, and a German/Frenchman in the street". Two centuries later, Jewish identity in multicultural Australia might well be summarized as: "Australian Jew in one's community; Jewish Australian on the commons". For all the ambivalence, clearly this is another way of being "forever Australian".

Notes

This chapter is part of a larger research project on Jews and multiculturalism, for which I would like to acknowledge the support of The British Academy Visiting Fellowship scheme. I am grateful to the Centre for the Study of Ethnicity and Citizenship, University of Bristol, and its Director, Professor Tariq Modood, for hosting my visit there in 2002. I also thank Professor Laksiri Jayasuriya for comment on some aspects, and Tiziana Torresi for research assistance.

1 Transcript of the Prime Minister The Hon John Howard MP Address at the National Multicultural Advisory Council Issues Paper Launch *Multicultural Australia: The Way Forward*, Melbourne Town Hall, 11 December 1997. See also Bernard Freedman, "Howard applauds role of East European Jews",

Australian Jewish News [henceforth *AJN*] 26 December 1997. All references to the *AJN* are to the Sydney edition.

2 See, for example, Paul Kelly, "The curse of the M-word", *The Australian* 30–31 August 1997; Editorial, "The politics of the M-word", *Sydney Morning Herald*, 16 December 1997; and Bernard Freedman, "Howard allergic to 'multiculturalism'", *AJN*, 23 May 1997.

3 Count Clermont-Tonnerre quoted in "The French National Assembly: Debate on the Eligibility of Jews for Citizenship (December 23, 1789)", in Paul Mendes-Flohr and Jehuda Reinharz, eds, *The Jew in the Modern World*, second edition (Oxford: Oxford University Press, 1995), p. 115.

4 On the trajectories of Jewish emancipation in different countries, see Pierre Birnbaum and Ira Katznelson, eds, *Paths of Emancipation: Jews, States, and Citizenship* (Princeton, N.J.: Princeton University Press, 1995).

5 Hilary L. Rubinstein et al., *The Jews in the Modern World: A History Since 1750* (London: Arnold; New York: Oxford University Press, 2002), p. 273.

6 Israel Getzler, *Neither Toleration nor Favour: The Australian Chapter of Jewish Emancipation* (Melbourne: Melbourne University Press, 1970), p. 11.

7 English Jews won the right to sit as parliamentary members in 1858. In the United States, Rhode Island secured Jewish equality in 1842, and North Carolina in 1868.

8 Suzanne D. Rutland, *Edge of Diaspora: Two Centuries of Jewish Settlement in Australia*, 1st edn (Sydney: Collins, 1988), p. 106.

9 See Rubinstein et al., *Jews in the Modern World*, pp. 417–38.

10 The small numbers and high degree of integration of the predominantly Anglo-Australian Jewish community up to the 1930s did raise questions about its ultimate assimilation. The arrival of Eastern European Jewish immigrants before and after World War II arrested this trend and reinvigorated the Jewish community *qua* a distinct community. See, for example, Peter Y. Medding, *From Assimilation to Group Survival: A Political and Sociological Study of an Australian Jewish Community* (Melbourne: Cheshire, 1968).

11 W. D. Rubinstein, *Judaism in Australia* (Canberra: Australian Government Publishing Service, 1997), pp. 48–52.

12 See Medding, *From Assimilation to Group Survival*.

13 For elaboration on this theme, see Daniel J. Elazar and Stuart A. Cohen, *The Jewish Polity: Jewish Political Organization from Biblical Times to the Present* (Bloomington: Indiana University Press, 1985).

14 That Zangwill's vision wholly excluded the situation of African and Native Americans means, of course, that it was less than fully democratic.

15 See respectively, Israel Zangwill, *The Melting-Pot: Drama in Four Acts* (New York: Macmillan, 1912); Horace M. Kallen, *Culture and Democracy in the United States* (New York: Boni and Liveright, 1924); and Will Herberg, *Protestant, Catholic, Jew: An Essay in American Religious Sociology*, 1st edn (Garden City, NY: Doubleday, 1955).

16 See Department of Immigration and Multicultural Affairs, *The Abolition of the 'White Australia' Policy*, Fact Sheet No. 5 (2001).

17 Australian Bureau of Statistics, *Migration*, Cat No. 3412.0 (1999–2000), p. 93.

18 See, e.g., Department of Immigration and Multicultural Affairs, *The Evolution of Australia's Multicultural Policies*, Fact Sheet No. 8 (2001).

19 Mark Lopez, *The Origins of Multiculturalism in Australian Politics 1945–1975* (Melbourne: Melbourne University Press, 2000), pp. 54–5.

20 The two main blueprints of Australian multiculturalism are the *National Agenda for a Multicultural Australia* (1989) launched by the Hawke Labor Government, and *A New Agenda for Multicultural Australia* (1999), launched by Howard's conservative Coalition. For a critical interpretation of these documents, see Geoffrey Brahm Levey, "The Political Theories of Australian Multiculturalism", *University of New South Wales Law Journal* 24 (2001): 869–81.

21 Lopez, *Origins of Multiculturalism in Australian Politics*, pp. 37–8.

22 Nathan Glazer and Daniel Patrick Moynihan, *Beyond the Melting Pot: The Negroes, Puerto Ricans, Jews, Italians, and Irish of New York City*, 2nd edn (Cambridge, MA: MIT Press, 1970), p. 290.

23 See Milton M. Gordon, *Assimilation in American Life: The Role of Race, Religion, and National Origins* (New York: Oxford University Press, 1964); and Kallen, *Culture and Democracy*. Kallen's vision of cultural pluralism involved territorially based, largely self-governing cultural communities on the model of the Swiss cantons and the national regions in Great Britain. In Australia, "cultural pluralism" conveys no such formal territorial and institutional autonomies, but rather the idea that retention of one's particular cultural background and heritage is simply accepted. On this meaning – which I adopt in this chapter – society resembles, in the popular image, a "salad bowl" of distinct cultural identities under a common political authority.

24 On this contrast, see Jon Stratton, *Coming Out Jewish: Constructing Ambivalent Identities* (London: Routledge, 2000), chaps. 8 and 9.

25 David Biale, Michael Galchinsky, and Susannah Heschel, "Introduction: The Dialectic of Jewish Enlightenment", in D. Biale, M. Galchinsky, and S. Heschel, eds, *Insider/Outsider: American Jews and Multiculturalism* (Berkeley: University of California Press, 1998), pp. 1–13.

26 Michael Galchinsky, "Glimpsing *Golus* in the Golden Land: Jews and Multiculturalism in America", *Judaism* 43 (1994): 360–8 at p. 365.

27 On American Jewry's reorientation from the "liberal politics of individual rights" to the "pluralist politics of group survival", see Peter Y. Medding, *The Transformation of American Jewish Politics* (New York: American Jewish Committee, 1989).

28 See, for example, Walter M. Lippmann, "Australian Jewry: Can it Survive?", *The Bridge* (Jan. 1973): 6–11.

29 Lopez, *Origins of Multiculturalism*, p. 5.

30 See, respectively, Lopez, *Origins of Multiculturalism in Australian Politics*, pp. 109–10; Jean Martin, *The Ethnic Dimension: Papers on Ethnicity and Pluralism*, edited and introduction by S. Encel (Sydney: George Allen & Unwin, 1981); Andrew Jakubowicz, "State and Ethnicity: Multiculturalism as Ideology", *Australian and New Zealand Journal of Sociology* 17 (1981): 4–13; and Frank Knopfelmacher, "The Case Against Multi-culturalism", in Robert Manne, ed., *The New Conservatism in Australia* (Melbourne: Oxford University Press, 1982), pp. 40–64.

31 Australian Council on Population and Ethnic Affairs, *Multiculturalism for all Australians: Our Developing Nationhood* (Canberra: Australian Government Publishing Service, 1982).

32   Council of the Australian Institute of Multicultural Affairs, *Looking Forward: A Report on Consultations Concerning the Recommendations of the Committee of Review of the Australian Institute of Multicultural Affairs* (Melbourne: The Institute, 1984).

33   Stratton, *Coming Out Jewish*, pp. 234–5.

34   Sol Encel, "Anti-Semitism and Prejudice in Australia", *Without Prejudice* 1 (1990): 37–47 at p. 44.

35   Peter Scott, "Ethnic, religious, or just peculiar?" *Australian Jewish Times*, 27 November, 1975. I am grateful to Louise Leibowitz for bringing this report to my attention.

36   Although, reputedly, Lippmann also had made many enemies in the Melbourne Jewish community (Lopez, *Origins of Multiculturalism*, p. 442).

37   Scott, "Ethnic, religious, or just peculiar?".

38   Stratton, *Coming Out Jewish*, p. 220.

39   On similar attitudes among Jews in Queensland, see Uri Themal, "Making Multicultural Music in Ethnic Affairs", *Generation* 5 (June 1995): 3–5.

40   For example, in 1996 the Kennett Liberal government in Victoria reconstituted its long-standing Ethnic Affairs Commission as the Victorian Multicultural Commission, and in 1998 the Beattie Labor government replaced Queensland's Bureau for Ethnic Affairs with Multicultural Affairs Queensland.

41   Bob Carr quoted in Editorial, "Ethnic Australians: Have we moved on?", *AJN*, 23 March 2001.

42   See Vic Alhadeff, "Government's ethnic body 'ethnic' no longer", *AJN*, 23 March, 2001; and the conspiratorial critique by Andrew Jakubowicz, "Are ethnic affairs over for New South Wales?", *AJN*, 7 May 1999.

43   Editorial, "End to ethnic focusing", *Sydney Morning Herald*, 19 April 1999.

44   *Community Relations Commission and Principles of Multiculturalism Act 2000* (NSW).

45   Sharon Labi, "Mixed reaction as Premier dumps 'ethnic' affairs", *AJN*, 16 April 1999.

46   Vic Alhadeff, "How a non-event became part of the story", *AJN*, 7 November 2003.

47   See, for example, the ECAJ's "Open letter to political, religious, civic and community leaders of Australia" of 25 March 2003 [www.ecaj.org.au].

48   See John Goldlust's chapter this volume, and A.C. Gariano and S. D. Rutland, "Religious Intermix: 1996 Census Update", *People and Place* 5 (1997): 10–18.

49   See Sharon Labi, "50 percent intermarriage", *AJN*, 18 June 1999, reporting a study of intermarriage among 20–29 year old Sydney Jews.

50   Victor Kleerekoper, "Hawke stuns Jews, praises intermarriage", *AJN*, 16 July 1999; "Intermarriage remark clarified", *AJN*, 23 July 1999.

51   See Bernard Freedman, "Unease over a cleric G-G", *AJN*, 4 May 2001, citing reservations by then ECAJ president, Nina Bassat.

52   Sharon Labi, "Mixed Jewish reaction to Santa at School", *AJN*, 11 December 1998.

53   Editorial, "December dilemma", *AJN*, 11 December 1998.

54   On the multicultural idea in this context, see Geoffrey Brahm Levey, "A santa schmanta response: Jews and Christmas", *The Australian*, 18 December 1998.

On the liberal idea, see the Jewish father's outraged letter on the lack of Jewish community support: Mr A., "I will proudly walk alone", *AJN*, 18 December 1998; and Stephen M. Feldman, *Please Don't Wish Me a Merry Christmas: A Critical History of the Separation of Church and State* (New York: New York University Press, 1997), esp. pp. 1–9.

55 See, for example, Margaret Safran, "Jews rally against racism", *AJN*, 13 December 1996; Bernard Freedman, "Australian Jewry condemns Hanson", *AJN*, 9 May 1997; and Margaret Safran, "Howard attacked for weak handling of Hanson", *AJN*, 18 September 1998.

56 See Bernard Freedman, "Second ethnic coalition formed", *AJN*, 26 June, 1998; and Sharon Labi, "Platform of diversity", *AJN*, 12 March 1999.

57 See Jacqui Seemann, "Racial Vilification Legislation and Anti-Semitism in NSW: The Likely Impact of the Amendment", *Sydney Law Review* 12 (1990): 596–615.

58 Toben v Jones [2003] FCAFC 137 (27 June 2003).

59 Executive Council of Australian Jewry & Anor v Olga Scully & Anor [1998] 66 FCA (13 February 1998).

60 Jeremy Jones quoted in "ECAJ can complain about racist acts", *AJN*, 27 February 1998.

61 AIP Consultancy [1998] VADT 1 (16 June 1998); and AIP Consultancy No. 2 [1998] VADT 2 (28 August 1998).

62 AIP Consultancy No. 2 [1998].

63 AAP, "Dating agency can be strictly kosher, tribunal decides", *Sydney Morning Herald*, 29 August 1998.

64 Another such case is infant male circumcision. See, for example, David Richards, "Male Circumcision: Medical or Ritual?", *Journal of Law and Medicine* 3 (1996): 371–6. See also Geoffrey Brahm Levey, "Circumcision or circumscribed?", *AJN*, 23 May 1997; and the subsequent letters exchange: Rabbis Raymond Apple and Moshe Gutnick, "Disservice", *AJN*, 30 May 1997; and Geoffrey Brahm Levey, "Best defence is tackling issues head-on", *AJN*, 6 June 1997.

65 See Sigrid Kirk, "Jews defend right to animal slaughter", *Sydney Morning Herald*, 4 July 1991.

66 Sweden, for example, has outlawed *shechita* for livestock, whilst allowing it for fowl.

67 Elizabeth Jurman, "Proposals to change animal slaughter laws anger Jews", *Sydney Morning Herald*, 18 January 1993.

68 Stefan Bialoguski, "Concern voiced, but *eruv* approved", *AJN*, 9 June 2000.

69 Michelle Gunn, "A multiculturally sound solution to the debate over public holidays", *The Australian*, 14 April 1993.

70 "Chanukah in New York – in Sydney", *AJN*, 11 December 1998.

71 Editorial, "Australia at 100: A great nation of nations", *AJN*, 26 January 2001.

12 | Inside AIJAC – An Australian Jewish Lobby Group

CHANAN REICH

This chapter deals with the major Australian Jewish lobby group AIJAC – The Australia Israel and Jewish Affairs Council – and its activities in the Australian political process. AIJAC fits well into Keith Abbott's definition of pressure groups as "political organizations that seek to encourage governments to adopt the policies they advocate . . . [It is] an independent, non-party organization with an organizational structure and formally affiliated members that have shared interests, which represents or claims to represent those interests by bringing organized pressure to bear on the political process of government".[1] A former editor of AIJAC's *Review*, Adam Indikt, defined its role in terms of pro-Israel and Jewish advocacy "to confront the enemies of plurality and democracy, and defend the interests of the State of Israel". Similarly, its National Chairman, Mark Leibler, claimed that AIJAC's campaigns in support of Israel and against terrorism, hatred, racism, Holocaust denial, and on war crimes had benefited not only the Jewish community, but also Australia as a whole.[2]

AIJAC evolved out of the amalgamation of two earlier Jewish organizations. The first established was Australia-Israel Publications (AIP) in 1974, under the joint chairmanship of Robert Zablud and Isador Magid, both key Melbourne Jewish personalities. Its formation reflected the realization by the Zionist Federation of Australia that it was losing the public relations battle. Its main purpose was to present pro-Israel perspectives within the media and in political debate, and to achieve this aim it began the publication of a monthly journal, the *Australia-Israel Review*, with Sam Lipski as its first editor. AIP became the best resourced of Australian Jewish organizations under the leadership of Isador Magid and, later, Mark Leibler, with appointments, at the editorial level, of full-time southern and northern directors in 1982 and of a director of public affairs in 1987. The second organization was the Australian Institute of Jewish Affairs (AIJA), which was founded in 1984 by two Melbourne businessmen, Isi Leibler and Richard Pratt. Its purpose was to conduct and promote research into issues of concern to the Jewish community. In 1997, AIP and AIJA amalgamated to form the Australia/Israel & Jewish Affairs Council (AIJAC), now generally recognized as the main, albeit unofficial, Jewish advocacy body in Australia.

AIJAC Executive Director, Dr Colin Rubenstein, emphasizes that his organization's primary responsibility and interest is in Australia and the Australian Jewish community:

> We are an Australian organization, and are very interested in promoting the sort of fabric of Australian multicultural democracy. We believe that it is in Australia's interest to . . . contain extremism; to promote resolution of deadly conflicts like the Arab–Israeli; to support democracies and democratization. Obviously we believe that Australian support for Israel is warranted but in a very balanced way. It is not inconsistent with Australian support for other Middle Eastern countries, but not Australian support for irredentist regimes and terrorism. We see ourself promoting Australian interests and Australian society, Australian democracy; and therefore we take very seriously our role in exposing extremism and racism on the far left as well as obviously on the far right . . . the League of Rights, La Rouche and the whole cluster of lunar far right organizations and individuals; and of course we take a certain degree of pride in taking the lead in exposing the implications and the ravages of [Pauline Hanson's] One Nation [Party] were causing . . . We do take seriously the regional context and the ravages of terrorism and Islamism but also the importance of working with like-minded and positive elements and that's why for example we struck up a very good rapport with President Wahid in Indonesia.[3]

Rubenstein describes his organization as an independent think-tank generating reliable analysis and information about the Middle East and conveying it to opinion-makers in the media and within bureaucracies, and to politicians, academics, and individuals and organizations dealing with international affairs and the Middle East. While readily conceding that the main reason for establishing AIJAC, and its current primary focus, is the Middle East, he emphasizes that AIJAC also has a domestic agenda, including war criminals, Holocaust deniers, anti-Semitism and racism, promoting multiculturalism and dealing with the security concerns of Jewish institutions as part of the general problem of security in Australia.[4]

Rubenstein is adamant that unless AIJAC can generate credible, quality, and reliable information and analysis it won't get anywhere. He is confident that advancing an understanding of the situation is the best way of promoting both Israel's interests and the interests of moderate elements across the Middle East that are open to the possibility of development and democratization, reconciliation and co-existence:

> Call it what you will – lobbying, propaganda; but the fact is we are always trying to provide the best possible analysis of what's happening. Because we are confi-

dent that the case of Israel is a good one there is no point gilding the lilies or covering up or pulling punches; that you call a spade a spade and especially in the Australian context. I think all of us underestimate how complex the Middle East really is. So many people simply operate out of a lack of understanding for what is a very complex set of realities . . . We think the best contribution we can make is try and shed a little bit of light on those realities and [leave the rest to] the democratic instincts of Australians and democratic reality of Israel.[5]

According to Rubenstein, key opinion-makers constantly approach AIJAC for information and comments. In turn, AIJAC often provides information to journalists known to have an interest in certain issues. AIJAC also brings speakers out to Australia to meet "serious journalists", politicians and bureaucrats. Rubenstein and Mark Leibler lobby the Department of Foreign Affairs and parliamentarians, including those critical of Israel such as the Australian Labor Party (ALP) MHR Tanya Plibersek, who met with AIJAC officials and visited the Holocaust museum in Sydney. In 2003 former Israeli Prime Minister Ehud Barak visited Australia and addressed a well-attended dinner of a bi-partisan parliamentary group, including Australian Foreign Minister, Alexander Downer, then federal Opposition and ALP Leader, Simon Crean, and the Opposition spokesperson on Foreign Affairs, Kevin Rudd.

At the end of 2003, AIJAC launched a new scheme, the Rambam Israel Fellowship Program, which aims to promote educational and fact-finding missions to Israel for opinion-leaders drawn from areas of public life such as politics, the media, trade unions and the academic community.[6] The first such group to visit Israel comprised eight prominent young political leaders who undertook a comprehensive week-long program of activities in July 2003. This activity was followed in December when a five-member Coalition parliamentary group spent a week in Israel as Rambam fellows. A third Rambam bipartisan parliamentary delegation to Israel took place in February 2004, including Senators Stephen Conroy (Labor, Vic.), Linda Kirk (Liberal, SA) and Ursula Stephens (Labor, NSW), and Liberal MPs Steven Ciobo, Sophie Panopoulos, and Andrew Southcott.

Rubenstein believes AIJAC enjoys good access on both sides of the political spectrum because "what we represent and the information that we bring helps policy makers . . . in their jobs in serving Australian interest . . . ".[7] At the same time he scoffs at the notion of "the powerful Jewish lobby", maintaining that he regularly encounters great difficulty in getting his articles published in Australia, which he attributes to pressure by Arab-Australian organizations. While accepting as perfectly legitimate Arab-Australian organizations' activities to counter negative stereotyping, racism or discrimination, he takes exception to what he regards as its activities against AIJAC. He criticised the Arab lobby's attitude to the federal Racial Vilification Bill, maintaining that they had opposed the legislation "because they thought it would be used against them, but when it was passed they were the first to use it". He is also very critical of Arab newspapers and radio programs in Australia, which he regards as extreme.

In November 1995, AIJAC's predecessor, AIP, came into conflict with the Australian Arabic Council (ACC) over a statement by David Pryce-Jones at a function at Beth Weizman following the assassination of Yitzhak Rabin. The *Herald Sun* in Melbourne quoted Pryce-Jones as having said "to shoot one's prime minister is what Arabs do, not what Jews do". Consequently the ACC lodged official complaints against the *Herald Sun* and AIP with the Australian Press Council and with the Human Rights and Equal Opportunity Commission. The conflict was resolved in December 1997 with an agreement for a public apology by AIP, which was published in the *Herald Sun*.[8]

Palestinian officials are very critical of AIJAC. The Head of the General Palestinian Delegation to Australia, Ali Kazak, accused AIJAC – "the Israeli lobby" – of attempting to prevent any factual reporting on the Palestine–Israel conflict by the Australian media. He was referring to AIJAC's report to SBS titled "SBS-TV and the Middle East", which, he claimed, "was full of deliberate deceptions and distortions of facts aiming to prevent SBS from covering any factual reporting on Israel's internationally-condemned bloody occupation, violations and war crimes committed on a daily basis against the defenceless Palestinian people on the pretext that such coverage is pro-Palestinian".[9]

AIJAC liaises closely with other Jewish organizations including the Executive Council of Australian Jewry (ECAJ) – the official representative roof body of Australian Jewry. AIJAC also tries to be a resource and a liaison to other Jewish organizations, although co-operation varies. It has naturally close links with the Zionist Federation of Australia (ZFA), with which it co-organizes functions. AIJAC also co-hosts visitors with the ZFA, ECAJ, and the state Jewish Boards of Deputies, and works closely with the Jewish National Fund and the United Israel Appeal (UIA). AIJAC also regards itself as a resource for students through the World Union of Jewish Students and offers assistance to other Jewish organizations in obtaining access to the media. Rubenstein acknowledges and laments past examples of competition with other Jewish organizations, which he claims were gratuitous and unnecessary.[10]

Rubenstein is accountable to a Board of Directors. Originally the two Directors were the prominent Australian Jewish businessmen Isidor Magid and Bob Zablud. Currently he is accountable to Mark Liebler, whom he described as having "added even further organizational discipline and strength to AIJAC", and to the Board. AIJAC is "a very tightly run organization in terms of our financing and our accountability", and raises funds within the Jewish community. Though it does not have public fund-raising appeals, it solicits support from like-minded leaders in the community, mainly in Melbourne and Sydney. AIJAC's ability to obtain funds for its operation depends on its ability to satisfy Jewish leaders and ordinary people.[11]

Rubenstein maintains that AIJAC is under-resourced for what it is trying to do. "Functionally we are a combination of the American Israel Public Affairs Committee and the American Jewish Committee. Both are huge organizations. We have a huge agenda and very modest resources". AIJAC's staff has grown, and at the end of 2003 it had 5 in Sydney and 10 in Melbourne. Believing that the issues are growing domestically, regionally and internationally, Rubenstein's aims are to professionalize and institutionalize AIJAC's role as a think-tank and to build broad coalitions on a variety of issues of importance to the Jewish community and to Australia. He is convinced that without his organization's activities "things would be a lot worse".[12]

The Australian Jewish community does not speak with one voice. Over the years, the main dissenting group has been the Australian Jewish Democratic Society (AJDS), discussed elsewhere in this book.[13] Rubenstein, while maintaining that he personally can live with dissent within the Jewish community, claims that it does present a problem for the community:

> If someone in a telephone box claims to be a Jewish leader we can tell them that that person, whoever he or she is, is not a Jewish leader. He might be leader of an anti-Jewish or certainly an anti-Israel lobby. The fact that he is born Jewish does not make him a Jewish leader. So we have to talk the realities and also we deal with the arguments that any fringe group might be able to advance, I mean that they are representative when they are not; and that they are mainstream when they are not. If they want to have a view that's fine; but they can't [mis]represent who they are and the position that they are taking. So, you know, it's a free country just so long as people do not operate under false pretences saying that they are what they are not.[14]

Rubenstein came to AIJAC from an academic career and maintains that his activities are based on the same strict academic standards. He has not received any instructions and has been given a high degree of professional independence to pursue AIJAC's objectives. He believed that AIJAC would only be able to achieve things if it did quality work, which requires a degree of autonomy and independence within the realm of pursuing "agreed objectives". AIJAC claims to be strictly bi-partisan in pursuing the interests of the Australian Jewish community. Its aim is to win friends on both sides of the political divide and to deal with critics and even enemies from whichever side of politics they come.[15]

In May 1997, AIJAC and the American Jewish Committee established institutional ties to advance joint interests. They agreed that while each organization would retain full autonomy and independence they would be collaborating on key Jewish communal and international policy issues, including defending the rights of Jews and other minorities and strengthening understanding between Jews and other ethnic and religious groups in their own countries and around the world; advocating for Jewish concerns in Asia and the Pacific Rim; enhancing Israel's security, peace and diplomatic normalization; combating hate groups and strengthening the forces of democratic pluralism; preventing the dissemination of Holocaust revisionism and other manifestations of antisemitism; countering the influence of Islamic extremism and other movements inimical to the welfare of the Jewish people; monitoring and raising awareness about the activities of Iran and other rogue states that engage in terrorism, seek to acquire destabilizing weapons, and in other ways threaten international security; and encouraging greater dialogue and understanding within the Diaspora, and between Israelis and Jews in other lands. They also agreed on joint sponsorship of research and publications, conferences, symposia, exchange programs, and fact-finding missions to Third World countries, especially in Asia and the Pacific region.[16]

AIJAC has continued to publish *The Review*, a monthly journal highlighting developments in the Middle East affecting Israel and public policy issues of concern to the Australian Jewish community. *The Review* was established in Melbourne by AIP in 1977 originally under the title of *Australia-Israel Review*. As noted, its first editor was Sam Lipski, a well-known journalist, and was dedicated "to putting Israel's case to Australia's opinion-makers". The newsletter had an editorial board, which initially consisted of Rubenstein, Professor Ronald Taft, Dr Rodney Gouttman, Rabbi John Levi and Professor W. D. Rubinstein. *The Review* went out to every member of every parliament, state and federal, in Australia, a practice that continues to this day. It was also sent to leading clergymen, academics and journalists. By the late 1980s it had a circulation of 3,600.[17] Over time, it was transformed from a densely packed eight-page newsletter into a glossy twelve-page magazine in 1994.

AIP's work included giving lectures, conducting seminars on university campuses, publishing and distributing booklets, appearing on television and radio, and organizing visits to Israel by parliamentarians, political and trade union leaders, journalists and film makers. According to its founder, Isidor Magid, there was a very good reaction from all quarters in the public. "They knew that everything in those days in the press was anti-Israel and pro-Arab and that Israeli publications had an official line . . . [Lipski, in contrast] took a neutral line". Magid attributed *The Review*'s editorial independence to the fact that he personally and not the State of Israel had financed it. Similar magazines were established in Brussels and San Francisco, with which *The Review* exchanged material. Lipski's successor as editor was Michael Danby, currently the federal Parliament's only Jewish MP. In the 1980s *The Review* began to devote attention to the far right in Australia. By 2000, *The Review* was devoting far more attention to Australian issues and local politics.[18]

Lipski emphasized the "all important psychological link between the local Jewish condition and Israel's standing". He regarded the driving force behind AIP's establishment "as much the growing discomfort and anxiety of Australian Jews at what was happening to their sense of security in this country, as it was their undoubted concern for Israel's security in the international arena". Similarly, Indikt claims that *The Review* represented an important statement that the Australia Jewish community would not stand by and allow a biased media coverage to affect Israel's image in Australia. In that respect, the establishment of AIP was a response to the hostility to Israel by the Labor Government of Gough Whitlam and the National Party, and to the growth of a large Arab community in Australia that had developed its own access and influence with politicians and the media.[19]

In 1988 *The Review* became national with the opening of its office in Sydney. Since 1994, *The Review* has evolved from a newsletter providing background information into an advocacy journal with original researched and breaking stories. It also tracked a consistent increase in activity by far right extremist organizations throughout Australia. *The Review* campaigned strongly against the entrance to Australia of individuals with a history of extremist agitation, such as David Irving, Louis Farrakhan, and members of the LaRouche cult. According to Indikt, Pauline Hanson's One Nation Party and far right and neo-Nazi organizations were politically destroyed by *The Review*.[20] Yet, while AIJAC may have contributed to the downfall of One Nation, the Party's leaders Pauline Hanson and David Ettridge also mightily contributed to this themselves through adopting procedures that produced legal investigations and ultimately prison terms for them.[21]

While maintaining a strongly pro-Israel editorial line, in the 1990s *The Review* carried interviews with Palestinian leaders, including Hanan Ashrawi, Yasser Arafat and Nabil Shaath as well as Israeli leaders Benjamin Netanyahu, Moshe Arens and Shimon Peres. *The Review* maintained a strong interest in the proliferation of weapons of mass destruction and, in particular, "rogue Middle East nations" seeking to acquire nuclear weapons capability.[22]

AIJAC has its critics. Former Australian diplomat, Richard Woolcott, a proponent of "a more balanced approach to the Middle East" by the Australian government, laments: "The Jewish lobby in Australia, although relatively small compared with that in America, was also influential and had the ear of Prime Minister Hawke".[23] According to Woolcott, "the combination of American and Jewish pressure made it difficult for Australia to move to a more balanced position".[24] AIJAC also has occasionally come in for severe criticism from within the Jewish community. Its decision in 1998 to publish One Nation's secret membership list caused considerable controversy in the community, as did its proactive opposition to the award of the Sydney Peace Prize to Palestinian activist Hanan Ashrawi in 2003 (analyzed in detail in the next chapter).[25] For example, David Langsam maintained that AIJAC's "relentless [disinformation] campaign against

Sydney Peace Prize recipient Dr Hanan Ashrawi has been very successful – at making the Jewish community look like bullies determined to get their own way at any cost". He expressed his dismay that AIJAC's lobbying had led to "a perception that it is a representative organization, its world view is Jewish public opinion and its methods are supported by the Jewish community. To the wider community they are bullies, but within the community they act like guard dogs keeping us from saying publicly what we think, should we dare to disagree with their worldview".[26]

AIJAC has dedicated a lot of its energies fighting what it has regarded as anti-Israel bias in the media and in certain organizations. Thus in January 2003, following a review undertaken by AIJAC of SBS *World News* over the calendar year of 2001, Daniel Mandel accused SBS of a consistent anti-Israel bias in its reporting, including a pattern of factual inaccuracy, bias in selection of facts and distribution of emphasis in reportage, biased choice of language, and reportage that regularly spills over into covert or overt editorializing. He also accused SBS of a "lack of responsiveness, indeed negativity, to reasoned and documented complaints". Mandel claimed that AIJAC's analysis of SBS documentaries and current affairs programming revealed a decade-long pattern of favouring overwhelmingly pro-Palestinian documentaries or material severely critical of Israel, no matter how biased and unreliable. The exception to this had been SBS' current affairs program *Dateline*, which had exhibited greater responsibility and balance. According to Mandel, when a single pro-Israel documentary – "A Nation is Born" written and narrated by the late Abba Eban – was screened on SBS in 1996, it took the unusual step of including an introductory disclaimer, describing it as "a partisan view". This practice, according to Mandel, had never been adopted for even the most blatantly pro-Palestinian programming over many years. Mandel also claimed that when, in the early 1990s, a Melbourne documentary filmmaker, Monique Schwarz, submitted to SBS a documentary she had produced about the effect on Israeli families of the Iraqi Scud missile attacks during the Gulf War, she was told by an SBS staff member that while SBS found the documentary interesting, it could never show a program on the Middle East "which did not contain an Arab point of view". Mandel concluded: "A track record that speaks as clearly as this is enough to indicate why the Australian Jewish community is concerned about SBS. It's time SBS provided some answers – and remedies – namely, an independent complaints procedure".[27]

AIJAC maintains close links with its former staffer, Michael Danby, in federal Parliament. Rubenstein praised Danby for being very helpful by raising certain issues in Parliament and providing a particular perspective. Although he is convinced that "you don't have to be Jewish to be pro-Israel", Rubenstein wishes there were more Jewish members of the national Parliament, including in the Liberal/National Party Coalition. He is proud of the fact that "we['ve] got a lot of good friends of Israel in Parliament", and that the Parliamentary Friends of Israel group is active and the largest such group in Parliament.[28]

AIJAC also maintains strong connections with Prime Minister Howard and other sympathetic parliamentarians. For example, Howard addressed an AIJAC/UIA dinner in Melbourne in November 2000. He spoke of his visit to Israel in April, and applauded the genuine Israeli efforts to reach a peace agreement with the Palestinians. He argued that the generous Israeli peace plan proposed by Israeli Prime Minister Ehud Barak the previous July should have been accepted by the Palestinian Authority. "It was an offer that should have been accepted and it is tragic in the extreme that it has not been accepted . . . I believe Barak displayed very great courage and he should be encouraged for the efforts that he has so far displayed". Mark Leibler commended Howard for "understanding that Israel has made serious, unrewarded efforts to reach a just and lasting peace which the Palestinians should have accepted". Rubenstein called on international leaders "to join Mr Howard in urging renewed commitment to the peace process. Instead of reciprocating with violence and terrorism, the Palestinians should recognise the need for a negotiated settlement".[29]

Similarly, in June 2001 the Australia-Israel Parliamentary Friendship Group expressed its condolences to the people and government of Israel for the recent deaths of 20 Israeli youngsters killed by a Palestinian suicide bomber. Christopher Pyne, Chairperson of the Group, said, "Both the Australian Government and Opposition had called on Palestinian Authority Chairman, Yasser Arafat to commit to a ceasefire by all elements of the Palestinian Arabs". Michael Danby, secretary of the Friendship Group, claimed that Australian parliamentarians supported these sentiments. Pyne and Danby added, "If the Palestinian Authority are to have even a shred of credibility Arafat must effectively implement, in deed as in word, the ceasefire before any further progress can by made".[30]

AIJAC and other Jewish organizations have been particularly critical of ALP backbencher Julia Irwin, one of Labor's strongest Palestinian supporters and who, in November 2002, moved in Parliament "That this House:

(1) notes the continued occupation by the State of Israel of the West Bank and Gaza Strip in contravention of United Nations Resolution 242 passed on 22 November 1967;
(2) supports the right of Israel to exist within secure borders;
(3) calls on the United Nations to insert a peace keeping force into the occupied territories of the West Bank and Gaza and the unconditional withdrawal of Israeli forces;
(4) calls for the recognition of the State of Palestine based on the pre-1967 borders of the West Bank and Gaza; and
(5) calls on the international community to encourage and support the

resolution of outstanding differences between the State of Israel and the State of Palestine based on the Oslo and Camp David Agreements".

Rubenstein described Irwin's private motion as "one-sided", "ignorant of the legal and political complexities inherent in the conflict" and "completely unhelpful" to achieving an end to the current violence and promoting peace. He added,

> by asking nothing of the Palestinians, [it] essentially seeks to reward terrorism. It is simply appalling that the day after a gunman working for the Al-Aqsa faction of Yasser Arafat's own Fatah party infiltrated an Israeli Kibbutz and shot dead five people, including two children, that a parliamentary motion which does not even call on the Palestinians to end terrorism and arrest terrorists, as required by international law, is even being considered. Moreover, this motion claims that Israel is violating UN Security Council Resolution 242, and implies that 242 calls for an unconditional Israeli withdrawal to the pre-1967 armistice lines, both of which are simply not true . . . Peace in the Middle East has never been more needed than today. But this one-sided and ignorant resolution . . . is completely unhelpful to that goal.

Consequently AIJAC called on Australian parliamentarians who cared about a just and lasting peace in the Middle East "to treat it with the disdain it deserves".[31]

ALP backbenchers' criticism of Israel caused great concern to Michael Danby, the ALP MHR for Melbourne Ports – an electorate comprising 90,000 voters, around 25 percent of whom are Jewish. Since he holds his seat by a margin of only 6 percent, he warned his party about the amount of coverage that the anti-Israel comments got and how it impacted on people in the electorate. A number of Jewish leaders informed then Opposition leader Crean of their discontent. Consequently Foreign Affairs Shadow Minister Kevin Rudd told a meeting of 800 people in Melbourne that the ALP was not moving to the left on the Middle East and that its policy would not change. Similarly, Crean told Jewish community leaders at a function in St Kilda to ignore criticisms of Israel from his backbench and assured them that his party's support for Israel remained strong. At question time, at the end of Mr Crean's speech, members of the audience accused several ALP MPs of anti-Semitism and racism. But Crean rejected their concerns, assuring his audience of his life-long support for the State of Israel.[32]

Crean came under criticism from Peter Rodgers, Australia's former Ambassador to Israel, who claimed in an open letter, published in *The Age*, that the Opposition Leader had an opportunity to speak frankly about Israel, but instead of offering a close, critical examination, he ducked for cover behind platitudes. According to Rodgers, the real challenge for Israel, and its friends, was to drain the pool of anger and bitterness. Yet, all too often Israel and its supporters try to shut down legitimate debate by accusing critics of being "anti-Israeli" or, worse, of being "anti-Semitic". If criticism of Israeli policies is the yardstick for defining anti-Semitism, you'll know from your own visits that there's an awful lot of it in Israel! . . . Unless we are honest with Israelis and their friends, as well as with Palestinians, we do them – and ultimately ourselves – no favours.[33]

In contrast, Rubenstein praised Crean's speech as "powerful, perceptive, appropriate and straight-forward" and criticized Rodgers' open letter. Rubenstein hailed Crean's forceful approach to terrorism, including his call for the isolation of the terrorist leaders, their deliverance to justice, the destruction of their networks and their moral justifications exposed as the rationalizations of fanatics. He praised the ALP leader for acknowledging "the indivisibility of terrorism; that it does not distinguish between Israeli, Indonesian, Iraqi or Australian victims, and that the fight against terrorism is as relevant in Bali or Baghdad as in Jerusalem. Anything less would have created a most unacceptable double standard". According to Rubenstein, Crean was balanced in the correct way with regard to Israel and the Palestinians, acknowledging the legitimate needs of both sides; applying equal standards in judging their behaviour; recognising Israel's right to fight attacks on its civilians; and calling on all parties to the conflict to exercise maximum restraint.[34]

Although Israel and the Middle East command AIJAC's focused attention, it also concerns itself with a range of other international and local issues. A number of these may briefly be canvassed here.

Islamism and Terrorism in Asia and the Pacific

In 1999, AIJAC in association with the American Jewish Committee produced a detailed research study, *Islam in Asia: Changing Political Realities.* The study looked specifically at the role of Islam in four regional centres: Indonesia, Malaysia, the southern Philippines and southern Thailand. In the wake of the challenge presented by the September 11 terrorist atrocities, AIJAC fully supported the US-led coalition in the war against terrorism, including the campaign in Afghanistan and the action in Iraq. AIJAC regarded the growth of Islamic extremism in Asia as constituting an important issue not only for all Australians, but Israel and the Australian Jewish community in particular.

According to Rubenstein, "The interest of Australia, of the US, and of AIJAC and the American Jewish Committee, is in a peaceful, stable, democratic and prosperous Southeast Asia . . . This timely current study offers the chance to understand and work with the local Islamic forces that can contribute to bringing this about". Jason Isaacson, Director of the Asia and Pacific Rim Institute of the American Jewish Committee emphasized the importance of the study in the light of the election of moderate Muslim cleric Abdurrahman Wahid as the new President of Indonesia. Professor Bruce Grant, former Australian High Commissioner in India, launched the study in Melbourne. Grant emphasized the value of the Report given the lack of understanding in Australia of the role of Islam within the Asia region. Also present for a panel discussion following the launch were Professor Arief Budiman, Chair of Indonesian Studies at Melbourne University; Michael O'Connor, Executive Director of the Australian Defence Association; and Dr. Greg Barton, Senior Lecturer in Religious Studies at Deakin University and author of the chapters in the report on Indonesia and Malaysia.[35]

According to Rubenstein, after the Bali bombing AIJAC's and *The Review*'s credibility were enhanced among a lot of people in government and the media. Rubenstein travelled in Malaysia and South Korea, and AIJAC exposed the Australian links of Ramsy Yusef, the convicted bomber of the World Trade Centre.[36] AIJAC also established close links with moderate leaders in the region such as Abdurrahman Wahid, President of Indonesia (1999–2001) and leader of the world's largest Muslim organization, the 25 million-member *Nahdatul Ulama*.

Racial and Religious Intolerance

AIJAC also defends and promotes efforts to further Australia's development as "a tolerant and harmonious multicultural society". Often acting in concert with other ethnic community organizations, AIJAC has exposed instances of racism and anti-Semitism in Australia and has lobbied governments to develop legislative and educative measures to counteract these phenomena. Thus, Rubenstein supported the Victorian Government's Racial and Religious Tolerance legislation:

> Freedom of speech is very important but has to be balanced with the right of all Victorians to be free from harassment, vilification and incitement to violence which often does result from hate speech. This move acknowledges and enhances the multicultural nature of Victorian society and will bring our state into line with virtually the rest of Australia.[37]

International Jewry

AIJAC has highlighted and campaigned against those in Australia and other parts of the world who have sought to deny or distort the history of the Nazi Holocaust – "the greatest single tragedy of all for the Jewish people". In addition to its campaign against a visit to Australia by David Irving, it strongly condemned the publication by Melbourne's *Herald Sun* of a poll asking readers to phone in to register whether or not they "agree with historian David Irving's views on the Holocaust". AIJAC National Chairman Mark Leibler insisted that

> the reader's poll was not only in terrible taste, and offensive to Melbourne's many Holocaust survivors, it was positively destructive. The aim of Holocaust deniers like Irving is to legitimize right-wing extremism and anti-Semitism by creating in the public mind a belief that the Nazi Holocaust against Jews is a debatable issue, that it a mere matter of opinion whether it did or did not happen. The *Herald Sun*, with its readership poll, has lent credibility and legitimacy to the politically motivated claim of deniers that the Nazi Holocaust, probably the best researched historical event of the twentieth century, is merely a "theory".

Subsequently, Leibler contacted the newspaper's editor in order to communicate the Jewish community's profound concern and disappointment with the publication of the poll.[38]

In May 2000, AIJAC condemned the Australian Government's decision to vote in favour of two loans by the World Bank to Iran, totalling US$232 million. The loans had been opposed by the United States Government, which had argued that the loans were inappropriate at a time when the Iranian regime had been holding a closed-door espionage trial of thirteen Jewish men. The trial had been widely condemned by diplomatic observers and human rights groups. The United States' stance had gained support for a postponement of the loans from Canada and France, but Australia declined to follow the United States' lead and voted in favour of the loans. Rubenstein claimed the loans sent the signal that the Iranian regime can continue to engage in gross religious discrimination, terrorism and other major violations of international norms and still enjoy improved relations with the outside world. Moreover, rather than strengthening the forces of moderation within Iran, the decision to approve these loans would only enhance the power of the extremist elements which still dominated the Iranian judiciary and security forces.[39]

When in July 2000 Iran convicted ten of these Iranian Jews on the fabricated charges of spying for Israel and the United States, AIJAC acted in concert with other Jewish groups internationally to protest this grave injustice. Rubenstein commended the Australian government "for its efforts to prevent this gross violation of human rights", and called for the Australian government to maintain its pressure against Iran until such time as the verdicts were reversed. He also asked the Australian government to review its diplomatic and commercial relationship with Iran "so as to maximize ongoing pressure until such time as these verdicts are reversed".[40]

War Crimes Justice

AIJAC has campaigned extensively to ensure that alleged Nazi war criminals in Australia face justice, either in Australia or overseas via deportation or extradition. To this end, AIJAC has called for the federal government to re-establish a specialized war crimes investigation unit to pursue suspects from the Nazi era and more recent conflicts, as well as assist international efforts to secure war crimes justice. [41] By 1995 *The Review* had tracked down Latvian Konrad Kalejs living in a retirement village in Melbourne, having escaped justice for 56 years for alleged war crimes in which thousands of prisoners, many of them Jews, died.

In 1997, AIJAC located Australia's highest-ranking Nazi war criminal, Lt Karlis Ozols.[42] In a media release on 29 September 2000, AIJAC welcomed the news that Kalejs had been indicted by Latvia and called upon the federal government to ensure that he was available for extradition.[43] Subsequently, on 13 December 2000, AIJAC welcomed reports that the Latvian authorities were formally lodging a request with the Australian government for the extradition of Kalejs and praised Australia for having taken "the principled step earlier in the year to institute extradition arrangements with Latvia for such an eventuality".[44]

When Kalejs died in November 2001 aged 88, Jewish community leaders responded to the news of his death with calls for the establishment of a similar investigative unit to pursue those in Australia suspected of genocide in East Timor, Rwanda, Bosnia, Cambodia, Afghanistan and other countries. Rubenstein said the new federal government should also equip itself with powers to deprive suspected war criminals of citizenship as Canada and the United States had done. These concerns were strongly supported by the Australian Democrats law and justice spokesman Senator Brian Greig.[45]

In March 2000 AIJAC called on the federal government to reopen its investigations into Nazi war criminal suspect Antanas Gudelis in light of new revelations aired on the SBS *Dateline* program. Rubenstein maintained that the serious allegations against Gudelis and the fact that several new witnesses in Lithuania had been found placed the onus on the government to fully investigate the evidence with a view to prosecution or extradition. Among the allegations against Mr Gudelis, an Adelaide resident, were that he had been a commanding officer at massacres of civilians in Nazi-occupied Lithuania and that he had been directly involved in the execution of prisoners. *Dateline* had also identified several individuals who had claimed to witness Gudelis' participation in such crimes. Rubenstein claimed that Australians wanted to see their government dealing effectively with the recurring problem of war criminals and to erase the image that Australia had become a safe haven for war criminals.[46]

Conclusion

AIJAC, in cooperation with other Jewish organizations, has been very active as an interest group in the Australian political system. Its main areas of concern have been the Australian Jewish community, the State of Israel and world Jewry. It regards these interests as integrally linked to the predominant Australian and Western values of democracy, human rights, freedom of speech and religious and ethnic freedom. Hence, its leaders are deeply convinced that when they campaign for the State of Israel and world Jewry they also campaign for values held sacred by most Australians. AIJAC therefore does not really believe there is room for such dissenting Jewish organizations as the Australian Jewish Democratic Society, and regard it as being at best led by misguided people, and at worst as self-hating Jews who have collaborated with left-wing, anti-Israel movements.

AIJAC's activities have been conducted through its *Review*, internet updates, direct contacts with the media, the Department of Foreign Affairs and politicians from the government and the opposition. Its critics argue that AIJAC has been biased and overzealous in its activities, creating an image of "an all powerful Jewish lobby" feared by politicians and government officials. By the very nature of its aims it is very difficult if not impossible to ascertain its success. Its aims do not render themselves easily to accurate measurement. AIJAC's officials, headed by Rubenstein, are however convinced that without their tireless efforts to combat prejudice against Israel and Jews, "things would be a hell of lot worse".

Notes

I thank Dr. Colin Rubenstein for granting me an interview and providing me with material on AIJAC. I would also like to thank Andrew Markus and Suzanne Rutland for historical material on AIJAC's establishment.

1 Keith Abbott, *Pressure Groups and the Australian Federal Parliament* (Canberra: Australian Government Publishing Service, 1996), p. 10.
2 Adam Indikt, "The Need For The Review"; Mark Liebler, "Toward The Future", *The Review*, January 2000: 18–19.
3 Interview of Rubenstein with the author, Melbourne, 10 September 2003.
4 *Ibid.*
5 *Ibid.*
6 *Ibid.*
7 *Ibid.*
8 Ghassan Hage, ed., *Arab-Australians Today: Citizenship And Belonging* (Melbourne: Melbourne University Press, 2002), pp. 184–9.
9 "Israel lobby attempts to prevent factual reporting", Press Release: General Palestinian Delegation, *Scoop*, 9 February 2004: www.scoop.co.nz/mason/stories/WO0402/S00057.htm.
10 *Ibid.*
11 *Ibid.*
12 *Ibid.*
13 See Philip Mendes's chapter, this volume.
14 Interview of Rubenstein with the author, Melbourne, 10 September 2003.
15 *Ibid.*
16 http://www.ajc.org/WhoWeAre/InternationalPartners.asp.

17   Suzanne D. Rutland, *Edge of the Diaspora: Two Centuries of Jewish Settlement in Australia*, 2nd edn (New York: Holmes & Meier, 2001), pp. 384–5.

18   Isador Magid, "In The Beginning"; Sam Lipski, "Remembrance Of The Early Years", *The Review*, January 2000: 15–16.

19   Sam Lipski, "Remembrance Of The Early Years"; Adam Indikt, "The Need For The Review", *The Review*, January 2000: 16. See also Chanan Reich, *Ethnic Identity And Political Participation: The Jewish And Greek Communities In Melbourne* (unpublished Ph.D. thesis, Monash University, 1983), chapter 9.

20   Michael Kapel, "New Agendas"; Adam Indikt, "The Need For The Review", *The Review* January 2000: 17–19.

21   Bernard Freedman, "Hanson, to stand trial", *AJN*, May 31 2002.

22   Michael Kapel, "New Agendas", *The Review*, January 2000: 17.

23   Robert James Lee (Bob) Hawke was Australian Prime Minister 1983–1991.

24   Richard Woolcott, *The Hot Seat: Reflection on Diplomacy from Stalin's Death to the Bali Bombings* (Sydney: Harper Collins, 2003).

25   See "Gothcha! One Nation's Secret Membership List", *Australia/Israel Review* July 1998; and the ensuing controversy in the pages of the *AJN*, 17 July 1998.

26   David Langsam, "AIJAC's hollow victory", *AJN* November 7 2003. On the Ashrawi episode, see chapter 13, this volume.

27   Daniel Mandel, "Imbalance all the time: How SBS violates its Code of Practice", *The Review*, January 2003: http://www.aijac.org.au/ review/2003/ 281/sbs–281.html.

28   *Ibid.* Rubenstein and Danby clashed, however, over AIJAC's response to the 2003 Sydney Peace Prize being awarded to Hanan Ashrawi. See Michael Danby, "Over the Top Protest Down Under", *Forward* (New York), 14 November 2003; and Colin Rubenstein, "No Appeasement on Ashrawi Award", *Forward* (New York), 21 November 2003.

29   Media Release: "Howard commended for lauding Israeli peace plan rejected by Palestinians", *AIJAC*, November 2000.

30   "Australia-Israel Parliamentary Friendship Group: Arafat must deliver cease-fire", HVP No. 58, 13 *Israel and Palestine*, 11 November 2002, p. 539.

31   Media Release: "Parliamentary Motion on Arab–Israel Conflict 'Ignorant' and 'Unhelpful'", 11 November 2002: www.aijac.org.au/media_releases/ 2002/ irwin_motion.html.

32   "Lone Jewish MP caught in the middle", *The Australian*, 14 July 2003. "Crean woos Jewish community", 1 Sep 2003: www.abc.net.au/news/justin/weekly/ newsnat-1sep2003–9.htm.

33   "Memo Simon Crean: be honest in dealing with Israel", *The Age*, 4 September 2003.

34   Colin Rubenstein, "Crean's analysis of Israel is compelling", *The Age*, 9 September 2003.

35   Media Release, 11 November 1999, "AIJAC and AJC release new study – Islam in Asia: Changing Political Realities": ww.aijac.org.au/media_releases/ 1999/asiastudy.html.

36   Interview of Rubenstein with the author, Melbourne, 10 September 2003.

37   Media Release: "AIJAC welcomes Victorian Racial and Religious Tolerance Discussion Paper", AIJAC, 18 December 2000.

38 Media Release: "AIJAC condemns Herald Sun Irving Poll", 14 January 2000: www.aijac.org.au/media_releases/2000/irvingpoll.html.

39 Media Release: "AIJAC condemns Australian Government's vote on new World Bank loans to Iran", 9 May 2000: www.aijac.org.au/media_releases/2000/iranloans.html.

40 Media Release: "AIJAC condemns 'Show Trial' verdicts against 10 Iranian Jews", 3 July 2000: www.aijac.org.au/media_releases/2000/verdict.html. See also Media Release: "Iran stands condemned by its travesty of justice", *The Review*, 22 September 2000.

41 http://www.aijac.org.au/main-pages/issues.html.

42 Michael Kapel, "New Agendas", *The Review*, January 2000: 17.

43 http://www.aijac.org.au/media_releases/2000/kalejs_indicted.html.

44 *Ibid.*

45 Bernard Freedman, "Kalejs: the last chapter", *AJN*, 16 November 2001.

46 Media Release: "New evidence on war crimes suspect requires renewed investigations", 31 March 2000: www.aijac.org.au/media_releases/ 2000/ gudelis2.html.

13 | The Hanan Ashrawi Affair: Australian Jewish Politics on Display

GEOFFREY BRAHM LEVEY AND PHILIP MENDES

In August 2003, the Sydney University Peace Foundation announced that prominent Palestinian intellectual Dr Hanan Ashrawi had won the 2003 Sydney Peace Prize. The announcement provoked a wave of criticism from bodies in the Australian Jewish community that reached a crescendo at the time of the presentation to Ashrawi in early November 2003. Yet the media and public debate focused on the activities of the so-called "Jewish lobby" rather than on Ashrawi's suitability for the prize. Many in the Jewish community and beyond were concerned at this turn of events; others seemed to welcome it. Almost everyone appeared surprised by it. From a broader perspective, however, the Ashrawi affair was entirely predictable. The affair simply replayed some longstanding features of Australian Jewish politics and attitudes in the broader Australian community. If there was anything new about the episode, then it was that it made these things suddenly and dramatically apparent.

The Sydney Peace Prize

The University of Sydney's Peace Foundation awards the Sydney Peace Prize annually upon the recommendation of a six-member selection committee. Worth 50,000 Australian dollars, previous winners of the award include former Australian Governor-General Sir William Deane, East Timorese President Xanana Gusmao, Archbishop Desmond Tutu, and former UN High Commissioner for Human Rights Mary Robinson. The prize was awarded to Hanan Ashrawi for "her commitment to human rights, to the peace process in the Middle East and for her courage in speaking against oppression, against corruption and for justice".[1] As is customary, the New South Wales Premier Bob Carr agreed to present the prize at a public ceremony. A long-time supporter of both Israel and Australian Jewry, Carr defended his decision to present the award on the basis that it could help to promote peace between Israel and the Palestinians. He would impress on Ashrawi the need for the Palestinians to renounce violence and accept a two-state solution.[2]

Awarding the prize to Ashrawi was always going to be controversial. First, honouring someone representing one side of the Middle East conflict rather than a joint award to a Palestinian and an Israeli would inevitably be interpreted as showing political bias.[3] Second, Hanan Ashrawi is no ordinary peacenik. On occasion, she has articulated extremist views and used inciting language against Israel.[4] Yet, there is also little doubt that she is a relative moderate within the Palestinian spectrum of opinion. She has generally endorsed a two-state solution, opposed violence against civilians, and specifically condemned suicide bombings. She also maintains good relations with sections of the Israeli peace movement. Overall, Ashrawi appears to be a shrewd and articulate advocate of the Palestinian cause who pragmatically varies her message according to her audience.[5]

Jewish concerns about the 2003 prizewinner were expressed from the beginning. Jeremy Jones, President of the Executive Council of Australian Jewry (ECAJ) – the national Jewish roof body – argued that Ashrawi had failed to contribute to peace and reconciliation and was merely "an old style propagandist".[6] However, it was a conservative Israeli academic, Gerald Steinberg of Bar-Ilan University, who drove the initial protest. Steinberg, an advocate of tough Israeli security policies, issued a statement denouncing peace studies in general and the peace prize to Ashrawi in particular.[7] He also initiated a petition calling on Carr not to present the prize on this occasion. The petition was widely distributed within the Australian Jewish community and attracted over 50,000 signatures. Most Australian Jews seemed to accept Steinberg's criticisms of Ashrawi, and thus of Carr, without question or verification.[8]

The New South Wales Jewish Board of Deputies (NSWJBD) took responsibility for directing the community's campaign given that the prize was to be awarded in Sydney, the NSW capital. However, the ECAJ, the Zionist Federation of Australia, and the private, Melbourne-based think tank, Australia/Israel & Jewish Affairs Council (AIJAC)[9] also had significant input. In addition, the newly formed Australian Academic Friends of Israel was involved in promoting the anti-Ashrawi petition to academics. All groups pushed the view from the start that Ashrawi was an extremist, rather than engage in a reasoned debate about her suitability for the prize.[10] AIJAC, for example, published a "fact sheet" featuring a handful of Ashrawi quotes and accompanying interpretations to demonstrate her allegedly extremist views.[11] There was also a general failure to present potential alternative candidates from either the Palestinian or the Israeli side.[12] Overall, the lobbying seemed very hardline, and intended to polarize opinions about Ashrawi and the Israeli–Palestinian conflict. The message to outsiders seemed to be that either you are with us all the way or you are against us.[13]

Internal Divisions

The orchestrated Jewish opposition to Ashrawi soon gave way to divisions over both the tone and content of the campaign. The NSWJBD favoured a relatively low-key, behind-the-scenes approach, whilst AIJAC encouraged public debate and division.[14] In addition, the NSWJBD issued only mild public criticisms of Carr, whereas other Jewish groups were less restrained.[15] These divisions reflected a range of organizational, political, interstate, and personal factors and rivalries. Chief among them was the key issue of who speaks for Australian Jews.

The NSWJBD is an elected body representing a range of views and opinions within the 40,000 strong NSW Jewish community. It is entitled to its claim of being the official voice of the NSW Jewish community. In contrast, AIJAC is a privately funded body that is accountable only to its Board. It is well resourced (far more so than either the NSWJBD or the ECAJ), respected for its professional research and media savvy, and politically well connected. Its national chairman Mark Leibler, for example, is a prominent tax lawyer with excellent access to the major political parties.[16] The problem is that many policy-makers and journalists either think that AIJAC is the official representative of Australian Jewry or treat it as if it were. This was apparent during the Ashrawi debate when a number of media outlets sought the opinions of AIJAC spokespeople rather than of the elected communal leaders.[17] As the *Australian Jewish News* noted, the matter is not helped when the ECAJ President, Jeremy Jones, is also AIJAC's Director of International and Community Affairs and manager of its Sydney office, housed in the same building as the ECAJ and NSWJBD offices.[18]

Another source of tension is ideological. As already noted, Carr has a long history of friendship toward Israel and Australian Jewry,[19] and a number of leading NSWJBD figures are active in the NSW Labor Party. NSWJBD president Stephen Rothman, for example, was an unsuccessful candidate for Labor preselection in the federal seat of Dobell in 2003.[20] In contrast, AIJAC is widely regarded as more politically conservative; its Executive Director Dr Colin Rubenstein is a prominent Liberal Party activist and a member of the Howard Government's Council for Multicultural Australia.[21] In June 2004, AIJAC had Howard receive the American Jewish Committee's highest honour, the American Liberties Medallion, and in January 2002 it was the AJCommittee's Distinguished Public Service Award at a ceremony in New York. "No one in Australia is more deserving of this honour than Prime Minister Howard", Rubenstein told those assembled.[22] Whilst AIJAC claims to be politically bipartisan with links to all mainstream parties, its campaigns against Ashrawi and Premier Carr were widely viewed as unbalanced. According to the editor of the Melbourne edition of the *Australian Jewish News*, Dan Goldberg, "many (Jews) consider AIJAC's politics – which can be described as conservative – as too right-wing. Despite Mark Leibler's claim that it is not partisan, it does appear to be aligned to a political ideology".[23]

Many Jewish supporters of the ALP felt that AIJAC's criticisms of Carr provoked an unnecessary dispute with a prominent and sympathetic politician. Stephen Rothman accused AIJAC of using inappropriate and overzealous methods to lobby Premier Carr and the Sydney Peace Foundation.[24] In particular, he attacked AIJAC for making the awarding of the prize an issue of party political contention within the NSW state Parliament.[25] Walt Secord, the NSW Premier's Director of Communications and a former *Australian Jewish News* reporter, expressed similar concerns.[26] The *Australian Jewish News* would later describe the actions of AIJAC as "enormously counterproductive", "ill-considered", and "intemperate".[27]

A number of prominent Jewish Labor Party figures – including former Jewish Community Council of Victoria officer Adam Slonim, Jewish Labor Forum Executive member George Newhouse, former federal MP and Minister Barry Cohen, former Federal Court Judge Marcus Einfeld, and former Australia Israel Publications (AIP) Director and current federal MP Michael Danby – defended Carr, and criticized the nature of the anti-Ashrawi campaign.[28] Danby accused Jewish leaders of drawing undue media attention to the award, and argued that AIJAC had "stirred up opposition not just from the usual anti-Israel chorus, but from people usually supportive of Israel".[29] Einfeld asked "why the knife was turned toward's one of Israel's most stalwart friends in public life in NSW Premier Bob Carr".[30] Another Labor supporter of Israel, Michael Easson, decried "the alienation of friends of Israel".[31] Carr would later comment: "I have got a lot of friends in the Jewish community who have said [to the lobbyists] Hang on, don't attack Bob over this. He's been a long-time supporter of the Israeli cause".[32]

More explicit criticisms of the Jewish leadership came from Jewish left groups such as the Australian Jewish Democratic Society (AJDS), and Jews Against the Occupation (JAO).[33] AJDS issued a press release criticizing the campaign against Ashrawi as lacking balance or moderation, whilst not necessarily endorsing her selection for the Peace Prize.[34] The more radical Sydney-based JAO publicly presented Ashrawi with a bouquet of flowers, and was included in a national television discussion of the debate.[35] Other Jews supporting the award included NSW Greens MP Ian Cohen[36] and University of NSW political scientist Ephraim Nimni. Nimni solicited support for Ashrawi from a number of Israeli academics and activists, including Hebrew University sociologist Professor Baruch Kimmerling, journalist Haim Baram, and – through the former Deputy Speaker of the

Israeli Knesset (parliament) Professor Naomi Chazan – the Coalition of Women for Peace in Israel. Their various statements defending Ashrawi's views and her receipt of the Peace Prize contrasted sharply with the anti-Ashrawi position of the hawkish Israeli Professor Gerald Steinberg noted above.[37] However, their efforts appeared to have little influence in the Australian Jewish community.

The Media Coverage

To the consternation of many within the Jewish community, media coverage of the Ashrawi affair quickly turned to focus on the alleged power and bullying tactics of Jewish lobby groups.[38] According to the *Australian Jewish News*, "The furore has focused overwhelmingly on the perception that the Jewish community – or the so-called Jewish lobby – has inappropriately used political and financial clout in an attempt to discredit Dr Ashrawi, have the prize rescinded, and pressure Carr, Councillor Turnbull and the University of Sydney to dissociate themselves from it".[39] It was also widely implied in media reports that criticisms of the prizewinner by public and political figures reflected a self-interested kowtowing to Jewish pressure, rather than genuine concerns about Ashrawi's views and merits.[40]

A number of examples of alleged Jewish bullying or undue influence were cited, including:

- Attacks by the NSW Liberal Party state member for Vaucluse Peter Debnam, the Opposition Leader John Brogden, and the Deputy Opposition Leader Barry O'Farrell on Premier Carr for agreeing to award the prize.[41] Most media reports made reference to Debnam as representing an electorate with a large proportion of Jewish voters;[42]
- The withdrawal of use of Sydney University's Great Hall for the award ceremony;[43]
- Alleged pressure on companies funding the Peace Prize such as Rio Tinto, PBL and Citigroup to withdraw their support;[44]
- Alleged pressure from prominent Jewish business figures such as Frank Lowy on the NSW Premier;[45]
- Abusive phone calls to the Peace Foundation's secretary;[46]
- The boycotting of Ashrawi's award presentation by Sydney Lord Mayor Lucy Turnbull despite her Council's sponsorship of the Prize. This action was attributed to her husband Malcolm Turnbull's participation in a Liberal Party preselection battle for the NSW federal seat of Wentworth, which has a large number of Jewish voters.[47]

Sydney Peace Foundation Director Stuart Rees subtly exploited these perceptions in order to depict criticisms of the Ashrawi award as illegitimate, referring, for example, to alleged "bullying and intimidation" by members of a powerful lobby group.[48] Elsewhere, he described the Jewish lobby as "one of the most powerful lobbies in the world".[49] Press support for Jewish concerns was limited primarily to a small number of conservative commentators such as Piers Akerman, Gerard Henderson, Paul Sheehan, and Padraic McGuiness.[50]

Interestingly, in contrast to the media's obsession with Jewish lobby groups, little reference was made to the views of the Australian Arab community, which is more than twice the size of the Jewish community and arguably more electorally significant.[51] Historically, Australian Arabs have failed to exert significant political influence due to a number of factors, including political and religious divisions, language barriers, and lack of resources. However, over the last decade, the Arab community has become far more articulate and organized,[52] and groups such as the Palestinian Human Rights Commission, Women for Palestine, and the Australian Arabic Council were vocal in expressing support for Ashrawi. They issued a number of press releases, and organized a pro-Ashrawi petition that secured over 6,000 signatures.[53] However, with few exceptions,[54] the media ignored these interventions, and no serious attempt was made to balance Jewish opinions of Ashrawi with Arab views.

The role of the *Australian Jewish News*, finally, cannot be overlooked. The weekly, which appears in a Melbourne and a Sydney edition (albeit with considerable overlap), has in recent years often taken positions to the left of the political sensibilities of many Jewish organizations and, judging from the letters to the editor, of many individual Jews as well. Throughout the controversy, the paper took a middle ground position of objecting to Ashrawi as a worthy recipient of the peace prize, whilst strongly criticizing players in the Jewish community over their handling of the issue. In addition, it gave the affair enormous oxygen by reporting extensively on the various angles of the debate and opening its pages up to opinion columns by Jewish community leaders and to letter writers.

The Affair as Symptomatic

For all its interest and spectacle, the Ashrawi affair had less to do with the specific details of the case than with underlying features of Australian Jewish politics and society. The episode was a fiasco waiting to happen. If it weren't Hanan Ashrawi and the peace prize, then soon enough it would have been some other issue. One reason for this has already been explored: the competing interests and approaches of AIJAC and official Jewish bodies. But four rather more longstanding contextual factors allowed the Ashrawi affair to play out predictably. These relate to Australian Jews' general sense of insecurity, reflex pro-Israelism, and political style, and to non-Jewish Australia's contrasting sense of Jewish success and excess. Let us look briefly at each.

Despite their high socioeconomic status and considerable resources, many Jews feel insecure within Australian society and are still traumatized by memories of the Holocaust. While this sense of insecurity is understandably reinforced by particular acts or episodes, such as the recent wave of attacks on Jewish persons and property in the wake of current events in the Middle East,[55] it does not require particular precipitating events. Rather it is a generalized anxiety and attitude. In a 1991 survey of Melbourne Jewry, for example, some 63 percent saw anti-Semitism as a "very or quite a serious problem in Australia today".[56] Such generalized feelings of anxiety are also widespread in other successful Western Jewish communities, including that in the United States. In a 2002 survey of American Jewish opinion, for example, 29 percent of respondents agreed that anti-Semitism in the US is currently a very serious problem and 66 percent thought it was somewhat of a problem.[57] Literary critic George Steiner perhaps best caught the condition of post-Holocaust Jewry when he described Jews (of which he is one) as a "traumatized [and] crazed people".[58] This sense of insecurity and trauma often informs the heightened or exaggerated reactions among Jews to perceived provocations against sites of Jewish identification. Israel represents one such important site.

On almost every available measure – visitation, resident relatives, emotional attachment, and philanthropy – Israel figures centrally in Australian Jewish identity.[59] Indeed, Zionism or pro-Israelism is curiously stronger among Australian Jews than many other diasporic Jewish communities. To take one example, despite the greater distance and cost involved, Australian Jews are more than twice as likely as American Jews to have visited Israel (73 to 31 percent).[60] Just why Israel looms so large in the local Jewish consciousness is not entirely clear. No doubt it is partly related to the Holocaust and Jews' sense of victimhood and Israel as the countervailing bastion of Jewish power and rights; a comparatively high proportion of Australian Jewry are Holocaust survivors or children of survivors. It may also have to do with the smallness of the community here and its remoteness from centres of Jewish life. When an Israeli academic visiting Sydney in 1998 suggested that Israel no longer needs the local community's financial support and that it would be better directed to the community's own needs, a local Jewish leader indignantly protested that Australian Jewry feels the need to give money to Israel even if Israel doesn't need to receive it.[61]

But the centrality of Israel to Australian Jewish identity doesn't explain the direction this attachment takes. As an exhibit in Amsterdam's *Joods Historisch Museum* (Jewish Historical Museum) puts it, while "the tie with the Land of Israel remains, [e]very Jew feels and expresses this in a different way. Some choose to make '*Aliyah*' – to emigrate to Israel. Others may voice their criticism of the political situation that has developed in Israel".[62] The latter sentiment, however, is scarcely countenanced by Australian

Jewry. On the Middle East conflict, the official community refuses critically to assess Israeli positions and actions or to welcome Jews who do. It is unlikely that any local Jewish leader would join the Chief Rabbi of the British Commonwealth, Jonathan Sachs, in stating that "Zionism is categorically not, as it is sometimes claimed to be, 'My people right or wrong'".[63] In mid-2003, World Jewish Congress president Edgar Bronfman urged US President George W. Bush to pressure Israel and the Palestinians to follow the "road map" peace plan and Israel to rethink its controversial security wall. Isi Leibler, the WJC vice-president and former Australian Jewish leader, demanded that Bronfman apologize or resign.[64] In this milieu, then, simply being critical of Israeli policies, let alone a Palestinian critic, would be enough to alienate the Australian Jewish community. A peace prize for any such person is literally unthinkable.

Pivotal to the Ashrawi affair was also a certain Australian Jewish political style. While by no means adopted by all Jewish organizations and leaders, at least all the time, it is common enough to be significant. Borne largely in the wake of the rise of identity politics in the 1960s and '70s, first in the United States and then elsewhere, and sharpened by training from American public affairs committees, the political style involves mobilizing and being heard on every issue that touches on Jewish concern. Nothing of this sort is left to pass or, if it can be helped, to chance. The Holocaust experience demands eternal vigilance. The style is thus proactive and often aggressive, although there tends here to be a difference between the Sydney and Melbourne communities. As noted earlier, the Sydney approach is to work "behind the scenes", while the Melbourne approach tends to be direct and "in your face". Or as Sam Lipski has put it, "Softly, softly" versus "Mount the barricades!".[65] However, what the two approaches share is, in our view, more important than their outward differences. Successful lobbying typically requires that complex issues be simplified for their target audiences. The Australian Jewish political style – whether in Sydney, Melbourne or any other city – is to simplify issues by polarizing them into Manichaean struggles between good and evil, friends and enemies. Because the stakes *always* involve potential peril, the imperative is on winning or prevailing as the only acceptable goal and outcome. This means that when the going gets tough, as it did in the Ashrawi case, the Jewish community's considerable resources and connections are often called on.

All of this leads to a disjuncture between Jews' self-perceptions and how they are perceived in the wider community. Whereas many Jews appear genuinely to see Ashrawi and leading Palestinians as potential threats to the security and safety of Jews to be confronted at all costs, many in the broader community simply do not share or understand the intensity of Jewish concerns about Middle East politics. Rather, they view the expression of such concerns as disproportionate, and designed to stifle free speech and suppress legitimate criticisms of Israeli policies. Where Jews feel themselves to be an insecure minority, in the broader Australian community they are viewed as affluent, privileged, and influential.[66] The perspectives of each confirm the suspicions of the other. Jews interpret criticism of the manner of Jewish lobbying as a denial of their right to lobby in a pluralist democracy and as evidence of anti-Semitism.[67] To others, the intensity and reach of Jewish *politiking* seem to confirm the stereotypes of Jews as a powerful and unyielding minority, and one that cries anti-Semitism whenever it is criticized.

Against this background, Hanan Ashrawi appears as really quite an innocent bystander.

The Fallout and the Upshot

The Ashrawi affair is another example of the increased globalization of Australian policy debates.[68] With the advent of e-mail and the internet it is no longer possible for significant local debates about Middle East politics to be conducted in isolation. As we have seen, the affair included significant international interventions both for and against the Ashrawi award. The debate was also widely reported in the international media. In Australia, as the media story became the powerful Jewish lobby rather than the suitability of the prizewinner, voices within the Jewish community began calling for a community inquiry into this "public relations disaster".[69] It was not long before those involved in the campaign were defending their roles as beyond reproach and, in the case of some, arguing that the alleged disaster was, in fact, a triumph.

AIJAC contended that the campaign was an "indisputable political and media success", and that its critics were simply political opportunists or appeasers.[70] Two reasons were given for the campaign's supposed success. First, it had obliged Ashrawi to condemn Palestinian terrorism and to moderate her speeches regarding Israel.[71] Prior to Ashrawi's visit, however, AIJAC had been criticizing her, among other things, for always moderating her message to international audiences and, during her visit, complained that she continued to prevaricate and use "weasel words".[72] Second, AIJAC pointed to the opposition to Ashrawi voiced by prominent politicians and commentators, including the Prime Minister.[73] Yet, such statements from Howard and his senior ministers would seem to reflect the success of AIJAC's cultivated relationship with them over many years, as noted above, rather than specifically of the anti-Ashrawi campaign. Likewise, it seems a stretch to claim credit for the critical reaction to Ashrawi's award by sections of the Australian press given their standard, conservative positions on the Middle East conflict. As for regrets, Rubenstein nominated only that the campaign "was sidetracked by some Jewish leaders, who when confronted by claims that the community was bringing anti-Semitism on itself by speaking out, engaged in scapegoating other Jewish organizations rather than repudiating this canard".[74] It would appear, however, that there was concern in AIJAC's offices that the organization was acquiring a reputation for being extremist; variations of the phrase "all mainstream organizations, including AIJAC" punctuated Rubenstein's spate of articles during and after the episode.

The opposing view abroad in the Jewish community was that the campaign failed to change the views of either the Sydney Peace Foundation or Premier Carr. Moreover, it produced serious divisions within the Jewish community, alienated many previously committed supporters of Israel, and reinforced stereotypes about Jewish influence and power being used to stifle free speech and debate. Even critics of Ashrawi such as *The Australian* referred to "self-inflicted wounds" and the "own goal of Australia's Jewish community".[75] Similarly, the *Australian Jewish News* opined, "the Jewish community's image has been battered and bruised".[76] Ashrawi's actual visit also seems to have been a great success. Her public lecture was sold out and attended by 1,500 people, and media coverage was enormous. Ashrawi delivered a moderate speech supporting a two-state solution and condemning violence against civilians from both sides, which fundamentally disarmed her strongest critics. She argued "neither side can lay claim to a monopoly of pain and suffering in the same way as it cannot claim exclusivity of narrative and legitimacy. Clearly, peace cannot be made incumbent upon converting all Palestinians to Zionism or transforming all Israelis to espouse Palestinian nationalism".[77]

From a tactical perspective, it could be argued that the major mistake of Jewish campaigners was to confuse challenging the worthiness of Ashrawi for the award with attacking Premier Carr for agreeing to present it. It was this side of the campaign that clearly alienated many supporters of the Labor Party both within and outside the Jewish community. But such considerations distract from the real lessons to be learned from the affair. Put simply, pro-Israel campaigns in Australia *do* seem disproportionate precisely because they are based on a zero-sum notion of manning the Middle East frontline here. The defence of Israel and its interests is invariably, but unnecessarily framed in terms of opposing any Palestinian arguments.[78]

Judging from Jewish leaders' comments and the post-mortems of the affair, the signs are not promising that the episode will make any real difference to Australian Jewish politics and outlook. Attention has simply focused on avoiding "negative perceptions" by playing the old game better: improved co-ordination among Jewish organizations, a closer grip on public comment by Jews, a more concerted effort to deny that there is any division within the community, and so on. The concern is about how the community's *modus operandi* came to backfire, not whether the *modus operandi* might itself be flawed. There is a deep assumption that the established traditions of Australian Jewish politics have served the Jewish community well. There is an inability to ask whether there might now be other approaches that are more fitting and more effective.

The Ashrawi affair nonetheless had one positive consequence, however inadvertently. It confirmed that Australian Jewry is not altogether politically monolithic. Whilst there is a broad pro-Israel consensus, there remains a wide diversity of views about how this consensus should be applied in Australian political debates, particularly when party politics are involved. For Australian society in general, this much is likely to have been educative. For the Jewish community, or at least sections of it, it may have been cathartic.

Notes

We are grateful to Israeli Professors Naomi Chazan, Baruch Kimmerling, and Peter Medding, and our Australian colleague Ephraim Nimni for clarifying certain international aspects of this affair. We also thank NSW Premier Bob Carr's media adviser Walt Secord for providing relevant information.

1 Sydney Peace Foundation, "Who has won the prize and why were they selected?" [www.spf.arts.usyd.edu.au/peace.html].
2 Bob Carr, "Speech to NSW Parliament on Israel and Hanan Ashrawi", 16 October 2003. In his speech at the Peace Prize dinner, Carr argued: "The Palestinians have no homeland. Israel has no peace. In one fact lies the solution to the other", 6 November 2003.
3 Peace Foundation Director, Professor Stuart Rees acknowledged that his organization had considered sharing the prize with an Israeli peace activist, but cited "logistical obstacles as too great". See Alana Rosenbaum, "Jewish communal leaders are outraged", *Australian Jewish News* [hereafter *AJN*], 22 August 2003. All references to the *AJN* are to the Melbourne edition.
4 See her speech to the September 2001 United Nations Conference on racism in Durban [www.miftah.org]. Reprinted in *AJN*, 7 November 2003.
5 Hanan Ashrawi, *This Side of Peace* (New York: Simon & Schuster, 1995), pp. 59–63; Barbara Victor, *A Voice of Reason: Hanan Ashrawi and Peace in the Middle East* (New York: Harcourt Brace, 1994), pp. 142–6, 273–4. See also the website of the Palestinian Initiative for the Promotion of Global Dialogue & Democracy, which she directs [www.miftah.org].
6 Tony Stephens, "Palestinian Crusader Wins Peace Prize", *Sydney Morning Herald*, 9 August 2003.
7 Gerald Steinberg, "Terror under the banner of Peace Studies", September 2003 [www.faculty.biu.ac.il/~steing/conflict/conflict.html].
8 Steinberg's statement ran: "By awarding Hanan Ashrawi its peace prize, the Sydney Peace Foundation and Centre for Peace and Conflict Studies, with the participation of Premier Bob Carr, are actually honouring war, murder and hatred, while debasing the concept of peace and reconciliation". Steinberg also happens to be Israel correspondent for the Australia/Israel & Jewish Affairs Council (AIJAC) monthly journal, *The Review*. On AIJAC, see below and the previous chapter.
9 Until 1997, AIJAC was called Australia-Israel Publications. For a brief official

history of AIJAC, see Colin Rubenstein, "25 Years and More", *The Review*, January 2000.

10 For example, AIJAC's Colin Rubenstein described Ashrawi as an "incendiary" who had given "unyielding support to violence". See Elizabeth Colman, "Jewish fury over Carr prize plan", *The Australian*, 2 October 2003. AIJAC Board member and current Liberal Party staffer Michael Kapel labelled Ashrawi a "mouthpiece for terror". See "Award raises the volume of terrorist mouthpiece", *The Australian*, 29 October 2003. AAFI convenor Jack Frisch argued that honouring Ashrawi was "a bit like Goebbels getting the peace prize". See Dani Cooper, "Anxiety forges a Jewish network", *The Australian*, 29 October 2003. And former NSWJBD President Peter Wertheim called Ashrawi "a hard-line maximalist, who has condoned terrorism, and denied the Holocaust". See Alana Rosenbaum, "Leaders to lobby Carr on Ashrawi", *AJN*, 10 October 2003. The claim that Ashrawi was a Holocaust denier is unfounded. See interview with Ashrawi on Richard Glover on 2GB Radio, 22 October 2003.

11 "Tainted prize", *The Review*, November 2003. The "fact sheet" matched a similar production issued by the Zionist Organization of America during Ashrawi's visit to Colorado in September 2002. That visit was also marred by a furious public debate over Ashrawi's views. See "Hanan Ashrawi, Apologist for Terror" [www.campus-watch.org].

12 An exception is AIJAC researcher Gedaliah Afterman, "Awarding prize to Ashrawi blots process and ignores genuine candidates", *Canberra Times*, 3 November 2003, who suggested a number of possible alternative Palestinian candidates. However, this proposal came far too late to impact on the public debate.

13 Pro-Ashrawi journalist Antony Loewenstein accurately described the campaign as "an attempt to delegitimize the Palestinian cause". See "Hanan Ashrawi and the Price of Dissent", *Znet*, 23 October 2003. *The Age* newspaper, whilst not uncritical of Ashrawi, argued that the Jewish campaign "distorted her views". See its editorial, "Hanan Ashrawi and the peace prize", 8 November 2003. For an attempted justification of the Jewish allegations against Ashrawi, see Michael Lipshutz, Jeff Morrison and Colin Rubenstein, "Who has distorted Ashrawi's message?" *The Age*, 12 November 2003.

14 Henry Benjamin, "Australian Jews left feuding after Ashrawi gets an award", *Jewish Telegraphic Agency*, 13 November 2003.

15 For example, the President of the Jewish Community Council of Victoria Michael Lipshutz accused Carr of "placing himself in the camp of the appeasers". See Dan Goldberg, "Petition against Ashrawi Prize", *AJN*, 17 October 2003.

16 For example, Leibler was among the small group of people recently invited by Prime Minister Howard to attend a private barbeque with US President George Bush. See Bernard Freedman, "Bush to Leibler: US will stand by Israel", *AJN*, 31 October 2003.

17 Dan Goldberg, "The Tempest", *AJN*, 21 November 2003. For example, Glenn Milne cited Colin Rubenstein at length, used material verbatim from AIJAC's "fact sheet" on Ashrawi, and made no reference to any elected Jewish leader. Glenn Milne, "Labor stumbles into another divide", *The Australian*, 13 October 2003. Similarly, the ABC TV *7.30 Report* described Colin

Rubenstein as "the man driving the anti-Ashrawi campaign" (5 November 2003), and the Channel Nine *Sunday* program cited Rubenstein as "the most prominent Jewish opponent of Ashrawi", 9 November 2003.

18 Editorial, "The Ashrawi Affair", *AJN*, 7 November 2003; Editorial, "Memo to the ECAJ", *AJN*, 28 November 2003.

19 Carr was Founding President of Labor Friends of Israel in 1977.

20 Aviva Bard, "Dispute erupts over Rothman's Labor candidacy", *AJN*, 14 November 2003.

21 Rubenstein was an unsuccessful candidate for Liberal Party preselection for the federal seat of Bruce in 1990.

22 For the speeches, see the American Jewish Committee website www.ajc.org/InTheMedia/Publications.asp?did=432&pid=1029].

23 Goldberg, "The Tempest". Similar comments were made by the Sydney *AJN*; see editorial, "Memo to the ECAJ".

24 Jim Hanna, "Jewish leader concedes community damaged by lobbying", *AAP General News*, 3 November 2003.

25 Stephen Rothman, "Melbourne's lack of discipline compounded Ashrawi fiasco", *AJN*, 7 November 2003. Rothman argued that AIJAC had "turned a cleverly-devised strategy into a fiasco".

26 Elisabeth Wynhausen, "Take the free out of speech", *The Australian*, 4 November 2003.

27 Editorial, "The Ashrawi affair".

28 Aviva Bard, "Cohen Slams Stupidity", *AJN*, 31 October 2003; Marcus Einfeld, "The changing face of Hanan Ashrawi", *AJN*, 31 October 2003; Adam Slonim, "Who really represents the Jewish community of Australia?" *AJN*, 28 November 2003; Michael Danby, "Over the Top Protest Down Under", *Forward* (New York), 14 November 2003.

29 Danby, "Over the top protest". Danby is also cited in Sharon Labi, "Jews lobby Carr to rethink prize presentation to Ashrawi", *Australian Associated Press General News*, 9 October 2003, and Alana Rosenbaum, "Leaders to lobby Carr on Ashrawi".

30 Marcus Einfeld, "An inquiry must be launched", *AJN*, 14 November 2003.

31 Michael Easson, "An informed outsider's assessment of the Ashrawi debacle", *AJN*, 21 November 2003.

32 Charlie Hamilton, "Jewish lobbying polite", *AAP General News*, 23 October 2003.

33 Tony Stephens, "Sydney will be judged by Ashrawi fight: Davis", *Sydney Morning Herald*, 29 October 2003.

34 Anon, "Jewish group rejects campaign against Hanan Ashrawi", *Green Left Weekly*, 29 October 2003; Dan Goldberg, "Jewish democrats slam demonising of Ashrawi", *AJN* 31 October 2003; Sol Salbe, "Ashrawi fracas – AJDS takes lead", *AJDS Newsletter*, November 2003, p. 3.

35 See interview with Angela Budai from JAO on ABC TV *7.30 Report*, 5 November 2003; and Mike Steketee and Emma-Kate Symons, "Ashrawi lauds resolute Carr", *The Australian*, 6 November 2003.

36 Mike Carlton, "Cohen gives peace prize a chance", *Sydney Morning Herald*, 25 October 2003.

37 Elizabeth Colman and Megan Saunders, "Ashrawi protests shameful: Israeli

academic", *The Australian*, 1 November 2003. See also letters in *AJN*, 7 November 2003.

38 Typical was the description of the Jewish lobby as "powerful, well coordinated and usually gets its way". Jim Hanna, "Carr digs in his heels again", *AAP General News*, 24 October 2003. Similarly, Phillip Adams accused Jews of attacking free speech. "Handing a club to anti-Semites", *The Australian*, 28 October 2003, and Margo Kingston referred to "a powerful, minority Jewish lobby with lots of money and power". See "Ashrawi and Brandis: the great debate" [www.smh.com.au]. Even *The Australian*, which was critical of the awarding of the prize to Ashrawi, referred to "undue pressure being brought to bear" and "the perception that prominent Jews tried twisting arms, both politically and financially" ("Time for outbreak of peace on the prize", 5 November 2003).

39 Vic Alhadeff, "Ashrawi flies into storm", *AJN*, 7 November 2003.

40 For a criticism of this argument, see Mark Leibler, "Differences are between friends", *The Australian*, 6 November 2003.

41 For example, see Barry O'Farrell's speech to the NSW Parliament, 16 October 2003.

42 Jim Hanna, "Carr defends upcoming meeting with Palestinian leader", *Australian Associated Press General News*, 16 October 2003; Alan Ramsey, "From Great Hall to messy brawl", *Sydney Morning Herald*, 8 November 2003.

43 Alan Ramsey, "Here's Lucy, Caving In, Taking Flight", *Sydney Morning Herald*, 25 October 2003.

44 Tony Stephens, "Jews Push Carr On Awarding Peace Prize", *Sydney Morning Herald* 18 October 2003; Stuart Rees, "A craven approach to peace and justice", *Sydney Morning Herald*, 22 October 2003.

45 Louise Perry, "Carr hits back at clanking colonel", *The Australian*, 3 November 2003; Paula Abood and Alissar Gazal, "Who's afraid of Hanan Ashrawi", *Green Left Weekly*, 5 November 2003. See the denial from Frank Lowy, "There's no plot, just disquiet over Ashrawi", *Sydney Morning Herald*, 30 October 2003. In fact after discussing the matter with Carr, Lowy declined to sign the anti-Ashrawi petition. See Jo Mazzocchi, "Carr opens Lowy Institute", ABC Radio *AM* program, 26 November 2003.

46 Ramsey, "Here's Lucy".

47 Emma Ambler, "Nothing but conflict for Australia's only peace prize", *AAP General News*, 22 October 2003; Tony Stephens, "Lord Mayor Boycotts Awards Amid Row", *Sydney Morning Herald*, 22 October 2003; Andrew Clark, "The war over the peace prize", *Australian Financial Review* 1 November 2003. Turnbull defended her decision on the basis of concerns around Ashrawi's track record. See "Lucy Turnbull explains the Ashrawi boycott", 27 October 2003 [www.crikey.com.au].

48 Ramsey, "Here's Lucy".

49 Louise Perry and Megan Saunders, "Vote on Ashrawi award not split", *The Australian*, 24 October 2003.

50 Piers Akerman, "Sydney's peace prize hijacked", *Daily Telegraph*, 23 October 2003; Gerard Henderson, "Dump the peace prize to avert a war of words", *The Age*, 28 October 2003; Padraic McGuiness, "Prizes for prejudice of a particular kind", *Sydney Morning Herald*, 11 November 2003. See also the

Editorial, "Carr gets no peace on Ashrawi's prize", *The Australian*, 23 October 2003.

51 The Australian Jewish population has been estimated at between 84,000 and 112,000 compared to over 250,000 Arab Australians. See Wynhausen, "Take the free out of speech", and chapter 1, this volume.

52 Ray Jureidini and Ghassan Hage, "The Australian Arabic Council: anti-racist activism", in Ghassan Hage, ed., *Arab-Australians Today* (Melbourne: Melbourne University Press, 2002), pp. 173–91.

53 See Australian Arabic Communities Council website [www.arabcouncil. org.au].

54 These include Katherine Danks, "Row deepens over peace prize boycott", *AAP General News*, 23 October 2003; Kim Arlington, "Arabic leader supports Carr's Ashrawi peace prize stand", *AAP General News*, 2 November 2003; Anon, "Arabs back Carr", *The Advertiser*, 3 November 2003; Peter Kohn, "Most agreed – Arabic Council", *AJN*, 21 November 2003. See also the two articles by Arab community activist Joe Wakim, "Boycott affects people, not prize", *Canberra Times*, 28 October 2003; and "Boycott an insult to peace-prize jury", *Canberra Times*, 29 October 2003.

55 See Diana Bagnall, "Anti-Semitism: the vicious circle", *The Bulletin*, 6 April (2004): 28–9.

56 See John Goldlust, *The Jews of Melbourne: A Community Profile* (Melbourne: Jewish Welfare Society Inc, 1993), p. ii. See also Sam Lipski, "We can't measure anti-Semitism by 'incidents'", *AJN*, 1 December 2000.

57 *2002 Annual Survey of American Jewish Opinion* (New York: American Jewish Committee, 2003) [www.ajc.org/InTheMedia/PublicationsList.asp].

58 George Steiner, "The Long Life of Metaphor: An Approach to 'the Shoah'", *Encounter* 68 (1987): 57.

59 John Goldlust, *The Melbourne Jewish Community: A Needs Assessment Study* (Canberra: Australian Government Publishing Service, 1997), pp. 32–4.

60 See respectively *ibid.*, p. 33; and Sidney Goldstein, "Profile of American Jewry: Insights from the 1990 National Jewish Population Survey", *American Jewish Year Book 1992* (New York: American Jewish Committee, 1993), p. 139.

61 Address by Professor Gabriel Sheffer, Hebrew University of Jerusalem, at Shalom College, Sydney, February 1998.

62 "Tie with Israel and Zionism" exhibit, Joods Historische Museum, Amsterdam, October 2003.

63 Leader, "Our dulled nerve", *Guardian Unlimited* [www.guardian.co.uk], 18 November, 2003.

64 Joe Berkofsky, "Bronfman letter on fence revives debate on Jewish criticism of Israel", *Jewish Telegraphic Agency* [www.jta.org], 13 August, 2003.

65 Sam Lipski, "Melbourne vs Sydney: echoes of an historic division", *AJN*, 5 December 2003.

66 Cameron Stewart, "Falling out with friends", *The Australian*, 5 September 2003.

67 See Tzvi Fleischer, "The libel against the lobby", *AJN*, 7 November, 2003; Michael Visontay, "Free speech for some, others pay", *Sydney Morning Herald*, 14 November 2003; and Colin Rubenstein, "No Appeasement on Ashrawi Award", *Forward* (New York), 21 November 2003.

68   Philip Mendes, *Australia's Welfare Wars* (Sydney: UNSW Press, 2003), pp. 51–66.

69   Editorial, "Inquiry needed into where it went wrong", *AJN*, 14 November 2003; Einfeld, "An inquiry must be launched".

70   See respectively, Colin Rubenstein, "Ashrawi revisited", *The Review*, December 2003; and Colin Rubenstein, "No Appeasement on Ashrawi Award", *Forward* (New York), 21 November 2003. See also Colin Rubenstein, "AIJAC will still lobby", *AJN*, 28 November 2003.

71   Dan Goldberg and Aviva Bard, "It was a success, insists Leibler", *AJN*, 14 November 2003; Rubenstein, "No Appeasement".

72   See respectively, "Tainted prize"(reproduced later as "Dr Hanan Ashrawi – A Brief Introduction" [www.aijac.org.au/resources/ashrawi_docs/ ashrawi_profile.html]); and Colin Rubenstein, "Passion obscures a politicised, misguided award", *Weekend Australian*, 8 November, 2003.

73   Rubenstein, "No Appeasement"; Rubenstein, "Ashrawi revisited".

74   Rubenstein, "No Appeasement".

75   "Time for outbreak of peace on the prize".

76   Dan Goldberg, "From The Editor", *AJN*, 7 November 2003.

77   Alison Caldwell, "Ashrawi gives speech amid protest", ABC Radio *AM* program, 6 November 2003.

78   Easson, "An informed outsider's assessment of the Ashrawi debacle".

CONCLUSION

Australian Jewish Politics in Comparative Perspective

PETER Y. MEDDING

Varying definitions of politics abound, but common to many of them is the view that politics is an activity or process concerned with the acquisition and exercise of authority, the establishment of order, the determination of public affairs and the conduct of collective pursuits. Accordingly, we may understand Jewish politics as concerned with the authoritative ordering and conduct of the Jewish group and its collective pursuits. Outside of Israel, a fundamental given of Jewish politics is the embeddedness of the Jewish group within a much larger, surrounding non-Jewish society. Thus constant negotiation of the Jewish group's relationship with the surrounding society has become an integral and unavoidable element of Jewish politics. Obviously, given their long history and worldwide dispersion, Jewish communities have engaged in a myriad of collective pursuits focused on a wide range of internal and external issues and goals. However, all Jewish communities have had to address the four defining primary group needs of identity, autonomy, security, and survival.

The first primary need, **identity**, refers to the Jewish group's conception of itself and its place in the universe – its cultural heritage in the widest sense – as expressed and transmitted in beliefs, values, norms, ritual practices, texts, historical experiences, and so forth. These cultural elements are constitutive of the Jewish group, shaping it over time, and distinguishing it fundamentally from all other groups that do not share its beliefs and values. The second primary need, **autonomy**, relates to the Jewish group's capacity to conduct its collective affairs independently, determine and implement its collective goals, and be the sole arbiter and authoritative interpreter of its own values and history. The third primary group need for **security** relates to the inviolability of Jews (individually and collectively) to attacks upon them due to their group origins, affiliation or identification, and to attacks upon the Jewish group's intrinsic worth or the legitimacy of its presence in a given society or specific sphere of life. Finally, the most elemental denial of security – loss of life – terminates not only individual survival but also the group's **survival** (and thus also its identity and autonomy). But even when the elemental physical survival of individuals is not at issue, the Jews' continued existence as a group is contingent upon the maintenance of its distinctive culture.

During the second part of the twentieth century, four major developments – the establishment and welfare of the State of Israel; the meaning, memory and commemoration of the Holocaust; communism and its collapse and the related extension of globalization; and the advent of multiculturalism – had profound implications for all aspects of Australian Jewish politics, as for Jewish politics everywhere. This was especially so with regard to Israel and the Holocaust, which introduced new elements of primary group needs that reshaped the issues and concerns on the Jewish political agenda.

The Establishment and Welfare of the State of Israel. Prior to 1948, Australian Jews, like Jews everywhere, had been divided over the ideology of Zionism, that is, over the desirability, feasibility and prudence of establishing a sovereign Jewish state in the homeland of Palestine. In particular, for some Australian (and British and American) Jewish leaders, Zionism raised the issue of conflict *between* Jewishness and citizenship, generating apprehensions that public support for the establishment of a sovereign Jewish state (to which Britain was opposed) would lead to accusations of disloyalty and undermine their legal status and social acceptance within their societies. As is well known, throughout the Jewish world this issue was soon resolved overwhelmingly on the side of Zionism and Israel. Empirical evidence from many countries indicates that Jews today are overwhelmingly united in their concern for Israel's wellbeing, such that one cannot be a Jewish communal and political leader – or, indeed, often an active politician – today if one does not actively support Israel publicly.

There are many reasons for this, but the main one relates to the central role that Israel has come to play in Jewish group identity over the past half-century. This is manifest at a number of levels and in a number of ways. First, the State of Israel, as the ultimate realization of Jewish peoplehood, is the fullest expression of shared kinship, family, and home, in the sense that every family has a home and every member of that family always has a place in that home, irrespective of whether they actually reside there. Or in the memorable and oft-quoted words of Robert Frost, a "place where they have to take you in, when you have to go there." Second, Israel's existence has fundamentally changed the status of the Jews as a group throughout the world, putting them on an equal footing with all other ethnic nations and peoples. Whereas other states have granted Jews equal status as individuals, the existence of the state of Israel gives the Jews that standing as a group, thus enfranchising the Jews everywhere as individuals. Third, both Jews and non-Jews automatically associate Jews and Israel, both positively and negatively. Thus, it has become the conventional wisdom in the Jewish world that whatever weakens Israel weakens all Jewish communities, and that whatever strengthens Israel strengthens all Jewish life. Conversely, and contrary to fundamental Zionist assumptions, strong disapora communities are good for Israel, and weak ones deprive it of needed support, and hence, for this reason, it is in Israel's interest to act to strengthen and maintain diaspora communities. Fourth, the establishment of Israel is a reversal of history, ongoing evidence of the fracturing of the Jews' hitherto universal inferior and downtrodden status, and an undermining of the minority syndrome that was deeply embedded in Jewish group identity and at the heart of Jewish politics over the centuries. Israel adds to Jewish group identity everywhere the confidence that the Jews are, in one place, the societal majority and in control of public authority, where they are able to shape their own fate. Finally, for all of the above reasons, the existence of the State of Israel is an immense and obvious source of ethnic and personal pride, and has become a major factor in enhancing Jews' self-image and self-esteem.

It is for precisely the same reasons, however, that issues generating dissonance and conflict between the existence of Israel and the realities of Israel are particularly troubling to Jews. Because they are united about the existence of Israel, Jews may freely criticize and oppose the government of Israel, its policies, its political leaders, its parties, its society, its religious laws and establishment, its lack of religious pluralism, its secularism, its treatment of its non-Jewish citizens, and its Palestinian neighbours, and so forth. What are the limits of such criticism, where and how should it be expressed, and whether such opposition and criticism will eventually erode the hitherto positive impact of Israel on Jewish group identity, are all far from clear.

Most troubling of all politically is the question of public dissent by Jewish organizations, leaders and individuals from Israeli policies. Not only is this thought by many Jews to be morally unacceptable – as such matters should only be decided by those who bear the responsibility for and consequences of those policies, namely the citizens of Israel – but Jewish communities and their leaders worry that internal disunity is likely to be regarded as a sign of weakness by other political actors, and hence hamper the community's efforts to gain governmental and public support of Israel. Whether this actually is the case in liberal democracies, where multiple interests, disunity and disagreement are the name of the game, is a moot point. Certainly, political and media debate of matters relating to Israel is a predictable, if not unavoidable, occupational hazard for those seeking to influence the making of public policy, and perhaps, as Harry Truman put it, those who can't stand the heat shouldn't be in the kitchen.

Holocaust Meaning and Memory. The second fundamental change in the definition and content of the Jews' primary group needs relates to the meaning and implications of the Holocaust. Obviously, the Holocaust underscored the primary group need for Jewish physical survival. The major political question has been what has to be done to ensure that survival, and the litmus test of any political phenomenon or activity is its implications for that end. This interest suffuses and overarches the Jews' other primary group needs.

To a large degree, this suffusion stemmed from the manner in which the Holocaust fundamentally changed the Jews' understanding of the age-old problem of anti-Semitism. The Nazi case showed clearly how in a civilized and advanced industrial society the systematic fanning and progressive intensification of anti-Semitism culminated in the Final Solution. The historical conclusion was inescapable: the Holocaust was the end-result of anti-Semitism, and without anti-Semitism the Holocaust could not and would not have occurred. The question, however, was what this meant for the assessment of the current dangers and future course of anti-Semitism in other societies. Did the existence of anti-Semitism portend a recurrence of the Holocaust, could such an end be averted, and, if so, what counter-measures were required? Thus, the question was not so much how to deal with actual instances of prejudice and discrimination and verbal and phys-ical hostility against Jews than one of anti-Semitism's "Holocaust potential" and how to deal with that.

Answers to these questions required analysis of the nature of anti-Semitism – whether its various manifestations from the most minor to the most extreme were of the same order, whether it tended inherently to inten-sify and spread, whether it was avoidable or stoppable. In other words, the issue is whether even the most minor manifestation of anti-Jewish expres-sion contains the seeds of another Holocaust or, as it is sometimes starkly put, whether "every anti-Semitic remark has the whiff of Auschwitz about it". Broadly, this search for answers had two foci: one psycho-cultural, which dealt with the cultural sources of, and psychological needs served by, individual and mass support for anti-Semitism; and the other, socio-political, which examined how such support could erode social order and undermine democracy. Signficantly, both approaches addressed anti-Semitism from the perspective of the whole society, which had profound implications for the Jews' collective pursuits. If anti-Semitism was no longer an interpersonal or intergroup question of threats to a small and marginal sub-group, but one of danger to the political order itself, then combating it was vital to the health of democratic society as a whole. The terms and strategy of Jewish collective politics broadened accordingly.

The concerns with Israel and the Holocaust came together in the poli-tics of survival. This was fed primarily by apprehensions about the threat of Israel's physical destruction, heightened by the historic irony that the State which was established to ensure Jewish security and survival now faced major problems of security and survival of its own, and by the accompanying fear that if indeed Israel were to be destroyed, it is unlikely that Jewish life elsewhere would survive such a mortal blow. It was also fed by varying manifestations of anti-Semitism in other countries and the potential threat to Jewish life that these posed. Another compelling lesson followed from the Jews' "reading" of the Holocaust: the attainment of their primary group needs of security, survival and continuity were directly dependent on Jewish political mobilization and its efficacy in shaping public policy. In short, Jews learnt the necessity of marshalling and committing resources to the exercising of political power. Keeping a low profile, not to utilize resources to exercise political power, and not to play a public societal role makes Jews dispensable, as were the Jews of Europe, and to that the politics of survival says NEVER AGAIN! Over the past decades, such political activism seems to have borne fruit throughout the world, including Australia, with public declarations of support for the security and survival of Israel now commonplace amongst the political leaders and candidates for high office in western countries.

Clearly, then, not only have the various aspects of the Jews' primary group needs been redefined, with new elements added, they have also become ever more closely intertwined. If nothing else, this makes it difficult to do what effective *politiking* generally requires, and that is to clearly define the issues and determine the goals accordingly. Thus, for example, with Israel, the Holocaust, anti-Semitism, group identity, group security and group survival, and much more, so closely connected, who can say with any certainty what the issue is at any time? This is what lies behind Geoffrey Levey and Philip Mendes' observation about a certain Jewish political style in Australia, where "the stakes *always* involve potential peril" and "the imperative is on winning or prevailing". The inseparability of Jewish primary group needs raises – or appears to raise – the political stakes, particularly of failure.

The Demise of Communism and Rise of Globalization. Australian Jewish politics has also been profoundly affected by the collapse of communism and the extension of globalization during the last decades of the twentieth century. With the fall of communism in Europe, for the first time in two millennia almost nowhere in the world were Jews subjected to governmental and/or popular discrimination, repression and persecution (a minor exception being the recent treatment of Jews in Iran). In fact, almost half of the Jews in the world now lived in Israel, while most of the rest lived in its major democracies. As a result, one of the major agenda items of the Jews' collective pursuits both domestically and internationally for more than 150 years – assisting and rescuing Jews living in distress – virtually disappeared.

Also brought to an end was the central and complicating influence on the Jewish political agenda of the struggle between communism and democracy, especially the conflict between the Soviet bloc and the countries of the Free World led by the United States. This conflict, not least the support and arming of the Arab states by the communist bloc in their conflict with Israel, directly informed Jewish life and politics during the second half of the twentieth century. Especially traumatic for Jews were the 1967 and 1973 Arab–Israel wars, and the repression of Jewish life in and ban on Jewish emigration from the Soviet bloc. The latter led to a coordinated international movement to free Soviet Jewry, involving Jewish lobbying of governments throughout the world to enlist their support for this cause, to which a number of chapters in this book refer in the Australian context. In short, with the end of the Cold War, a large part of the international Jewish political agenda also expired.

For countries like Australia, globalization signalled the end of the tyranny of distance, replacing it with the tyranny of the internet. If the fall of communism signified the end of history, then globalization brought about the end of geography. As a result, Jewish communities everywhere now pursue much the same agenda and respond to problems in essentially the same manner. As in the past, many of the items on that agenda are broached internationally, with Jewish communities in many countries acting on issues affecting their brethren in some other country, for example, by lobbying their own governments to intervene diplomatically or petitioning the appropriate international bodies. But in addition, many of the issues of concern to Jews now transcend their own specific interest and are truly global, such as international terrorism, Islamic fundamentalism, and oil embargoes. Consequently, seemingly isolated incidents in one country are perceived to be a link in a global chain or global threat, especially when reinforced by history and memory. Thus, for example, the defacing of tombstones in a French country cemetery with swastikas may be perceived as part of a global threat with grave consequences for human civilization on the basis of the political lessons derived from the Holocaust. The problem suddenly is not simply a defaced tombstone, but anti-Semitism/Holocaust/racism/genocide. The nature of the global threat is exacerbated when it is discovered that the perpetrators are Muslims from a Middle Eastern country, and that the defacing comes in response to some action by the Israeli government or armed forces. So what by any standards is a minor manifestation of anti-Semitism somewhere is now viewed as a threat to Jewish existence everywhere, and hence is a matter of major concern to Jews in all countries. One swastika, and there is a presumed global problem.

Global problems and global threats create a global Jewish political agenda – the same items pursued in the same manner in many different places. Whatever domestic issues are the focus of Australian Jews' collective pursuits, the prime concern seems to be with the items on this global Jewish political agenda, as is clearly demonstrated by the Ashrawi affair over the Sydney Peace Prize in 2003. Here, too, what by all accounts might be regarded as a minor issue, initiated from outside Australia, became a cause celebre and a matter of concern to Jews everywhere, because it was perceived as contributing to a global problem of terror, and in this case was exacerbated by appearing, in the eyes of some, to reward terror with a prize. The Ashrawi affair also fed into another major theme in the globalization of the Jewish political agenda – the connection between anti-Semitism and anti-Zionism, which in many cases is presented as mere criticism of the Israeli government's policies and activities, while it often means to deny the right of Israel to exist and to call for its dismemberment, and, as such, represents a fundamental threat to Jewish existence. Hence, it is often referred to as the "new anti-Semitism".

Finally, global issues, global threats and a global Jewish political agenda turn the Jewish group's domestic political opponents into global enemies. Moreover, while much domestic opposition in Australia (and other western countries) to the Jewish group's political agenda, especially relating to criticism of Zionism and Israel, is presented in ideological terms and claimed to be based on universally applied moral considerations, Jews throughout the world commonly perceive it as applied solely and selectively to them. They believe that they are systematically singled out for criticism, held to higher standards and subjected to harsher moral judgments than is any other state or would-be state actor, and conclude that this is another mutation of classic anti-Semitism, however much dressed in universal ideological garb.

These perceived elemental attacks on the Jewish group create major dilemmas for the conduct of its collective pursuits in a global and multicultural world. Their concentration on the left was a further rend in the sundering of seemingly natural ideological affinities and political alignments between Jews and the left that was central in modern Jewish politics for almost a century. Jewish individuals who sought to combine both left and Jewish commitments simultaneously – that is, to act within the left to maintain and promote Jewish concerns, and to act within the Jewish group on the basis of a left world-view – were, as Philip Mendes points out, highly unpopular in both, and pursued a difficult and painful course to maintain. For the Jewish group, the break with the left narrows its base of potential political support. A stable alliance is replaced with ongoing confrontations that constitute a significant barrier to the gaining of support for any of its collective pursuits amongst the organizations and individuals associated with that political sector. Moreover, if the break with the left does not result in a new political marriage between the Jews and the right, their quest for political support is likely to result in fluid, *ad hoc*, and pragmatic relationships with different partners. While such shifting and split alliances may be integral to multicultural politics, they add to the instability of the Jewish group's conduct of its collective pursuits and generally are more difficult to negotiate, operate and maintain than lasting, broad and stable coalitions anchored in a clear ideological divide.

In his discussion of the more recent manifestations of the break between the left and the Jews in Australia, Mendes demonstrates that "much of the . . . left . . . explicitly rejects Zionist or pro-Israel agendas". This also holds true in other western countries. Furthermore, although such opposition to Israel is concentrated on the left, the fact that it also extends across the whole political spectrum amplifies the global threat to Jewish existence and increases its impact on Jewish politics.

Multiculturalism. The fourth major development that has had a profound impact on Jewish politics in Australia is multiculturalism. Although its meaning varied over the years, Australian multiculturalism, as it emerges from Geoffrey Levey's summary of its enduring elements, tolerates and permits, rather than encourages or celebrates, differing group identities and cultures. It is cast in a procedural, instrumental and individualist vein, and might be regarded as no more than a minor gloss on the established Australian pattern of democratic government and traditions of fair play. Indeed, as Levey's chapter makes clear, multiculturalism made few demands upon Australian Jews (or of other groups) in the way of a distinctive group contribution to the whole. Similarly, as a group, the Jews asked little of Australian multiculturalism beyond protection from discrimination and vilification, and accommodation of religious practices, while taking for granted the Christian character of Australian society, and expecting that the majority would make allowance for its Jewish needs, so long as this did not impinge upon the majority.

Nevertheless, even if primarily procedural and instrumental, a genuine governmental commitment to multiculturalism as a mode of coping with cultural diversity is potentially of profound significance for Jewish politics. To begin with, such a declared societal commitment alone creates conditions and an ambience that facilitate the maintenance by the Jewish group (and others) of separate group existence and the perpetuation of distinctive group values and identities. Second, it is likely to improve the actual situation of Jews by lessening prejudice and hostility at both the societal and intergroup levels, and lowering intergroup tensions. (In those countries, such as Australia, where the latter have been low for decades, and the actual treatment of Jews leaves little, if anything, to be desired, the impact is more likely to be psychological than real, and to address apprehensions about the potential of prejudice.) Third, multiculturalism further grounds Jews' claims to protection from discrimination and vilification. Fourth, multiculturalism warrants the participation of the Jewish group as a group (and not merely as an association of individuals or citizens) in the political process, thus according its collective pursuits heightened legitimacy. Finally, the introduction of multiculturalism encourages the development of a pattern of group politics that may cut across the usual party, parliamentary, and federal politics.

This analysis leaves two important questions in abeyance. What impact does the maintenance of separate Jewish identity, commitments, and community have on a Jewish person's Australian-ness? Conversely, what is the impact of Australian-ness on a Jewish person's Jewishness? Clearly, the answers to these questions are key to understanding the place and collective politics of Jews in Australian society. It seems fairly clear from the analysis in this book that the predominant view amongst Australian Jews is that these two sets of identities and commitments are compatible, that both can be maintained fully and simultaneously, but that essentially they are on separate planes and address different aspects of individual and group existence. That is, they are not integrated in a manner that allows Jews to participate fully in all aspects of Australian life, without either being hampered by conflicts between them or without these questions constituting a major agenda item.

Contrast this situation with that in the United States where, although there is no official government policy of multiculturalism, a long tradition of cultural pluralism prevails. There, Jewish collective pursuits are driven and shaped by visions of the good society, anchored in and informed by Jewish values. Moreover, consistent with their understanding of cultural pluralism, American Jews operate in the public arena on the premise that it is their *right and duty* as citizens and as members of a culturally distinct group to contribute their vision of what is good for American society to the ongoing debate in the public square, and in the belief that they may have something unique or of value to add to the whole society. Inevitably, therefore, their visions of the good society involve them in activities and programs directed toward the improvement of American society. Major American Jewish organizations pursue rich and varied domestic political agendas, which cover the whole gamut of issues under discussion in American society at any point in time.

Multiculturalism in Australia does not beckon groups to participate in the public square in anything like this way. Jewish individuals and groups, including the representative bodies of the Jewish community, rarely if ever operate politically on the basis of presenting their visions of the good society for consideration by the whole, and rarely are their collective pursuits directed at societal improvement. As some contributors to this volume note, in recent years, representative Jewish organizations have voiced their concerns, albeit in muted tones, on a few social issues, such as Aboriginal rights and the treatment of asylum seekers. There is little evidence, however, of any parallels to the belief reportedly held by many American Jews "that the better an American one is, the better Jew one is", and to the phenomenon of regarding American liberal values as Jewish values and Jewish values as liberal values.[1] This lack of integration and compartmentalization – where Australian values do not enrich Jewish values and Jewish values do not enrich Australian values or inform Australian Jews' collective pursuits – nevertheless means that Australian values do not melt Jewish values and identity, but rather let Jews remain identifiable in the Australian mosaic. As Levey observes, it enables them to be Australian Jews as much as Jewish Australians and, certainly, "Australians, pure and simple".

This consideration of the major post-World War II developments on Jewish politics leads us to consider, finally, the patterns of Jewish voting behaviour in Australia. Because voting is compulsory in Australia, the participation of eligible individuals in elections is nigh-universal, whilst a small proportion of Australian Jews are involved in the activities of civic associations and political parties at various levels, with a few of the latter becoming members of parliament and government ministers. Interestingly, this proportion is far lower than that amongst American and British Jews. In the United States, in recent years, there have been as many as 11 Jewish Senators (11 percent), 32 Jewish members of the House of Representatives (over 7 percent), in addition to Jewish members of the cabinet, state governors and mayors of major cities, and a Jewish vice-Presidential nominee, whilst in Britain, the number of Jews elected as MPs averaged 22 between 1945–59, 40 between 1964–79, and 23 between 1992–2002, with a high of 46 in 1974 (about 7 percent of the total) and an overall average of 29 Jewish MPs (about 4.4 percent).[2]

In the United States, throughout the twentieth-century the vast majority of Jews active in politics were Democrats, but in Britain a major change occurred in 1983: till then the vast majority of Jewish MPs represented the Labour Party (over 90 percent until 1970, about 75 percent in 1974, and 65 percent in 1979). Ever since that year's election, however, some 60 percent of Jewish MPs have been Conservatives. Moreover, at one point there were five Jewish ministers in Margaret Thatcher's Cabinet, and in 2003 the Conservatives elected a Jew as party leader. Significantly, in both countries these developments mirrored Jewish political loyalties and voting preferences: in presidential elections for example, Jews have voted overwhelmingly for the Democratic candidate – Clinton and Gore both received about 80 percent amongst them, and generally the proportion of Jews voting Democrat has exceeded the national average by some 25 percentage points. Similarly, American Jews are overwhelmingly Democratic in terms of party activism, membership and campaign contributions. In Britain, too, the party distribution of Jewish MPs has been broadly consistent with the voting preferences of British Jews: whereas, until some time in the 1960s some two-thirds supported Labour, since 1974 electoral surveys have indicated that 60 percent or more of British Jews vote Conservative.

In Australia, as in Britain, for several decades the majority of Jews voted Labor in federal elections until the late 1960s, but then moved to the right, and since then, support for the Liberals appears to have hovered around 60 percent. Yet, interestingly, Jewish party membership and activism appear, to date, not to have followed the changes in Australian Jews' voting preferences, and are still located mainly on the Labor rather than the Liberal side of the political divide. In other words, even though some 60 percent of Australian Jews currently vote Liberal, and have done so for at least thirty years, most prominent Jewish politicians and activists are associated with the ALP. The other main difference is that whereas in the United States and Britain, Jewish representation in the legislature and the cabinet has been significant both absolutely and relative to their proportion of the total population (2–3 percent in the US, 0.45 percent in Britain), that in Australia is miniscule, only matching, more or less, their proportion of the total population (0.5 percent). Why has there been such a radical change in the voting preferences of Australian and British Jews over the past thirty to forty years but not in those of American Jews? Why have Australian and British Jews moved from left to right, abandoned Labor/Labour and transferred their allegiance to the Liberal and Conservative parties, respectively, while their brethren in America continue to support the Democratic Party and its candidates so over-whelmingly? The relatively high proportion of Jews at the middle and upper levels of the socio-economic scale in all three countries increases the puzzle in two ways. First, there are strong correlations between high socio-economic status and voting for the party to the right of centre, and between low socio-economic status and voting for the party to the left-of-centre. Second, those who move up the socio-economic ladder, as did the Jews, tend to adjust their voting preference accordingly.

On this basis, it might seem that the voting behaviour of Australian and British Jews conforms to expectation, whilst that of American Jews is anomalous and requires explanation. Things, however, are not this simple. After all, there is a century-long history of universal support by Jews for left-of-centre parties, ideologies and values, so much so that this was and often still is regarded as the Jewish political norm or tradition. From this perspective, it is the voting behaviour of the Australian and British rather than the American Jews that departs from that norm and requires expla-nation, and this view is reinforced by evidence from other countries (e.g. Canada, South Africa, and France) indicating continued majority Jewish support for left-of-centre parties despite high socio-economic status and upward mobility. Clearly, what is or is not anomalous and in need of expla-nation depends upon what is regarded as the norm.

A better way to approach the issue, therefore, is not to assume any Jewish voting norm, but rather seek to determine how Jews vote in varying circum-stances, and under which conditions they may tend to vote left, centre, or right. This serves to focus attention specifically on a number of critical factors. These include: first, the status of the Jews in society, both legal and actual – whether this is an issue or a problem for the society, and how this impinges both on the society and on the Jews; second, the nature and substance of the specific issues on the societal and Jewish political agendas; third, the manner and extent to which both the society's and the Jews' polit-ical agendas are informed by an overall ideological or value perspective, and its nature – be it left, right, liberal, conservative, Christian, or, in the case of the Jews, Judaic; fourth, which political and societal actors best support and which most oppose what Jews stand for and seek to attain.

In explaining the move from left- to right-of-centre voting amongst Australian Jews, I would thus emphasize the following factors.

For a number of decades, the place of Judaism, Jewishness and the Jews in society has not been at issue in Australia. Thus, the questions of their constitutional and legal standing and their symbolic status have not been on the societal agenda, the subject of political debate or a focal point of division between the major political parties. In particular, the place in it of Judaism and Jewishness does not impinge upon Australian society's understanding of itself, collective identity, self-image, or the defining values of Australian-ness. To be sure, matters relating to the actual treatment or actions of Jews in Australia arise from time to time, especially those relating to prejudice and discrimination and to mobilization on behalf of Israel, but these are passing concerns. They are of an entirely different order from the complex of issues that place Judaism, Jewishness and the Jews centre stage in American politics, courtesy of that society's debates over the role of religion in society, the constitutional warrant for establishing a strict wall of separation between church and state, and the ongoing societal and political battles between the proponents of Christian America and those who oppose their initiatives on a variety of grounds.

With the increasing cultural diversity of the Australian population since the 1960s, the Jews are no longer what they were at least until the end of World War II – the most numerous, prominent and distinctive non-British and non-Christian group in Australian society. In addition, by highlighting the different national, cultural, linguistic, racial and religious groups comprising Australian society, the policy of multiculturalism de-emphasized the singularity of the Jewish group. Moreover, multiculturalism, which preached that all cultural groups have their place in society, encouraged good relations between them as the means to defuse tensions and foster societal harmony. As a result, the speedy resolution of prejudice and discrimination and the like was for the good of society as a whole and not just for the Jews.

Third, at any point of time, Australian Jews' collective pursuits focus on domestic matters relating to their actual treatment in and by Australian society, and on global matters, such as those relating to Israel, terrorism, the Holocaust and the like. Rarely, do they focus directly on the various domestic items on the Australian political agenda. Indeed, the representative Jewish organizations have tended to take a principled stand *eschewing* involvement in the political thicket on issues dividing the major parties, whether because it is unfeasible (they themselves are internally divided along party lines); because it is imprudent (taking sides between the parties risks the loss of possible future support); or because they lack a mandate to do so.

Unlike their American counterparts, representative Australian Jewish communal organizations do not engage in Australian politics on the basis of some overall vision of the good society, a blueprint for Australia, or a coherent ideology of any kind – Liberal, Socialist, Conservative, or even Multicultural. Neither do they, nor the rabbis and synagogue organizations, view it as their function to participate in Australian politics on the basis of the Jewish obligation "to repair the world" (*Tikkun Olam*) by offering society the benefit of some overall Jewish vision of the good society, or even take a public political stance on the basis of their under-standing of Jewish religious, prophetic or moral values. Thus, there is nothing to compare with the religious liberal Jewish vision of the good society put forward by the lay organizations of Reform Judaism in America, or the secular liberal Jewish vision of the good society put forward by National Jewish Public Affairs Council (till recently known as the National Jewish Community Relations Advisory Council). Similarly, there is nothing to compare with the statements issued in the 1980s by the former and current Chief Rabbis in Britain, finding support in the Hebrew Bible for and giving ethical legitimacy to major elements of Conservative domestic legislation in the Thatcher era.

To a large degree, of course, Australian Jewry's pragmatic, *ad hoc* approach to the conduct of its collective pursuits reflects the dominant mode in Australian politics, where discussion of the good society does not generate much light or heat in the public square. Neither is it manifest in party contestation and manifestos. Thus, according to former Liberal MHR, Peter Baume, his colleagues were like most people, few of whom have "thought-through political views based on a coherent ideology. Most people are 'middle of the road' with no very strong views". Historically, much of Labor's vision of the good society fell by the way-side with its abandonment of the commitment to nationalization and the socialization of industry, production, distribution and exchange, the rolling back of the welfare state, the loss of faith in the capacity of the state to intervene in social life justly and efficiently, not only to provide services and to protect the weak, but also to bring about the creation of the good society. Moreover, although the Liberal Party moved right – in Baume's words, gave up its progressive stance and became less compas-sionate – they do not seem to have developed a coherent and comprehensive conservative or neo-conservative vision of the good society.

Of obvious importance is also the question of which political and soci-etal actors best support and which most oppose what Jews stand for and seek to attain. Two main foci are relevant here. The first concerns the formal political actors – the parties, both in government and opposition. A situation in which both the main parties are equally responsive or unre-sponsive to the Jews' concerns is less likely to influence Jewish voting behaviour than a situation where there is a clear difference between the parties in this regard.

The second focus is the various groups in society engaged in advocacy and contestation on matters relating to the Jews' collective pursuits. Here, the question is how the major parties relate to these groups; for example, are they closely associated with groups strongly antipathetic to Jews or to views the Jews stand for, and hence will they be influenced by this asso-ciation on matters of concern to Jews? Alternatively, do parties act to distance themselves from such groups even when not closely associated with or dependent on them? In general, these factors, may serve to reinforce, weaken, or cancel out the tendency of Jews to vote for a party.

Australian Jewish voting patterns, it seem to me, may be explained along the above lines. Put simply, there is no clear or powerful factor that upsets the predicted predisposition of Jews to vote as do others in the society of similar socio-economic status, with those at the top levels tending to vote Liberal, and those at the lower levels tending to vote Labor. Also, there may be specific factors strengthening the propensity to vote Liberal and diminishing the degree of Jewish support for Labor in recent decades, such as the belief shared by many Australian Jews since the Whitlam era that Labor's Middle East policies indicate a lack of support for Israel's security and survival. I would also contend that the same broad lines of explanation apply in Britain. Similarly, understanding the different manner in which these factors present themselves and are interrelated in the United States also serve to explain the very different voting behaviour of American Jews. Finally, the latter serves as a reminder of the fluidity of politics. That is, a change in any of the above factors – for example, a serious and prolonged out break of anti-Semitism in Australia, and an assessment amongst Jews that the party in power has not acted decisively enough to curb it, or a changed policy in the Middle East that leads to a distancing from Israel, or failure to act strongly enough in opposing and condemning efforts to delegitimize Israel, or a rolling back of the policy of multiculturalism – could all have a significant impact on the voting behaviour of Australian Jews. This is not to say that any of the above will occur, but recognizing its possibility serves to place the explanation of the current situation in proper context.

Notes

1   Cited in Jonathan D. Sarna, *American Judaism: A History* (New Haven: Yale University Press, 2004), p. 371.

2   On the United States, see L. Sandy Maisel and Ira N. Forman, *Jews in American Politics* (Lanham: Rowman and Littlefield, 2001), pp. 445–80. On Britain, see Geoffrey Alderman, "The Political Conservatism of the Jews in Britain", in Peter Y. Medding, ed., *Values, Interests and Identity: Jews and Politics in a Changing World: Studies in Contemporary Jewry*, vol. 11 (New York: Oxford University Press, 1995), pp. 101–16.

APPENDIX

Jewish Parliamentarians in Australia, 1849 to the Present

COMPILED BY HILARY L. RUBINSTEIN

FEDERAL PARLIAMENT

1901–45

(Sydney) Max Falstein
b. 1914, Coffs Harbour, N.S.W.
d. 1967, Concord, N.S.W.
Barrister.
M.H.R. (Watson, N.S.W.) 1940–49.
ALP; defeated as Independent.

(Sir) Isaac Isaacs (Knighted 1928)
b. 1855, Melbourne, Vic.
d. 1948, South Yarra, Vic.
Barrister, formerly schoolteacher.
M.H.R. (Indi, Vic.) 1901–6.
Attorney-General, 1905–6 .
(see also Victoria).

Pharez Phillips
b. 1855, Mount Blackwood, Vic.
d. 1914, Scotland
Farmer and storekeeper.
M.H.R. (Wimmera, Vic.) 1901–6.
(see also Victoria).

Elias Solomon
b. 1839, London.
d. 1909, Fremantle, W.A. Merchant.
M.H.R. (Fremantle, W.A.) 1901–3.
Free trader.
(see also Western Australia).

Vaiben Louis Solomon
b. 1853, Adelaide, SA.
d. 1908, Adelaide, SA.
Merchant, formerly storekeeper and
  newspaper proprietor.
M.H.R. (Boothby, S.A.) 1901–3.
Free trader.
(see also South Australia).

1945–present

Peter Erne Baume
b. 1935, Sydney.
Medical practitioner.
Senator (N.S.W.) 1974–91.
Minister for Aboriginal Affairs,
  1980–82.
Minister for Health, 1982.
Minister for Education, 1982–83.
Minister for Education and Youth
  Affairs, 1983–85.
Shadow Minister, Community
  Services & Status of Women,
  1985–87 (res.)
Liberal.

Joseph Max Berinson
b. 1932, Perth, W.A.
Barrister.
M.H.R. (Perth, W.A.) 1969–75.
Minister for the Environment, 1975.
ALP.
(see also Western Australia).

Moss (Moses Henry) Cass
b. 1927, Western Australia.
Medical practitioner.
M.H.R. (Marybyrnong, Vic.)
 1969–83.
Minister for Environment and
 Conservation, 1972–75.
Minister for Media, 1975.
Shadow Minister for Health,
 Immigration and Ethnic Affairs,
 1975–83.
ALP.

Barry Cohen
b. 1935, Griffith, N.S.W.
Businessman.
M.H.R. (Robertson, N.S.W.)
 1969–90.
Minister for Home Affairs &
 Environment, 1983–84.
Minister assisting the Prime Minister
 for the Bicentennial, 1984–87.
Minister for the Arts, Heritage &
 Environment, 1984–87.
ALP.

Samuel Herbert Cohen
b. 1913, Bankstown, N.S.W.
d. 1969, Adelaide, SA.
Barrister.
Senator (Vic.) 1962–69.
Deputy Leader of Opposition in
 Senate, 1967–69.
ALP.

Michael Danby
b. 1955, Melbourne, Vic.
Political activist and adviser; editor,
 Australia-Israel Review.
M.H.R. (Melbourne Ports, Vic.)
 1998–
Opposition Whip, 2001–
ALP.

Sydney David Einfeld
b. 1909, Sydney.
d. 1995, Sydney.
Company director.
M.H.R. (Phillip, N.S.W.) 1961–63.

ALP.
(see also New South Wales).

Lewis Kent (originally Kapolnai)
b. 1927, Belgrade, Yugoslavia.
Former stationmaster, Vic. Rail.
M.H.R. (Hotham, Vic.) 1980–90.
ALP.

Richard Emanuel Klugman
b. 1924, Vienna, Austria.
Medical practitioner.
M.H.R. (Prospect N.S.W.) 1969–90.
ALP.

NEW SOUTH WALES

1859–1901

Maurice Alexander
b. 1820, London.
d. 1874, Sydney.
Merchant.
M.L.A. 1861–72.

Morris Asher
b. 1818, London.
d. 1909, Potts Point, N.S.W.
Merchant.
M.L.A. 1859–60.

Henry Emanuel Cohen
b. 1840, Port Macquarie, N.S.W.
d. 1912, at sea (bur. Sydney).
Barrister; judge.
M.L.A. 1874–80, 1882–85.

John Jacob Cohen
b. 1859, Grafton, N.S.W.
d. 1939, Sydney.
Civil engineer; architect; barrister;
 judge.
M.L.A. 1898–1919.
Speaker, 1917–19.

Samuel Cohen
b. 1812, London.
d. 1861, Sydney.

Merchant.
M.L.A. 1860.

Charles Collins
b. 1850, Goulburn N.S.W.
d. 1898, Tamworth, N.S.W.
Storekeeper and merchant.
M.L.A. 1885–87, 1890–98.

Samuel Emanuel
b. 1803, Portsmouth, U.K.
d. 1868, Sydney.
Merchant.
M.L.A. 1862–64.

Solomon Herbert Hyam
b. 1837, Jamberoo, N.S.W.
d. 1901, Katoomba, N.S.W.
Produce merchant and cattle breeder.
M.L.A. 1885–87.
M.L.C. 1892–1901.
Protectionist but supported
    Robertson's Free Trade ministry.

Samuel Aaron Joseph
b. 1824, London.
d. 1898, Woollahra, N.S.W.
Merchant.
M.L.A. 1864–68.
M.L.C. 1881–85, 1887–93.

1901–45

John Jacob Cohen
(see above).

Albert Ernest Collins
b. 1868, Goulburn, N.S.W.
d. 1956, Killara, N.S.W.
Storekeeper and merchant.
M.L.A. 1901–10.
Liberal, later independent.

Hyman Goldstein
b. 1876, London.
d. 1928, Coogee, N.S.W.
Businessman.
ML.A. 1922–25, 1927–28.
Nationalist.

Abram Landa
b. 1902, Belfast, N. Ireland.
d. 1989, Sydney.
Solicitor.
M.L.A. 1930–32, 1941–65.
Minister for Labour & Industry, and
    for Social Welfare, 1953–56.
Minister for Housing, 1956–65.
Minister for Co-operative Societies,
    1959–65.
ALP.
N.S.W. Agent-General in London.

(Sir) Daniel Levy (Knighted 1929)
b. 1872 London.
d. 1937 Darling Point, N.S.W.
Barrister.
M.L.A 1901–37.
Speaker, 1919–25, 1927–30, 1932–37.
    Attorney General and
Minister of Justice, 1932
Liberal and Reform; Nat. United
    Australia Party.

Ernest Samuel Marks
b. 1872 West Maitland, N.S.W.
d. 1947 Sydney.
Wool merchant.
M.L.A. 1927–30.
Liberal and Reform; Nat. (Lord
    Mayor of Sydney 1930).

Ernest Meyer Mitchell
b. 1875, Sydney.
d. 1943 Sydney.
Barrister.
M.L.C 1934–43.
U.A.P.

Simeon Phillips
(see above)

*(Sir) Saul Samuel (Knighted 1882,
    Baronet, 1898)*
b. 1820, London.
d. 1900, London.
Merchant and Pastoralist.
M.L.A. 1859–60, 1862–72.
M.L.C. 1872–80.

Colonial Treasurer, 1856–60,
1865–66, 1868–70.
Postmaster-General, 1872–75, 1877,
1878–80.
NSW Agent General in London,
1880–97.

Leyser Levin
b. 1830, Prussia.
d. 1908, St. Kilda, Vic.
Storekeeper.
M.L.A. 1880–85.

Lewis Wolfe Levy
b. 1815, London.
d. 1885, Sydney.
Merchant.
M.L.A. 1871–72, 1874.
M.L.C. 1880–85.

Solomon Meyer
b. 1823, London.
d. 1902, Goulburn, N.S.W.
Storekeeper.
M.L.A. 1874–76.

Jacob Levi Montefiore
b. 1819, Bridgetown, Barbados.
d. 1885, U.K.
Merchant and pastoralist.
M.L.A. 1856–60, 1874–77.

Philip George Myers
b. 1839, Sydney.
d. 1881, Brisbane, Qld.
Auctioneer, stock and station agent.
M.L.A. 1880–81.

Harris Levi Nelson
b. 1835, Prussia.
d. 1883, Cooks River, N.S.W.
Storekeeper.
M.L.A. 1872–77.

Simeon Phillips
b. 1847, Parramatta, N.S.W.
d. 1925, Rose Bay, N.S.W.
Jeweller.
M.L.A. 1895–1904.

Joseph George Raphael
b. 1818, London.
d. 1879, Sydney.
Merchant
M.L.A. 1872–74.

(Sir) Julian Emanuel Salomons
(Knighted 1891)
b. 1835, Edgbaston, Birmingham,
U.K.
d. 1909, Woollahra, N.S.W.
Barrister.
M.L.C. 1870–71, 1887–99.
Solicitor-General, 1869–70.
N.S.W. Agent-General in London,
1899–1900.

1945–present

Morton Barnett Cohen
b. 1913 Paddington, N.S.W.
d. 1968 Vaucluse, N.S.W.
Bank officer and businessman;
formerly schoolteacher.
M.L.A. 1965–68.
Liberal.

Ian Cohen
b. 1951, Sydney.
M.L.C. 1995–
Greens.

Margaret Alayne Elizabeth Davis (née
Alexander)
b. 1933, Sydney.
Pharmacist.
M.L.C. 1967–78.
Liberal.

Sydney David Einfeld
(see also Federal)
M.L.A. 1965–81.
Minister for Consumer Affairs,
1976–80.
Minister for Co-operative Societies,
1976–81.
Minister for Housing, 1978–80.
ALP.

Derek David Freeman
b. 1924, Sydney.
Dental surgeon.
M.L.C. 1973–84.
Liberal.

(Sir) Asher Alexander Joel (Knighted 1971)
b. 1912, Stanmore, N.S.W.
d. 1998, Sydney.
Public relations and advertising executive.
Director of Public Relations for the Liberal Party (Victoria), 1945.
M.L.C. 1958–78.
Independent; joined Country Party 1959.
Treasurer, 1971–72.
Member Central Executive 1971–?

Abram Landa
(see above)

(David) Paul Landa
b. 1941, Sydney.
d. 1984, Sydney.
Solicitor.
M.L.C. 1973–84.
Minister for Industrial Relations, and Minister for Planning and the Environment, 1976–80.
Vice-President of the Executive Council, 1976–81; 1983–84.
Minister for Education, 1980–81.
Minister for Energy and Minister for Water Resources, 1981–83.
Leader of the Government in the Legislative Council, Attorney General, Minister of Justice and Consumer Affairs, 1983–84.
ALP.

Leon Samuel Snider
b. 1897, Melbourne.
d. 1965, Sydney.
Theatre proprietor.
M.L.C. 1943–65.
Liberal; transferred to Country Party 1959.

VICTORIA

1860–1901

(Sir) Benjamin Benjamin (Knighted 1889)
b. 1834, London.
d. 1905, East Melbourne.
Merchant and speculator.
M.L.C 1889–92.
(Mayor of Melbourne 1887–89).

Edward Cohen
b. 1822, London.
d. 1877, East Melbourne.
Auctioneer, later merchant.
M.L.A 1861–65, 1868–?
(Mayor of Melbourne 1862–63).

Charles Dyte
b. 1818 London.
d. 1893 Ballarat, Vic.
Auctioneer and estate agent.
M.L.A 1864–71.

Benjamin Josman Fink
b. 1847, Guernsey.
d. 1909, London.
Financier.
M.L.A. 1883–89.

Theodore Fink
b. 1855, Guernsey.
d. 1942, Melbourne.
Solicitor and newspaper proprietor.
M.L.C. 1894–1904.

(Sir) Isaac Alfred Isaacs
(see under Federal).
M.L.A. 1892–1901.
Solicitor-General 1893;
Attorney-General 1894–99, 1900–1.

John Alfred Isaacs
b. 1863, Yackandandah, Vic.
d. 1944, Auburn, Vic.
Barrister.
M.L.A. 1894–1902.

Daniel Barnet Lazarus
b. 1866, Bendigo, Vic.
d. 1932, Melbourne.
Mining director,
M.L.A. 1893–97, 1900–2.

1901–45

Harold Edward Cohen
b. 1881, St. Kilda, Vic.
d. 1946, South Yarra, Vic.
Solicitor, soldier, company director.
M.L.C. 1929–35.
M.L.A. 1935–43.
Assistant Treasurer 1932–35.
Minister of Public Instruction and
    Solicitor General, 1935
Nat., U.A.P.

Henry Isaac Cohen
b. 1872, Melbourne.
d. 1942, Armadale, Vic.
Barrister.
M.L.C. 1921–37.
Minister without Portfolio, 1923–24.
Minister of Public Works and of
    Mines, 1924.
Attorney-General and Solicitor-
    General, 1924.
Minister of Public Instruction,
    1928–29.
Minister of Water Supply and of
    Electrical Undertakings, 1935.
Nat., U.A.P.
(Government leader, L.C., 1928–29;
    Unofficial leader, L.C., 1922–28,
    1935–37).

Theodore Fink
(see above)

Max (Maximilian) Hirsch
b. 1852, Cologne, Prussia.
d. 1909, Vladivostok.
Social economist, writer.
M.L.A. 1902–3.
Free trader; single tax proponent; bid
    unsuccessfully to enter Federal
    Parliament.

John Alfred Isaacs
(see above).

Daniel Barnet Lazarus
(see above).

Nathaniel Levi
b. 1830, Liverpool, U.K.
d. 1908, St. Kilda, Vic.
Merchant.
M.L.A. 1861–65, 1866–67.
M.L.C. 1892–1904.

Jonas Felix Levien
b. 1840, Williamstown, Vic.
d. 1906, St. Kilda, Vic.
Merchant.
M.L.A. 1871–77, 1880–1906.
Anti-Chinese migration.

Sidney Ricardo
b. 1819, London.
d. 1896, Melbourne.
Farmer.
M.L.A. 1857–59.

Samuel Samuel
b. 1834, Dublin.
d. 1892, Melbourne.
Solicitor.
M.L.A. 1892.
Labor.

Emanuel Steinfeld
b. 1828, Neisse, Prussia.
d. 1893, Adelaide, SA.
Furniture manufacturer.
M.L.C. 1892–93.
Federationist.

Joseph Sternberg
b. 1852, London.
d. 1928, Melbourne.
Businessman.
M.L.C. 1891–1928.
Eventually "father of the House".

Nathaniel Levi
(see above).

Jonas Felix Levien
(see above).

(Sir) Archie Michaelis (Knighted 1952)
b. 1889, SI. Kilda, Vic.
d. 1975, South Yarra, Vic.
Company Director.
M.L.C. 1932–52.
Minister without Portfolio, 1945.
Speaker, 1950–52.
U.A.P., Liberal.

1945–present

David Leon Frank Bornstein
b. 1940, Carlton, Vic.
Journalist.
M.L.A. 1970–75.
ALP.

Walter Jona
b. 1927, Hawthorn, Vic.
Business executive.
M.L.A. Hawthorn 1962–84.
Minister of Immigration and Ethnic
    Affairs, and Assistant
Minister of Health, 1976–79.
Minister of Community Welfare
    Services, 1979–82.
Liberal.

(Sir) Archie Michaelis
(see above).

Baron David Snider
b. 1917, Caulfield, Vic.
d. 1966, Ivanhoe, Vic.
Management consultant.
M.L.A. 1955–64.
M.L.C. 1964–66.
Liberal.

Marsha Rose Thomson
b. 1955, Pascoe Vale, Vic.
Electorate and Research officer.
M.L.C. 1999–
Minister for Consumer Affairs,
    1999–2002.
Minister for Small Business, 1999–

Minister for Information and
    Communication Technology,
    2002–
ALP.

SOUTH AUSTRALIA

1857–1901

(Sir) Lewis Cohen (Knighted 1924)
b. 1849, Liverpool, U.K.
d. 1933, Glenelg, SA.
Merchant.
M.H.A. 1887–93, 1902–6.
Protectionist.
(Mayor of Adelaide 1889–91, 1901–4,
    1909–11;
Lord Mayor 1921–23).

Morris Lyon Marks
b. 1826, London.
d. 1893, Albert Park, Vic.
Merchant.
M.H.A. 1857–58.

Maurice Salom
b. 1832, London.
d. 1903, North Adelaide, S.A.
Auctioneer.
M.L.C. 1882–91.

Emanuel Solomon
b. 1800, London.
d. 1873, Adelaide, SA.
Merchant.
M.H.A. 1862–65.
M.L.C. 1867–71.

Judah Moss Solomon
b. 1818, London.
d. 1880, Adelaide, SA.
Auctioneer.
M.H.A.1858–60, 1871–75.
M.L.C. 1861–66.
(Mayor of Adelaide 1869–70).

Saul Solomon
b. 1836, London.

d. 1929, Northam, WA.
Photographer, later businessman.
M.H.A. 1887–90.

Vaiben Louis Solomon
(see also Federal).
M.H.A. 1890–1, 1905–8.
Premier and Treasurer, 1–8 December
   1899.
Free trader, Federationist, anti-
   Chinese migration.

1901–45

(Sir) Lewis Cohen
(see above).

Vaiben Louis Solomon
(see above).

WESTERN AUSTRALIA

1849–1901

Matthew Louis Moss
b. 1863, Dunedin, N.Z.
d. 1946, London.
Barrister and solicitor.
M.L.A. 1895–97.
M.L.C. 1900–1, 1902–14.
Colonial Secretary 1901.
Minister without Portfolio 1902–4,
   1905–6.
(To U.K. 1914; Acting Agent-General
   for WA. 1934)
Liberal.

Lionel Samson
b. 1798, London.
d. 1878, Fremantle, W.A.
Merchant.
M.L.C. 1849–56, 1859–68.

Elias Solomon
(see also Federal)
M.L.A. 1892–1901.
Independent.

1901–45

Harry Boan
b. 1860, Dunolly, Vic.
d. 1941, Melbourne.
Businessman.
M.L.C. 1917–18, 1922–24.
Nationalist.
Matthew Louis Moss
(see above)

(Sir) Charles Nathan (Knighted 1928)
b. 1870, Christchurch, N.Z.
d. 1936, Perth, W.A.
Business Manager.
M.L.C. 1930–34.

1945–present

Joseph Max Berinson
(see also Federal).
M.L.C. 1980–93.
Minister Assisting the Treasurer and
   Chief Secretary, 1983.
Minister for Inter-Govt. Relations and
   Defence Liaison, 1983.
Minister for Prisons, 1983–87.
Deputy Leader of Govt. in L.C.,
   1983–87.
Attorney-General 1983, Minister for
   Budget Management,
1988–90.
Minister of Corrective Services,
   1987–93.
ALP.

QUEENSLAND

1878–1901

Louis Goldring
b. 1857, London.
d. 1934, Townsville, Qld.
Storekeeper.
M.L.A. 1888–93.

Jacob. Horwitz
b. 1830, East Prussia.
d. 1920, Berlin.

Storekeeper, flourmiller.
M.L.A. 1878–87.

Francis Benjamin Kates
b. 1830, Berlin.
d. 1903, Dalveen, Qld.
Storekeeper and flourmiller, later
    grazier.
M.L.A. 1878–81, 1883–88,
    1899–1903.
Liberal.

Isidore Siegfried Lissner
b. 1832, Posen, Prussia.
d. 1902, Brisbane, Qld.
M.L.A. 1883–93, 1896–99.
Secretary for Mines and Public
    Works, 1893.

1901–45

Francis Benjamin Kates
(see above).

TASMANIA

1860–1901

Joseph Cohen
b. 1826, London.
d. 1893, place unknown.
Auctioneer.
M.H.A. 1860–61.

John Davies
b. 1813, London.
d. 1872, Penrith, N.S.W.
Actor, reporter, newspaper proprietor,
    etc.
M.H.A. 1861, 1862–72.

Possibly Jewish origin

VICTORIA

Adolphus Goldsmith
dates unknown
Pastoralist.
M.L.C. 1851–53.

Albert Harris
b. 1842, London.
d. 1910, St. Kilda, Melbourne (bur.
    Anglican).
Storekeeper.
M.L.A. 1883–89, 1899–1904,
    1904–10.

George Collins Levey
b. 1831, Surrey, U.K. (Washington,
    U.S.A. according to Walter Jona).
d. 1919, Richmond, Surrey, U.K. (?
    Presbyterian).
Writer.
M.L.A. 1861–67.

QUEENSLAND

Eugen Hirschfeld
b. 1866, near Breslau, Prussia
    (Wroclaw, Poland).
d. 1946, Inglewood, Qld. (bur.
    Anglican).
Medical practitioner and pastoralist.
M.L.C. 1914.

[i] Revised and reprinted with the author's
    and publisher's permission from Hilary
    L. Rubinstein, "Jewish Parliamentarians
    in Australia, 1849 to the Present: A
    Complete Listing", *Australian Jewish
    Historical Society Journal* 10, 4 (1988):
    295–316; and Hilary Rubinstein,
    "Australian Jewish Parliamentarians: An
    Addendum", *AJHSJ* 10, 6 (1989):
    542–43.

The Contributors

Peter Baume, AO is a physician and is Chancellor of Australian National University. He has been Professor of Community Medicine, University of New South Wales; Chair of the Australian Sports Drug Agency; Deputy-Chair of the Australian National Council on AIDS; Commissioner of the Australian Law Reform Commission; President of the Public Health Association (NSW Branch); Director, Sydney Water Corporation; and Governor, Foundation for Development Cooperation. He was Senator for New South Wales from 1974–91, during which time he was Federal Minister for Aboriginal Affairs, Minister for Health, and Minister for Education.

Danny Ben-Moshe directs Social Diversity Research at Victoria University, Melbourne, and is Adjunct Professor at Gratz College, Philadelphia, teaching Zionism and Israeli studies. He was previously Israel Director of the British Israel Public Affairs Centre and Australian Director of the B'nai B'rith Anti-Defamation Commission. He has published widely on Israeli politics, contemporary anti-Semitism, and Israel–Diaspora relations in journals such as *Israel Affairs*, *Israel Studies Forum* and the *Modern Middle East Source Book Project* (Oxford University Press). He is currently co-editing a book on *Israel and Diaspora Jewish Identity* (Sussex Academic Press).

Barbara Bloch is a doctoral candidate at the Centre for Cultural Research, University of Western Sydney. Her thesis is titled *Unsettling Zionism: Diasporic Consciousness and Jewish Australian Communal Identity*, and she has recently published "David vs Goliath: Australian Jewish Perceptions of Media Bias in Reporting the Israeli–Palestinian Conflict", *Media International Australia*, 109 (2003). She has been a long time feminist activist in Sydney and London, and has worked on many social justice issues, including anti-racism campaigns, employment and educational rights, and equal opportunities for women, especially those from non-English speaking backgrounds.

Eva Cox, AO currently lectures in Social Inquiry at the University of Technology, Sydney. She is a long-term member of Women's Electoral Lobby and an unabashed feminist. She has undertaken many research projects for Government, the private sector and community groups. She has published widely and eclectically in books, journals and newspapers. Her 1995 Boyer lectures on ABC Radio, *A Truly Civil Society*, popularized the concept of social capital.

Sol Encel is Emeritus Professor of Sociology at the University of New South Wales, and was previously Reader in Political Science at the Australian National University. He is currently Honorary Research Associate at the Social Policy Research Centre, UNSW. He has written or edited more than 20 books on a variety of social issues. His publications include *The NSW Jewish Community: A Survey* (UNSW Press, 1978), *The Arab–Israel Conflict* (Jirlac Educational, 1984), and *Continuity, Commitment, and Survival: Jewish Communities in the Diaspora* (Praeger, 2003).

John Goldlust teaches in the School of Social Sciences at La Trobe University. He researches in the areas of immigration, ethnicity and multiculturalism, mass media and popular culture and social history. Recent publications include "Jewish Continuity in Australia" in L. Stein and S. Encel (eds) *Continuity, Commitment and Survival: Jewish Communities in the Diaspora* (Praeger, 2003), "Globalizing Community: Jews in Space", *Social Analysis*, 45:1 (2001), and "Soviet Jews" in James Jupp (ed.), *The Australian People: An Encyclopedia of the Nation, Its people and Their Origins* (Cambridge University Press, 2001).

Geoffrey Brahm Levey is Senior Lecturer in Politics and International Relations, and foundation Coordinator of the Program in Jewish Studies, University of New South Wales, Sydney. His publications have appeared in such journals as *Political Theory*, *British Journal of Political Science*, *Philosophy of the Social Sciences*, and *Studies in Contemporary Jewry*, and in several edited volumes, including *Essential Papers on the Talmud* (New York University Press, 1994), *Encyclopedia of American Religion and Politics* (Facts on File, 2003), *National-Cultural Autonomy and Its Contemporary Critics* (Routledge, 2004), and *The Oxford Companion to Australian Politics* (Oxford University Press, forthcoming).

Andrew Markus is Professor of History and Jewish Civilisation at Monash University, Melbourne. His research encompasses Australian race relations and immigration history, racial thought and the Holocaust. He is the sole author of four books and the editor or co-editor of more than ten others, including: *Race: John Howard and the Remaking of Australia* (Allen & Unwin, 2001), short-listed in two categories of the 2002 New South Wales Premier's Literary Awards, *Building a New Community. Immigration and the Victorian Economy*, editor (Allen & Unwin, 2001), and *Australian Race Relations 1788–1993* (Allen & Unwin, 1994).

Peter Y. Medding is the Dr Israel Goldstein Professor of the History of Zionism and the State of Israel in the departments of Political Science and of Contemporary Jewry at the Hebrew University of Jerusalem. He currently serves as Chair of the Political Science Department. He is an editor of the Oxford University Press annual, *Studies in Contemporary Jewry*; editor of *Jews in Australian Society* (Macmillan, 1973); and author of *The Founding of Israeli Democracy, 1948–1967* (Oxford University Press, 1990), *Mapai in Israel: Political Organisation and Government in a New Society* (Cambridge University Press, 1972), and *From Assimilation to Group Survival: A Political and Sociological Study of an Australian Jewish Community* (Cheshire, 1968).

Philip Mendes is Senior Lecturer in Social Policy and Community Development in the Department of Social Work, Faculty of Medicine, Monash University. He is author of *The New Left, the Jews and the Vietnam War, 1965–1972* (Lazare, 1993) and *Australia's Welfare Wars* (UNSW Press, 2003), and co-editor with James Rowe of *Harm Minimisation, Zero Tolerance and Beyond: The Politics of Illicit Drugs in Australia* (Pearson Education, 2004).

Chanan Reich is Senior Lecturer in Political Science at the Yizre'el Valley Academic College in Israel, and Visiting Lecturer at Haifa and Monash Universities. He graduated in Political Science and Sociology at the Hebrew University, Jerusalem, and earned his Ph.D. from Monash University for his thesis, *Ethnic Identity and Political Participation: The Jewish and Greek Communities in Melbourne.* He is the author of *Australia and Israel: An Ambiguous Relationship* (Melbourne University Press, 2002).

Hilary L. Rubinstein is Associate Editor of the Victorian issues of the *Australian Jewish Historical Society Journal.* A Fellow of the Royal Historical Society in the UK, where she currently resides, she is well-known as a historian of Australian Jewish life. Her books and numerous articles include *The Jews in Victoria, 1835–1985* (Allen & Unwin, 1985), *Chosen: The Jews in Australia* (Allen & Unwin, 1987), and *The Jews in Australia: A Thematic History. Volume One 1788–1945* (Heinemann, 1991). She has been a Research Fellow in History, University of Melbourne, and has taught Modern Jewish History at Monash and Lampeter universities.

William D. Rubinstein is Professor of Modern History at the University of Wales-Aberystwyth. Born and educated in the United States, he lived in Australia from 1976 till 1995, when he was Professor of Social and Economic History at Deakin University. He has written in many fields, including *The Jews in Australia: A Thematic History, Volume Two 1945–Present* (Heinemann, 1991), and, as editor, *Jews in the Sixth Continent* (Allen & Unwin, 1986). From 1988–1995, he edited the issues section of the *Journal of the Australian Jewish Historical Society.* In 2002–2004 he served as president of the Jewish Historical Society of England.

Suzanne D. Rutland is Associate Professor and Chair of the Department of Hebrew, Biblical & Jewish Studies at the University of Sydney. She is author of numerous articles, chapters in books and books on Australian Jewish history. Her major publications include *Edge of the Diaspora: Two Centuries of Jewish Settlement in Australia* (Collins, 1988; 2nd edn, Brandl & Schlesinger, 1997, 2001). She has held numerous leadership positions, including current president of the Australian Jewish Historical Society, Sydney.

Colin Tatz is Director of the Australian Institute for Holocaust and Genocide Studies, adjunct Professor of Politics at Macquarie University, and Visiting Professor of Political Science at the Australian National University. He is the author of seventeen books, including *Shadow and Substance in South Africa* (University of Natal Press, 1962), *Race Politics in Australia* (University of New England Publishing, 1979), *Obstacle Race: Aborigines in Sport* (UNSW Press, 1995), *One-Eyed: A View of Australian Sport,* with Douglas Booth (Allen & Unwin, 2000), and *With Intent to Destroy: Reflecting on Genocide* (Verso, 2003).

INDEX